A Church for the World

A Church for the World

The Church's Role in Fostering Democracy and Sustainable Development

Edited by Samuel Yonas Deressa
and Josh de Keijzer

Foreword by Gary M. Simpson

LEXINGTON BOOKS/FORTRESS ACADEMIC
Lanham • Boulder • New York • London

Published by Lexington Books/Fortress Academic
Lexington Books is an imprint of The Rowman & Littlefield Publishing Group, Inc.
4501 Forbes Boulevard, Suite 200, Lanham, Maryland 20706
www.rowman.com

6 Tinworth Street, London SE11 5AL, United Kingdom

Copyright © 2020 by The Rowman & Littlefield Publishing Group, Inc.

"Church and Development in Post-Colonial Africa: Revisiting African Development Plan and the Theology of Reconstruction through the Lens of the Capabilities Approach" was originally presented at the 2019 ALCF Annual Conference at Wittenberg University from October 4–5.

"Church and Development in Ethiopia: The Contribution of Gudina Tuma's Holistic Theology" by Samuel Yonas Deressa © 2017 Lutheran Society for Missiology. Used by permission.

All rights reserved. No part of this book may be reproduced in any form or by any electronic or mechanical means, including information storage and retrieval systems, without written permission from the publisher, except by a reviewer who may quote passages in a review.

British Library Cataloguing in Publication Information Available

Library of Congress Cataloging-in-Publication Data

Names: Deressa, Samuel Yonas, editor. | Keijzer, Josh de, 1965- editor.
Title: A church for the world : the church's role in fostering democracy and sustainable development / edited by Samuel Yonas Deressa and Josh de Keijzer ; foreword by Gary M. Simpson.
Description: Lanham : Lexington Books/Fortress Academic, 2020. | Includes bibliographical references and index. | Summary: "In A Church for the World, contributors from mostly non-Western theological communities offer historical, developmental, ecclesiastical, and theological perspectives on the church-world relationship, challenging misconceptions and practices that prevent the church from being salt and light in the world"-- Provided by publisher.
Identifiers: LCCN 2020007666 (print) | LCCN 2020007667 (ebook) | ISBN 9781978710771 (cloth) | ISBN 9781978710795 (pbk.) | ISBN 9781978710788 (epub)
Subjects: LCSH: Church and the world. | Democracy--Religious aspects--Christianity. | Sustainable development--Religious aspects--Christianity.
Classification: LCC BR115.W6 C5645 2020 (print) | LCC BR115.W6 (ebook) | DDC 261.8/5--dc23
LC record available at https://lccn.loc.gov/2020007666
LC ebook record available at https://lccn.loc.gov/2020007667

To Dr. Thom Ries, President Emeritus of Concordia University, St. Paul,
and
to Mary de Keijzer-Mathew

Contents

Foreword: Toward a Postcolonial "Inescapable Network of Mutuality" — ix

A Church for the World: The Church's Role in Fostering Democracy and Sustainable Development — xi
Samuel Yonas Deressa and Josh de Keijzer

Part One: Historical Perspectives — 1

Chapter 1: Church and Development in Postcolonial Africa: Revisiting African Development Plan and the Theology of Reconstruction through the Lens of the Capabilities Approach — 3
Samuel Yonas Deressa

Chapter 2: Church and Development in Ethiopia: The Contribution of Gudina Tuma's Holistic Theology — 21
Samuel Yonas Deressa

Chapter 3: On Human Flourishing: A Call for Public Responsibility in Contemporary Ethiopian Christianity — 37
Andrew D. DeCort

Part Two: Developmental Perspectives — 65

Chapter 4: Church and Human Development: An Asian Perspective — 67
Lim Teck Peng

Chapter 5: The Critical Role of the Church in the Development of Asia — 81
Delfo C. Canceran, OP

Part Three: Ecclesiastical Perspectives 97

Chapter 6: Church and Development in Nigerian Context: Theological Foundation, Practical Appraisal, and Prophetic Call to Action 99
Ibrahim Bitrus

Chapter 7: Hospitality and Social Responsibility: The Church in the Age of Globalization 117
Nestor M. Ravilas and Wilfredo A. Laceda

Chapter 8: On Not Answering the Public Cry for Justice: The Silence of the Ethiopian Evangelical Churches in the Context of National Crisis 137
Wondimu Legesse Sonessa

Part Four: Theological Perspectives 167

Chapter 9: The Roles of Religions in Public Theology: An Asian Perspective on the Paradoxes of Religious Violence and Peace 169
David Thang Moe

Chapter 10: Justice and Peace Kiss Each Other (Psalm 85:10b): Integrating the Ethics of Justice and Peace in the World of Injustice and Violence 201
David Thang Moe

Chapter 11: To Be Like Christ: Decolonizing Theology for an Incarnational Church 219
Josh de Keijzer

Chapter 12: Capitalism as Divine Necessity: Toward a Political Theology of the Cross 233
Josh de Keijzer

Index 257

About the Contributors 261

Foreword

Toward a Postcolonial "Inescapable Network of Mutuality"

Reading Martin Luther King Jr. as an eighteen-year-old set me on a lifelong path where my Lutheran Christian upbringing was being continually juxtaposed with a world quite beyond my personal experience thus far, yet a world amazingly interconnected with that experience both for bane and for blessing. Like King, I am continually becoming "cognizant."

> Moreover, I am cognizant of the interrelatedness of all communities and states. I cannot sit idly by in Atlanta and not be concerned about what happens in Birmingham. Injustice anywhere is a threat to justice everywhere. We are caught in an inescapable network of mutuality, tied in a single garment of destiny. Whatever affects one directly, affects all indirectly. (Martin Luther King, Jr., *Letter from Birmingham Jail*)

In the following pages, editors Samuel Yonas Deressa and Jacobus (Josh) de Keijzer have assembled authors, principally from the Global South, who are once again amplifying my cognizance of the inescapable network of mutuality that is God's creation. More than one of these essayists retrieves the globally path-breaking "capabilities approach" to human flourishing and economic and social development put forth by political philosopher Martha Nussbaum and recently adopted by the United Nations. That she originated the capabilities approach by initially entering deeply into the everyday lives of women and girls in several countries of the Global South also makes me cognizant that this volume's authors are all male, and that networks of gender mutuality remain likewise inescapable.

Together with others from around the world, these global Christian authors are inventing Christian postcolonial public theologies of human and ecological flourishing. Here, in this still "fierce urgency of now," as Martin King liked to put it, you will meet their provocative interventions to decolonize and to emancipate democracy and human development.

How can I now ever "sit idly by" here in the Twin Cities, Minneapolis and St. Paul, "and not be concerned about what happens in" Ethiopia, or the Philippines, or the Netherlands, or Myanmar, or Nigeria, or Singapore, or, for that matter, in the atrociously colonized domains right here in my hometowns? How about you in your hometown?

Gary M. Simpson
St. Paul, Minnesota

A Church for the World

The Church's Role in Fostering Democracy and Sustainable Development

Samuel Yonas Deressa and Josh de Keijzer

We live in a world that is far more connected globally than ever before. Social media, in particular, have effectively created platforms for people living in different parts of the world to interact on a day-to-day basis on social, political, or other issues that occur unexpectedly on any given day or issues of common concern that require the attention of citizens of the world (such as environmental pollution, terrorism, human trafficking, immigration, and so on). This is the result of the common understanding that what happens in one part of the globe also affects people living in other parts of the world.

This reality has had its impact on how theology is being done and practiced in the last few decades. When we look at some theological institutions in the United States, for example, they have shifted from solely addressing local issues and developing theologies that were only applicable to their own context to adopting curriculums that fits the demand of global Christianity. We could observe such development during our graduate studies at Luther Seminary, in St. Paul, Minnesota, between 2011 and 2017), working as adjunct professors at Concordia University and Augsburg University in St. Paul between 2016 and 2018, and participating in academic seminars. Similar developments are also taking place among theological institutions in Africa, Asia, and Latin America.

Though they are few in number, books with multiple theological or theoretical perspectives are also being published and used as educational tools at these institutions. These books address social, economic, religious, and political issues from various theological perspectives that arise from different contexts and traditions. Our hope is that this book will be a valuable addition to these resources and be used as a means to create a platform for Christians worldwide who are engaged in dialogue on the issue of democracy and sustainable human development.

This book is about the role of the church in ensuring democracy and sustainable human development in a non-Western context. Why a book on development? People living in the Global South are demanding a response to the multifaceted forms of injustice that continue to condemn many persons to hunger, disease, displacement, and violent death resulting from civil conflicts, developmental stagnation, and so on. Countries are experiencing civil conflicts and wars, and political instability mainly because of problems related to development such as uneven distribution of wealth, unemployment, ignorance, or corruption. When it comes to countries in the Global North, even though most have ensured economic development for their citizens, they are still affected with different crises related to development, such as climate change, migration, or health care. As government data show, a significant number of their citizens are also experiencing extreme poverty. One good example is the United States where, according to the US Census Bureau's 2011 report, "46.2 million Americans are considered impoverished—15 percent of the country's population. Approximately 16.4 million American children—22 percent of the population younger than 18—live in poverty."[1] Therefore, development is one of the critical issues that needs to be addressed globally.

Why a Christian approach to development? Three reasons: firstly, the church in the Global South is experiencing phenomenal growth and expansion, and has become the center of Christianity. This phenomenon has put immense responsibility on churches in the Global South not only to lead the Christian churches worldwide toward the future or the new phase of Christianity, but to also translate the Christian faith in a way that they are able to address different challenges that people in their communities are facing in their day-to-day lives—including development. Secondly, the Christians in the Global South are notoriously religious people who do not distinguish between the sacred and the profane because they view life as a whole. They put faith at the center of their religious, social, economic, and political life. Therefore, in this part of the world, religion is part of all kinds of academic and nonacademic discourse. Thirdly, a Christian approach aims to bring the tremendous resources of the Christian message and spirituality as rooted in the person, teachings, and work of Jesus Christ to bear on the situation today. A call to development is a call to the church to return to the Gospel and to construct theologies that offer alternative ways of being together. As the community of Jesus, the church has much to offer by way of living out what this means.

Most of the contributors of this book are scholars from the non-Western world, especially Africa and Asia. One thing all authors do in this book, however, is to challenge some theoretical and theological frameworks that are used to define and describe development, the ways these frameworks are used to shape development plans as well as the ways in which these frameworks are enshrined in accepted but often harmful paradigms of church praxis and political organization. The contributors also address some misconceptions about how the word *development* is being used and how these misconceptions directly or indirectly affect the public role of churches in developing countries.

A common description of the term *development* emerged in 1960s after the publication of Walt Whitman Rostow's book, *The Stages of Economic Growth: A Non-Communist Manifesto*.[2] For Rostow, there exists a five-stage model for economic development. These stages are: "the traditional society" (characterized by limited growth), the commercial stage (where exploitation of agriculture begins to develop), the industrial stage (with an increasing manufacturing sector), leading to a penultimate stage (increase of industries and connections to the consumer market), and the stage of high mass consumption and exploitation of comparative advantage (the final stage of economic development).[3]

Rostow came up with his model for economic development based on a historical description of eighteenth- and nineteenth-century Europe and America. His model clearly implied that there exists only one way toward economic development, which is to follow the map laid out by the West. According to Rostow, all underdeveloped and developing countries should aspire to undergo these paths of development if they are to join the rest of the developed world. This argument by Rostow was extensively criticized in the past, mainly for not considering the fact that there exist significant differences between the social, cultural, and political contexts of developing countries and the West. Rostow's definition about development was also narrowly focused on economy and ignores other important aspects of development, such as social, political, and spiritual systems that create the opportunity for every human being to have the opportunity to fulfil their full human potential and live a dignified life.[4] As Justin Thacker put it rightly, what we see in Rostow's argument and Western scholars who follow the same line of thought is that such understanding simply promotes "a form of cultural imperialism that must be challenged."[5]

The fundamental assumptions promoted by Rostow, however, have been utilized as a foundation for the development models and ideals of democracy that were introduced to the Global South by the Western nations. The Western nations, and institutions such as the International Monetary Fund (IMF) and the World Bank, have been playing paternalistic roles by promoting and demanding that nations in the Global South adopt the same human rights and development models as they accept. This has resulted in heavy criticism of the West's approach to development in general.[6] Criticisms have included (but are not limited to) the following: that both institutions (the IMF and World Bank) were not paying enough attention to voices from the Global South, that they have their own standards of measuring development that were not compatible to the context of the Global South, and that they followed top-down or paternalistic and self-serving approaches.[7] Others also criticized these two international organizations mainly because of their emphasis on economic growth and their exclusion of social well-being of the community. As studies show, people in the Global South give equal value to social values as much as economic values, and these social values include a sense of dignity and respect, family security, and so on.[8]

Regardless of those critics, there are many nations in the non-Western world that attempted to adopt those models in their own context, with some form of conviction that these models might result in positive outcomes. The majority, however, adopted these development models with an understanding that they were the only options for securing funds from those two institutions. Their attempts, however, failed, with few exceptions where only minimal outcomes were achieved. The exceptions were Asian countries like China, Japan, India, and few others who managed to succeed in getting some deals on external trade relationships with Europe and America. Others, however, made little and painstaking progress that demanded revision of the economic plans. It was because of the points of criticism described previously and through such and similar experiences that most non-Western nations realized that effective development plans are the ones that emerge from within their own context, not the ones that are imported from another continent. This realization informed the Comprehensive Asian Development Plan and the New Partnership for Africa's Development, economic development plans adopted by nations in Asia and Africa, respectively, and for the creation of Partnership and Economic Development in Central America.

Countries in Asian, African, and Central America have been evaluating their own indigenous development plans mentioned previously in the last few decades. Many studies indicate the positive outcomes of these development plans and partnerships and also contain suggestions on how to improve weak areas.[9] To mention a few, a report by African Union and United Nations Economic Commission in Africa, entitled *The Young Face of NEPAD*;[10] studies by the Economic Research Institute for ASEAN and East Asia, such as *Exporting "Content" in the Face of Indifference*,[11] and others. Among these studies, very few are grounded on theological arguments. In fact, the development conversation has not generally involved the domains of theology until recent time. This is mainly due to mistaken understanding about religion as part of the problem of poverty rather than solution, particularly in the developing countries. Our main purpose in this book is to fill this gap and initiate the conversation between the church and theological institutions and other institutions in the Global South. This purpose is based on our conviction that, as Villa-Vicencio, following Gustavo Gutiérrez, rightly argues, "a theology which fails to address the most urgent questions asked by ordinary people is not theology at all."[12]

In addition to the topic of development, some of the contributions in this volume provide a critical perspective on the role of the church vis-à-vis society. They argue for a spirituality that is courageously world-engaging and that addresses the church's complicity in the Western exploitation of the non-Western world. This issue is rather closely related to that raised previously. If the ideology of development described here implied a form of cultural imperialism, we could also say that the ideal of democracy exported to the rest of the world conceals the fact that democracy itself is captive to the specter of global corporate capitalism and as such only serves to render non-Western countries vulnerable to imperialist exploitation. Ultimately, development demands both the active engagement of the local church in the non-Western world and the persistent engagement of western scholars and church leaders with scholars and leaders in the Global South.

As theologians and leaders of the church, we ask ourselves about our role, and the role of the churches in the Global South, in ensuring democracy and sustainable human development. As an institution, the church has distinct advantages that make it uniquely positioned for fostering democracy and human development. For many people, particularly the people in developing countries, the church is the center of all social activity. The church provides them with their needs: education, health, shelter, food, and so on. *The question is, how is the church enabled to understand these unique opportunities so that it can adequately address issues of democracy and human development? How can it develop a praxis of active engagement in the world born of a Christ-centered spirituality?*

The goals of the book are (1) to create awareness about the relationship between religion, democracy, economy, and human development in a non-Western context; (2) to help the global Christian mission organizations and churches reevaluate their role in ensuring sustainable human development and democracy; (3) to increase the involvement of the church in human development and democracy building and to stimulate the cooperation between the church and organizations involved in doing so. The book addresses questions like: What has Christianity to do with democracy and human development? How is the identity and mission of the church related to its public role? What are the advantages and the disadvantages the church has in fostering democracy and sustainable human development? What is the role of theology in helping the church become aware of its privileges and significance in helping nations to embrace and practice democracy and in fostering sustainable human development?

The essays in this volume all focus on the nature and role of the church as well as its responsibility vis-à-vis development, democracy, economy, and human flourishing. Yet some have a more historical orientation, while others take a more systematic approach. We have therefore grouped the essays under a number of perspectives: the historical, the developmental, the ecclesiastical, and the theological perspective. This will aid the reader in making the most of this volume and will facilitate its use in educational settings.

HISTORICAL PERSPECTIVE

Samuel Deressa takes a look at the historical development of the role of the Church in development after the colonial era in "Church and Development in Postcolonial Africa: Revisiting African Development Plan" and, again, in "The Theology of Reconstruction through the Lens of the Capabilities Approach." As the latter title suggests, he uses the capabilities approach developed by Martha Nussbaum to challenge, reframe, and rearticulate programs and strategies implemented across Africa.

Andrew D. DeCort looks at the Ethiopian Church in "On Human Flourishing: A Call for Public Responsibility in Contemporary Ethiopian Christianity." He does this from the perspective of human flourishing as developed by Nussbaum and William Schweiker. As a deeply biblical concept, this perspective lays bare the Ethiopian Church's failure at key moments in its recent history to develop a holistic vision of human flourishing. DeCort suggests ways in which such failure can be avoided in the future.

DEVELOPMENTAL PERSPECTIVE

Working with the Asian context, Lim Teck Peng, after developing the agential concept of capability, makes a case for reflective agency as indispensable for responsible and sustainable development in "Church and Human Development: An Asian Perspective." Such agency as reflection of its own cultural embeddedness and of its critical engagement with market-driven globalization can ideally come to flourish in Christian congregational life through emphasis on discipleship. In this way, the church can contribute to reflective democracy.

A similar role of analysis and examination for the church in society is argued by Delfo Canceran in "The Critical Role of the Church in the Development of Asia." Resisting subsuming the church's agency within existing neoliberal structures and analyzing the current economic situation in Asia, Canceran argues, with an approving nod toward liberation theology and help from postcolonial and postmodern theories, for an active political role of the church in advocating social justice and fostering the democratic process.

ECCLESIASTICAL PERSPECTIVE

In "Church and Development in Nigerian Context: Theological Foundation, Practical Appraisal, and Prophetic Call to Action," Ibrahim Bitrus examines the role of the church in the Nigerian context. He carefully evaluates the current praxis of the church against a solid theological framework that retrieves Luther's two-kingdom model and makes an argument for a specific contribution of the church toward development. Ibrahim Bitrus then issues a prophetic call for public engagement of the church with regard to its social and political vocation in "Church and Development in Nigerian Context: Theological Foundation, Practical Appraisal, and Prophetic Call to Action."

In "Hospitality and Social Responsibility: The Church in the Age of Globalization," Nestor Ravilas and Wilfredo Laceda, departing from the Parable of the Talents, examine the uneasy relation between money and spirituality within the context of globalization. Discussing the impact of the free market, individualism, and consumerism, as well as their easy adaptation by the church, the authors call the church to self-examination through a subversive reading of Jesus's parables.

Wondimu Sonessa provides a sobering account of the church's lack of response to the increasing abuse of human rights in Ethiopia in "On Not Answering the Public Cry for Justice: The Silence of the Ethiopian Evangelical Churches in the Context of National Crisis." Drawing on examples from the Ethiopian Church's own history as well as the life of Bonhoeffer, he calls the church to a retrieval of its task to be a dynamic presence in society.

THEOLOGICAL PERSPECTIVE

David Thang Moe engages in an effort of constructive public theology in "The Roles of Religions in Public Theology: An Asian Perspective on the Paradoxes of Religious Violence and Peace." He argues that in the Asian religiously pluralistic context, people of different religions need to build a vision together based on their common humanity. He does so by looking at the Chinese and the Burmese context, suggesting that Buddhists and Christians can resist evil governments together. The second article by Moe also explores the connection between justice and peace as the manifestation of shalom based on Psalms 85:10. His article discusses the theological concept and implication of justice and peace in a broken world corrupted by human sin.

In "To Be Like Christ: Decolonizing Theology for an Incarnational Church," Josh de Keijzer takes a fresh look at decolonization. With the help of Bonhoeffer's ideas about the church as the present Christ, he argues that decolonization is the only gateway through which the church can become genuinely incarnational and, as such, world affirming. Part of the colonial baggage that the church carries is the Western dichotomy between liberal and conservative theology, the latter of which receives special attention.

In "Capitalism as Divine Necessity: Toward a Political Theology of the Cross," Josh de Keijzer claims that the current economic climate is a secularized expression of the religious imagination of medieval Christianity. This desacralized religiosity needs to be exposed for what it is, he argues: idolatry. De Keijzer presents Luther's theology of the cross as the paradigm from which this momentous and urgent task may be accomplished.

ABOUT THE COVER

The Baobab tree is found in Africa, Madagascar, Arabia, and Australia. It was around before the continents drifted apart some two hundred million years ago. The Baobab tree can live to be five thousand years old. The tree is appreciated because of its fruit, which contains many nutrients. It is a succulent, which means that during rainy season, it stores vast quantities of water in its trunk, producing fruit even when everything else around it is arid and dry. No wonder, then, that in Africa, the tree is known as the Tree of Life, reaching high while its roots go deep in earth's soil. We see the Baobab tree as a metaphor for what the church ought to be.

NOTES

1. See "Poverty in the United States," *Debt.org*. Accessed October 17, 2019, from https://www.debt.org/faqs/americans-in-debt/poverty-united-states/.
2. W. Whitman Rostow, *The Stages of Economic Growth: A Non-Communist Manifesto* (Cambridge: Cambridge University Press, 1960).
3. Ibid., chapter 2.
4. Milburn Thompson, *Justice and Peace: A Christian Primer*, 3rd ed. (New York: Orbis, 2019), 48f.
5. Justin Thacker, *Global Poverty: A Theological Guide* (London: CSP, 2017), 161.
6. Ibid., Bade Onimode, et al., *Africa Development and Governance Strategies in the 21st Century* (London: Zed, 2004); Claude Ake, *Democracy and Development in Africa* (Washington DC: The Brookings Institution, 1996).
7. Bryant Myers, *Walking with the Poor: Principles and Practices of Transformational Development* (Maryknoll, NY: Orbis, 2011), 32.
8. Ibid.; see also Deepa Narayan-Parker, (ed.) *Measuring Empowerment: Cross-disciplinary Perspectives* (Washington, DC: World Bank, 2005).
9. For further detail on studies about development plans in the Global South and their contributions to the society, see Ferdinand Nwaigbo, "The Church and Repositioning the Maternal Care in Africa: A Project of the Millennium Development Goals," *OGIRISI: A New Journal of African Studies* 6, no. 1 (2009); Alex Addae-Korankye, "Causes of Poverty in Africa: A Review of Literature," *American International Journal of Social Science* 3, no. 7 (2014); Flora M. Musonda, "Myths and Realities of Poverty in Africa: The Impact of Debt and Global Policies on Local Economies," in *So the Poor Have Hope*, ed. Karen L. Bloomquist and Musa Panti Filibus (Geneva: LWF, 2007).

10. *The Young Face of NEPAD: Children and Young People in the New Partnership for Africa's Development.* African Union and The United Nations Economic Commission for Africa. 2002. Accessed October 17, 2019, from https://www.unicef.org/publications/files/NEPAD_FINAL.pdf.

11. "Research Institute Network." *Economic Research Institute for ASEAN and East Asia,* July 13, 2017. Accessed October 15, 2019 .

12. Charles Villa-Vicencio, *A Theology of Reconstruction: National Building and Human Rights* (Cambridge: Cambridge University Press, 1992), 41. See also Gustavo Gutiérrez, *A Theology of Liberation*, rev. ed. (London: SCM, 1988).

Part One

Historical Perspectives

Chapter 1

Church and Development in Postcolonial Africa

Revisiting African Development Plan and the Theology of Reconstruction through the Lens of the Capabilities Approach

Samuel Yonas Deressa

For some decades after African nations gained their independence (1960s and afterward), the main discussion among governments has been on how to achieve economic growth and sustainable development. The development agenda appeared, replacing the nationalist ideology of self-government, an ideology used to mobilize Africans to fight for freedom and independence. Pointing to the colonial legacy as a major factor contributing to the failure of the development enterprise in Africa, the new emerging leaders in postcolonial Africa became the main proponents for drafting a development plan with an indigenous character (i.e., by Africans for Africa).[1] After many attempts that took over forty years, the New Partnership for African Development (NEPAD) was set up in 2001.

Following the lead of political leaders, some religious institutions and organizations have also placed development at the center of their theological discussion and ministry. Particularly during the early 1990s, there existed an extended discourse on development that was initiated by the work of Kenyan theologian Jesse Mugambi. This was followed by the South African theologians such as Charles Villa-Vicencio and Archbishop Desmond Tutu who played a major role in developing a theology of reconstruction as a means for helping Christian churches develop a theological foundation for their ministry in society.[2] The theology of reconstruction addressed a wide range of issues related to development such as education, health care, poverty and inequality, faith and global warming, religion in conflict and peacemaking, gender roles, and others.[3]

The African economy, however, did not exhibit the expected result. Rather, health and education prospects have become poorer, malnutrition and poverty remain widespread, and the unemployment rate has continued to increase. As studies show, one of the main causes for this is the ineffectiveness of the development plans adopted in the past by African nations as well as the theology of development as articulated by African theologians. This article discusses weak areas of both NEPAD and the theology of reconstruction and proposes a rearticulation and reframing of both development plans based on Martha Nussbaum's human development theory, a capabilities approach designed as a means for ensuring sustainable human development in an African context. According to Nussbaum, the capabilities approach is "an approach to comprehensive quality-of-life assessment and theorizing about basic social justice."[4]

DISCOURSE ON ECONOMIC DEVELOPMENT IN POSTCOLONIAL AFRICA

The discussion on economic development in Africa was initiated when Emperor Haile Selassie presented at the conference held in Accra, Ghana, in 1958. This was the time African nations started to gain their independence from colonial powers. The Emperor's presentation became the means for the resolution adopted by the first meeting of the Organization of African Union, later named the African Union (AU), from May 22 through 25, 1963. This new resolution was called the *Areas of Cooperation in Economic Problems* (ACEP). At this meeting an economic committee was set up to study, design, and present an economic development plan that is applicable in an African context.

According to this first AU resolution (ACEP), the work of the economic study committee was to provide a broad framework to "protect Africa's infant industries, a commodities stabilizing fund, the freeing of African currencies from external attachment, the restructuring of international trade in Africa's favor, and the harmonization of African development strategies."[5] During the following years, the work of this committee could only result in subsequent resolutions passed by African nations such as the *African Declaration on Cooperation, Development, and Economic Independence* (1973 in Addis Ababa), *The Revised Framework of Principles for the Implementation of the New International Economic Order in Africa* (1977 in Libreville), and the *Monrovia Declaration of Commitment of the Heads of States and Governments of the Organization of African Unity on Guidelines and Meas-*

ures *for National and Collective Self-Reliance in Social and Economic Development for the Establishment of a New International Economic Order* (1979 in Monrovia).⁶

In early 1980, African nations moved from adopting resolutions to the actual drafting of an economic development plan developed by the economic study committee. The following plans were adopted accordingly: the *Logos Plan of Action for Economic Development* (1980–2000), *The Africa's Priority Program for Economic Recovery* (APPER 1986–1990), *The African Alternative Framework to Structural Adjustment Program for Socio-economic Recovery and Transformation* (AAF-SAP 1989), and *The African Charter for Popular Participation for Development* (UNN-NADAF 1990–1991).⁷

The Logos Plan, in particular, was the most comprehensive one, dedicated to ensuring "self-reliance (national and collective) and self-sustaining development."⁸ According to Ake, this development plan emphasized the need for self-reliance by "changing Africa's location in the existing international division of labor, changing the pattern of production from primary commodities to manufactured goods, and relying more on internal resources of raw materials, spare parts, management, finance, and technology."⁹ The necessity of self-reliance and sustainability was due to African nations' understanding that:

> Africa is susceptible to the disastrous effect of natural and endemic disease of the cruelest type and is a victim of settler exploitation arising from colonialism, racism, and apartheid. Indeed, Africa was directly exploited during the colonial period and for the past two decades; this exploitation has been carried out through neo-colonialist external forces which seek to influence the economic policies and directions of African States.¹⁰

A few years after the Logos Plan was adopted by African nations, another competitive development plan was proposed by the International Monetary Fund (IMF) and the World Bank named Accelerated Development (AD). Contrary to the Legos plan, which is indigenous in character, AD was a Western-oriented development plan incompatible with the African context. As noted by Justin Thacker, the AD plan was designed "to ensure that [African] countries grew economically as they *fallowed the path of economic development that had been pursued by the West.*"¹¹ This was the reason why some African leaders regarded it as "political and ideological documents masked as economics that attempts to induce its readers to accept largely false or misleading issues, irrelevant solutions, and a wrong agenda."¹²

For five years (1980–1985), African nations persisted in following their own plan without critically reacting to the proposal of the IMF and World Bank. In those years, however, they realized that they were too dependent and too weak to pursue their own development plan, and therefore agreed to reform their mega plan along the line of the two international organizations, resulting in a new plan named the *Structural Adjustment Program*. For over ten years, African nations attempted to implement this proposal in their own context, but the effect was, as rightly described by Josef Stiglitz (chief economist of the World Bank), increased poverty and "social and political chaos."[13]

In the new millennium, regretting their unwilling submission to international organizations' proposal for development, African nations came up with another comprehensive plan. A draft of this major document was signed by African nations and was known as the *New Partnership for Africa's Development* (NEPAD) in 2001.[14] NEPAD was a development plan that emerged as a result of African nations' desire to define their own path to development for the second time.

NEPAD was considered a blueprint for African sustainable development that ensures "pan-African structures that can lead to the social and economic transformation of the continent in a rapidly globalizing world."[15] A distinct characteristic of NEPAD is that it is a plan (like the Logos Plan) that emerged from the African leaders themselves and was not imposed on them by the developed nations. At the core of NEPAD's development plan is "poverty alleviation, independently and communally incorporating African countries into sustainable growth and development; discontinuing marginalization of Africa in globalization, and integration into the global economy; and hastening women empowerment."[16] It also promises to deliver "peace and security, democracy, [and] good political, economic, and corporate governance."[17]

NEPAD, however, was tested over the last seventeen years, and has not made as much of a difference as expected. Most African nations have neither achieved the expected economic development nor secured peace and stability in their respective countries. As rightly described by Chinua Achebe, the great African poet and novelist, Africa is "no longer at ease."[18] African societies are still in crisis and many men and women all too often fail to find appropriate responses to their life problems.[19]

What mainly contributed to the failure of NEPAD, according to some critics, is its lack of detailed guidance on how to implement the plan.[20] These critics also note that the absence of some basic concerns shared among African nations (such as HIV/AIDS) in both NEPAD base document and associated documents had its own major consequence.[21] Others also emphasize that its foundation, the "old neo-liberal models of development," is what contributed to its weakness in addressing the genuine concerns of the African continent.[22] One cannot deny that the political crisis more African nations have experienced in the past decades have also contributed to the failure of NEPAD. In many countries, politicians were so caught up in their own struggle for power that issues related to development were neglected. Therefore, as Claude Ake rightly emphasized, "political conditions in Africa [have become] the greatest impediment to development."[23] At present, Africa is in a critical situation awaiting a response from the churches. Poverty has reached its lowest stage, with the result that most African people have preferred to migrate to European countries by any means.

This makes us ask questions such as: If NEPAD is not effective, how can it be improved or rearticulated so that it becomes a solid foundation for sustainable economic and human development? What can religion or theology contribute in strategizing a new economic development plan? And what should be the role of the church in both developing and implementing the strategy? I will respond to these questions based on Nussbaum's capabilities approach. But first, I will briefly discuss how African churches and theologians have engaged the issue of economic development during the postcolonial period.

CHURCH AND DEVELOPMENT IN POSTCOLONIAL AFRICA

In the first two decades when African nations started to gain their independence (1950s and early 1960s), when the issue of economic development was at the center of the discussions held among leaders of African nations (as stated previously), African church leaders and theologians focused on formulating a distinct and indigenous theology that totally ignored the role of the church in fostering economic development in Africa. The theological current that evolved in postcolonial Africa had a narrow focus on the cultural-religious dimension, which was later named "inculturation theology." Its emphasis was on how to adapt the gospel message to suit the African situation and ethos by describing the relationship between pre-Christian cultural and religious heritage and Christian traditions.[24]

One may wonder why the African church leaders, radicalized by revolutionary struggles, did not develop a theological stance on liberation in its political and economic dimensions. The answer is that most African countries had been under colonial powers that mostly worked hand in glove with missions, and missions before 1960s, according to David Bosch, had "no concern for liberation."[25] Just as officially declared during the 1937 conference on "Church, Community, and State" held at Oxford, they "claimed that the church's task was supranational, supraclass and supraracial."[26] Therefore, for too long, churches in Africa were not taught about the relationship between church and society, and were therefore not sure if issues related to development has anything to do with God's mission in the world. As Flora Musoda rightly notes, "the church in Africa has been encouraged for too long to think that its role is to save souls and not bodies."[27]

Furthermore, just as African countries were gaining independence, African theologians as emerging indigenous leaders of the church had the conviction that their first task should focus on deconstructing the theology planted by the western missionaries who brought it a concomitant interest in "the seed of perpetual Western superiority and domination."[28]

It was in the late 1960s and 1970s that some African theologians started to call for a different type of theology, liberation theology, which they thought would address the whole aspect of human life in Africa. The two major voices of liberation theology in the African context are Jean-Marc Éla and Engelbert Mveng from Cameroon. In their writings, they criticized the church in Africa for being silent in the face of corrupt and brutal governments with less or no concern for the development of their countries. The churches were criticized for a lack of family spirit, their unwillingness to share, and their lack of active solidarity with persons struggling to break free from misery and oppression. They emphasized that the African theologians' and leaders' emphasis on gospel-culture relationship has resulted in the churches' activity being limited to charitable works among the needy, and that not enough was done to empower Christians to be courageous enough to confront the systems—be it political, social, economic, or other—in a prophetic manner.[29]

In the case of South Africa, there arose liberation (Black) theology in the context of Apartheid where the native blacks were dehumanizingly segregated by the white minority. Black theology was aimed at challenging and undoing the then-dominant ideology of white supremacy that materialized in harsh treatment of black people in the country. The *Kairos Document*,[30] a document that emphasizes theology in its prophetic mode, a theology that speaks to the particular circumstances of various social, economic, and political crises, is a reflection of the true nature of liberation theology in the South African context.

The significance of liberation theology was that it "challenged academics to join the 'masses' in the struggle for economic justice, rather than analyze social structures without commitment to change them."[31] This was particularly realized when Cameroonian and South African theologians called for a shift from emphasis on culture-religion to liberation theology. This gained much attention during the Pan-African Conference of Third World theologians held in Accra (1977), where African church leaders admitted their silence in the face of structural injustices in postcolonial states and agreed to adopt liberation theology—a theology that emphasizes liberation from cultural captivity and kinds of oppression (social, political, and economic). Hence, the Conference announced, "African theology must also be *liberation* theology."[32]

Liberation theology was also a challenge to some churches in Africa that limited their ministry to the spiritual spheres of life. Many African churches understood and defined the role of the church as being limited to evangelism (restoring people's relationship with God) and neglected their other (social, economic, and political) responsibilities. Their main argument was founded on the understanding that God's redemptive act is concerned solely with the spiritual realm of life, but not with "physical" or "social" realms. These churches have also at times described development as a vehicle for evangelism, but not as part and parcel of God's mission in the world. Those involved in development work treated their social and economic ministry as separate sectors from the central ministry of the church, which is mainly evangelism.[33] Being challenged with liberation theology, some of these churches started to play a more active role in the social, economic, and political life of their respective countries even though the majority of their churches were still largely absent from the agenda and discussions taking place among secular institutions on issues related to development.[34]

After the demolition of apartheid in South Africa in 1992, which marked the dawn of a new political landscape in the country in particular and the rest of tropical Africa in general, theology's focus shifted from liberation to reconstruction. At this period in Africa's history, the theology of reconstruction was found to be essential because the sociopolitical questions of democracy, human rights, equality, and justice had normally been in its infancy, despite different human-made calamities. The proponents of the theology of reconstruction were the Kenyan theologian Jesse Mugambi followed by South African theologians Charles Villa-Vicencio and Archbishop Desmond Tutu.[35]

Reconstruction theology, according to Mugambi, is a comprehensive approach to engaging postcolonial Africa, which includes several components such as personal reconstruction, cultural reconstruction, ecclesial reconstruction, socioeconomic reconstruction, political reconstruction, and so on. In other words, it is a theology that provides the tools for African church leaders and theologians to engage in the renewal and transformation of Africa.[36] It is the new theological task that replaced the decade-long discourse on enculturation and liberation with emphasis on serious dialogue on democracy, human rights issues, law-making, nation building, and economics.[37]

In the last two decades, other scholars have been critical of reconstruction theology in addressing some real challenges in African social, economic, and political life without suggesting a better alternative. One of these theologians is Justin Thacker, who argues that the main problem with the theology of reconstruction is the "absence of concrete examples which are genuinely transformative and which instates the theology being articulated renders the theology effectively moot."[38] That means that reconstruction theology must translate its utopian ideals into practical actions. Julius Gathogo also identifies the following shortcomings in the theological methodology adopted: "Not rooted in the historical factors," not ecumenical, "not . . . multi-disciplinary," and it does not follow a "critical re-evaluation of Biblical themes" of liberation and reconstruction.[39] And according to Musa Dube, a theology of reconstruction also "remain[s] quite blind to the superstructure of patriarchy, which must be deconstructed in order to reconstruct. Otherwise, it is founded on sand as long as it does not address major oppressive issues of both globalization and patriarchy."[40] It is for these reasons that I propose a rearticulating of the reconstruction theology based on the capabilities approach—this rearticulating may lead to transformation of reconstruction theology into a more practical and comprehensive theology that can address all aspects of human development.

CAPABILITIES APPROACH

The distinctive nature of the twentieth-century discussion on human development is the dynamic interaction and fusion of the individual in his or her context. Among these approaches, this article mainly focuses on the new theoretical paradigm in human development theory—the capabilities approach. The capabilities approach has been cultivated in development economics by Amartya Sen and was used by the United Nations Development Program's annual Human Development Reports in the 1990s.[41] It is an emerging theory in political philosophy, and has been applied to other fields such as education, computer science, gender studies, psychiatric work, and religion.[42]

Among the major theorists of the capabilities approach, this study mainly draws from Martha Nussbaum's theory of basic social justice. Nussbaum defines the capabilities approach as "an approach to comprehensive quality-of-life assessment and theorizing about basic social justice."[43] The capabilities approach is a theoretical framework that entails two core values. First, "the freedom to achieve well-being is of primary moral importance."[44] Second, the freedom to achieve well-being is understood in terms of the people's capabilities (and opportunities) to be or to do "what they have reason to value."[45] Nussbaum argues that capabilities theory should be "informed by an intuitive idea of a life that is worthy of the dignity of the human being."[46]

Quoting Nussbaum,

> The core idea is that of the human being as a dignified free being who shapes his or her own life in cooperation and reciprocity with others, rather than being passively shaped or pushed around by the world in the manner of a "flock" or "herd" animal. A life that is really human is one that is shaped throughout by these human powers of practical reason and sociability.[47]

The capabilities approach basically focuses on responding to the following practical questions: "What are people actually able to do and to be? What real opportunities are available to them?"[48] It is with these basic questions that the capabilities approach diverts the emphasis of policy and development analysis from utilitarian and even resource theories (which emphasize incomes at the micro-level and gross domestic product per capita at the national level) to people's actual capabilities.

The capabilities approach concentrates on the functioning of individuals in areas deemed central to the quality of life. It aims at discovering what people are actually able to do and to be in relation to their social and political context. It gives due consideration to the practical opportunities that are created by a combination of the abilities that exist inside a person (like capacities and skills) with their social, economic, and political environment.[49] It is also *"concerned with entrenched social injustice and inequality, especially capabilities failure that are the result of discrimination and marginalization."*[50]

In this theory, Nussbaum offers a concrete list of ten central capabilities that she hopes will serve as a standard for determining social justice. This list (as found in her latest book, *Creating Capabilities*) is a development from her critical question that she asked in her book *Women and Human Development and Frontiers of Justice*, where she asks her readers to consider what makes for a minimally just society. She argues that it is a duty of both government and nongovernment organizations to ensure that all people meet minimal thresholds of those capabilities: life; bodily health; bodily integrity; senses, imagination, and thought; emotions; practical reason; affiliation; other species; play; and control over one's environment.[51]

Nussbaum identifies two types of capabilities: internal and combined. Internal capabilities are the general characteristics of a person (physical, mental, emotional) that are developed through interaction with external features of society.[52] According to Nussbaum, examples of internal capabilities are "personality traits, intellectual and emotional capacities, states of bodily fitness and health, internalized learning, skills of perception and movement" and the like.[53] Combined capabilities are "internal capabilities plus the social/political/economic conditions in which functioning can actually be chosen."[54] As such, the two types of capabilities are interrelated, and cannot be separated within a society. In other words, as Nussbaum emphasizes, one cannot separate the two because "it is not possible conceptually to think of a society producing combined capabilities without producing internal capabilities."[55]

REFRAMING NEPAD AND THE THEOLOGY OF RECONSTRUCTION

As described previously, both the African development plan named NEPAD and the African theology of reconstruction have one common shortcoming, which is lack of a concrete plan for how African nations are able to put the plan or proposed theology into practice. African nations have embraced and have adopted NEPAD for the last two decades, but we are not given any concrete examples where this plan has resulted in economic, social, and political transformation. Reconstruction theology also lacks emphasis on practical outworking of the theology being articulated. Anyone reading Mugambi's and other African theologians' work on reconstruction theology would appreciate the sentiment, but at the same time will end up asking the following question: what does this theology mean in practice?

The significance of Nussbaum's capabilities approach is that it provides us with a tool to transform both NEPAD and reconstruction theology into a more practical development plan and a theology of development respectively. The capabilities approach is a practical theory we can use to understand and seek solutions "in an area of urgent human problems and unjustifiable human inequalities."[56] According to Nussbaum, "the capabilities approach is fully universal: the capabilities in question are important for each and every citizen, in each and every nation, and each is to be treated as an end."[57] What is helpful for this is Nussbaum's appropriate list of what she calls "central [basic] human functional capabilities" (see previous discussion). It is this list that provides the NEPAD Plan and the theology of reconstruction to identify the function that Africans ought to promote for one another, and that the African States ought, as far as possible, to underwrite for all their members.

Secondly, as Joseph Morbi contends, NEPAD's lack of "details on how to tackle certain social issues leads to the apparent omission of" some basic economic and social concerns.[58] In the same way, the theology of reconstruction is also criticized for not presenting a list of functions that must be addressed in the reconstruction process. Rather than its inspirational purpose in motivating Christian Africans to engage in development activities, it does not clearly identify the "functionings" which the church should aspire to promote for the communities they serve. This is the main reason why I argue in this article that for NEPAD and reconstruction theology to move one step ahead, they must engage and adopt the language of a human development theory, particularly the capabilities approach. The capabilities approach, and the list of "central [basic] human functional capabilities" in particular, provides NEPAD and reconstruction theology a framework through which one can evaluate the government's and church's engagement with its environment. For the Christian church in particular, this theory provides a practical tool that helps to bridge the church and its mission. More importantly, in the African context where churches are most often characterized by an inward-looking emphasis on edification of the saints and ministries limited to the spiritual realm of life, this approach helps to address the social implications of the gospel of Jesus Christ.

Thirdly, NEPAD's weakness is also not recognizing the role of religions in bringing true human development into the African context. In the African context, it is impossible to think of development without considering the African worldview, which is holistic in that it does not see the physical and spiritual life as separate, but as one and combined. J. Mbiti rightly states, "Africans are notoriously religious, and each people has its own religious system with a set of beliefs and practices. *Religion permeates into all the departments of life so fully that it is not easy or possible always to isolate it.*"[59] This is the reason why Komi Hiagne rightly argues that it is impossible to isolate religious institutions in Africa when talking about development because they play a major role in shaping people's thoughts and cultural reconstruction.[60]

My argument is that, in the African context, true human development occurs only when one is able to formulate a plan that integrates the economic, social, political, cultural, and spiritual domains.[61] As rightly articulated by Pope John Paul VI, "development cannot be limited to mere economic growth [as developed by development theorists]. In order to be authentic, it must be integral, that is, it has to promote the good of every man and the whole of man."[62] As Bryant Myers rightly states, any development approach devoid of the good news of the Gospel is fatally impoverished.[63] Therefore, he contends, a true and successful approach to development is creating a context in which the individual and the community experience transformation through discovering their identity "as human beings created in the image of God" and vocation "as productive stewards" in Christ and being reconciled to the triune God.[64]

Similarly, one of the shortcoming of reconstruction theology is that it does not follow a multidisciplinary approach. To fully address issues related to sustainable human development, the theology of reconstruction will have to borrow heavily from other related disciplines. It needs to dialogue with and employ methodologies adopted in the social sciences such as sociology, psychology, philosophy, environmental science, cultural studies, and so on.[65] As Mugambi also emphasized, "the multi-disciplinary appeal of reconstruction makes the concept [of reconstruction] functionally useful as a thematic focus for reflection in Africa during the coming decades."[66] The language of the capabilities approach provides us with a common language we can use to help both the government and religious institutions develop a shared vision.

Finally, the theory of capabilities is a significant theory to conceptualize the notion of functioning and capabilities as elements in the explanation of social phenomena, particularly for understanding how African nations and churches are functioning in creating capabilities. More importantly, the general classification between the two types of capabilities (internal and combined capabilities) helps to study how Africans flourish both as individuals and how their internal capabilities are nurtured by both governmental and nongovernmental institutions that serve them on a day-to-day basis (here, we take these institutions as combined capabilities).

African nations and churches are being criticized for focusing on responding to temporary problems (like relief) rather than promoting an increase in the people's personal and institutional capacities. In other words, the emphasis has been given to material and financial provisions (as a means to changing the situation of the poor) rather than human and institutional development.[67] Considering Nussbaum's approach helps Africa to promote the most important human capabilities by supporting both internal and combined capabilities through emphasis on "education, resources to enhance physical and emotional health, support for family care and love, a system of education, and much more."[68]

CONCLUSION

In the past sixty plus years, African nations have been struggling with issues related to ensuring sustainable human development. In their annual and biannual meetings, they have passed several resolutions that addressed a wide range of issues, which finally resulted in a development plan named NEPAD adopted in 2001. Similarly, in African Christian studies, the issue regarding the contribution of Christian faith to human development has been at the center of theological discourses since the early 1990s. These discourses were a way responding to situations in Africa in which the majority still live under conditions of economic deprivation. The most important outcome of the discourses has been the theology of reconstruction as articulated by Mugambi of Kenya. This theology aspires to contribute to the teaching and practice of African Christian communities in bringing change in the everyday life of people who are in crisis.

These two development plans, however, contributed much less than what they promised and what most Africans have probably expected. In Africa, hundreds of millions live in utter poverty, experiencing inhuman conditions. Rather than improving these conditions, leaders of African nations seemed more concerned about their own survival. Their focus on survival means that the goal of sustainable community development is neglected. Most religious institutions in Africa, on the other hand, define their mission as limited to spiritual activities of the church and relief work.

The theory of the capabilities approach provides us with a tool to challenge, reframe, and rearticulate the governments' plan (NEPAD) and the African churches' plan (or theology of reconstruction) in a way such that they both become productive in changing the lives of the African people. For this to happen, the combined interplay between theology, human development theories, and policies of the successive governments of African nations is required.

BIBLIOGRAPHY

Adesinia, J. "Development and the Challenges of Poverty: Nepad, Post-Washington Consensus and Beyond." In *Africa and Development Challenges in the New Millennium: The Nepad Debate*, edited by Adesinia J. and Olukoshi Y. London: Zed Books LTD, 2005.
Ake, Claude. *Democracy and Development in Africa*. Washington DC: The Brookings Institution, 1996.
Anand, P. "Capabilities and Health." *Journal of Medical Ethics* 31 (2005): 299–303.
Appiah-Kubi, Kofi, and Sergio Torres, eds. *Final Communiqué* African Theology En Route: Papers from the Pan African Conference of Third World Theologians, December 17–23, Accra, Ghana. Maryknoll, NY: Orbis, 1979.
Bediako, Kwame. "African Theology." In *The Modern Theologians: An Introduction to Christian Theology in Twentieth Century*, edited by David E. Ford. London: Blackwell, 1997.
Bediako, Kwame. "Understanding African Theology in the 20th Century." *Themelios* 20, no. 1 (October 1994).
Bosch, David Jacobus. *Transforming Mission: Paradigm Shifts in Theology of Mission*. Maryknoll, NY: Orbis, 1991.
Bragg, Wayne. "Beyond Development." In *The Church in Response to Human Need*, edited by Tome Sine. California: MARC, 1983.
Bujo, Bénézet. *African Theology in Its Social Context*. Maryknoll, NY: Orbis, 1992.
Challenge to the Church: Theological Comment on the Political Crisis in South Africa. Pcr Information: Reports and Background Papers. Geneva: World Council of Churches, Programme to Combat Racism, 1985.
Deressa, Samuel Yonas. "Church and State in Ethiopia: The Contribution of the Lutheran Understanding of the Community of Grace." *Word and World* 37, no. 3 (2017).
―――, ed. *Revisiting the History, Theology, and Leadership Practice of the Ethiopian Evangelical Church Mekane Yesus*. Minneapolis: Lutheran University Press, 2016.
Eide, Øyvind. "Integral Human Development." In *The Life and Ministry of Gudina Tumsa*, edited by Paul E. Hoffman, vol. 2. Hamburg: WDL, 2008.
Éla, Jean-Marc. *African Cry*. Maryknoll, NY: Orbis, 1986.
―――. *My Faith as an African*. Maryknoll, NY: Orbis, 1988.
Fashole-Luke, E. W. "The Quest for an African Christianity." *The Ecumenical Review* 27, no. 3 (1975).
Florian, L. "How Can Capability Theory Contribute to Understanding Provision for People with Learning Difficulties?" *Prospero* 14 (2008): 24–33.
Gathogo, Julius. "A Survey on an African Theology of Reconstruction (Ator)." *Swedish Missiological Themes* 95, no. 2 (2007).
―――. "The Tasks in African Theology of Reconstruction." *Swedish Missiological Themes* 96, no. 2 (2008).
Heinrich, Geoff, David Leege, and Carrie Miller. *A User's Guide to Integral Human Development*. Baltimore, MD: Catholic Relief Services, 2008.
Hiagbe, Komi. "The Church and Sustainable Development in Sub-Saharan Africa." *Studia Historiae Ecclesiasticae* 41, no. 2 (2015).
Hoffman, Paul, ed. *Church and Society: Second Missiological Seminar on the Life and Ministry of Gudina Tumsa, General Secretary of the Ethiopian Evangelical Church Mekane Yesus (1966–1979)*. Hamburg: WDL, 2011.
―――. "Ministry to the 'Whole Man' Revisited—a Look Back in Order to Look Ahead." In *Serving the Whole Person: The Practice and Understanding of Diakonia within the Lutheran Communion*, edited by Kjell Schlagenhaft. Minneapolis: Lutheran University Press, 2010.
Johnstone, J. "Technology as Empowerment: A Capability Approach to Computer Ethics." *Ethics and Information Technology* 9 (2007): 73–78.
Korgen, J. Odell. "Catholic Relief Services: Fostering Integral Human Development through Charity in Truth." In *Religious Leadership: A Reference Handbook*, edited by Sharon Henderson Callahan. Los Angeles: Sage.

Korten, David C. *Getting to the 21st Century: Voluntary Action and the Global Agenda.* West Hartford, CN: Kumarian, 1990.

Majawa, Clement. "African Quest for Original Index of Holistic Development: Church and State, 50 Years after Independence." *African Ecclesial Review* 56, no. 2 and 3 (2014).

Maluleke, Tinyiko. "The Bible and African Theologies." In *Interpreting the New Testament in Africa*, edited by M. Getui, T. Maluleke and J. Ukpong. Nairobi: Action, 2001.

Mbiti, John S. *African Religions and Philosophy.* New York: Praeger, 1969.

The Metaphysics Research Lab, Center for the Study of Language and Information. "The Capability Approach." *Stanford Encyclopedia of Philosophy.* Accessed October 13, 2015, from https://plato.stanford.edu/entries/capability-approach/.

Morbi, Joseph. Accessed April 10, 2018, from https://www.e-ir-info/2011/10/26/is-nepad-an-effective-development-organization/.

Mugambi, J. N. K. *Christian Theology and Social Reconstruction.* Nairobi: Action, 2003.

———. *From Liberation to Reconstruction.* Nairobi: EAEP, 1995.

Murage, Josiah Kinyau. "Development and Reconstruction Theologies of Africa." *Swedish Missiological Themes* 95, no. 2 (2007).

Musonda, Flora M. "Myths and Realities of Poverty in Africa: The Impact of Debt and Global Policies on Local Economies." In *So the Poor Have Hope*, edited by Karen L. Bloomquist and Musa Panti Filibus. Geneva: LWF, 2007.

Mveng, Engelbert. "Impoverishment and Liberation: A Theological Approach for Africa and the Third World." In *Paths of African Theology*, edited by Rosino Gibellini. London: CSM Press, 1994.

Myers, Bryant L. *Walking with the Poor: Principles and Practices of Transformational Development.* Maryknoll, NY: Orbis, 2011.

Nussbaum, Martha Craven. *Aristotle, Politics, and Human Capabilities: A Response to Antony, Arneson, Charlesworth, and Mulgan.* Chicago: University of Chicago Press, 2000.

———. *Creating Capabilities: The Human Development Approach.* Cambridge, MA: Harvard University Press, 2011.

———. *Frontiers of Justice: Disability, Nationality, Species Membership.* The Tanner Lectures on Human Values. Cambridge, MA: Belknap, 2006.

———. *Women and Human Development: The Capabilities Approach.* Cambridge, UK: Cambridge University Press, 2000.

Nyerere, Julius. *Freedom and Development: A Selection from Writing and Speeches 1968–1973.* Oxford: Oxford University Press, 1973.

Onimode, Bade, Mbaya Kankwende, S. O. Tomori, and Olu Ajakaiya. *Africa Development and Governance Strategies in the 21st Century.* London: Zed, 2004.

Organization of African Unity (OAU). "Logos Plan of Action for the Economic Development of Africa, 1980–2000." Geneva: International Institution for Labour Studies, 1982.

Prempeh, E. Osei Kwadwo. *Against Global Capitalism: African Social Movements Confront Neoliberal Globalization.* Aldershot, UK: Ashgate, 2006.

Shorter, Aylward. *African Christian Theology: Adaptation or Incarnation?* Maryknoll, NY: Orbis, 1977.

Stiglitz, J. *Globalization and Its Discontents.* New York: W. W. Norton, 2002.

Thacker, Justin. *Global Poverty: A Theological Guide.* London: CSP Press, 2017.

Villa-Vicencio, Charles. *A Theology of Reconstruction.* Cambridge, UK: Cambridge University Press, 1992.

Wayne, Bragg. "Beyond Development." In *The Church in Response to Human Need*, edited by Tome Sine. California: MARC, 1983.

NOTES

1. Claude Ake, *Democracy and Development in Africa* (Washington DC: The Brookings Institution, 1996), 8–9; Julius Nyerere, *Freedom and Development: A Selection from Writing and Speeches 1968–1973* (Oxford: Oxford University Press, 1973).

2. Charles Villa-Vicencio, *A Theology of Reconstruction* (Cambridge, UK: Cambridge University Press, 1992); J. N. K Mugambi, *Christian Theology and Social Reconstruction* (Nairobi: Action, 2003). Archbishop Desmond Tutu have not published a book on a theology of reconstruction. However, he is known for a proposal for a shift of paradigm from liberation to a reconstruction theology during his tenure as president of All Africa Council of Churches where this idea was first entertained based on Mugambi's presentation titled "Future of the Church and the Church of the Future in Africa."

3. In Ethiopia, similar theology, named the *theology of holistic ministry*, was developed by Gudina Tumsa, general secretary of the Ethiopian Evangelical Church Mekane Yesus (1966–1979). See Paul Hoffman, ed., *Church and Society: Second Missiological Seminar on the Life and Ministry of Gudina Tumsa, General Secretary of the Ethiopian Evangelical Church Mekane Yesus (1966–1979)* (Hamburg: WDL,- 2011); Paul Hoffman, "Ministry to the Whole Man' Revisited—a Look Back in Order to Look Ahead," in *Serving the Whole Person: The Practice and Understanding of Diakonia within the Lutheran Communion*, ed. Kjell Schlagenhaft (Minneapolis: Lutheran University Press, 2010); Samuel Yonas Deressa, ed. *Revisiting the History, Theology, and Leadership Practice of the Ethiopian Evangelical Church Mekane Yesus* (Minneapolis: Lutheran University Press, 2016); Øyvind Eide, "Integral Human Development," in *The Life and Ministry of Gudina Tumsa*, ed. Paul E. Hoffman, vol. 2 (Hamburg: WDL Publishers, 2008).

4. Martha Craven Nussbaum, *Creating Capabilities: The Human Development Approach* (Cambridge, MA: Harvard University Press, 2011), 18.

5. Ake, *Democracy and Development in Africa*, 21.

6. Ibid., 22.

7. Bade Onimode et al., *Africa Development and Governance Strategies in the 21st Century* (London: Zed, 2004), 3.

8. Ake, *Democracy and Development in Africa*, 23.

9. Ibid., 23

10. Organization of African Unity (OAU), "Logos Plan of Action for the Economic Development of Africa, 1980–2000," (Geneva: International Institution for Labour Studies, 1982), 3.

11. Justin Thacker, *Global Poverty: A Theological Guide* (London: CSP, 2017), 163. Emphasis mine.

12. Ake, *Democracy and Development in Africa*, 25.

13. J. Stiglitz, *Globalization and Its Discontents* (New York: W. W. Norton, 2002), 18; Thacker, *Global Poverty*, 164.

14. For discussion of the African Union in the past years, see the Millennium Partnership for the African Recovery Program, which was drafted by President Mbeki of South Africa, President Bouteflik of Algeria, President Obasanjo of Nigeria, and President Mubarak of Egypt, and the OMEGA plan drafted and presented by President Wade of Senegal. See Josiah Kinyau Murage, "Development and Reconstruction Theologies of Africa," *Swedish Missiological Themes* 95, no. 2 (2007). Also see New Partnership for Africa's Development, accessed February 15, 2018, from http://www.un.org/en/africa/osaa/peace/nepad.shtml.

15. Murage, "Development and Reconstruction," 151.

16. Ibid.

17. Ibid.

18. Quote in Clement Majawa, "African Quest for Original Index of Holistic Development: Church and State, 50 Years after Independence " *African Ecclesial Review* 56, no. 2 and 3 (2014): 109.

19. Jean-Marc Éla, *African Cry* (Maryknoll, NY: Orbis Books, 1986); Flora M. Musonda, "Myths and Realities of Poverty in Africa: The Impact of Debt and Global Policies on Local Economies," in *So the Poor Have Hope*, ed. Karen L. Bloomquist and Musa Panti Filibus (Geneva: LWF, 2007).

20. J. Adesinia, "Development and the Challenges of Poverty: Nepad, Post-Washington Consensus and Beyond," in *Africa and Development Challenges in the New Millennium: The Nepad Debate*, ed. Adesinia J. and Olukoshi Y. (London: Zed, 2005), 34.

21. Ibid.

22. E. Osei Kwadwo Prempeh, *Against Global Capitalism: African Social Movements Confront Neoliberal Globalization* (Aldershot, UK: Ashgate, 2006), 103–104.

23. Ake, *Democracy and Development in Africa*, 1.

24. See Kwame Bediako, "African Theology," in *The Modern Theologians: An Introduction to Christian Theology in Twentieth Century*, ed. David E. Ford (London: Blackwell, 1997); Kwame Bediako, "Understanding African Theology in the 20th Century," *Themelios* 20, no. 1 (October 1994); Bénézet Bujo, *African Theology in Its Social Context* (Maryknoll, NY: Orbis, 1992); E. W. Fashole-Luke, "The Quest for an African Christianity," *The Ecumenical Review* 27, no. 3 (1975); John S. Mbiti, *African Religions and Philosophy* (New York: Praeger, 1969).

25. David Jacobus Bosch, *Transforming Mission: Paradigm Shifts in Theology of Mission* (New York: Orbis Books, 1991), 433. The issue that dominated the ecumenical discussions for over thirty years after the first Church and Society Conference held in Stockholm in 1925 was "the problem of the West and the (Marxist) East." See ibid.

26. Ibid.

27. Musonda, "Myths and Realities," 61.

28. Aylward Shorter, *African Christian Theology: Adaptation or Incarnation?* (Maryknoll, NY: Orbis, 1977), 150.

29. Kofi Appiah-Kubi and Sergio Torres, eds., *Final Communiqué* African Theology En Route: Papers from the Pan African Conference of Third World Theologians, December 17–23, Accra, Ghana (Maryknoll: Orbis, 1979); Éla, *African Cry*; Jean-Marc Éla, *My Faith as an African* (Maryknoll, NY: Orbis, 1988); Engelbert Mveng, "Impoverishment and Liberation: A Theological Approach for Africa and the Third World," in *Paths of African Theology*, ed. Rosino Gibellini (London: CSM Press, 1994).

30. *Challenge to the Church: Theological Comment on the Political Crisis in South Africa*, Pcr Information: Reports and Background Papers (Geneva: World Council of Churches, Programme to Combat Racism, 1985).

31. Mugambi, *Christian Theology and Social Reconstruction*, 29.

32. Appiah-Kubi and Torres, "*Final Communiqué*," 194. Emphasis added.

33. The term *evangelism* is a loaded term with different meanings. In this article, it refers to the verbal proclamation of the gospel.

34. Samuel Yonas Deressa, "Church and State in Ethiopia: The Contribution of the Lutheran Understanding of the Community of Grace," *Word and World* 37, no. 3 (2017).

35. Villa-Vicencio, *A Theology of Reconstruction*; Mugambi, *Christian Theology and Social Reconstruction*. Archbishop Desmond Tutu has not yet published a book on a theology of reconstruction. However, he is known for a proposal for a shift of paradigm from liberation to a reconstruction theology while he was the president of All African Council of Churches (AACC) where this idea was first entertained based on Mugambi's presentation titled "Future of the Church and the Church of the Future in Africa" (see the work cited above).

36. Mugambi, *Christian Theology and Social Reconstruction*.

37. For details, see Julius Gathogo, "The Tasks in African Theology of Reconstruction," *Swedish Missiological Themes* 96, no. 2 (2008); Tinyiko Maluleke, "The Bible and African Theologies," in *Interpreting the New Testament in Africa*, ed. M. Getui, T. Maluleke, and J. Ukpong (Nairobi: Action, 2001).

38. Thacker, *Global Poverty*, 175.

39. Gathogo, "The Tasks in African Theology of Reconstruction," 165–177.

40. Quoted in Julius Gathogo, "A Survey on an African Theology of Reconstruction (Ator)," *Swedish Missiological Themes* 95, no. 2 (2007): 128.

41. Martha C. Nussbaum, *Aristotle, Politics, and Human Capabilities: A Response to Antony, Arneson, Charlesworth, and Mulgan* (Chicago: The University of Chicago, 2000), 65.

42. P. Anand, "Capabilities and Health," *Journal of Medical Ethics* 31 (2005): 299–303; L. Florian, "How Can Capability Theory Contribute to Understanding Provision for People with Learning Difficulties?" *Prospero* 14 (2008): 24–33; J. Johnstone, "Technology as Empowerment: A Capability Approach to Computer Ethics," *Ethics and Information Technology* 9 (2007): 73–78.

43. Nussbaum, *Creating Capabilities*, 18.

44. The Metaphysics Research Lab, Center for the Study of Language and Information, "The Capability Approach," *Stanford Encyclopedia of Philosophy*, accessed October 13, 2015, from https://plato.stanford.edu/entries/capability-approach/.
45. Ibid.
46. Martha Craven Nussbaum, *Women and Human Development: The Capabilities Approach* (Cambridge, UK: Cambridge University Press, 2000), 5.
47. Ibid., 72.
48. Nussbaum, *Creating Capabilities*, x, 14. Nussbaum has also developed this theory in her other works such as Nussbaum, *Women and Human Development*; Martha Craven Nussbaum, *Frontiers of Justice: Disability, Nationality, Species Membership*, The Tanner Lectures on Human Values (Cambridge, MA: Belknap, 2006).
49. Nussbaum, *Creating Capabilities*, xi–xii, 20.
50. Ibid., 19. Emphasis original.
51. Ibid., 33–34.
52. Ibid., 23.
53. Ibid., 21.
54. Ibid., 22.
55. Ibid.
56. Ibid., xii.
57. Ibid.; Nussbaum, *Aristotle, Politics, and Human Capabilities*, 125.
58. Joseph Morbi. Accessed April 10, 2018, from https://www.e-ir-info/2011/10/26/is-nep-ad-an-effective-development-organization/.
59. John S. Mbiti, *African Religions and Philosophy* (New York: Anchor Books, 1970) 1.
60. Komi Hiagbe, "The Church and Sustainable Development in Sub-Saharan Africa," *Studia Historiae Ecclesiasticae* 41, no. 2 (2015): 10.
61. Geoff Heinrich, David Leege, and Carrie Miller, *A User's Guide to Integral Human Development* (Baltimore, MD: Catholic Relief Services, 2008), 2. The term *integral human development* was first coined by Pope Paul VI in 1967 in his letter to the bishops (encyclical) entitled *Populorum Progressio* (Development of the People). See J. Odell Korgen, "Catholic Relief Services: Fostering Integral Human Development through Charity in Truth," in *Religious Leadership: A Reference Handbook*, ed. Sharon Henderson Callahan (Los Angeles: Sage), 498.
62. Heinrich, Leege, and Miller, *A User's Guide*, 2.
63. Bryant L. Myers, *Walking with the Poor: Principles and Practices of Transformational Development* (Maryknoll, NY: Orbis, 2011), 3.
64. Ibid.
65. Gathogo, "The Tasks in African Theology of Reconstruction," 172.
66. J. N. K Mugambi, *From Liberation to Reconstruction* (Nairobi: EAEP, 1995), 2.
67. David C. Korten, *Getting to the 21st Century: Voluntary Action and the Global Agenda* (West Hartford, CN: Kumarian, 1990). Wayne Bragg also argues in his article that a biblical understanding of development requires churches to go beyond relief, and include components such as equity (equitable distribution of resources), justice (in all social, economic, and political relationships), dignity and self-worth (feeling fully human), freedom (from all kinds of oppression), participation, reciprocity (between poor and rich), cultural fit (respect of all cultures), and ecological soundness. See Wayne Bragg, "Beyond Development," in *The Church in Response to Human Need*, ed. Tome Sine (California: MARC, 1983), 37–95.
68. Nussbaum, *Creating Capabilities*, 21.

Chapter 2

Church and Development in Ethiopia

The Contribution of Gudina Tuma's Holistic Theology

Samuel Yonas Deressa

Evangelical Christianity was introduced to Ethiopia over a hundred years ago. Through their ministries, evangelical Christians have been playing a major role in shaping the values and attitudes of individuals and societies in terms of social behaviors and political and economic activities. In the past few decades, however, religious instructions (particularly among Evangelicals) have largely been absent from the agenda of development. As studies indicate, this absence is due to teachings and practices that separate between the spiritual and physical realms.[1]

The Ethiopian evangelical churches' approach to development is influenced by two major emphases: the Western missions' emphasis on development as against evangelism and the Pentecostal church's teaching and practice that waters down all except the spiritual activities of the church. These two approaches to development have resulted in mission activities in Ethiopia suffering longstanding dichotomization between evangelism and development, "which have been considered as mismatching pair that exist and operate in their own differing worlds."[2]

Development activities of faith-based organizations in Ethiopia have either been used as a vehicle for evangelism or were considered as the sole purpose of Christian mission. Both these approaches are problematic since faith and development belong together. This chapter, which is based on Gudina Tumsa's understanding of holistic theology, proposes a holistic approach to development as a critique and an alternative to the previously mentioned one-sided and partial practices of service in a society.

Chapter 2
CHALLENGES TO A HOLISTIC APPROACH TO MISSION

Ethiopia is one of the oldest Christian nations. Christianity was introduced to Ethiopia in the fourth century. Adopting the Eastern Orthodox tradition, the Ethiopian Orthodox Church (EOC) was established as a national church. The history of evangelical churches in Ethiopia, however, begins with the first attempt of Lutheran missionaries to reform the EOC in the seventeenth century, followed by the first successful mission endeavor of the Swedish Evangelical Mission (SEM), which happened at the end of the nineteenth century.[3]

The first three missionaries of the SEM, Lars-Johan Lange, Per-Eric Kjellberg, and Johan Carlsson, were sent to reach Ethiopians, particularly the Oromo tribe, via Sudan in 1866.[4] However, when they arrived at Kunama (a town in today's Eritrea), they were faced with two major problems. First, the missionaries learned that the River Nile was too unstable for expedition. Second, the Ethiopian emperor, Emperor Tewodros, had closed all the ways to the Oromo territory out of suspicion of the missionaries' desire to connect with that part of the country. Therefore, the missionaries were forced to remain in Kunama and work among the people of that area until the situation changed.[5]

Because of local wars among the Kunama, the SEM missionaries had to move to a new location called Massawa in 1870, and later build their mission station at Imkulu. According to Eric Virgin, Imkulu, "the territory around and to the west of Massawa, was at the time a no-man's-land" divided between Ethiopia and Egypt.[6] This situation created a favorable context for the SEM to feely engage in mission, which would be a strong foundation for the start of evangelical churches in Ethiopia. Here, the SEM had to wait for a period of twenty-eight years to realize their primary mission of reaching the Oromo territory.

The SEM's understanding of mission at the time can be understood from the general policy they adopted in 1871, which says, "mission should not only be a mission of preaching, but also a mission of service which in the beginning lays more stress on carrying for those in need."[7] At Imkulu, they opened a fully equipped school that provided a Western form of education to the local community. Carpentry and metalwork were also part of the curriculum. Additionally, they established a printing press and started to publish Scriptures translated into local languages.[8] In this way, the SEM founded a mission station that provided holistic service to the community. This approach helped the SEM to win souls around their mission station. As a result of mutual interaction between the SEM and the Reformed EOC clergy, the Eritrean Evangelical Church was also founded. However, as Halldin Norberg explains, "the work [of the SEM] in Eritrea was regarded only as a station on the way to the Oromo."[9]

The work of the SEM in providing religious as well as other forms of education at Imkulu resulted in a different, but fruitful, strategy to reach the Oromo with the gospel. It was this little seed planted by the SEM at Imkulu that would grow like a tree throughout Ethiopia as indigenous converts trained at this institution became pioneers of Evangelical faith among the Oromo. These converts were freed Oromo slaves, poor fugitives, and exiled reformers—Eritrean clergy who were in conflict with EOC for adopting the Evangelical faith. The SEM's holistic approach to evangelism became a strong foundation and a viable strategy for indigenous missionaries that, following their footsteps, reached out to other parts of Ethiopia. From this time on, evangelization was linked with the holistic services that the church provides for the community it serves: education, health services, providing shelter and food, and advocating and voicing for the poor and the marginalized.

Gebre-Ewostatewos Ze-Mikael (1865–1905) and Daniel Debela (1866–1904) were the two indigenous missionaries (both trained at Imkulu) who reached the Oromo for the first time in 1898. They were engaged in evangelism and development work from the day they started ministering among the people. Besides religious instructions and changing the livelihood of the community, both Ze-Mikael and Debela organized a team and together started an elementary school where they introduced modern education to the local community and where "students who were born by landless parents were encouraged to take up manual crafts which promoted local economy and social change."[10] They also discouraged slavery, and paid from their own pockets to free as many slaves as possible.[11] They were later joined by Onesimos Nesib and two women, Aster Ganno and Feben Hirpe, all freed slaves trained at Imkulu by the SEM.[12]

Indigenous pioneers have also contributed to the indigenization of the Ethiopian Evangelical Church Mekane Yesus (EECMY) by using local languages in worship; translating Scriptures, liturgies, and hymn books into local languages; and using cultural concepts in translating and evangelizing the communities. It was Nesib who played a major role in translating hymn books that contained one hundred songs in 1887, which he named *Galata Waaqayyoo Gooftaa Maccaa* (Glory to the Everlasting God). He also translated the New Testament (1893), the whole Bible (1899), Luther's *Small Catechism*, and Dr. Barth's *Bible Story* with the assistance of Ganno and Hirpe. In addition, he wrote a book, *Jalqaba Barsiisaa*, also known as *The Readers* (1894), with the assistance of Ganno and Hirpe.[13] One may ask what translation has to do with helping the Christian community in becoming active in the socioeconomic life of its country. As Andrian Hastings rightly argues, translation of the Bible and other literatures into vernacular languages results in the building of the national consciousness.[14] It was the availability of these translations coupled with other forms of indigenization (as mentioned previously) that has continued to shape congregational ministries (which is holistic) and is how the EECMY continued to be engaged in nation building.[15]

When the door was opened for missionaries to work in Ethiopia, evangelical Christianity was already an established movement following the tradition of the SEM. Upon their arrival, the missionaries strengthened the work and helped in the establishment of congregations. This took place until the Italian occupation (1936–1945). Upon Italy's invasion, European missionaries were expelled and indigenous leaders continued to plant congregations and provide holistic service to the communities they served. As Eide states, "[F]rom the very beginning of the evangelical enterprise in Ethiopia, we see that wherever there is a congregation there is a school. Wherever a group of evangelical Christians gathered they established a school."[16]

Following Ethiopia's liberation from the Italian occupation in 1941, Western mission organizations started to come back to Ethiopia after Emperor Haile Selassie I permitted them to freely work in the country. The freedom, however, was given with certain restrictions. One was on the work of evangelism, which limited the missionaries' spheres of evangelical work to the so-called mission-open areas—areas not designated to the EOC.[17] According to the Emperor's autobiography, this permission was granted to missionaries because of their contribution to education and health services. The Emperor's goal was to modernize the country using mission organizations as a means for the introduction of modern education, social services, and medical services in all parts of the country.[18]

The missionaries provided modern education coupled with theological training, which enhanced the ministry of the church. They played a major role in providing modern education to the communities they served. The training centers, hospitals, schools, and other institutions planted by missionaries were meant to meet the spiritual and physical demands of the community. As Eide emphasizes, this approach "led to a re-establishment of the dignity and the identity of ethnic groups, which in turn came to play a role in the Ethiopian revolution."[19]

The shift in the missionaries' approach to mission, however, started to change in the early 1960s. This shift was from a holistic approach to mission to a new emphasis on social action and community development.[20] This shift was preceded by the new concept of development that emerged in the West after the Second World War, particularly in the 1950s, "to describe the wellbeing of the poor."[21] During those years, the intellectual discourse was focused on economics mainly because it was the time when Western nations were under pressure to grant political independence to their respective colonies in Africa.[22] In this discourse, the term *civilization* was equated with "Christianization," which led to promotion of economic prosperity as a means of redeeming Africa to Christ.[23]

This shift resulted in an imbalance in funding received from the West for development projects over against projects that supported the evangelistic outreach of churches in Africa, particularly the EECMY. The Western mission organizations were "readily prepared to assist in material development, while there seemed to be little interest in helping the church meet her primary obligation to proclaim the Gospel."[24] As Megersa Guta also noted, there were also labels put on machinery used in development projects of the church that read "not for evangelism work."[25] This stipulation was of course the requirement of some governments that were able to contribute resources to church programs, for example, agricultural development, but not to church programs in evangelism. Even though the EECMY was not convinced by the new approach of the Western mission organizations, its traditional holistic approach to mission was challenged. To the present time, Western partner churches of the EECMY hold onto similar theological positions that give little or no attention to the evangelistic mission of the church. Therefore, how the church continues to uphold its holistic theology and practice remains a challenge.

Besides the theology and practice introduced by Western missionaries, the EECMY's understanding of mission, particularly related to development, was also influenced by the Pentecostal movement that started in the early 1950s.[26] This movement was started by the Swedish Philadelphia Church Mission and the Finish mission. In the 1960s, many young Ethiopians were attracted to the movement, and the first Pentecostal church, the Ethiopian Full Gospel Believer's Church, was established as a result in 1967. Their application to be registered as a national church was rejected the same year by the Ministry of the Interior, which entailed the closure of the church's meeting places.[27] This resulted in the influx of a large number of Pentecostal believers into the mainline denominations, including the EECMY, until they were allowed to have their own worship places in 1991.

As Gemecho Olana states, "one of the dominant features of the [Pentecostal] movement in Ethiopia is their reluctance to engage in social action or prophetic ministry. [They] are indifferent to the social implication of the gospel and take no interest in politics."[28] They emphasized the "otherworldliness" of Christians, which encouraged political and economic passivity. In their teaching, they discouraged members from having commitment to anything other than the spiritual aspects of life. According to Mamusha Fanta, one of the main Pentecostal leaders, "the major reason that made [Pentecostals] passive when it comes to economic and political things was that [they] perceived that the government [that persecuted them] was anti-Christian."[29]

The teaching of the Pentecostal movement that emphasizes the spiritual aspect of life and gives little or no value to social, economic, and political matters has influenced most of the EECMY members. Its major impact was on creating two separate worldviews about reality: the sacred (good) and secular (evil). Spiritual practices (worship, preaching, and so on) are considered as heavenly and other activities (in the social, economic, and political realms) are described as evil or other-worldly.[30]

THE EECMY ON HOLISTIC MINISTRY (EVANGELISM VS. DEVELOPMENT)

The EECMY's theology, commonly described as "holistic theology," was developed by Gudina Tumsa, the General Secretary of the EECMY (1966–1979) in response to the two challenges mentioned previously: the West's emphasis on development over against evangelism and the influence of the Pentecostal movement on members of the EECMY (which highlighted the spiritual aspect of mission). For Tumsa, God's mission could not be dichotomized between the spiritual and physical because it was holistic in nature.[31]

Tumsa's distinct contribution to the church worldwide can be viewed from his perspective on holistic ministry. He was a holistic thinker who believed in the undivided human reality. Tumsa's concept of holism is built on Africans' view of life in its totality. This became most obvious in the context of international church and development work through the EECMY's 1972 document "On the Interrelation between the Proclamation of the Gospel and Human Development."[32]

This document addressed the theological basis of human development involved in the development efforts of the EECMY in collaboration with partnering churches, established the EECMY's theology of "serving the whole person," and has guided its development programs ever since. The core of this theology is the notion of "holistic ministry," which serves both the spiritual and material needs of the human person. This particular brand of "holistic ministry" is deeply rooted in an African concept of the place of human beings vis-à-vis God's creation and it centers on the idea of "integral human development," which views proclamation of the gospel and human development as having the same objective—transforming the human being in society.

In the document, Tumsa and EECMY's leaders define development from a Christian point of view as "a process of liberation by which individuals and societies realize their human possibilities in accordance with God's purpose."[33] This process starts with being freed from one's own "self-centered greed" by the liberating power of the Gospel of Jesus Christ.[34] It is this freedom that leads to "development of the inner man [which is] a pre-requisite for a healthy and lasting development of [the] society."[35] The spiritual freedom and maturity is basic for lasting development because it "enables [individuals and the society to] responsibly handle material development."[36]

Otherwise, "what was intended to be a means of enhancing the wellbeing of man can have the opposite effect and create new forms of evil" that results in the destruction of the society.[37]

Tumsa and other EECMY leaders articulated this theological statement at the height of the so-called golden age of development and presented these ideas as a critique of the dominant ecumenical debate over the nature of the relationship between the new independent churches in the developing world and their missionary counterparts in the West. The leaders were trying to communicate to their Western partners that in the church's involvement in God's mission there exists no dichotomy between the sacred and the profane, the physical and the spiritual, the religious and the moral. In the main, the religious and the moral permeate the physical, material, political, and social concerns of the people. They emphasized that churches should strive to promote the well-being of the members of society, and Christians must promote the well-being of community and restore it when it is disrupted.

In this document, Tumsa and other leaders of the EECMY addressed the Lutheran World Federation (LWF) with the following statement:

> We believe that an integral human development, where spiritual and material needs are seen together, is the only right approach to the development question in our society. . . . The division between witness and service or between proclamation and development is harmful to the church and will ultimately result in a distorted Christianity. . . . The development of the inner person is a prerequisite for a healthy and lasting development of society.[38]

According to Johnny Bakke, the EECMY letter of 1972 "accused the missions and the Western churches in general of splitting the task of the church into an evangelism and development ministry, distorting its vocation to serve the whole person."[39] This letter indicates that "to strip development activities of the evangelistic aspect means to accept that man can be treated in parts"—which is incompatible with an African worldview. Therefore, according to Bakke, "the main purpose of the letter was a reminder to the donor agencies that man may not be divided arbitrarily as soul, body and mind and ministered to in sections."[40]

For Tumsa and other EECMY leaders, both aspects of the church work, mission and human development, must not be separate—they are part and parcel of the church's responsibility in carrying out God's mission in this world. This was an absolute challenge to the mission organizations that are shaped by ideologies that believed in compartmentalization of the dualistic Western worldview and organizational structures.

Tumsa's concept of holism is built on Africans' view of life in its totality. His argument was focused both on challenging the Western churches to understand the holistic nature of the gospel and on challenging his fellow Africans to adopt a theology based on an African holistic worldview that is compatible to the gospel. This is mainly reflected in his letter to Carl-J. Hellberg, director of the LWF Department of Church Cooperation in 1992, where he stated that "an African view assumes the totality of man which is not in line with the Western ways of thinking,"[41] and that it is such an understanding that should guide the way African theology is to be developed.

For Tumsa, a theology shaped by an African holistic view is what enables the church "to rededicate itself to living for others, serving the whole human person, meeting the spiritual as well as the physical needs."[42] Such an understanding of Christian ministry is compatible with the gospel of Jesus Christ, the gospel that not only sets us free from spiritual bondage or "eternal damnation," but also from "economic exploitation, political oppression, etc. Because of its eternal dimension the Gospel of Jesus Christ can never be replaced by any of the ideologies invented by men throughout the centuries."[43]

For Tumsa, the church's role in the society is to serve as a means through which God provides healing. This healing, according to Tumsa, is not simply a question of medical care, but "has to do with the restoration of man to liberty and wholeness."[44] In his address to the LWF consultation held in Nairobi, Kenya, in 1974, Tumsa states that this ministry of the church is founded on the understanding that in the ministry of Jesus, "forgiveness of sins and healing of the body, feeding the hungry and spiritual nurture, opposing dehumanizing structures and identifying himself with the weak were never at any time divided or departmentalized. He saw man as a whole and was always ready to give help where the need was most obvious."[45]

Tumsa, in "Report on Church Growth in Ethiopia" presented in Tokyo 1971, two years before the EECMY letter was written, had also argued that "central to the proclamation and witness of the believers is the idea that Jesus saves." As he contends, "[from the African point of view] there is no distinction between curing from malaria, pneumonia and saving from sin. 'Jesus Christ saves' means that he literally cures from physical diseases as well as from the burden of sin. The simple preaching of the Gospel was very often accompanied by healing, exorcism or by some other signs that were interpreted to be the new God demonstrating His power."[46]

One can argue that the EECMY's understanding of holistic theology is mainly informed by Luther's distinction between the two kingdoms or realms. According to Luther, on his "left hand," through secular governors, God rules over the whole universe. On his "right hand," through the church, God provides mercy and grace.[47] As Luther indicates, God's kingship is not limited to the spiritual spheres of life. He is the Lord of the whole universe.[48] Through these two kingdoms, God provides holistic ministry to his creation.

Holistic theology adopted by the EECMY is also founded on the Scriptures. A closer look at the ministry of Jesus and his disciples, particularly in the Gospel of Luke and the book of Acts, reveals that their ministry was holistic. It was holistic because their focus was "a wholehearted embrace and integration of both evangelism and social ministry so that people experience spiritual renewal, socioeconomic uplift, and transformation of their social context."[49] Jesus has come to this world to restore his people (Luke 4:16–21). This restoration is to be manifested in the lives of the poor and the oppressed as compassion and justice prevail.

In the book of Acts, the disciples' life and ministry is described as a continuation of this liberating ministry of Jesus Christ—which is holistic. Holistic ministry in Acts is three-dimensional: *evangelistic, fellowship* (communion), and *prophetic*. The *evangelistic* aspect of the church's ministry is vividly expressed in Acts, where the disciples are described as those committed to teaching and preaching—"preaching the word of God" (Acts 6:2) and "the ministry of the word and sacrament" (Acts 6:4). In Acts, Luke gives emphasis to the actual story of the lives of the apostles focused on teaching in the ongoing life of the Christian community. In Ephesians, Paul continually taught for two years (Acts 19:8). Apollos, after being instructed by Priscilla and Aquila, was also engaged in teaching the word of God (Acts 18:24–28). These and other similar stories about the commitment of the apostles to teach and instruct the church show the intention of Luke to illustrate to his readers that this particular characteristic of the church is needed for the nourishment and guidance of the believing community.

The social ministry of the church is described in Acts within the *fellowship* and communion shared among believers. One of the areas on which Luke focused while describing the life and ministry of the apostles in the book of Acts is that they devoted themselves to *fellowship*, the breaking of bread, and helping the needy (Acts 2:42ff; 4:32ff). They had "everything in common" to the extent that they were "one soul" (Acts 2:44; 4:32).[50]

The socioeconomic and transformational ministry of the church, which others describe as the *prophetic* role the church plays among the community it serves, is demonstrated in the life and ministry of the apostles of Jesus Christ—in that the mission for which they are being commissioned is the same as that attributed to Jesus: healing the sick, casting out demons, and preaching the kingdom of God (Luke 4:43; 8:1; 9:11; 11:20).

Balancing the Church's Ministry in a Society

In this section, I discuss the implication of Tumsa's holistic theology for understanding the church's role in society. As stated in the previous sections, the Lutheran church in Ethiopia has been deeply involved in development, especially in the areas of education and health. This involvement is due to its longstanding understanding of God's mission, which encompasses all aspects of life. This understanding, however, is being challenged by two different views held by Western missionaries and the Ethiopian Pentecostals.

The Western missionaries' emphasis on development and the Pentecostals' emphasis on spiritual ministries resulted in the distorted or "unbalanced" understanding of mission. Tumsa's holistic theology responds to this challenge by indicating that the church's mission has to be holistic. For Tumsa, both positions are unacceptable because they "are equally harmful to the local churches in Developing Countries, which see it as their obligation to serve the whole man."[51]

The Western missionary's emphasis on development results from an understanding that separates the spiritual and physical domains of life. This approach, according to Tumsa, should be criticized because it is "a threat to the very values which make life meaningful if carried out without due attention to a simultaneous provision to meet spiritual needs."[52] It also has the capacity to "weaken the spiritual life of the church and turn away those who long for the Gospel."[53] This assumption not only controls the intellectual inquiry and practice of missions, but also impacts the ministry of non-Western churches working in partnership with them. The EECMY, as indicated previously, is a case in point. Many members of the EECMY and other evangelical churches in Ethiopia have succumbed to this Western worldview and have allowed themselves to be relegated to the spiritual world.

The Pentecostal emphasis on the spiritual aspects of ministry is also another challenge that results in a focus on spiritual activities (evangelism) over other ministries. Other ministries, such as development and advocacy, are considered as nonessential for salvation, and are therefore considered secondary or supportive ministries. This understanding has also influenced many members of the EECMY and other evangelical churches in Ethiopia, resulting in withdrawal from all kinds of development activities.

Tumsa's holistic theology challenges these two understandings by interpreting the Scripture from various dimensions and considering God's mission as concerned with all aspects of human life. As Tumsa articulates in the 1972 document, God's mission, in which all churches are invited to participate, is holistic in nature in that it encompasses all dimensions of life. The significance of adopting a holistic approach (holistic theology) is that it provides us with a profound foundation to critically engage all forms of complacency and silence of such congregations. It provides us with the tools to stand alongside persons struggling to break free from multifaced oppression. More importantly, the concept of holistic ministry in the EECMY is mainly focused on people's development (both spiritual and physical), not just material or economic development.

As Tumsa contends,

> [The problem among Ethiopian evangelicals is that] the Gospel was not understood as the Good News for the whole man, and salvation was given a narrow individualistic interpretation, which was foreign to [Africans'] understanding

of the God–Man relationship. God is concerned about the whole man, and this concern is demonstrated in the Gospel. [Therefore], the imbalance created by some Missionary [and Pentecostal] attitudes has been harmful to the Church in its consequences.[54]

CONCLUSION

The majority in Ethiopia live under conditions of economic deprivation. Hundreds of millions live in utter poverty, experiencing inhuman conditions. This economic condition also affects members of Evangelical churches. Evangelical churches, however, are being challenged by nonholistic approaches to mission, which minimize their contribution to changing the lives of the community they serve. As I try to argue in this article, Tumsa's holistic theology can serve as both a critique and foundation for further development of theology and practice in African context.

The interplay between theology and development is not new to Ethiopian churches, as the African worldview is also dominated by a holistic view of life. The problem, however, is that in Ethiopian Christian studies, the issue regarding the contribution of Christian faith to development has been ignored for so long. This shows that there is a long way to go to introduce this in Ethiopian Christian and academic traditions.

BIBLIOGRAPHY

Addo-Fenning, Robert. "Christian Mission and Nation-Building in Ghana: An Historical Evaluation." In *Uniquely African? African Christian Identity from Cultural and Historical Perspectives*, edited by James Cox and Gerrie ter Haar, 193–212. Trenton, NJ: –Africa World Press, 2003.

Aren, Gustav. "Onesimos Nesib: His Life and Career." *EECYM Information Release*, 1981.

Arén, Gustav. *Envoys of the Gospel in Ethiopia: In the Steps of the Evangelical Pioneers, 1898–1936*. Stockholm: EFS Förlaget, 1999.

———. *Evangelical Pioneers in Ethiopia: Origins of the Evangelical Church Mekane Yesus*. Stockholm: EFS Förlaget, 1978.

Bakke, Johnny. *Christian Ministry: Patterns and Functions within the Ethiopian Evangelical Church Mekane Yesus*. Atlantic Highlands, NJ: Humanities Press International, 1987.

Bartlett, David Lyon. *Ministry in the New Testament*. Minneapolis: Fortress Press, 1993.

Birri, Debela. *Divine Plan Unfolding: The Story of Ethiopian Evangelical Church Bethel*. Minneapolis: Lutheran University Press, 2014.

Deressa, Samuel Yonas, ed. *Emerging Theological Praxis: Journal of Gudina Tumsa Theological Forum*. Minneapolis: Lutheran University Press, 2012.

Eide, Øyvind. "Gudina Tumsa: The Voice of an Ethiopian Prophet." *Svensk MissionsTidskrift* 89, no. 3 (2001).

———. "Political Dynamics in the Wake of Missionary Efforts within the Realm of Human Rights: The Case of Ethiopia." *Swedish Missiological Themes* 89, no. 4 (2001): 473–85.

———. *Revolution and Religion in Ethiopia: The Growth and Persecution of the Mekane Yesus Church, 1974–85*. Oxford: J. Currey, 2000.

Eshete, Tibebe. *The Evangelical Movement in Ethiopia: Resistance and Resilience*. Waco, TX: Baylor University Press, 2009.

Fantini, Emanuele. "Transgression and Acquiescence: The Moral Conflict of Pentecostals in Their Relationship with the Ethiopian State." *PentecoStudies* 12, no. 2 (2013).

Grenstedt, Staffan. *Ambaricho and Shonkolla: From Local Independent Church to the Evangelical Mainstream in Ethiopia, the Origins of the Mekane Yesus Church in Kambata Hadiya.* Uppsala, Sweden: Uppsala University, 2000.

Gurmessa, Fakadu. *Evangelical Faith Movement in Ethiopia: Origins and Establishment of the Ethiopian Evangelical Church Mekane Yesus*, edited by Ezekiel Gebissa. Minneapolis: Lutheran University Press, 2009.

Guta, Megersa. "A Reflection Paper on the 1972 EECMY Letter: 'On the Interrelation between Proclamation of the Gospel and Human Development.'" In *Serving the Whole Person: The Practice and Understanding of Diakonia with the Lutheran Communion*, edited by Kjell Nordstokke. Minneapolis: Lutheran University Press, 2009.

Haile, Selassie, and Edward Ullendorff. *My Life and Ethiopia's Progress, 1892–1937: The Autobiography of Emperor Haile Sellassie I.* Oxford: Oxford University Press, 1976.

Hansen, Rich. "Transforming the Dualistic Worldview of Ethiopian Evangelical Christians." *International Bulletin of Missionary Research* 39, no. 2 (2015).

Hastings, Andrian. *The Construction of Nationhood, Religion, and Nationalism.* New York: Cambridge University Press, 1997.

Hoffman, Paul E. "Gudina Tumsa's Ecclesiology: His Understanding and Vision of the Church." In *Church and Society.* Hamburg: WDL Publishers, 2010.

Jennings, Willie. *The Christian Imagination: Theology and the Origins of Race.* New Haven: Yale University Press, 2010.

Jörg, Haustein. *Writing Religious History: The Historiography of Ethiopian Pentecostalism. Studien Zur Aussereuropaischen Christentumsgeschichte.* Wiesbaden: Harrassowitz Verlag 2011.

Luther, Martin. "On Secular Authority." In *Martin Luther: Selections from His Writings*, edited by John Dillenberger. New York: Doubleday 1961.

Myers, Bryant L. *Walking with the Poor: Principles and Practices of Transformational Development.* Maryknoll, NY: Orbis Books, 2011.

Norberg, Viveca Halldin. *Swedes in Haile Selassie's Ethiopia, 1924–1952: A Study in Early Development Co-Operation.* Uppsala, Sweden: Almqvist and Wiksell International, 1977.

Olana, Gemechu. "An Empowering and Reconciling Presence: Public Ministry in the Ethiopian Evangelical Church Mekane Yesus, a Brief Historical Perspective Review with Some Prospective Remarks." In *Emerging Theological Praxis: Journal of Gudina Tumsa Theological Forum*, edited by Samuel Yonas Deressa. Minneapolis: Lutheran University Press, 2012.

Pankhurst, Richard. "The Role of Foreigners in Nineteenth Century Ethiopia Prior to the Rise of Menelik." Boston: Boston University Papers on Africa, 1966.

Pieper, F. *Christian Dogmatics.* Vol. 2. St. Louis, MO: Concordia, 1951.

Preus, Robert, ed. *The Church and Her Fellowship, Ministry, and Governance.* St. Louis, MO: Luther Academy, 1990.

Sider, Ronald J., Philip N. Olson, and Heidi Rolland Unruh. *Churches That Make a Difference: Reaching Your Community with Good News and Good Works.* Grand Rapids: Baker, 2002.

"Strategic Plan Presented to the EECMY General Assembly." Ethiopian Evangelical Church Mekane Yesus, 2013.

Tumsa, Gudina. *Witness and Discipleship: Leadership of the Church in Multi-Ethnic Ethiopia in a Time of Revolution.* Vol. 1. Hamburg: WDL, 2008.

Virgin, Eric. *The Abyssinia I Knew.* London: Macmillan, 1936.

NOTES

1. Johnny Bakke, *Christian Ministry: Patterns and Functions within the Ethiopian Evangelical Church Mekane Yesus* (Atlantic Highlands, NJ: Humanities Press International, 1987); "Strategic Plan Presented to the EECMY General Assembly" (Ethiopian Evangelical Church Mekane Yesus, 2013).

2. See http://egst.edu.et/workshop-on-redefining-development-from-faith-perspective-conducted/#more-1559, accessed 2/13/17. According to Misgana Mathewos, "one of the major hurdles that exacerbate such dichotomy in Ethiopia is the policies of the successive governments that do not recognize religious/theological education on the basis of separation of state and religion in the past four decades and the churches' unqualified reception of those policies."

3. These missionaries were Peter Heyling from Germany (1607–1652), missionaries sent by the Church Mission Society such as Gobat from Switzerland and Christian Kugler from Germany, Johann Ludwig Krapf and Karl William Isenberg, and several missionaries from the German Hermansburg Mission. For details, see Gustav Arén, *Evangelical Pioneers in Ethiopia: Origins of the Evangelical Church Mekane Yesus* (Stockholm: EFS Förlaget, 1978); Debela Birri, *Divine Plan Unfolding: The Story of Ethiopian Evangelical Church Bethel* (Minneapolis: Lutheran University Press, 2014); Tibebe Eshete, *The Evangelical Movement in Ethiopia: Resistance and Resilience* (Waco, TX: Baylor University Press, 2009); Fakadu Gurmessa, *Evangelical Faith Movement in Ethiopia: Origins and Establishment of the Ethiopian Evangelical Church Mekane Yesus*, edited by Ezekiel Gebissa (Minneapolis: Lutheran University Press, 2009).

4. Arén, *Evangelical Pioneers in Ethiopia*, 30.

5. Gurmessa, *Evangelical Faith Movement*, 128–29.

6. Eric Virgin, *The Abyssinia I Knew* (London: Macmillan, 1936), 109.

7. Arén, *Evangelical Pioneers in Ethiopia*, 163.

8. Richard Pankhurst, "The Role of Foreigners in Nineteenth Century Ethiopia Prior to the Rise of Menelik" (Boston: Boston University Papers on Africa, 1966), 164.

9. Viveca Halldin Norberg, *Swedes in Haile Selassie's Ethiopia, 1924–1952: A Study in Early Development Co-Operation* (Uppsala: Almqvist & Wiksell International, 1977), 105.

10. Gustav Arén, *Envoys of the Gospel in Ethiopia: In the Steps of the Evangelical Pioneers, 1898–1936* (Stockholm: EFS Förlaget, 1999), 62–63.

11. Ibid.

12. Gustav Aren, "Onesimos Nesib: His Life and Career," *EECYM Information Release*, 1981, 8; Øyvind Eide, *Revolution and Religion in Ethiopia: The Growth and Persecution of the Mekane Yesus Church, 1974–85* (Oxford: J. Currey, 2000), 51.

13. Ibid.

14. Andrian Hastings, *The Construction of Nationhood, Religion, and Nationalism* (New York: Cambridge University Press, 1997), 12; Willie Jennings, *The Christian Imagination: Theology and the Origins of Race* (New Haven: Yale University Press, 2010), 209.

15. A significant number of studies describe how Nesib adopted Oromo patterns of thought in his translation, and how that impacted the ministry of the EECMY. See Arén, *Evangelical Pioneers in Ethiopia*, 396; Bakke, *Christian Ministry*, 42, 127–128; Eide, *Revolution and Religion in Ethiopia*, 74–76.

16. Eide, *Revolution and Religion in Ethiopia*, 51.

17. Staffan Grenstedt, *Ambaricho and Shonkolla: From Local Independent Church to the Evangelical Mainstream in Ethiopia, the Origins of the Mekane Yesus Church in Kambata Hadiya* (Uppsala: Uppsala University, 2000), 79ff.

18. Selassie Haile and Edward Ullendorff, *My Life and Ethiopia's Progress, 1892–1937: The Autobiography of Emperor Haile Sellassie I* (Oxford: Oxford University Press, 1976), 69.

19. Øyvind Eide, "Political Dynamics in the Wake of Missionary Efforts within the Realm of Human Rights: The Case of Ethiopia," *Swedish Missiological Themes* 89, no. 4 (2001): 473–474.

20. Gudina Tumsa, *Witness and Discipleship: Leadership of the Church in Multi-Ethnic Ethiopia in a Time of Revolution*, vol. 1 (Hamburg: WDL, 2008), 62.

21. Bryant L. Myers, *Walking with the Poor: Principles and Practices of Transformational Development* (Maryknoll: Orbis Books, 2011), 26.

22. Ibid., 27.

23. This is also a well-established fact in African mission history. See Robert Addo-Fenning, "Christian Mission and Nation-Building in Ghana: An Historical Evaluation," in *Uniquely African? African Christian Identity from Cultural and Historical Perspectives*, ed. James Cox and Gerrie ter Haar (Trenton, NJ: Africa World Press, 2003), 193–212.

24. Tumsa, *Witness and Discipleship*, 83.
25. Megersa Guta, "A Reflection Paper on the 1972 Eecmy Letter: 'On the Interrelation between Proclamation of the Gospel and Human Development,'" in *Serving the Whole Person: The Practice and Understanding of Diakonia with the Lutheran Communion*, ed. Kjell Nordstokke (Minneapolis: Lutheran University Press, 2009), 183.
26. For a detailed history of Pentecostalism in Ethiopia, see Haustein Jörg, *Writing Religious History: The Historiography of Ethiopian Pentecostalism. Studien Zur Aussereuropaischen Christentumsgeschichte*. (Wiesbaden: Harrassowitz Verlag 2011).
27. Ibid., 2–7, 138–151.
28. *Social concern*, according to Olana, refers to social actions such as "politics, and social and economic developments." Gemechu Olana, "An Empowering and Reconciling Presence: Public Ministry in the Ethiopian Evangelical Church Mekane Yesus, a Brief Historical Perspective Review with Some Prospective Remarks," in *Emerging Thelogical Praxis: Journal of Gudina Tumsa Theological Forum*, ed. Saamul Yonas Deressa (Minneapolis: Lutheran University Press, 2012), 65.
29. Quoted in Emanuele Fantini, "Transgression and Acquiescence: The Moral Conflict of Pentecostals in Their Relationship with the Ethiopian State," *PentecoStudies* 12, no. 2 (2013): 214. According to Eide, the Pentecostals were also accused of being "dangerous for the nation" because they adopted a pacifist position. See Eide, *Revolution and Religion in Ethiopia*, 62.
30. According to Rich Hansen, the dualistic worldview among evangelical Christians in Ethiopia is caused by the Ethiopian Orthodox tradition, protestant missionaries, and ideology of the socialist government (1974–1991). See Rich Hansen, "Transforming the Dualistic Worldview of Ethiopian Evangelical Chrstians," *International Bulletin of Missionary Research* 39, no. 2 (2015). Though the argument of Hansen may have some realities, other studies indicate that the dualistic worldview adopted by many evangelical believers is the result of Pentecostal movements in Ethiopia. See Bakke, *Christian Ministry*; Eide, *Revolution and Religion in Ethiopia*; Olana, "An Empowering and Reconciling Presence"; Tumsa, *Witness and Discipleship*.
31. Tumsa was the former general secretary of the EECMY (1966–1979) who was murdered in 1979 by a communist military junta that ruled Ethiopia from 1974 to 1991. When he was named general secretary of the EECMY in 1966, the church leaders faced multiple challenges relating to establishing the EECMY as a national evangelical church. Before his death, Tumsa wrote papers of global significance while leading an exemplary life. Many scholars have called him the Dietrich Bonhoeffer of Africa. See Samuel Yonas Deressa, ed. *Emerging Theological Praxis: Journal of Gudina Tumsa Theological Forum* (Minneapolis: Lutheran University Press, 2012); Øyvind Eide, "Gudina Tumsa: The Voice of an Ethiopian Prophet," *Svensk MissionsTidskrift* 89, no. 3 (2001); Paul E. Hoffman, "Gudina Tumsa's Ecclesiology: His Understanding and Vision of the Church," in *Church and Society* (Hamburg: WDL Publishers, 2010).
32. Tumsa, *Witness and Discipleship*, 85ff.
33. Ibid., 89.
34. Ibid., 90.
35. Ibid., 89.
36. Ibid.
37. Ibid.
38. Ibid.
39. Bakke, *Christian Ministry*, 230.
40. Ibid.
41. Tumsa, *Witness and Discipleship*, 115–16.
42. Ibid., 82.
43. Ibid.
44. Tumsa, *Witness and Discipleship*, 121.
45. Ibid., 122.
46. Ibid., 135.
47. Martin Luther, "On Secular Authority," in *Martin Luther: Selections from His Writings*, ed. John Dillenberger (New York: Doubleday 1961), 368. As F. Pieper reiterates, God's "right hand" is the church "which is truly the kingdom of Christ." For him, "the Kingdom of Grace is

synonymous with the church of God on earth." See F. Pieper, *Christian Dogmatics*, vol. II (St. Louis, Missouri: Concordia Publishing House, 1951), 385.

48. For more details, see Robert Preus, ed. *The Church and Her Fellowship, Ministry, and Governance* (St. Louis, MO: Luther Academy, 1990), 174ff.

49. Ronald J. Sider, Philip N. Olson, and Heidi Rolland Unruh, *Churches That Make a Difference: Reaching Your Community with Good News and Good Works* (Grand Rapids: Baker Books, 2002), 17.

50. For more reading on this particular aspect of the ministry of the church, refer to David Lyon Bartlett, *Ministry in the New Testament* (Minneapolis: Fortress Press, 1993), 134ff.

51. Tumsa, *Witness and Discipleship*.

52. Ibid., 88.

53. Ibid.

54. Ibid.

Chapter 3

On Human Flourishing

A Call for Public Responsibility in Contemporary Ethiopian Christianity

Andrew D. DeCort

At the beginning of Germany's political crisis, Dietrich Bonhoeffer wrote, "It is time for a final break with our theologically grounded reserve about whatever is being done by the state—which really only comes down to fear. 'Speak out for those who cannot speak'—who in the church today still remembers that this is the very least the Bible asks of us in such times as these?"[1] Bonhoeffer's words call to mind those of the prophet Ezekiel: "When the wall collapses, will people not ask you, 'Where is the whitewash you covered it with?'" (Ezekiel 13:12).

This essay explores four questions of crucial importance for Christians who care about human flourishing in Ethiopia as the country continues its journey toward democracy and development. These questions are given urgency by the present moment in Ethiopia marked by crisis, uncertainty, and hopes for new beginnings.

First, what is human flourishing? This question asks about what we should be aiming for when we talk about a robust vision of development and human well-being.[2] Here I look at the work of Martha Nussbaum and William Schweiker.

Second, is human flourishing a Christian concept and commitment or a "secular" idea foreign to Christian conviction? Here I look at the work of David Gushee on the "sacredness of human life" in Scripture.

Third, how are Ethiopian churches doing at promoting human flourishing for the common good in key moments of sociopolitical crisis when religious leadership is most badly needed? Here I look at Ethiopian churches' responses to the 2005 and 2015–2018 crises.

Finally, what are some ways forward for our churches to more faithfully promote human flourishing in Ethiopia today and tomorrow? Here I offer three constructive suggestions in conclusion.

Taken together, I hope this chapter stimulates expanded moral imagination and public responsibility in Ethiopian churches and society for the flourishing of all neighbors.[3]

WHAT IS HUMAN FLOURISHING? TOWARD AN EXPANDED MORAL IMAGINATION

According to the renowned philosopher Charles Taylor, "Every person, and every society, lives with or by some conception(s) of what human flourishing is: What constitutes a fulfilled life? What makes life really worth living?" For Taylor, the question of flourishing is one "we can't help asking."[4]

From this perspective, we could argue that the question of flourishing is fundamental to what it means to be human. Humans not only live, seek pleasure, avoid pain, and die. We also question our lives' value, interrogate their meaning, and sometimes seek to live more fully or faithfully in ways that transcend ourselves, even if this requires struggle and sacrifice.

Human development is an urgent priority in Ethiopia. The Ethiopian People's Revolutionary Democratic Front (EPRDF) has enshrined "developmental statism" as its core ideology and used development progress as the cornerstone of its political legitimacy. The new prime minister, Dr. Abiy Ahmed, declared in his inaugural address, "The crux of the matter is to catapult our country to a higher level of development."[5] A survey of recent statistics indicates that Ethiopia is making encouraging progress in key areas but that poverty, injustice, and human suffering remain enormous problems attacking human flourishing in Ethiopia.[6]

If Taylor is right that we can't help asking about human flourishing and if development is central to Ethiopia's present and future pursuit of human flourishing, how might we understand human flourishing and how might that contribute to a richer vision of development? In this section, I briefly explore the work of Martha Nussbaum, professor of law and philosophy, and William Schweiker, professor of theological ethics, both at the University of Chicago. Whether we are fully persuaded by their respective visions of human flourishing or not, their work importantly argues that flourishing cannot be reduced to any one factor and must, instead, integrate a plurality of interconnected dimensions of our humanity, including our capacities for intellectual life, free speech, and public engagement. They both agree that the opposite of "poverty" is much more than financial or material abundance.

Chapter 3

Martha Nussbaum's Capabilities Approach and Human Flourishing

According to Martha Nussbaum, the dominant model in development theory has assumed that a society's growth should be measured solely by a rising gross domestic product (GDP).[7] But Nussbaum argues that this model "distorted human experience" and ignored radical inequality.[8] For example, a society like Ethiopia might boast an impressive GDP, but this economic growth may not actually improve the lives of many impoverished Ethiopians, because the increased GDP is siloed off by the wealthy few. Nussbaum compares this monodimensional GDP model to a government announcing that there is a beautiful painting and delicious feast in a private parlor to which the poor have no access.[9] Its cheerfulness is often matched by its exclusivity and cruelty.

By contrast, Nussbaum argues for "a new theoretical paradigm," which she and others like Amartya Sen have called "the capabilities approach."[10] This model, which she describes as "a relatively unified approach to a set of questions about both quality of life and basic justice,"[11] starts with simple questions: "What are people actually able to do and be?"[12] and "which are the [capabilities] that a minimally just society will endeavor to nurture and support?"[13]

For Nussbaum, our "central capabilities" are precisely our answers to these two questions about our "doings and beings," what Nussbaum calls our "opportunities to choose and act" and Sen calls our "substantial freedoms."[14] Thus, Nussbaum, Sen, and others see "development" as much more than material increase, and centralize the freedom of human persons to exercise their moral agency to pursue a life worth living. This is a subtle but significant anthropological claim: humans are much more than producers and consumers of material but creatures of moral meaning, value, freedom, and action.

Thus the capabilities approach builds on the assumption that "the quality of a human life involves multiple elements"[15] or "plurality and nonreducibility,"[16] combined with the moral axiom that "freedom has intrinsic value."[17] In other words, "lives that are worthy of their human dignity"[18] depend upon our ability to act and grow through access to interconnected relationships, freedoms, and opportunities that empower "the complexities of human life and human striving."[19] Nussbaum notes that "the approach is influenced by philosophical views that focus on human flourishing"[20] and is heavily dependent on "notions of respect and dignity."[21]

On this theoretical basis, Nussbaum expounds a list of "central capabilities," which she believes summarize what humans need to flourish and whose protection and promotion define "the decent society."[22] These ten central capabilities integrate "basic capabilities" (a person's "innate faculties" that can be trained and developed[23]), "internal capabilities" ("trained or developed traits and abilities" like critical thinking and confidence[24]), and "combined capabilities" ("internal capabilities plus the social/political/economic conditions in which functioning can actually be chosen"[25]). The notion of *combined* capabilities is important, because a society may develop its people's internal capacities for, say, free speech and assembly but not allow them to exercise them.[26] Human flourishing requires both. Indeed, Nussbaum boldly insists, "The political goal for all human beings in a nation ought to be the same: all should get above a certain threshold level of combined capability, in the sense not of coerced functioning but of substantial freedom to choose and act."[27]

What I wish to highlight here is the interconnected, multidimensional nature of Nussbaum's vision of human flourishing, ranging from bodily health to creative imagination to political freedom. For Nussbaum, the life worth living is not reducible to a certain amount of money above a poverty line or to bodily survival and security. A society overflowing with money that thwarts the internal capabilities or oppresses the combined capabilities of its citizens is still impoverishing and cannot be said to promote flourishing or development.[28]

The list that follows is Nussbaum's attempt to answer the fundamental question, "What does a life worthy of human dignity require?"[29]:

1. *Life*. Being able to live to the end of a human life of normal length. . . .
2. *Bodily health*. Being able to have good health [including reproduction, food, and shelter]. . . .
3. *Bodily integrity*. Being able to move freely from place to place [including safety from violence and sexual assault]. . . .
4. *Sense, imagination, and thought*. Being able to use the senses, to imagine, think, and reason [through educational cultivation protected by political, religious, and artistic freedom]. . . .
5. *Emotions*. Being able to have attachments to things and people outside ourselves . . . in general, to love, to grieve, to experience longing, gratitude, and justified anger. Not having one's emotional development blighted by fear and anxiety [including support for associations that develop emotional wholeness].
6. *Practical reason*. Being able to form a conception of the good and to engage in critical reflection about the good and to engage in critical reflection about the planning of one's life [which entails protection for the liberty of conscience and religious observance].
7. *Affiliation*. (A) Being able to live with and toward others [cultivating empathy and social interaction, and protecting related institutions, assembly, and political speech]. (B) Having the social bases of self-respect and nonhumiliation; being able to be treated as a dignified being whose worth is equal to that of others [including nondiscrimina-

tion for "race, sex, sexual orientation, ethnicity, caste, religion, national origin"]. . . .
8. *Other species.* Being able to live with concern for and in relation to animals, plants, and the world of nature.
9. *Play.* Being able to laugh, to play, to enjoy recreational activities.
10. *Control over one's environment.* (A) *Political.* Being able to participate effectively in political choices that govern one's life; having the right of political participation, protections of free speech and association. (B) *Material.* Being able to hold property . . . having the right to seek employment on an equal basis with others; having the freedom from unwarranted search and seizure. In work, being able to work as a human being, exercising practical reason and entering into meaningful relationships of mutual recognition with other workers.[30]

Nussbaum's "proposal" is complex and merits detailed unpacking.[31] But my purpose here is simply to illustrate the multidimensional richness of her conception of human flourishing, which grows out of her philosophical understanding of human personhood and community. Rather than one element defining a developing society (e.g., GDP), Nussbaum thinks that these ten elements are required for "a dignified and minimally flourishing life,"[32] such that a government cannot deliver in one area and use that as an excuse to ignore or deny the others.[33] In short, "respect for human dignity requires that citizens be placed above an ample (specified) threshold of capability, in all ten of those areas,"[34] including critical thinking, freedom of speech and assembly, and public engagement.[35]

William Schweiker's Integrity of Life Ethics and Human Flourishing

Similar to Nussbaum's critique of GDP as the sole measure of development, William Schweiker critiques personal piety and group identity as the primary markers of a faithful spiritual life. In his coauthored manifesto *Religion and the Human Future*, Schweiker argues for a theological vision of human flourishing that emerges out of his account of "theological humanism," which emphasizes God as the creator, sustainer, and redeemer of all life in its vast complexity.[36]

Schweiker's Christian theology grounds and energizes his ethics of "the integrity of life" in which human flourishing requires the harmonious integration of diverse goods. Simpler than Nussbaum's ten capabilities, Schweiker describes four interlocking goods or spheres of life that must be "respected and enhanced" in response to "the imperative of responsibility."[37] Schweiker summarizes:

> Humans are situated in existence through interlocking modes of life, each marked by vitalities and vulnerabilities. Human beings are *living creatures* within and not against the wide community of finite life on this planet. We are *social beings* who sustain and also threaten our existence through relations with others. Human beings are *reflective creatures* who seek to understand their lives, their world, and others.[38]

In what follows, I briefly unpack Schweiker's conception of each good.

1. *Locational Goods*: Goods of locale "are always located in space and time" and include our planet, natural environment (e.g., air, soil, forests), and the diverse species that co-inhabit earth.[39] Here we experience the longing for belonging and vulnerabilities related to global warming, environmental degradation, and species extinction, as well as homelessness, migration, and displacement caused by political violence.[40] To flourish, humans need a locale that is clean, safe, and enlivening. (Compare capacities 3, 8, 10b cited previously.)
2. *Basic Goods*: Natural or basic goods "inhere in finite life independent of human choice, but are necessary to sustain human agency," such as "our bodies, the taste for beauty, the fear of death, force of enjoyment and delight, the need for food and shelter."[41] Basic goods include a minimal daily caloric intake to sustain our bodies and develop our brains. We experience basic goods in our longing for pleasure and vulnerability to pain, experiences that Schweiker emphasizes are universal across human differences and should stimulate our sympathy for others.[42] (Compare capacities 1–3, 10b, cited previously.)
3. *Social Goods*: Social goods "depend on . . . action and choice in concert with others" and require our participation in communities with their "standards, customs, rights, practices and beliefs," which sustain "the conditions of cooperative thinking, speaking, and acting."[43] Within this broad category, Schweiker refers to "family, economic and political institutions, friendship, patterns of interaction with other species, and even the means to think, speak, and act together with others."[44] We experience social goods in our longing for recognition and praise and in our vulnerability to shame and blame. Here Schweiker emphasizes the importance of the Golden Rule and the finality of others (e.g., the refusal to instrumentalize people) for human flourishing.[45] (Compare capacities 5, 7, 9, 10, cited previously.)
4. *Reflective Goods*: Reflective or spiritual goods "enable human agents to be knowingly responsible for themselves and others."[46] They include "interpretation and assessment," "a truthful life, meaningfulness, and self-understanding," and "the entire domain of symbolic, linguistic, and practical meaning systems," including our capacity to question and seek transcendent reality.[47] Reflective goods unfold in

our longing for justice and innocence and our vulnerability to abuse and guilt. For Schweiker, reflective goods should awaken us to "the moral density of the world," the "gravity of one's life," and the importance of respecting the autonomy of persons amidst our interdependence as moral agents.[48] (Compare capacities 4–6, 10a.)

As with Nussbaum, what interests me here in Schweiker's vision of human flourishing is its multidimensionality within a rigorous intellectual framework aspiring to a larger integrity.[49] Nussbaum argues for the capabilities approach in which human flourishing is realized through the empowerment of our ten central capabilities. Schweiker argues for a theological ethics in which human flourishing comes to fruition in the integrity of life uniting locational, bodily, social, and reflective goods.

Whether we are ultimately persuaded or not by either, both illustrate an expanded moral imagination in which human flourishing cannot be reduced to a single metric but requires the integration of multiple dimensions of life, including human thought, speech, and action in community with others for common goods. Material abundance and an industrial infrastructure devoid of these other dimensions, if even achievable by themselves alone, are still impoverished and far short of human flourishing.[50]

IS HUMAN FLOURISHING A CHRISTIAN CONCEPT AND COMMITMENT?

If the question of human flourishing is unavoidable, its relationship to Christian faithfulness is not unambiguous. As Charles Taylor notes, "The injunction 'Thy will be done' isn't equivalent to 'Let humans flourish.'"[51] Thus we must ask if the wider vision sketched previously is a Christian concept and commitment or a "secular" agenda that should be held in suspicion or even resisted. Here I turn to David Gushee's brilliant work in *The Sacredness of Human Life: Why an Ancient Biblical Vision Is Key to the World's Future*.[52]

According to Gushee, the Bible and traditional Christian theology teach the sacredness of human life, which "*means that God has consecrated each and every human being—without exception and in all circumstances—as a unique, incalculably precious being of elevated status and dignity.*" Thus, God promises to "*hold us accountable for responding appropriately*" to human beings, which requires that we embrace "*a posture of reverence*" toward every person and "*a full-hearted commitment to foster human flourishing.*"[53] For Gushee, this ancient biblical vision provides a radical foundation for human flourishing today and amounts to "the greatest moral contribution of the Christian tradition to world civilization."[54] Indeed, Gushee argues that "the ultimate origin" of modern convictions about human equality and inviolable rights is found in "Christian civilization" shaped by this biblical ethics.[55]

As Gushee looks at today's world, he sees "a race between forces that motivate us to honor our neighbors and forces that motivate us to desecrate them,"[56] as we will see in the section on Ethiopian society later in this chapter. Thus the sacredness of human life is not merely a biblical dogma but "a desperately urgent task facing anyone who would claim to be in covenant with God."[57] This is the reason Gushee subtitles his book *Why an Ancient Biblical Vision Is Key to the World's Future*.

Gushee systematically unpacks impressive evidence to demonstrate that the sacredness of human life is a biblical concept that demands "a full-hearted commitment to foster human flourishing." Here I summarize over one hundred pages of argumentation in a few short paragraphs.

Human Sacredness and Flourishing in the Old Testament

In his survey of the Old Testament, Gushee provides four fundamental pieces of evidence that demonstrate God's original and relentless will for human sacredness and flourishing:

1. *Creation, Humanity, and the Image of God*: In Genesis 1, God creates all of reality and calls it "very good" (1:31). As the climax of God's good creation, God makes humanity in God's own "image and likeness" (1:26), which in the ancient Near East was an elevated status restricted to male kings and priests to represent the gods and rule on their behalf. But Genesis 1 radically affirms that *all* men *and all* women are made in God's sacred image to rule the earth and bring creation to fruitfulness, which Gushee calls "an implicit primal human *egalitarianism* and *unity*" against any hierarchy based on gender, race, wealth, status, or ability. Long after the Fall, Genesis continues to affirm humans as God's image-bearers, which grounds its teaching on the inviolability of human life and condemnation of violence (Genesis 9:6; 6:11). Gushee concludes, "To violate human rights is to violate God's rights"[58] and sees "this elevation of collective human dignity" as "a staggering contribution to human culture."[59]
2. *God's Compassionate Care and Liberating Deliverance*: In Exodus, God listens to the cry of the suffering and brings liberation to the oppressed. Against the Egyptians' genocidal enslavement of an ethnic minority, God practices a "preferential option for the poor" and struggles for their deliverance.[60] Here Gushee quotes James Cone's powerful summary of the ethical implications of the exodus: "There is no knowledge of Yahweh except through his political activity on behalf of the weak and helpless."[61] Thus, rather than ignoring or marginaliz-

ing "suffering, victimized human beings," Exodus affirms that God has a radical commitment to the flourishing of the most vulnerable.
3. *Biblical Law*: Building on creation and the exodus, Gushee shows that the Old Testament roots moral law in God's transcendent will (contra legal positivism), which is equally binding on all (contra favoritism). Thus biblical law "reinforces momentum toward human equality before the law"[62] and builds a crucial protection for human flourishing. This includes the radical implication that *human* law should only be obeyed when it is just and corresponds to God's law for the flourishing of all without discrimination, which is illustrated in the Hebrew midwives' courageous disobedience to Pharaoh (Exodus 1:15–22).[63]
4. *The Prophetic Demand and Yearning for Shalom*: Finally, in the Old Testament's vision for the ultimate future, Gushee unpacks God's promise to renew the earth and reconcile all people. For example, the prophet Isaiah foresees that "all nations" will be brought together, "they will beat their swords into plowshares," and "the earth will be filled with the knowledge of the Lord" (Isaiah 2:1–5; 11:6–9). Rather than abandoning humanity and destroying the earth, God promises to re-create the earth and to resurrect humanity (Isaiah 65:1, 17). Thus the prophets repeatedly reject empty religion and political injustice, and demand that God's people struggle for peace, justice, reconciliation, and the restoration of creation (see Isaiah 1:13–17 and 58:6–9; Micah 6:6–8; Amos 5:21–24). This prophetic vision of shalom grounds and energizes sociopolitical reform for human flourishing in the present based on God's promise for the future.

Human Sacredness and Flourishing in the New Testament

Gushee then turns to argue that the New Testament expands and intensifies the Old Testament's affirmation of human sacredness and flourishing, again unpacking four major pieces of evidence.

1. *Jesus's Ministry*: Throughout his ministry, Jesus opposed violence and taught peace, included the marginalized (e.g., women, children, the sick, the disabled, the poor, foreigners), and proclaimed God's saving love for all people. Gushee summarizes, "Jesus did much to overturn the religious, cultural, economic, and political barriers of his context and demonstrated love, respect, and inclusion toward people of all descriptions, in doing so often shocking and scandalizing those around him."[64] Jesus universalized the concept of "neighbor," and insisted that his followers must love all people, including enemies, and work for their flourishing like God does (Matthew 5:43–48; Luke 6:27–36).

2. *Jesus's Incarnation, Cross, Resurrection, and Ascension*: Jesus's incarnation affirms that God sanctifies and embraces our humanity into God's own life, especially the poor and oppressed like Jesus himself: "The incarnation elevates the status of every human being everywhere on the planet at every time in human history."[65] Jesus's crucifixion demonstrates that humanity is worth saving at the price of his own torture and execution: "Everyone must matter to us, because everyone matters to God . . . all have sinned; all need salvation; Christ suffered and died for all."[66] Jesus's resurrection embodies God's will for human life to triumph over death in new creation: "Human life never ceases to be bodily. . . . All that wars against life is enemy to God, and God has defeated it proleptically at the cross [and resurrection]."[67] Jesus's ascension astonishingly means that a human person shares God's throne and rules for human flourishing.
3. *Jesus's Image*: Returning to Genesis 1, Gushee argues that Christ "*repairs and restores* the image of God in fallen humanity."[68] Even if sin distorted or destroyed God's image in us, Christ has renewed it, launching "a pioneering community determined to treat all human beings with a dignity proper to the redemptive work that God has done on humanity's behalf in Jesus Christ."[69]
4. *The Expansive Reach of the Body of Christ*: The church that Jesus founded and that we see in the Book of Acts embodied a multicultural, cosmopolitan, generous, and justice-seeking community. Referring to Galatians 3:28, Gushee argues, "All humanly significant distinctions are transfigured and overcome by and in and through Jesus Christ. . . . This [the church] would be a multiethnic, multilinguistic, multiracial, gender-inclusive, class-inclusive community, and a community that would not accept dehumanization and degradation of any category of people."[70]

Taken together, the Old and New Testaments affirm the sacredness of human life and God's will for human flourishing. Rather than a secular innovation or heterodox misinterpretation, Gushee convincingly concludes, "The moral conviction that each and every human life is of equal and incalculable value is embedded in the Christian faith and goes with Christianity wherever it goes—even when Christian people fail to live up to its implications, as is so often the case."[71] Thus Gushee stands on a solid biblical foundation when he calls human sacredness and flourishing "the greatest moral contribution of the Christian tradition to world civilization,"[72] which should energize "*a full-hearted commitment to foster human flourishing.*"[73]

While Taylor rightly pointed out that obedience to God may require us to sacrifice our own personal flourishing like Jesus, the purpose and importance of that sacrifice is always to restore God's original (Genesis 1), incarnate

(John 1), and ultimate (Revelation 21–22) will for human flourishing. The second-century theologian Irenaeus beautifully encapsulates this biblical vision: "The glory of God is humans fully alive."[74]

HOW ARE ETHIOPIAN CHURCHES DOING AT PROMOTING HUMAN FLOURISHING IN KEY MOMENTS OF SOCIOPOLITICAL CRISIS?

If we should embrace something approximating the multidimensional vision of human flourishing, sketched previously in the second section, as an authentically Christian concept and commitment, described in the third section, how are Ethiopian churches doing at promoting human flourishing in key moments of sociopolitical crises? Here it is especially important to remember James Cone's summary of the Exodus God: "There is no knowledge of Yahweh except through his political activity on behalf of the weak and helpless."[75]

I focus on these crisis moments because they are times when human flourishing is most endangered, the moral values of society are most at stake, the practical commitments of the church are most tested, and principled leadership is most urgently needed. These decisive moments, while obviously not fully representative, can also be viewed as windows into the health of communities in less tumultuous times when the status quo may conceal neglected values and hidden problems.

The 2005 Crisis, Public Dismembering, and Church Failure

Most Ethiopians see the May 15, 2005, national election and its aftermath (commonly referred to as *2005* or *zetena sebat*) as the most important event shaping public life in recent Ethiopian history. In this decisive season, Ethiopian citizens attempted to exercise their agency (à la Nussbaum's capabilities[76] and Schweiker's social and reflective goods[77]) to determine what they saw as a more flourishing future with unprecedented participation.[78]

While the events surrounding the election are controversial, this much is clear. The election results were disputed by the opposition parties, tense public demonstrations followed, and security forces responded with mass arrests and killings (most violently on June 6–8 and November 1–2).[79] The BBC published a story titled "Ethiopian Protesters 'Massacred'" and reported that at least 193 citizens had been killed, 20,000 had been detained, and over 100 opposition leaders, journalists, and others were put on death row on disputed charges of subverting the constitution and inciting genocide.[80]

What began as one of the most dynamic, hopeful moments in recent Ethiopian history for an expanded human flourishing rapidly deteriorated into a terrible dismembering of the body politic. Amid disappearances, torture, and killing, the Ethiopian public was traumatized and torn apart with loss, grief, fear, rage, and disenchantment. Human life was desecrated.

Now, if the Christian community is called by God to celebrate and defend human flourishing, as we have argued in this chapter, how did its leaders respond in this time when human flourishing, on personal and public levels, was so terribly devastated?

Unfortunately, there is virtually nothing to report, because the churches were almost entirely silent and passive. To my knowledge, the Orthodox and Evangelical churches, representing around 65 percent of the Ethiopian population and nearly 99 percent of Ethiopian Christians, made no public response whatsoever.[81] Abebe Tadesse summarizes, "They [Evangelical leaders] did not say a word about the killing of their fellow citizens when the world condemned the events. . . . Instead to get favor or not to enter into disagreement with the government, they chose to remain silent. Indeed, this is a shameful act in the history of the Ethiopian Evangelical Churches Fellowship."[82]

The Ethiopian Catholic Secretariat was the only church body to respond, issuing a public statement on June 19 titled "Post-Election Message of Bishops of the Ethiopian Catholic Church," in which eleven clerics declared:

> We abhor violence of any kind, and in the name of God we appeal for peace, tolerance and goodwill. We deeply regret this and offer our deepest sympathy to those families who subsequently have tragically lost their members. We urge all those concerned to enhance the quality of the people's lives by creating an atmosphere of mutual respect, since that leads to peace, stability and development. To that end and, indeed, for the common good of all Ethiopians, we encourage all concerned to take steps in promoting tolerance and mutual respect. . . . [W]e appeal to you to be responsible citizens who pray for the gift of peace, unity, love and mutual understanding.[83]

However brief, this was an exemplary message that (1) condemned violence, (2) expressed sympathy for the dead and grieving, and (3) called for moral principles to guide leaders and citizens alike. Even so, the Catholic Church only represents around 0.7 percent of the Ethiopian population, and I am not aware of any further statement when the violence escalated in November.

Thus, with the exception of a single statement, when moral leadership was desperately needed to defend the sacredness of human life, Christian churches said and did nothing in public. Sadly, "2005" can be judged a total failure of Christian public responsibility for human flourishing. Of course, calls for prayer were heard, but as Martin Luther King, Jr. rightly argued,

> The idea that man [sic] expects God to do everything leads inevitably to a callous misuse of prayer. . . . Prayer is a marvelous and necessary supplement of our feeble efforts, but it is a dangerous substitute. . . . [W]e must also use our minds to develop a program, organize ourselves into mass nonviolent

action, and employ every resource of our bodies and souls to bring an end to . . . injustice.[84]

In my view, having interviewed a wide spectrum of Ethiopians about these events, the most plausible explanations of the churches' silence include the following. First, the leadership didn't consider "politics" as important to their dualistic vision of Christian "ministry."[85] Second, in their decades-long honeymoon after the brutal communist regime known as the Derg (1974–1991), they were afraid of being punished—whether through arrest, loss of legal registration, the denial of land for church construction, or more subtle forms of reprisal—if they condemned the violence, called for justice, and organized nonviolent action for peace. Third, the church itself lacked the moral authority to speak and act given its own problems with corruption, division, and ethnocentrism.

Thus, in what is arguably the most important public event in recent Ethiopian history, the Christian churches were mostly invisible, inaudible, and irrelevant, safely carrying on with what Isaiah called "meaningless offerings," "detestable incense," "worthless assemblies," and rejected prayers (Isaiah 1:13–17), while the conditions for human flourishing in Ethiopia were terribly impoverished and publicly devastated. Many believe that whatever moral authority the churches had for providing public leadership was nearly bankrupted at this time.[86]

The 2015–2018 Crisis, Public Dismembering, and Limited Church Responsibility

Since October 2015, the Christian churches have had another chance to exercise moral leadership for human flourishing in a time of sociopolitical crises.[87] Far exceeding the upheaval of 2005, Ethiopia has been swept with demonstrations and strikes starting in Oromia and spreading to the Amhara and Southern regions. In response, security forces have killed around a thousand people and arrested some twenty-five thousand others, with brutal accounts of torture following.[88] A ten-month state of emergency was declared on October 8, 2016 (ending August 4, 2017), and a second state of emergency was declared on February 16, 2018, a day after Prime Minister Hailemariam Desalegn resigned amid a widespread sense of urgent national crisis. Many have described this extended season of upheaval as a nightmarish repetition of 2005 but on a greater scale.

Initially, it appeared that church leaders would repeat their failure in 2005 and remain silent and passive in the face of societal crisis. Indeed, there were many months of total silence. But as the crisis has intensified, some public statements have emerged defending basic justice and God's will for human flourishing.

The Catholic Church (August 15, 2016)

Once again, the Catholics took the lead and issued a public statement in a press conference led by Cardinal Berhaneyesus on August 15, 2016, that condemned the chaos, prayed for the souls of killed children and their grieving families, and called for dialogue, peacemaking, and economic development for the poor. Government officials were called to listen to the people, elders were asked to work for reconciliation in their communities, and the youth were challenged to "stay calm and maintain peace."

> We ask all people to cooperate in building a society free of all hatred that we can pass on to the next generation. . . . We ask in the name of God all Ethiopians living in the country and abroad, Ethiopians involved in different fields of expertise and government officials to make the pillars of a society which are Truth, freedom, justice and love your working principles and maintain our peace, cooperation, conflict resolution through dialogue.[89]

The Inter-Religious Council of Ethiopia (September 11, 2016)

A month later, the government-run *Ethiopian Herald* published a short article reporting on a holiday meeting in which representatives from the Orthodox Church, the Islamic Affairs Supreme Council, the Catholic Church, the Mekane Yesus Church, and the Evangelical Churches Fellowship of Ethiopia made short statements emphasizing "the need to further strengthen Ethiopian [sic] long held tradition of peaceful coexistence."[90] While better than silence, their messages were brief and generic, suggesting no practical action plan for believers or the wider public. Based on the paper's record, nothing was said about justice, forgiveness, or reconciliation.

The Full-Gospel Believers' Church (Mid-September 2016)

In mid-September 2016, the Full-Gospel Believers' Church broke the denominational silence, and its forty-second General Assembly posted a three-page "Statement of the EFGBC Concerning the Current Situation of Our Country."[91] Claiming to represent six million members, the statement begins, "The church has been giving holistic ministry both in the past and present" and underscores its commitment "to provide biblical teaching" on the situation, to prioritize "peace and stability," to urge conflict resolution through dialogue and condemn violence (which harms Ethiopia's image, causes death, and destroys property), and to "execute the Great Commission" by praying for leaders and national peace.

The statement then makes nine points about the church: that it (1) grieves for "the spilled blood, lost life, and damaged properties," warns against this happening again, and calls for prayers for peace; (2) affirms human equality against divisive labeling; (3) preaches love and unity against "hatred and division"; (4) believes that God "appoints and invalidates governments"; (5) urges the government to patiently "entertain various questions"; (6) "does not support any violent act . . . from any party"; (7) does not endorse any human ideology, government, or opposition; (8) "do[es] not serve as a tool for any political agenda"; (9) praises the government for its "development works" and urges it to "address questions coming from the public in a fair and legal way."

This statement made important affirmations and was an encouraging break from the silence. But its points were not unpacked, could be interpreted as self-defensive, and failed to offer any concrete action plan going forward to interrupt the mounting crisis. Oddly, it said nothing about the church's active responsibilities beyond prayers and beliefs. Moreover, after this statement, the church said nothing further, even as the crisis expanded and escalated thereafter.

Mekane Yesus (February 24, 2018)

After seventeen months of ecclesial silence, on February 24, 2018—now into the second state of emergency and long after different public massacres without a response—the Ethiopian Evangelical Churches Mekane Yesus (EECMY) published a statement on its social media platform addressed to "the Federal Democratic Republic of Ethiopia, people of Ethiopia, opposition political parties, and Christian communities" titled "A Call from EECMY regarding the Current Situation of Our Country."[92]

This two-page statement begins by reminding readers that the Bible "teaches (with the highest emphasis) that both the church and the government should execute their responsibility given to them, from God and the people, faithfully in righteousness," and calls the church "an ambassador of God on this Earth" that is "duty-bound to teach, advise, and urge both people and government to execute their responsibility with the fear of God."

The statement continues to say that the country's situation is "very worrisome," especially with regard to the "handling of human rights, democracy, justice and good governance," because of which "many lost their lives in sad ways, others lost their body parts, and properties are destroyed." About the denomination's own action, it claims that it has been praying for "peace and reconciliation characterized by justice"; "urging the government, both independently and with other religious organizations, to swiftly respond to the public demand appropriately and in a justified manner" (no details are offered about what this is referring to); and "urging the public to present its questions in a peaceful manner." The statement then commends the government for "asking an apology to the people of Ethiopia" and releasing some prisoners.

Looking toward the future, the EECMY statement calls for national unity, public peace, and "communal understanding" between the government and the people. It then directly addresses the Ethiopian government with four paragraphs. The first names "the public" as the "source and cause" of "every government" (a polite allusion to popular sovereignty) and calls on the government to prioritize the people's peace, security, and unity over its own "political ideology." The second declares that Ethiopia's peace depends on cultivating the "virtue of co-existence" and urges the government to open "a platform which allows all political parties with varied ideologies, civil societies, scholars, known public figures, religious leaders and elders to come together." The third expresses worry that the second state of emergency would "affect the hope of peace and agreement" and requests the government either to retract it "if possible" or, if not, to exercise "utmost care . . . not to violate the basic right of citizens and human right." The fourth urges the government to increase its efforts at good governance by "entertaining diverse ideas and releasing prisoners."

In its two paragraphs addressed to "Opposition Political Parties," the statement urges them to prioritize "public safety" and "peace" over their "principles and interests" and to "promote diverse opinions in a peaceful way through dialogue and contribute for common understanding and peace."

Its two sentences addressed to the "People of Ethiopia" call on the youth to "forward their questions with utmost responsibility and great discipline in peaceful ways" and highlight "the dangerous trends" of "ethnic-based conflicts" and the need for "our virtue of long-lived companionship and solidarity."

The final paragraph addressed to "All the Christian Community" reminds them that "the sovereign God is the rescuer of our country and the mother of nations and nationalities." Thus it calls for prayer and fasting "until justice rolls down like a river," for Christians to be "salt and light" as "messengers of peace and reconciliation," and for "Christians to fulfill their duty of citizenship." What this duty means and requires is left undefined and ambiguous.

Kale Heywet (March 26, 2018)

A month later on March 26, the Ethiopian Kale Heywet Church (EKHC) posted to its social media platform a statement on "the current problems of our country" with an introduction and ten paragraphs, along with a photo of over fifty of its leaders.[93] The introduction states that Ethiopia's social situation affects EKHC's ministries, that the church is actively committed to "peace and development," that the church feels the pain of "the recent violence" (mentioning death, displacement, absence of peace and security, and destruction of property), that the church has visited victims, that the church is worried that the state of emergency may weaken Ethiopian unity, and that the church is praying for "peace and coexistence" as it makes this statement.

In the following ten paragraphs, the statement: (1) calls for prayer and fasting; (2) affirms that humans are made in God's image, expresses "deep-felt sorrow" for the violence, and calls for legal accountability for perpetrators; (3) praises the government for responsive actions like "releasing prisoners" and "transferring power" (presumably the Prime Minister's resignation), and calls on the government to continue on this path; (4) "calls the people to work for true justice, forgive each other, and stand together" citing Isaiah 58; (5) expresses further grief for the victims and calls on "the government and the public" to care for the distressed; (6) "urges [members and citizens] to preach love, unity, equality, peace and development" rather than spreading divisive language; (7) calls on everyone "to get rid of the lack of good governance in the country which caused the people to be dissatisfied" and affirms "the right to express one's dissatisfaction as an individual and as a group"; (8) condemns divisive abuses of "ethnicity, religion, diverse opinion" leading to violence and calls the church to "reject and fight such actions" that can only "curse" Ethiopia and "create regional chaos"; (9) calls on the community to serve the youth (mentioning job creation), "so that they stop hating their country and stop choosing the path of exile/migration"; and (10) "cautions that utmost care be taken to protect the dignity of precious life in the process of implementing the State of Emergency" and "call[s] upon a transparent meeting to be held between religious leaders, elders, and government with the aim of seeking to reverse the situation [the state of emergency]." Nothing further is said about the what, where, when, or how of this "meeting."

The statement concludes, "[W]e call upon all concerned bodies, the Ethiopian government, political parties, civil society organizations, and other organizations (that are contributing to the development of our country), citizens living here and abroad, members of KHC, and all Christians in general to respond positively to this call for peace."

Summary

While these statements came woefully late, carefully avoided referring to any specific injustices, and neglected to map any concrete action plans, they were far superior to the foregoing silence. They expressed grief for victims and employed a rich moral vocabulary to call for fundamental ideals that promote human flourishing like love, justice, forgiveness, dignity, equality, unity, democracy, and the common good.

Nonetheless, since I started teaching at the Ethiopian Graduate School of Theology in August 2016, I have required each of my students to conduct and write up an "ecclesiography," during each semester of the crisis to the present. These compact studies of their churches' preaching and practice were based on fifteen weeks of detailed observation and represented the major denominations and independent churches in Ethiopia, including Mulu Wongel, Mekane Yesus, and Kale Heywet. In over eighty reports, I cannot recall even one paper that described a local church with any active preaching or practice related to social justice. Students repeatedly reported that their churches were either silent on the crisis or restricted themselves to prayers for peace.

Several of my students wrote critically of their churches' silence and passivity in the face of the extreme injustice and human suffering in their society. One student, then working as a federal prosecutor, powerfully summarized what I found to be the overwhelming pattern among my students' ecclesiographic research:

> There is great chaos in the country . . . which resulted in great suffering for millions of people, including women and children. . . . But I have never seen the church trying to help, collect offerings, sending clothes or anything to anyone who suffered from natural or manmade crisis. . . . [T]he church is not serving her purpose, and I am afraid God is not accepting our rituals (Amos 5:21–24). . . . The church is so passive in relation to the sociopolitical concerns of the society. All the church has been doing is pray, and the church has used the prayer as an excuse for her inactiveness. The leaders and the congregations don't realize that prayer doesn't replace action. Some of the leaders and members who have some affiliations with the ruling party somehow try to influence others to believe everything is ok. But injustice and violence is not ok.[94]

This student's ecclesiography was echoed in an interview I conducted with a senior leader with decades of experience in one of Ethiopia's largest denominations. When I asked him, "Do you know of a pastor who prioritizes social justice in his or her ministry?" he paused briefly and then answered confidently, "I haven't met one yet."[95] Thus, while we should celebrate and encourage the church statements summarized here, their congregational reach and implementation appear to be ineffectual and severely limited.

I am not aware of any public statement or action organized by the Ethiopian Orthodox Tewehado Church,[96] the Evangelical Churches Fellowship of Ethiopia, the Inter-Religious Council of Ethiopia (aside from the short New Year's messages in 2016 prior to both states of emergency), or the mushrooming independent churches in Ethiopia.[97] To my knowledge, they have been publicly silent and passive, and have offered no public leadership.[98]

Did the churches learn from their failure in 2005 and speak or act to defend God's will for human flourishing in 2015–2018? Yes and no. Responses were slow in coming, of varying substance, limited in reach, and nebulous in application. But they were a significant improvement compared to the previous silence. What became clear in this second national crisis is that the contemporary church has yet to produce a Christian leader comparable to Martin Luther King Jr., Oscar Romero, or Desmond Tutu, not to mention Ethiopia's own past church leaders like Aba Estifanos (c. 1380–1450),[99] Abuna Petros (1892–1936),[100] Abuna Tewoflos (1910–1979),[101] and Gudina Tumsa (1929–1979),[102] who can provide authoritative moral leadership on the national level.

The brief discussion in this chapter should not be misunderstood. I am not saying that the Ethiopian churches' commitment to human flourishing is reducible to the public statements they make during times of sociopolitical crisis. However, public statements or their absence during these times are important windows into what churches consider to be worthy of public record (and risk) and the calls they think should be issued to the entire church and wider community. Thus they can be used as an important metric for measuring the seriousness of the churches' commitment to the Bible's vision of multidimensional human flourishing in times when this is most endangered or destroyed.

WHAT IS THE WAY FORWARD?

In this essay, I have attempted to sketch a multidimensional vision of human flourishing with Nussbaum and Schweiker, to demonstrate that human flourishing is a fundamental Christian concept and commitment with Gushee, and to evaluate how Ethiopian churches have done at promoting human flourishing during two recent moments of sociopolitical crisis. After the grievous failure of 2005, a few of the major denominations at least appear to be finding a public voice for human flourishing in 2016 and 2018.

According to David Gushee, the sacredness of human life—its inviolable value and right to flourish as God's good creation—stands as "the greatest moral contribution of the Christian tradition to world civilization."[103] Gushee continues, "To violate human rights is to violate God's rights."[104] If this is so, then the question of human flourishing and the Christian community's defense of it cannot be seen as marginal or academic matters. Instead, they are urgent and practically important for the Christian community commanded by Christ to love neighbors left for dead on the roadside (Luke 10:25–37), to treat others the way we ourselves want to be treated (Matthew 7:12),[105] to visit prisoners (Matthew 25:36), and "to remember those in prison as if you yourselves were together with them in prison, and those who are mistreated as if you yourselves were suffering" (Hebrew 13:3).

If the evidence I have surveyed in this chapter is remotely accurate, Ethiopian Christianity finds itself amid a sociopolitical crisis that is no less a theoecclesiological crisis raising ultimate questions: Who is God? What does God want? And how should the Christian community respond to and represent God's will, especially in critical moments? In short, what is the way forward, if the Christian community is to honor the Creator God and obey God's will for human flourishing?[106]

Here I offer three very brief suggestions in conclusion for critical dialogue and practical action.

First, our churches must struggle to define and devote themselves to a holistic vision of human flourishing. Do we have a multidimensional concept of human flourishing, and are we convinced that this is God's will for us and our neighbors? The relative silence and practical inaction sketched here indicate that churches need a dramatically expanded moral imagination and deepened conviction about public responsibility, which I believe could be assisted by critically engaging the work of Nussbaum, Schweiker, and others.[107] It will take courage to challenge the Ethiopian government's entrenched postcommunist suspicion of religion and its role in society, as well as the Ethiopian churches' entrenched dualism, evacuation theology, and mushrooming prosperity gospel.[108]

Second, our churches must self-examine, repent, and confess our failures to responsibly address terrible human desecration and devastation. It seems that the Christian community has very little moral authority left, because the problems convulsing society (e.g., authoritarian leadership, ethnocentric division, moral corruption) are rampant in the church as well. Many believe that the church is so slow to respond (or doesn't respond at all) to sociopolitical crises, because it knows that its severe hypocrisies will be called out by the government and the public. Here Dietrich Bonhoeffer can lead the way for the metanoiaic practice we need:

> The church confesses that it has witnessed the arbitrary use of brutal force, the suffering in body and soul of countless innocent people, that it has witnessed oppression, hatred, and murder without raising its voice for the victims and without finding ways of rushing to help them. It has become guilty of the lives of the weakest and most defenseless brothers and sisters of Jesus Christ.[109]

Third, we need to formulate a practical action plan to promote human flourishing in times of crisis, and we need to start courageously practicing it now. Of course, such strategies must be carefully contextualized, but there is enduring wisdom in the steps outlined by Dr. Martin Luther King Jr. in his "Letter from Birmingham Jail" written to the silent and passive pastors of his time: "In any nonviolent campaign there are four basic steps: collection of the facts to determine whether injustices exist; negotiation; self-purification; and direct [nonviolent] action."[110]

Without this intentional and urgent process of defining and devoting ourselves to God's will for human flourishing, self-examining and confessing our failures, and formulating and practicing a concrete plan for faithfulness in the mist of crisis, I fear that Dr. King's indictment will remain true of us:

> [T]he judgment of God is upon the church as never before. If today's church does not recapture the sacrificial spirit of the early church, it will lose its

authenticity, forfeit the loyalty of millions, and be dismissed as an irrelevant social club with no meaning for the [twenty-first] century. Every day I meet young people whose disappointment with the church has turned into outright disgust.[111]

Alas, this indictment against the church was already raised nearly fifty years ago and only seems to be growing today:

> Students asserted that the church's teachings—to endure poverty and exploitation—had contributed to the underdevelopment of Ethiopia. . . . What had become of the Christian tradition of fearlessly assailing national evils? Where were the voices of the Jeremiahs, Ezekiels, and Daniels? 'History will judge the Church for its silence when thousands go to bed without any food.' . . . The view that religion was the opiate of the people was prevalent among many activists.[112]

There is no time to waste.

BIBLIOGRAPHY

Abebe, Tadesse. *The Role of the Evangelical Church in Promoting Justice in Relation to Ethiopian Election 97*. Unpublished BTh paper, Addis Ababa: Mekane Yesus Seminary, 2008.
Abiy, Ahmed. "Inaugural Address" on April 2, 2018. Translated by Dr. Hassen Hussein. Available at https://www.opride.com/2018/04/03/english-partial-transcript-of-ethiopian-prime-minister-abiy-ahmeds-inaugural-address/.
Alehegne, Mersha. "Abune Petros." In *Encyclopedia Aethiopica*, vol. 4, ed. Siegbert Uhlig. Wiesebaden: Harrassowitz Verlag, 2010, 140–141.
Balsvik, Randi Rønning. *Haile Sellassie's Students: The Intellectual and Social Background to Revolution, 1952–1974*. Addis: Addis Ababa University Press, 2005.
"Ethiopia Profile—Timeline." *BBC*, April 3, 2018. Available at http://www.bbc.com/news/world-africa-13351397.
Bonhoeffer, Dietrich. *Ethics*, ed. Clifford Green, trans. Reinhard Krauss, Charles West, and Douglas Stott. Minneapolis: Fortress, 2005.
———. *London, 1933–1935*, Vol. 13 of *Dietrich Bonhoeffer: Works*, edited by Keith Clements, translated by Isabel Best. Minneapolis: Fortress, 2007.
Carter Center. "Observing the 2005 Ethiopia National Elections: Final Report." Atlanta, GA: Carter Center, 2009.
Cone, James. *God of the Oppressed*, rev. ed. Maryknoll, NY: Orbis, 1997.
Debele, Serawit Bekele. "Religion and Politics in Post-1991 Ethiopia: Making Sense of Bryan S. Turner's 'Managing Religions.'" *Religion, State and Society* 46, no. 1 (2018), 26–42.
DeCort, Andrew. "Authority, Martyrdom, and the Question of Axiality in Ethiopian Political Theology: From Ancient Aksum to Abba Estifanos toward Addis Ababa." *The Journal of Ethiopian Religious Studies* (forthcoming).
———. *Bonhoeffer's New Beginning: Ethics after Devastation*. Lanham, MD: Lexington/Fortress Academic, 2018.
———. "The Obedience of Disobedience: Political Violence, the Bible, and Romans 13." *The Ethiopian Journal of Theology* (forthcoming).
Deressa, Samuel Yonas. "Church and Development in Ethiopia: The Contribution of Gudina Tumsa's Holistic Theology." *Lutheran Mission Matters* 25, no. 1 (May 2017): 150–67.

———. "Church and State in Ethiopia: The Contribution of the Lutheran Understanding of the Community of Grace." *Word and World* 37, no. 3 (Summer 2017): 281–91.

———, ed. *The Life, Works, and Witness of Tsehay Tolessa and Gudina Tumsa, the Ethiopian Bonhoeffer.* Minneapolis, MN: Fortress, 2017.

"Dry Bones + Word" (unpublished sermon). Addis Ababa: Beza International Church, February 19, 2018.

Ejo, Desalegn Abebe. "Where Does the Meserete Kristos Church Stand in Christian Political Engagement: Keeping the Anabaptists' Political Pacifism or Endorsing the Drifting of Its Key Members into Political Participation?" MA thesis, Ethiopian Graduate School of Theology, Addis Ababa, 2016.

Eshete, Mengistu. "Factors Affecting Attitudes of Evangelical Christians toward Politics: A Case of Ye Ethiopia Birehanena Hiwot Betekeristian." MA thesis, Ethiopian Graduate School of Theology, Addis Ababa, 2014.

"Ethiopia Profile—Timeline." *BBC*, April 3, 2018. Available at http://www.bbc.com/news/world-africa-13351397.

"Ethiopian Catholic Bishops Call for Peaceful Dialogue to Resolve Conflicts," *Ethiopian Herald*, August 15, 2016. Accessible from http://www.ecs.org.et/index.php/8-news-slider/90-ethiopian-catholic-bishops-call-for-peaceful-dialogue-to-resolve-conflicts.

Ethiopian Catholic Secretariat Newsletter 3, no. 2 (June 2005).

"Ethiopian Protesters 'Massacred.'" *BBC*, October 19, 2006. Available at http://news.bbc.co.uk/2/hi/africa/6064638.stm.

"Ethiopian Religious Leaders Urge Political Parties to Conduct Peaceful Election." *Strategic Thinking on East Africa*, April 30, 2015. Accessed from http://www.strathink.net/ethiopia/ethiopian-religious-leaders-urge-political-parties-to-conduct-peaceful-election/.

Ethiopian Evangelical Churches Mekane Yesus. "A Call from EECMY regarding the Current Situation of our Country." Unpublished, Addis Ababa, February 2018.

Ethiopian Kale Heywet Church. Untitled Statement. Unpublished, Addis Ababa, March 2018.

Full-Gospel Believers' Church. "Statement of the EFGBC Concerning the Current Situation of Our Country." Unpublished, Addis Ababa, September 2016.

The Ge'ez Acts of Abba Estifanos of Gwendawende: Corpus Scriptorum Christanorum Orientalism. Translated by Getachew Haile. Leuven, Belgium: Peeters, 2006.

Gerbi, Wake Jeo. *Evangelical Christianity and Politics in the Oromo Context in Ethiopia.* Stockholm: Författares Bokmaskin, 2016.

Gushee, David. *The Sacredness of Human Life: Why an Ancient Biblical Vision Is Key to the World's Future.* Grand Rapids, MI: Eerdmans, 2013.

Hansen, Rich. "Transforming the Dualistic Worldview of Ethiopian Evangelical Christians." *International Bulletin of Missionary Research* 39, no. 3 (July 2015): 138–41.

Heliso, Desta. "Justified Fears: A Perspective on the Current Ethiopian Situation." *The Ethiopian Reporter*, December 10, 2016.

———. "The Relevance of the Study of Religion in Ethiopian Context." *The Ethiopian Reporter*, July 28, 2017.

Hill, Ruth, and Eyasu Tsehaye. *Ethiopia Poverty Assessment: 2014 Overview.* Washington, DC: World Bank Group, 2015.

"The Human Cost of Ethiopia's Sweeping State of Emergency: 'I Never Wanted to See Tomorrow.'" *Addis Standard*, December 20, 2016. Available at http://addisstandard.com/human-cost-ethiopias-sweeping-state-emergency-never-wanted-see-tomorrow/.

Klem, David, and William Schweiker. *Religion and the Human Future: An Essay on Theological Humanism.* Malden, MA: Blackwell, 2008.

King Jr., Martin Luther. "The Answer to a Perplexing Question." In *Strength to Love.* Minneapolis, MN: Fortress, 2010.

———. "Letter from Birmingham Jail." In *Why We Can't Wait.* New York: HarperCollins, 1964.

Michael, Admasu Gebre. "Cursed Be the Church." *Struggle* 3, no. 1 (1969).

Middleton, J. Richard. *The Liberating Image: The* Imago Dei *in Genesis 1.* Grand Rapids, MI: Brazos, 2005.

Myers, Bryant. *Walking with the Poor: Principles and Practices of Transformation Development*, rev. ed. Maryknoll, NY: Orbis, 2011.
Nussbaum, Martha. *Creating Capabilities: The Human Development Approach*. Cambridge, MA: Harvard University Press, 2011.
———. *The Fragility of Goodness: Luck and Ethics in Greek Tragedy and Philosophy*. Cambridge, NY: Cambridge University Press, 2001.
Schweiker, William. *Dust That Breathes: Christian Faith and the New Humanisms*. Malden, MA: Wiley-Blackwell, 2010.
———. *Responsibility and Christian Ethics*. New York: Cambridge University Press, 1995.
———. "Responsibility and the Integrity of Life." Unpublished Niebuhr Lecture given at Elmhurst College, IL, February 23, 2011.
Sen, Amartya. *Development as Freedom*. New York: Oxford University Press, 1999.
Siedentop, Larry. *Inventing the Individual: The Origins of Western Liberalism*. London: Penguin, 2015.
Taylor, Charles. *A Secular Age*. Cambridge, MA: Harvard University Press, 2007.
Teklu, Theodros Assefa. *The Politics of Metanoia: Towards a Post-Nationalistic Political Theology in Ethiopia*. Frankfurt am Main: Peter Lang, 2014.
Teshome, Mengisteab, and Haftu Gebreegziabher. "Religious Fathers Convey New Year's Messages." *Ethiopian Herald*, September 11, 2016. Accessed at http://www.ethpress.gov.et/herald/index.php/news/national-news/item/5925-religious-fathers-convey-new-year-s-message.
"Timeline: Human Rights Situation in Ethiopia." Underrepresented Nations and Peoples Organization, March 5, 2018. Accessed from http://unpo.org/article/19573.
United Nations Habitat. *The State of Addis Ababa 2017: The Addis Ababa We Want*. Nairobi, Kenya: United Nations Human Settlements Program, 2017.
United States Congress, House Resolution 128, passed on April 10, 2018.
Zelalem, Zecharias. "Woldia Massacre: Ethiopian Security Forces Kill a Dozen, Turning a Holiday Procession into Nightmare," *OPride*, January 22, 2018. Accessed from https://www.opride.com/2018/01/22/woldia-massacre-ethiopian-security-forces-kill-dozen-turning-holiday-procession-nightmare.

NOTES

1. Dietrich Bonhoeffer, letter on September 11, 1934, to Erwin Sutz, in *London, 1933–1935*, Vol. 13 of *Dietrich Bonhoeffer: Works*, ed. Keith Clements, trans. Isabel Best (Minneapolis, MN: Fortress, 2007), 217.

2. The goal of this essay is not to discuss the concept of development. For a constructive model, see Bryant Myers, *Walking with the Poor: Principles and Practices of Transformational Development*, rev. ed. (Maryknoll, NY: 2011).

3. On the concept of responsibility in Christian ethics, see William Schweiker, *Responsibility and Christian Ethics* (New York: Cambridge University Press, 1995).

4. Charles Taylor, *A Secular Age* (Cambridge, MA: Harvard University Press, 2007), 16.

5. Abiy Ahmed, "Inaugural Address" on April 2, 2018, translated by Dr. Hassen Hussein and available online at https://www.opride.com/2018/04/03/english-partial-transcript-of-ethiopian-prime-minister-abiy-ahmeds-inaugural-address/.

6. For recent figures, see Ruth Hill and Eyasu Tsehaye, *Ethiopia Poverty Assessment: 2014 Overview* (Washington, DC: World Bank Group, 2015), 2–3 and the United States Congress's House Resolution 128 passed on April 10, 2018.

7. Martha Nussbaum, *Creating Capabilities: The Human Development Approach* (Cambridge, MA: Harvard University Press, 2011).

8. Ibid., ix.

9. Ibid., 13.

10. For Sen's most famous articulation, see *Development as Freedom* (New York: Oxford University Press, 1999).

11. Nussbaum, *Creating Capabilities*, 20.

12. Ibid., x, 14, 18.
13. Ibid., 28.
14. Ibid., 20.
15. Nussbaum, *Creating Capabilities*, x.
16. Ibid., 18.
17. Ibid., 25. This axiom is important in the Ethiopian context, where the EPRDF's "developmental statism" seems to reject the intrinsic value of freedom.
18. Ibid., 1, 15.
19. Ibid., x.
20. Ibid., 23.
21. Ibid., 26; see 29–31.
22. Ibid., 21.
23. Ibid., 24.
24. Ibid., 21.
25. Ibid., 22.
26. Ibid., 21.
27. Ibid., 28. For Nussbaum's attempt to articulate a normative ethical basis for this approach, see chapter 4 "Fundamental Entitlements," 69–100.
28. Ibid., 31.
29. Ibid., 32.
30. Ibid., 33–34.
31. Ibid., 36.
32. Ibid., 33.
33. Ibid., 35.
34. Ibid., 36.
35. For Nussbaum's discussion of moral tragedy (e.g., when a poor family needs its children to work and thus not to attend school), see 37–42. Nussbaum calls for "ingenuity and effort" driven by expectations that are "aspirational but not utopian" rather than resigning ourselves. See Martha Nussbaum, *The Fragility of Goodness: Luck and Ethics in Greek Tragedy and Philosophy* (Cambridge, NY: Cambridge University Press, 2001).
36. David Klem and William Schweiker, *Religion and the Human Future: An Essay on Theological Humanism*, Blackwell Manifestoes (Malden, MA: Blackwell, 2008). Schweiker defines "theological humanism" as "a stance and orientation in life that combines humanistic aspirations with a genuine theological outlook" (18).
37. See William Schweiker, "Responsibility and the Integrity of Life," unpublished Niebuhr Lecture given at Elmhurst College, IL, February 23, 2011.
38. Ibid, 75. See William Schweiker, *Responsibility and Christian Ethics* (New York, NY: Cambridge University Press, 1995), 117; and William Schweiker, *Dust That Breathes: Christian Faith and the New Humanisms* (Malden, MA: Wiley-Blackwell, 2010), 49.
39. Klem and Schweiker, *Religion and the Human Future*, 79.
40. Ibid., 80.
41. Ibid., 76.
42. Ibid., 77.
43. Ibid., 77.
44. Ibid., 78.
45. Ibid., 81.
46. Ibid., 78.
47. Ibid., 78.
48. Ibid., 79.
49. For Schweiker's critique of Martha Nussbaum's position and other neohumanists, see *Dust That Breathes*, chapter 5, "Voices of Neohumanism."
50. If this essay were longer, I would discuss United Nations Habitat's report, *The State of Addis Ababa 2017: The Addis Ababa We Want* (Nairobi, Kenya: United Nations Human Settlements Program, 2017), which commendably analyzes five key areas of human development: economy, housing, services, environment and quality of life, and the role of citizens in deciding public policy. Still, the report says nothing about happiness, morality, activism, dialogue, faith,

hospitality, art, love, friendship, or other factors, and thus falls far short of describing the city Addis Ababans actually want. The report works with an impoverished imagination of what it means to be human and thus struggles to inspire the change it seeks.

51. Taylor, *A Secular Age*, 17.

52. David Gushee, *The Sacredness of Human Life: Why an Ancient Biblical Vision Is Key to the World's Future* (Grand Rapids, MI: Eerdmans, 2013).

53. Ibid., 33. Italics in original.

54. Ibid., 1.

55. Ibid., 4. See Larry Siedentop, *Inventing the Individual: The Origins of Western Liberalism* (London: Penguin Books, 2015) for a similar argument.

56. Gushee, *The Sacredness of Human Life*, 6.

57. Ibid., 14.

58. Ibid., 52.

59. Ibid., 47. For an extended demonstration of Gushee's argument, see J. Richard Middleton, *The Liberating Image: The* Imago Dei *in Genesis 1* (Grand Rapids, MI: Brazos, 2005).

60. Gushee, *The Sacredness of Human Life*, 58.

61. Ibid., 60. For Cone's full argument, see James Cone, *God of the Oppressed*, rev. ed. (Maryknoll, NY: Orbis, 1997).

62. Gushee, *The Sacredness of Human Life*, 62.

63. For a study of numerous cases of political disobedience in the Bible, see Andrew DeCort, "The Obedience of Disobedience: Political Violence, the Bible, and Romans 13," forthcoming in the inaugural edition of *The Ethiopian Journal of Theology*.

64. Gushee, *The Sacredness of Human Life*, 92.

65. Ibid., 95.

66. Ibid., 102–103.

67. Ibid., 103–104.

68. Ibid., 107.

69. Ibid., 110.

70. Ibid., 111–13.

71. Ibid., 115.

72. Ibid., 1.

73. Ibid., 33.

74. Ibid., 121.

75. Cone, *God of the Oppressed*, 59.

76. Nussbaum, *Creating Capabilities*, 5–7, 10.

77. Klem and Schweiker, *Religion and the Human Future*.

78. See Carter Center, "Observing the 2005 Ethiopia National Elections: Final Report" (Atlanta, GA: Carter Center, 2009), 1–69.

79. According to official tallies, the Coalition for Unity and Democracy won 109 seats and requested reelection for 139 seats. The United Ethiopian Democratic Forces won 52 seats and requested reelection for 50 seats. Thus the opposition officially won 172 seats (including eleven for the Oromo Federal Democratic Movement), falling short of the 273 seats needed to form a government.

80. "Ethiopian Protesters 'Massacred,'" *BBC*, October 19, 2006. Accessed from http://news.bbc.co.uk/2/hi/africa/6064638.stm.

81. I'm not suggesting that individual Christians were not active in some cases. For example, Dr. Nebeyou Alemu has informed me that students from Holy Trinity theological college sent a statement condemning the violence to Addis Admas newspaper, but I have not been able to find this article. See the next footnote.

82. Tadesse Abebe, *The Role of the Evangelical Church in Promoting Justice in Relation to Ethiopian Election 97* (Unpublished BTh paper, Mekane Yesus Seminary, Addis Ababa, 2008), 7, 35. While the Evangelical Churches Fellowship of Ethiopia (ECFE) encouraged Christians to vote, sponsored trainings, and officially participated as an observer of the election with 234 delegates (mainly volunteers from local churches), Abebe concludes that the ECFE was totally silent and passive in the crisis after the election: "Thus they were not ready to manage the problems. Then the task force of ECFE did not give any official announcement. Ato Bekele

Geda, the coordinator and leader of the task force, said in his report, 'We finished our responsibility to help Christians to participate in the election and we accomplished our goal by getting more Christians in the parliament.' The report does not indicate a single word about the fairness or the destruction and loss of life. I asked the coordinator about this issue. He replied, 'It was beyond us, although it is the responsibility and right of the ECFE to say something based on their observation.' His personal opinion on this issue is 'general problem of leadership.' . . . Evangelical Churches did not want to say any word about the crisis but only asked the people to have patience on Ethiopian Television with other religious leaders of Ethiopia. They did not say any word different from the government's claim" (26, 29).

83. *Ethiopian Catholic Secretariat Newsletter* 3, no. 2 (June 2005): 16.

84. Martin Luther King, Jr., "The Answer to a Perplexing Question," in *Strength to Love* (Minneapolis, MN: Fortress Press, 2010), 138.

85. See Abebe, *The Role of the Evangelical Church*; and Rich Hansen, "Transforming the Dualistic Worldview of Ethiopian Evangelical Christians," *International Bulletin of Missionary Research* 39, no. 3 (July 2015): 138–41.

86. An Ethiopian scholar who reviewed this manuscript commented, "Most churches were experiencing internal conflict and their cases were before the government; hence they didn't have the moral ground to condemn the acts of the government."

87. For detailed descriptions of government injustice and public violence during these years, see the United States Congress's House Resolution 128 passed on April 10, 2018; "Ethiopia Profile—Timeline," *BBC*, April 3, 2018, accessed from http://www.bbc.com/news/world-africa-13351397; and "Timeline: Human Rights Situation in Ethiopia," Underrepresented Nations and Peoples Organization, March 5, 2018, accessed from http://unpo.org/article/19573. The numbers in these reports are highly disputed.

88. Again, these numbers are disputed. See "The Human Cost of Ethiopia's Sweeping State of Emergency: 'I Never Wanted to See Tomorrow,'" *Addis Standard*, December 20, 2016, accessed from http://addisstandard.com/human-cost-ethiopias-sweeping-state-emergency-never-wanted-see-tomorrow/.

89. "Ethiopian Catholic Bishops Call for Peaceful Dialogue to Resolve Conflicts," *Ethiopian Herald*, August 15, 2016. Accessible from http://www.ecs.org.et/index.php/8-news-slider/90-ethiopian-catholic-bishops-call-for-peaceful-dialogue-to-resolve-conflicts.

90. Mengisteab Teshome and Haftu Gebreegziabher, "Religious Fathers Convey New Year's Messages," *Ethiopian Herald*, September 11, 2016. Accessed from http://www.ethpress.gov.et/herald/index.php/news/national-news/item/5925-religious-fathers-convey-new-year-s-message. See also "Ethiopian Religious Leaders Urge Political Parties to Conduct Peaceful Election," *Strategic Thinking on East Africa*, April 30, 2015, at http://www.strathink.net/ethiopia/ethiopian-religious-leaders-urge-political-parties-to-conduct-peaceful-election/.

91. I'm grateful to Dr. Nebeyou Alemu for translating this and other unpublished Amharic documents for this essay.

92. The EECMY claims over three thousand ministers, twelve thousand congregations, and 8.3 million members.

93. The EKHC claims some seven million members and eight thousand churches.

94. Ecclesiography from Introduction to Christian Ethics. No further information is given to protect the author's anonymity.

95. The interview was conducted on March 29, 2018. Again, no further information is given to protect anonymity.

96. See Zecharias Zelalem, "Woldia Massacre: Ethiopian Security Forces Kill a Dozen, Turning a Holiday Procession into Nightmare," *OPride*, January 22, 2018, accessed from https://www.opride.com/2018/01/22/woldia-massacre-ethiopian-security-forces-kill-dozen-turning-holiday-procession-nightmare/: "there have been no public statements or messages of condolences by anyone affiliated to the Church's governing body or the Patriarch Abune Mathias."

97. Rather than addressing the crisis, the large independent church Beza International published a sermon entitled "Dry Bones + Word" on February 19, 2018—days after the Prime Minister resigned and the second state of emergency was imposed—in which it declared, "Stop

watching the news" and "if you call [your situation] blessed, heaven will decree it so!" Thus the sermon instructed the congregation to ignore the suffering of their neighbors and the injustice of their society, because of their word of faith. See https://mailchi.mp/7550575e8143/god-is-not-after-worship-but-the-worshiper-2612321?e=be0d55431b.

98. See Serawit Bekele Debele, "Religion and Politics in Post-1991 Ethiopia: Making Sense of Bryan S. Turner's 'Managing Religions,'" *Religion, State and Society* 46, no. 1 (2018): 26–42 on state silencing and cooptation of religion.

99. See *The Ge'ez Acts of Abba Estifanos of Gwendawende: Corpus Scriptorum Christanorum Orientalium*, trans. Getachew Haile (Leuven, Belgium: Peeters, 2006) and Andrew DeCort, "Authority, Martyrdom, and the Question of Axiality in Ethiopian Political Theology: From Ancient Aksum to Abba Estifanos toward Addis Ababa," *The Journal of Ethiopian Religious Studies* (forthcoming).

100. See Mersha Alehegne, "Abune Petros," in *Encyclopedia Aethiopica*, vol. 4, ed. Siegbert Uhlig (Wiesebaden: Harrassowitz Verlag, 2010), 140–41.

101. See "Tewoflos (B)," on the *Dictionary of African Christian Biography* website.

102. See Samuel Yonas Deressa, ed., *The Life, Works, and Witness of Tsehay Tolessa and Gudina Tumsa, the Ethiopian Bonhoeffer* (Minneapolis, MN: Fortress, 2017) and Samuel Yonas Deressa, "Church and Development in Ethiopia: The Contribution of Gudina Tumsa's Holistic Theology," *Lutheran Mission Matters* 25, no. 1 (May 2017): 150–67. For contemporary work, see Theodros Assefa Teklu, *The Politics of Metanoia: Towards a Post-Nationalistic Political Theology in Ethiopia* (Frankfurt am Main: Peter Lang, 2014); Wake Jeo Gerbi, *Evangelical Christianity and Politics in the Oromo Context in Ethiopia* (Stockholm: Författares Bokmaskin, 2016); Samuel Yonas Deressa, "Church and State in Ethiopia: The Contribution of the Lutheran Understanding of the Community of Grace," *Word and World* 37, no. 3 (Summer 2017): 281–91; and Desta Heliso, "Justified Fears: A Perspective on the Current Ethiopian Situation," *The Ethiopian Reporter*, December 10, 2016 and "The Relevance of the Study of Religion in Ethiopian Context," *The Ethiopian Reporter*, July 28, 2017. For unpublished research, see Mengistu Eshete, "Factors Affecting Attitudes of Evangelical Christians toward Politics: A Case of Ye Ethiopia Birehanena Hiwot Betekeristian" (MA Thesis, Ethiopian Graduate School of Theology, Addis Ababa, 2014) and Desalegn Abebe Ejo, "Where Does the Meserete Kristos Church Stand in Christian Political Engagement: Keeping the Anabaptists' Political Pacifism or Endorsing the Drifting of Its Key Members into Political Participation?" (MA Thesis, Ethiopian Graduate School of Theology, Addis Ababa, 2016).

103. Gushee, *The Sacredness of Human Life*, 1.

104. Ibid., 52.

105. Who wants to be seized and tortured while others remain safely silent and passive?

106. See Andrew DeCort, "Public Theology in Ethiopia: State, Church, and Neighbor-Love," in *What Does Theology Do, Actually?* eds. Matthew Ryan Robinson and Inja Inderst (Evangelische Verlagsanstalt, forthcoming).

107. See Myers, "Toward a Christian Understanding."

108. See Hansen, "Transforming the Dualistic Worldview."

109. Dietrich Bonhoeffer, *Ethics*, ed. Clifford Green, trans. Reinhard Krauss, Charles West, and Douglas Stott (Minneapolis, MN: Fortress, 2005), 139. For an extensive discussion of practices of new beginnings in Bonhoeffer's work, see Andrew D. DeCort, *Bonhoeffer's New Beginning: Ethics After Devastation* (Lanham, MD: Lexington/Fortress Academic, 2018), particularly chapter 5, "'The Dawning of the New World, the New Order': Practices of New Beginning in Bonhoeffer's Thought."

110. Martin Luther King Jr., "Letter from Birmingham Jail," in *Why We Can't Wait* (New York, NY: HarperCollins, 1964), 78.

111. Ibid., 92.

112. Randi Rønning Balsvik, *Haile Sellassie's Students: The Intellectual and Social Background to Revolution, 1952-1974* (Addis: Addis Ababa University Press, 2005), 241. The internal quotation is from Admasu Gebre Michael, "Cursed Be the Church," *Struggle* 3, No. 1 (1969), 7.

Part Two

Developmental Perspectives

Chapter 4

Church and Human Development

An Asian Perspective

Lim Teck Peng

THREE FACETS OF DEVELOPMENT

Since its inception, the church has a longstanding history of engagement in benevolent acts (Acts 2:44–45; 6:1–5). Through the centuries, most notably during crisis periods such as the Black Death, countless Christians, men or women, wealthy or humble, have participated in humanitarian acts, sometimes to the extent of risking their lives.

Despite the widespread confidence in economic growth during the last century, problems of poverty, deprivation, and inequality persist. This persistence has prompted a series of reflections and public declarations from the church, including Pope John XXIII's *Mater et Magistra* issued in 1960, a report titled *Liberation, Justice, Development* published by the East Asia Christian Conference in 1970, and *Hope for a Global Future: Toward Just and Sustainable Human Development* published by the Presbyterian Church (USA) in 1996.[1] These publications, while reflecting the rich traditions of Christian compassion, employ also contemporary concepts of development, testifying therein to both the proximity and tension between religious and secular views of human flourishing.

While deliberating the contemporary approaches of a just, sustainable, and human development, *Hope for a Global Future* explicates the distributive, ecological, and agential aspects of development, bringing into view development principles such as distributive justice, responsibilities to future generations, and the enhancement of the quality of life. The report offers a good example of how Christians can critically and productively engage contemporary development discourse and practice.

Taking the aforementioned three facets of development as its starting point, the present paper concentrates on one particular aspect that receives only cursory mention in the Presbyterian report: building up human agency. Beginning with the economist and Nobel Laureate Amartya Sen's influential notion of capability, the first part of my paper examines how it helps the church adopt a broader framework for Christian social involvement and provide a new focus (besides the distributive and preservative aspect of development) for reflection and discussion. The second section then highlights the ambiguity of a one-sided emphasis on the subjectivity of agency (personal choice and freedom, etc.) by bringing into focus two things: the cultural embeddedness of agency, and the encroachment of market-driven globalization that shapes human desires as much as economic activities. Giving epistemic priority to the sociocultural embeddedness of human agency, and keeping in view the contestable aspects of development, the importance of reflective agency is then explored.

The third section of the paper focuses on the efficacy of Christian congregational living, concentrating on its reflective and interactive aspects. This is followed by an examination of how these dimensions of congregational life render the church an important player in the development process, moving toward what political theorist Robert Goodin calls "reflective democracy."[2]

HUMAN DEVELOPMENT: WELL-BEING AND AGENCY

The idea of human development was first developed by Mahbub Ul Haq, the mind behind the Human Development Report (HDR).[3] In contrast to the models of distributive and sustainable development, human development carries a distinct orientation as a

> development of the people for the people by the people. Development of the people means investing in human capabilities, whether in education or health or skills, so that they can work productively and creatively. Development for the people means ensuring that the economic growth they generate is distributed widely and fairly. . . . [D]evelopment by the people [means] giving everyone a chance to participate.[4]

This citation by the Presbyterian report is taken from the 1993 HDR. The Presbyterian report does not elaborate on the concept of human capability, which is an influential concept in the United Nations Development Programme made popular by Amartya Sen.

In contrast to the opulence-oriented approach that uses indicators such as gross domestic product to assess progress, Sen seeks to evaluate national development in terms of what the people can do or be. In an article titled "Well-being, Agency and Freedom," Sen develops the framework for his capability approach by first providing a rigorous conceptualization of well-being and agency.[5] Concerning the difference between well-being related to agency and human agency in general, Sen writes:

> People have aspects other than well-being. Not all their activities are aimed at maximizing well-being (nor does their activity contribute to it), no matter how broadly we define well-being within the limit of that general concept. There are goals other than well-being, and values other than goals.[6]

What is significant for the present study is that agency consists of value-driven actions motivated by particular visions of the good, and that these actions do not necessarily concern the well-being of the actor. Sen concedes: "In fact, some types of agency roles, e.g., those related to fulfilling obligations, can quite possibly have a negative impact on the person's well-being."[7]

To further unpack the idea of agency, Sen introduces the concepts of "capability" and "functionings." The former refers to a person's repertoire of possible actions to take or states to be in, whereas the latter refers to things or states that a person manages to do or to be in.[8] The notion of capability is akin to the meaning of the Greek word *dunamin*, sometimes translated as "potentiality."[9] And the concept of "functionings" includes basic human agency ranging from being adequately nourished and being in good health to achieving self-respect or being socially integrated. Using the dual notions of capability and functionings, Sen defines his capability approach to the aspect of well-being in human development as "a particular approach to well-being and advantage in terms of a person's ability to do valuable acts or reach valuable states of being."[10]

Going beyond the distributive model of development (whether the issue at hand is the distribution of resources within one generation or, in the case of sustainable model, the distribution of ecological resources across generations), the capability approach treats resources as means to human capability. The basic tenet of the capability approach is that poverty or inequality is identified not only as an unjust distribution of resources (income and food, etc.) but also as a deprivation of capability (living a minimally decent life as a human being and being adequately nourished, etc.).

By shifting the focus from wealth production to agential development, the capability approach provides an impetus for the church to include the development of agency in her vision of social and global engagement. Without necessarily replacing the concern for a just and sustainable development, this adds a new dimension to our reflection on the relationship between church and development. It does not mean that the philanthropic efforts of the church to provide basic needs to the disadvantaged, to voice concern over the enormous income-gap between rich and poor, and to advocate for environmentally friendly policy are unnecessary; it simply means that the concern of the church cannot stop here. Furthermore, the church needs to think in more concrete terms about the kind of capacities that are associated with Christian social actions.

THE EMBEDDEDNESS OF AGENCY AND DEVELOPMENT

The concept of freedom is pivotal to Sen's construal of well-being and agency. According to Sen: "A person's 'agency freedom' refers to what the person is free to do and achieve in pursuit of whatever goals or values he or she regards as important"; such freedom is not arbitrary but embedded with the person's "aims, objectives, allegiances, and—in a broad sense—the person's conception of the good."[11] Comparing the freedom associated with the well-being of a person and his or her freedom as an agent, Sen writes:

> Although well-being achievement is geared to a specific objective, and well-being freedom is seen in terms of the freedom to achieve that objective through the choice of functioning vectors, agency freedom cannot be examined in terms of any prespecified objective. The open conditionality referred to above is central to that concept.[12]

In my view, there is an ambiguity in Sen's rather abstract formulation of the "open conditionality" of agency freedom: from whose point of view does one decide that an agent's freedom "cannot be examined in terms of any prespecified objective"? If I am totally unrelated to a person, and we are growing up in two different life-worlds, it makes sense that "open conditionality" holds if I am to understand his or her way of exercising agency. However, if we were pals growing up together, socialized by the same community, breathing the same air of communal living, and sharing what Ludwig Wittgenstein calls the language-game, is it not natural and reasonable that my pal and I do share and hence expect from each other some kind of "prespecified objective" in our aspirations and concepts of the good? Are we then still free agents in Sen's view?[13]

Departing from Sen's formal and abstract way of conceptualizing agency, I intend to concretize the concept of agency by situating it specifically in the context of the majority world in which two realities stand out: (1) the sociocultural embeddedness of agency, and (2) the encroachment of market-driven globalization that constantly shapes desires through various forms of advertising and marketing. The first aspect is about the historical efficacy of lived traditions and cultures, embedded in human cognition, affection, and volition and hence constitutive of human agency. In contrast to the historicity of agency, the second aspect represents influences from outside exerted on a local community. It reflects the deeply intertwined relationship between development and globalization, in which the question of the good involves advertising and marketing companies as much as development practitioners and the local community.

Concepts of the good life (including the idea of freedom and progress) are therefore never neutral, nor are the soils in which these ideals are meant to take root. As the development trajectory moves from providing basic human needs to the enhancement of people's capability to undertake actions and ways of being considered good and desirable, the development process inevitably involves evaluative questions such as "What constitutes a good life?" In a development situation, the development practitioners and the recipients are equally entrenched in a tradition that influences their aspiration for a better life. In this regard, instead of making an *a priori* claim of open conditionality of human agency, I would argue that it is more productive to recognize the cultural embeddedness of human agency (including that of the development practitioner) and hence the contestable character of development.

The following citation from *The Quality of Life* demonstrates the contestable nature of the evaluative question concerning the good life in a development context:

> When standards are chosen to assess the quality of life of people in different parts of the world, one has to ask whose views as to the criteria should be decisive. Should we, for example, look to the local traditions of the country or region with which we are concerned, asking what these traditions have regarded as most essential to thriving, or should we, instead, see some universal account of good human living, assessing the various local traditions against it?[14] If we stick to local traditions, this seems to have the advantage of giving us something definite to point to and a clear way of knowing what we want to know.... It seems, as well, to promote the advantage of respect of difference.... On the other hand, most traditions contain elements of injustice and oppression, often deeply rooted; and it is frequently hard to find a basis for criticism of these inequities without thinking about human functioning in a more critical and universal way.

My question is: Besides being definite, clear and different, is it possible that the local traditions have something no less critical and universal than the Western traditions to offer to the world and its continuing development? Besides playing a supportive role to the Western ideas of progress and democracy, do non-Western cultures have anything unique and universal to contribute?[15]

Sen's capability approach aims to secure the liberty with which an individual is free to decide what he or she wants to do or be; in this sense it is less prescriptive than the opulence approach of development. However, in view of the deep entanglement between development and market-driven globalization, the rhetoric of personal freedom fails to provide the needed resistance against the tide of consumerism, propelled by a constant reproduction of human desire based on the logic of production and consumption.[16]

Raising a person's living standards and inculcating in him or her a sense of personal autonomy and capability do not necessarily lead to a deprivation of the local life-world and traditions. However, my contention is that neither will it, as a matter of fact, develop the kind of cultural agency needed for the renewal of local traditions and for resistance to cultural displacement.

The reclamation of the historicity and the communality of human agency, while not privileging local traditions from the need of a hermeneutics of suspicion, points positively to the need to cultivate *cultural response-ability towards one's inherited culture in such a manner that is just and responsible to the past, present and future generations.*[17] For the majority world, this aspect of human agency is critical not only from the human development point of view but also from the sustainable development point of view.[18] I will contend that the future of a particular local culture should not be left to the "invisible hand" of the market to decide, but to the local community,[19] of which the local church is a part.

REFLECTIVE AGENCY AND THE CHURCH

The church bears the marks of the love of God, the grace of Jesus Christ, and the fellowship of the Holy Spirit (*koinonia*, the Greek word for fellowship or communion, literally means participation and sharing). These marks are gifts from God deeply related to human flourishing. Whenever Christian discipleship is taken seriously, capabilities important to communal living will inevitably receive much emphasis. These include a capacity to "value others above yourselves, not looking to your own interests but each of you to the interests of the others" (Phil. 2:4–5).

The co-presence of divine agency and human agency makes the church a unique site of human development that is distinctly shaped by the grammar of the Christian story and theology.[20] As a *local* community, every Christian congregation, whose core belief and imagination are shaped by the incarnation of Jesus Christ, carries the *dunami* of becoming "incarnated" actors or agents. The deep sense of locality (i.e., association and identity beyond personal interest and utility), when coupled with the belief that the best elements of its cultures are part of the "glory and honour of the nations" (Rev. 21:26), provides a powerful motivation for the church to participate in the renewal of local traditions in a way that is both redemptive and productive.

The aforementioned cultural capability of Christians is exercised within and not apart from the lived reality of one's life-world. Instead of conceptualizing agency freedom in an *a priori* fashion as the autonomy of an agent against the efficacy of lived tradition, I argue that agency freedom is always instantiated in and through and not apart from one's lived tradition. It involves one's freedom to discern and make a judgment about the visions of the good life, including those embedded in the local wisdom and those reaching the shore of one's habitat through the tide of globalization. In this respect, what Paul teaches the Thessalonians concerning the discernment of prophetic claims is not irrelevant: "Do not treat prophecies with contempt but test them all; hold on to what is good, reject every kind of evil" (1 Thess. 5:20–22).

As part of the social fabric of local community, a local church can provide a space that is conducive for reflective agency. In this space, visions of the good life, modern or premodern, are allowed to be explicated, worked out, and tested. In the modern context of development and democratization, the development of such a reflective and discursive space is a concrete way for the church to seek the welfare the city (Jeremiah 29:7) by taking part in the renewal of traditions and cultures. This makes the local church an important player in local development. Using Thomas Groome's approach to Christian religious education as an illustration, the following paragraphs aim to explore how a facet of church life can be made conducive to the nurturing of reflective agency.

Among the different aspects of congregational living, its educational activities reflect most explicitly the effort of the church to nurture the agency of Christian discipleship. Few are as emphatic as Thomas Groome about the importance of reflection in religious education.[21] Groome describes his approach as "a relational, reflective and experiential knowing in which by critical reflection on lived experiences people discover and name their own story and vision and . . . the Story and Vision of the Christian community."[22] His approach promotes reflective capability through an opening question aimed to invite participants to articulate a personal statement based on a particular subject matter. Depending on the issue at hand, this may include "the participants' reactions, feelings, sentiments, overt activity, valuing, meaning making, understanding, beliefs, relationships, and the like."[23] The first movement will then be followed by a time of critical reflection that focuses on "why we do what we do and what our hopes are in doing it."[24] In Groome's own words: "In this the movement attempts to help participants to come to a consciousness of the social conditioning, norms, assumptions, and the like that are embodied in their present actions."[25] These explications are further brought into dialogue with the Christian Story and Vision through the remaining three movements of Groome's approach. For purposes of the present discussion, it suffices to say that Groome's approach emphasizes reflectivity as much as the objectivity of Christian Story, and that reflective capability plays a crucial role in Groome's construal as both the condition and the outcome of religious education.[26]

While direct and explicit reflective learning is important for the church, it is by no means the only way in which a reflective moment occurs in the Christian communal living. Christian worship, fellowship, services, and acts of proclamation are all possible contexts in which a reflective moment may occur at the personal, interpersonal, and corporate level. For example, Christian fellowship, which consists of interpersonal interactions, provides plenty of opportunities for participants across all ages and all walks of life to interact and engage with one another. It is through such deliberative and reflective processes that the local church becomes a site of development for the reflective agency crucial for the process of democratization.

THE DEVELOPMENT OF REFLECTIVE DEMOCRACY

In Asia, as in other parts of the majority world, reflective agency involves the task of sorting out the good and the bad elements of one's inherited traditions as well as of those ideas imported from the West. Without the provision of space for reflection and deliberation, any ideal, however well-intended it may be, risks being imperialistic. In the absence of reflective and discursive processes such as those offered in the church, any institutionalized ideal, democracy included, will in the long run become an impediment to human flourishing.

The democratic ideal by itself does not prescribe—let alone settle—the disputes concerning the trajectory and pace of democratization and development. Advocacy and contestation are therefore inevitable when democratization is coexistent with different social imaginations and divergent views and assessments concerning the manner and pace of development.[27] In view of the contestable nature of development, as it involves different orientations and preferences, one may argue that unreflective development is no less detrimental to human flourishing than is oppressive tradition. In the field of political theory, Robert Goodin has recently argued for the importance of reflective capability in his book *Reflective Democracy*.[28] Goodin's deliberations provide a good illustration of the importance of reflective agency in a democratic society.

Defining various models of democracy as "essentially preference-respecting systems,"[29] Goodin describes unreflective preferences in these words: "They might be *ill-considered*: half-baked, knee-jerk, top-of-the-head, not thought through. They might be unreflective in the connected sense of being *narrow*. Among the things that unreflective agents might have failed to think through are the full ramifications, either for themselves or others, either for the short term or especially the long term."[30]

Against the background of unreflective preferences, Goodin lists three common characteristics shared by reflective preferences:

- More *empathetic* with the plight of others
- More *considered*, and hence both better informed and more stable
- More *far-reaching* in both time and space, taking fuller account of distant periods, distant people, and different interests[31]

Against unreflective and hence indiscriminate openness to preferences and advocacies, Goodin argues for models of democracy "that enable us to respect preferences *reflectively*—to *differentiate* among preferences, respecting some but not others. Such models of democracy provide mechanisms, of various different sorts, for sifting among people's preferences and weighting some more heavily than others (and discounting still others altogether) in reaching social decisions."[32]

For the purpose of the present study, Goodin's concepts of "public deliberation" and "democratic deliberation within" are of special interest to us. Public deliberation refers to "open discussion in a public forum" characterized not only by "the obligation to give a public account of yourself and your reasons for favouring some particular course of action," but also by the capability of "listening carefully and directly to what one another has to say, and then reflecting upon what each of us has previously said in light of that."[33] In contrast to such intersubjective interaction, "democratic deliberation within" refers to one's inner dialogue based on "our internal reflections upon the perspectives of one another." It is a subjective reflection that "tries to come to grips with one another's perspectives in the most coherent (and in that sense, too, 'reflective') form."[34]

The threat of unreflective practice described by Goodin exists in development process as much as in democratic practices. And the reflective capability described by Goodin is as much needed in development as it is in the democratization process. Viewed in this light, the reflective potential embedded in ecclesial practices as described in the previous session carries public significance that goes beyond the four walls of the church. It enables people to resist all kinds of reductionism and polarization which, theologically speaking, are acts of idolization that aim to replace the Gospel of Christ with a particular human aspiration.

CONCLUSION

Christianity is not the only religion involved in philanthropy and human development. As observed by Matthew Clarke and Anna Halafoff, "there are many instances where development activities are being undertaken in religious locations. Such merging of sacred place and development space is not an exception but a daily occurrence across the globe that is yet to be fully appreciated."[35] With an increase in attention to the relationship between religion and development, it is crucial for the church to develop a more in-depth understanding of its unique contribution.

Of course, the manner and actual extent a Christian community is allowed to participate in the local development scene involves political legitimacy as much as self-understanding.[36] Regardless of the extent of participation, as a *local* religious community, what the church is doing within the four walls is not without public significance to the society at large insofar as what goes on in the church does reflect her vision of the common good and the possibility of a continuing transformation and flourishing of cultures and traditions. In this regard, I would like to end this paper by emphasizing the priority of discipleship over personal spiritual well-being and citizenship. The present paper argues that, both historically and theologically speaking, the agency of Christian discipleship should take precedence and priority over the needs of spiritual well-being and the agency of citizenship.

The New Testament testifies how the church, as the agential community in Jesus Christ, exercises its agency in a world ruled by others. The agency of the NT church is one of discipleship that can make the presence of Christ felt under any sociocultural and political condition. Hence, the contributions of the church in human development lie in its *being* as much as its *doing*.

BIBLIOGRAPHY

Clarke, Matthew, and Anna Halafoff. *Religion and Development in the Asia-Pacific: Sacred Places as Development Spaces*. London: Routledge, 2017.

Croker, David R. "Functioning and Capability: The Foundation of Sen's and Nussbaum's Development Ethics." *Political Theory* 20 (1992): 584–612.

East Asia Christian Conference, World Council of Churches, and Pontifical Commission Justice and Peace (Rome). *Liberation, Justice, Development*. Madras: Diocesan Press, 1970.

Fountain, P., R. Bush, and R. M. Feener. *Religion and the Politics of Development*. New York: Palgrave Macmillan, 2015.

Goodin, Robert E. *Reflective Democracy*. Oxford: Oxford University Press, 2010.

Gremillion, Joseph. *The Gospel of Peace and Justice: Catholic Social Teaching since Pope John*. New York: Orbis, 1976.

Groome, Thomas H. *Sharing Faith: Sharing Our Story and Vision*, 2nd ed. San Francisco: Jossey-Bass, 1999.

Lim, Teck Peng. "The Rise of Civil Society and the Fashioning of Christian Agency: An Asian Perspective." *Asia Journal of Theology* 31 (2017): 41–57.

Nussbaum, Martha C., and Amerya Sen, eds. *The Quality of Life*. Oxford: Clarendon Press, 1993.

Presbyterian Church (USA). *Hope for a Global Future: Toward Just and Sustainable Human Development*. Louisville, KY: The Office of the General Assembly Presbyterian Church (USA), 1996.

Sen, Amartya. "Capability and Well-being." In *The Quality of Life*, edited by Martha C. Nussbaum and Amerya Sen, 30–53. Oxford: Clarendon Press, 1993.

———. *Development as Freedom*. Oxford: Oxford University Press, 1999.

———. "Rights and Agency." *Philosophy and Public Affairs* 11 (1982): 3–39.

———. "Well-being, Agency and Freedom." *The Journal of Philosophy* 82 (1985): 169–221.

NOTES

1. See Joseph Gremillion, *The Gospel of Peace and Justice: Catholic Social Teaching Since Pope John* (New York: Orbis Books, 1976), 143–200; East Asia Christian Conference, World Council of Churches, and Pontifical Commission Justice and Peace (Rome), *Liberation, Justice, Development* (Madras: Diocesan Press, 1970); Presbyterian Church (USA), *Hope for a Global Future: Toward Just and Sustainable Human Development* (Louisville, KY: The Office of the General Assembly Presbyterian Church [USA], 1996).
2. Robert E. Goodin, *Reflective Democracy* (Oxford: Oxford University Press, 2010).
3. For the series of Human Development Reports published by the United Nations Development Programme, please visit the website of UNDP (www.hdr.undp.org).
4. United Nations Development Programme, *Human Development Report 1993* (New York: Oxford University Press, 1993), 3; cited in Presbyterian Church, *Hope for a Global Future*, 87.
5. Amartya Sen, "Well-being, Agency and Freedom," *The Journal of Philosophy* 82 (1985): 169–221. For another work by Sen on the notion of agency, see "Rights and Agency," *Philosophy and Public Affairs* 11 (1982): 3–39.
6. Sen, "Well-being, Agency and Freedom," 186.
7. Ibid., 187.
8. Sen writes: "*Functionings* represent parts of the state of a person—in particular the various things that he or she manages to do or be in leading a life. The *capability* of a person reflects the alternative combinations of functionings the person can achieve, and from which he or she can choose one collection." (Amartya Sen, "Capability and Well-being," in *The Quality of Life*, eds., Martha C. Nussbaum, and Amerya Sen [Oxford: Clarendon Press, 1993], 31, original italics) It is noteworthy that "the alternative combinations of functionings" refers to the spectrum of all the things or states that a person can possibly do or can possibly be in.
9. Ibid., 30, n.2.
10. Ibid., 30.
11. Sen, "Well-being, Agency and Freedom," 203.
12. Ibid., 204.
13. Concerning the agential conception of the good, it is possible that my pal and I (going back to my previous hypothetical illustration) may have different objectives under the same situation. Local cultural does not necessarily provide a monolithic answer to the evaluative question. However, such differences do not negate the reality of socialization and language-game that always precedes our consciousness and actions.
14. Nussbaum and Sen, *The Quality of Life*, 4.
15. Sen, in criticizing how Asian value "has often been invoked in recent years to provide justification for authoritarian political arrangements in Asia," emphasizes that the idea of personal freedom is not totally absent from Asian cultures (Sen, *Development as Freedom*, [New York: Anchor Books, 1999], 231). He then concludes: "The valuing of freedom is not confined to one culture only, and the Western traditions are not the only ones that *prepare us for a freedom-based approach to social understanding*" (Ibid., 240, italics added). I agree that the diversity of Asian cultures defies any crude simplification, and that the pursuit of freedom is not unique to the West. However, it is one thing to say that the value of freedom is not alien to a culture; it is quite another to say (as Francis Fukuyama has claimed) that Western liberal democracy is the only and final form of sociopolitical achievement that the human race can ever attain.
16. One scholar calls this "the manipulations of corporate advertising" (David R. Croker, "Functioning and Capability: The Foundation of Sen's and Nussbaum's Development Ethics," *Political Theory* 20 [1992]: 612, n.34). I will argue that the manipulation of human desires for economic gain is more detrimental than the unjust and oppressive elements of traditions, as the former are subtle and often clothed in a matter-of-fact manner.
17. The reclamation of the cultural embeddedness of agency does not imply that local culture should be put in a privileged position or preserved in toto. Neither does it mean that

there can never be tension between a person and his or her cultural life-world. In fact, there is no lack of references in the Bible about the oppressive elements of human traditions.

18. *Hope for the Global Future* asserts: "While we cannot know the precise need of future generations, we can reasonably anticipate (because they are our biological heirs) the general nature of their needs for sufficient and safe resources. The cultural and ecological heritage we pass on will shape our successors and their prospects profoundly, for good or ill"(82).

19. Cf. Sen, *Development as Freedom*, 240–42. Sen seems to have taken a position that the "invisible hand" of the market is fair and able to decide which culture or tradition is fit to survive. Such a view, I will contend, fails to account for the problem of consumerism.

20. What stands between the reflective potential that the church has and its actualization is the obstacle created by the privatization or politicization of Christian faith. While the former often leads to a form of religious escapism, the latter tends to short-circuit the hope of God's reign by turning it into a form of Christian political triumphalism.

21. Thomas H. Groome, *Sharing Faith: Sharing Our Story and Vision*, 2nd ed. (San Francisco: Jossey-Bass, 1999).

22. Ibid., 149.

23. Ibid., 208.

24. Ibid., 211.

25. Ibid.

26. Groome makes it clear that during the first movement, participants should feel free not to speak (Ibid., 210). Nevertheless, it goes without saying that it remains the responsibility of the teacher to design an opening question that is aimed to elicit responses from *all* and not just a few vocal participants.

27. The concepts of statehood, citizenship, and democracy were first introduced to Asia during the period of European expansion and colonialism. While these notions evolved in the West over a period of more than two hundred years, countries in the majority world have to master both the form and spirit of these concepts within a rather short span of time, constantly under the watchful eyes of the West. As a society is going through the process of democratization, the learning curve that the government and people need to climb is both steep and slippery. In this process, democratization is never a merely procedural matter nor solely dependent on the leadership capability of the elites. I have argued that, with the rise of civil society and its culture of advocacy and contestation—itself an important progress of modernization and democratization, discernment and judgment are important aspects of agency for the church as much as for society (see Lim Teck Peng, "The Rise of Civil Society and the Fashioning of Christian Agency: An Asian Perspective," *Asia Journal of Theology* 31 [2017]: 41–57).

28. Robert E. Goodin, *Reflective Democracy* (Oxford: Oxford University Press, 2010).

29. Ibid., 58.

30. Ibid., 7, italics original. Later in the book, Goodin elaborates in more detail two models of unreflective democracy. The first is a populist-style democracy in which "people's preferences are aggregated directly to form a social decision, with no intervening filters or substantive mediation anywhere along the way." The second unreflective model of democracy is a delegate-style model of representative democracy in which "representatives act on strict instructions from their electorates, serving merely as conduits passing along messages from the electorate without reflecting on the contents" (Ibid., 62). Commenting on how these models lack the impetus for judgment and discernment, Goodin asserts that "all such 'unreflective' models would have us respecting any and all of people's preferences, utterly without discrimination" (Ibid., 62). Under such unreflective models of democracy, "why people want what they say they want, whether getting it will satisfy their purposes, whether there is some other way of satisfying them better or at less cost to others' similar satisfactions, are all issues which simply cannot arise. Preferences are preferences, each as worthy of respect as the next" (Ibid., 62).

31. Ibid., 7, italics original.

32. Ibid., 63.

33. Ibid.

34. Ibid., 72.

35. Matthew Clarke and Anna Halafoff, *Religion and Development in the Asia-Pacific: Sacred Places as Development Spaces* (London: Routledge, 2017), 18.

36. On the political dimension of the complex interaction between the development project and religious communities, see P. Fountain, R. Bush, and R. M. Feener, *Religion and the Politics of Development* (New York: Palgrave Macmillan, 2015).

Chapter 5

The Critical Role of the Church in the Development of Asia

Delfo C. Canceran, OP

Ellis and te Haar have written, "Development in the twenty-first century will be shaped largely by religion. It is therefore important for any analysis or recommendations to take account of this."[1] Robin Bush, Philip Foujtaij, and R. Michael Feener write, "The field of religion and development is becoming increasingly exciting, and the arguments that are advanced today have the ability to shape the future of this field."[2] And Severine Deneuline observes, "Development studies recognize the important role of churches in delivering social services to the poor, in the absence of state-sponsored basic services."[3]

Development is a serious concern both of the churches and governments, not just in Asia but in the whole world.[4] Historically, churches,[5] whether Protestant or Catholic, have engaged in social service among the impoverished and the marginalized sectors of society. They work not just in charity during disasters but in social justice advocacy in the transformation of society. In fact, their social service predates the development programs of the governments among the poor sector of society. Although it is not yet formally called "development" at that time but social service in the form of charity works among the poor, it is nonetheless development in the form of assistance or aid. In this sense, we cannot separate church and development. Development in different forms is essentially a missionary work of the churches. It is fundamentally embedded in their identity. "Development is what adherents of a religion do because of who they are and what they believe in."[6]

However, we have to admit that religion acts either as barrier or catalyst to development. There are religious practices that can facilitate or hinder works of development to the people.[7] In this sense, the place of religion in development is ambivalent, but, at this juncture, we have to underline its positive contribution to development. In Asia, Christian churches remain a minority religion. Nonetheless, they can easily mobilize their resources and networks in development work. Historically, in the West religion has been excluded from development work and separated from other spheres of life. Eventually, development practitioners and policy makers have realized that religion is inevitable in development work. People on the ground invoke their religious sense in all spheres of their life. Religion intersects with economic, political, and social spheres and this intersection affects development work in the field. Politics involves decision-making and development makes such decision. "Development is political and politics shapes development."[8]

PRELIMINARY REMARKS

It is difficult to proceed discussing a topic if the concepts used are unclear or undefined. Although we can explore these concepts in the meantime since the combination of these concepts belongs to a nascent stage in the literature relating religion and development, we still need to know what will be included and excluded—the scope—in the discussion for the sake of clear understanding. We cannot just go on in a sporadic way because we may mess up our thoughts and fall short in communication. Thus, I will define my terms as clearly as possible, even if only tentatively.

Sociologically, in a structuralist-functionalist theory, *role* refers to the behavior expected of an individual or group that occupies a given social position in a system. This behavior is socially recognized by the system, providing a means of identifying and functioning of an individual or group in a given society. When an individual or group is recruited in a system, it should fit within it. In that way, the system will operate in a smooth working relationship. If not, the system will just malfunction because that part is alien or a misfit.[9] In effect, role defines the essence of the actor or agency. Using the concept of *role*, the church must fit with the system of development model already in use by government agencies in Asia. The dominant development model follows the neoliberal philosophy that promotes individual rights in a free market. Neoliberalism relies on a pro-market and a pro-capital development. According to neoliberalism, "to achieve desirable development outcomes, the government's role must be diminished, with private capitalists and entrepreneurs freed from state control to apply their energies to economic growth strategies."[10] Thus the church is recognized as an agency of development but only accommodated or assimilated within the system of neoliberalism. If we follow Fukuyaman's logic announcing that capitalism is the best and the last system,[11] then the church must fit within the capitalist system.

Sociologically, the church is a religious institution.[12] Structurally, religion includes "a set of symbols, invoking feelings of reverence and awe, and is linked to rituals or ceremonies engaged in by a community of believers."[13] In this way, religion describes worship as practiced by the people belonging to a church. As such, religion seen from the perspective of the leadership prescribes the allowed symbols, the proper feelings and legitimate rituals of the believers. It invokes the organization and the legislation of the church in terms of its hierarchy and dogma. If we follow this definition, the church is an organized religion such as the Catholic Church or the Protestant churches. These churches rely on organization and legislation in carrying out their mission of development. They cannot act on their own without the permission of the authority that will provide the rules of engagement in development programs. In the past, the institutional churches have been actively involved in charity programs such as education and health and in social services such as food programs and vocational courses for the poor.

Our dominant concept of a development model usually follows the economic blueprint that measures development in terms of economic development such as investment in business and income for workers. It is assumed that investment can create jobs that will employ people in the workforce. It is believed that in this arrangement, the wealth will trickle down from the rich to the poor and, in the long run, the poor will get out of poverty. However, this trickledown economics has failed since the poverty of the majority remains unchecked. Instead, the rich become richer and the poor become poorer. Wealth remains in the hands of the elite and their businesses have even ballooned. This dominant economic development has failed to rescue the poor and reduce poverty. Inspired by Amartya Sen's economics of human capability principle,[14] the United Nations has shifted in its Human Development Report to the human development paradigm that transcends material well-being to comprehensive human flourishing. Human development is "based on the priority of human well-being, aimed at ensuring and enlarging human choices leading to greater equality of opportunities for all people in society and empowerment of people so they participate in—and benefit from—the development process."[15]

Asian Continent

Asia is the biggest continent and most populated region in the world. It is "host to an extraordinary diversity of politics, development experience and religious traditions."[16] Admittedly, it is so huge that it is impossible to include all countries that compose it and to discuss each one of them in terms of their different Christian churches and their development practices. Even the Association of Southeast Asian Nations (ASEAN) has difficulty in its integration because historically the ASEAN are more familiar with the West than with the Orient. ASEAN has not developed that keen awareness of and affinity with the neighboring countries because they have not been well represented in knowledge and, if ever they are represented, they are underrepresented or even ill-represented in scholarship. We look down on the capacity of our neighbors or our neighbors are invisible to our knowledge. We always look up to the West as the superior race and model at the expense of the Orient.[17]

As a global player, Asia exhibits a contradictory picture. On a positive note, Asia is rapidly becoming more productive and influential in the globe. On a negative note, Asia shows that economic gulf between the rich (China, Japan, Hong Kong, Taiwan, and South Korea) and the poor in South Asia and Southeast Asia (India, Pakistan, Bangladesh, Sri Lanka, Afghanistan, Indonesia, the Philippines, Burma, Cambodia, and Laos). Although Asia is considered as a region of wealth creation and a center of growth, these are distributed unevenly among its members. The economic gains are concentrated in China and India. Across Asia, many countries have to resort to cutting labor costs so that they can compete in the world market. Workers have to abandon the agricultural sector in the rural areas and migrate to the urban centers in hope of better employment. Unsatisfied with the domestic markets, these workers look for employment overseas and risk working abroad for higher income.[18] They remit their income for their families. Remittances have become an important source of foreign currency and a hedge fund for financial sectors. Behind the success story of the newly industrialized countries (NICs) in Asia, we also have other countries dubbed "sitting ducks" because they cannot catch up with the global competition and are unready for takeoff in the global market.[19] A majority of Asian countries have experienced loads of problems such as persistent underdevelopment, extreme poverty, crowded urbanization, corrupt government, insurgency, criminality, and overpopulation, among others.[20]

In Asia, there is a transition from low-income countries to middle-income countries in the region. This transition shifts the development focus from the traditionally rich countries, transferring resources to poor countries to new rich countries having more internal responsibilities to their poor citizens and neighboring poor countries. Thus development assistance in the form of helping their people and region is no longer the sole responsibility of the rich industrialized countries but also the NICs. Because Asia is the home of major religious traditions, rich countries from the developing world can tie up with different religions and tap these churches in working together in their development programs. However, there has been little explicit attention to the political leverage that religious actors can exert in development. Although the religious actors are more trusted by the people, development actors continue to rely on their own and underestimate these religious actors.[21] There should be a cooperative partnership between the secular actors and the religious actors in their development efforts. However, development programs "will need to be based on a proper understanding and acceptance of Asian traditions."[22]

NATURE OF THE CHURCH

Although we have the historical and theological divide between the City of God and the City of Man, nonetheless the City of God operates in the City of Man. Jesus Christ provided the model to his followers. Jesus preached and taught to ordinary people and healed many who were sick. He set out from place to place and reached out to many different people. His dedication to his work and compassion for the people characterized His mission in building the reign of God. The leader set the model for the followers to emulate. The Father sent his Son to a mission of redemption and salvation by bringing the good news to the poor, liberty to captives, sight to the blind, and freedom to the oppressed. His followers should continue this mission. His followers are in the world but not of the world. They need to reach out to the world but not be absorbed by the world. They were sent and scattered in different parts of the world to spread the good news of salvation and redemption. Until now, the believers have been establishing churches and have been engaging in charity works. In imitation of Jesus's mission, churches work in the fields of educational institutions and health care. In this way, they extend and continue the mission of Jesus of preaching, teaching, and healing. For example, for the Catholic Church, development is an earthly mission entrusted by Jesus Christ to the believers.[23]

The Christian churches remain a minority religion in Asia. Christianity continues to be the majority religion in Armenia, Cyprus, East Timor, Georgia, the Philippines, and Russia and the minority religion in China, Hong Kong, India, Indonesia, Iran, Iraq, Israel, Japan, Jordan, Kazakhstan, Kyrgyzstan, Lebanon, Malaysia, Pakistan, Palestine, Singapore, South Korea, Syria, Vietnam, and other Asian countries. Buddhism, Hinduism, and Islam remain the dominant religions in Asia.[24] "In many parts of Asia, their impact is perhaps best measured not so much by the number of actual converts made, but rather by the broader effects that their activities have had on society at large—ranging from the provision of new models of doctrinal adherence, devotionalism, and institutional membership to organizational innovations in education, health care, publications and social welfare programmes."[25] In works of charity, religions remain a vital source of welfare in many developing countries where churches provide basic social services to the poor.[26] In this situation, it is important "to acknowledge that religious leaders are political actors and, moreover, that many political actors around Asia are explicitly and publicly affiliated with religious traditions and organizations."[27]

CHURCH AND SECULARIZATION

Modern society has been characterized as a secular city; in fact, modernity and secularity are synonymously identified. The secular city is described as the triumph of the profane world taking over the sacred world. Secularism assumes that religion will eventually decline in the public sphere and its practice will be relegated to the private sphere. However, this prognosis has failed because, despite modernization, many societies remain religious and their religiosity stays vibrant. Thus "the reality of life in developing countries shows that religion has a public face that can neither be ignored nor contained within certain boundaries."[28] In reality, religion remains living and expanding among people in various places. Religion cannot be evacuated from society and development cannot undermine religion. It plays a significant role in politics since it wields power in society. It is a way of life through which people find meaning in their everyday existence. "Religion is a political force in developing countries; trying to confine it to a private sphere is likely to encounter oppositions, if not to lead to a rejection of development models which do not recognize the inherent political nature of religion."[29] Governments and churches realize that "both secular and [religious] entities often shared similar development concerns, especially commitment to poverty alleviations the crucial first stage in a wider and deeper process of human development."[30] In a way, "one can say that most development work done by religious organizations falls under the rubric of the secular, in the sense of this-worldly focus on individual and collective betterment."[31]

In various disciplines in the social sciences, the place of religion has been played down in their theories and discourses.[32] In their treatment of religion, scholars see religion as instrumental, institutional, or immaterial. In an instrumental role, religion is looked upon as an obstacle or catalysis of development. The place of the church as a development actor can hinder or facilitate development because of its teachings or beliefs. In an institutional role, the church is seen mainly as an obstacle to development because of the incompatibility between religion and development. Development anchors its theories on modern rationality, while religion anchors on transcendental reality. In an immaterial role, the church is inessential to development because, predictably, religion will eventually disappear in modernity.[33] This treatment is unfair since the mission of the churches in works of charity has predated the development assistance and aid organized by governments. Historically, religion has a legacy of charitable works. In this sense, development is inherent in the religious traditions of the churches. These "development activities arise out of attempts by religious communities to live a 'good life' in accordance with the fundamentals of the religion in the context in which adherents live."[34]

Throughout much of Asia, the state itself is decidedly not a purely secular entity; it is mixed up with religion. "A number of modern Asian nations have provisions establishing an 'official religion' within their state constitutions" and the movement of establishing "official religion for the nation appears to have been exercising increasing appeal."[35] Some Asian nations have an implicit official religion, not just because their religion is the dominant or majority religion but because the influence of their religion is ubiquitous and imposing. In these cases, the secular and the religious spheres have intertwined among many Asian nations. The entanglements between different religious organizations and the state structures are both extremely profound and persistent. Asian societies are deeply religious and political leaders are religiously affiliated. Thus "the neat distinction between the religious and the secular [is] largely fictitious and constitutes a modern myth—or a mythos of modernity."[36] Religion acts as a moral basis that unites society. "Thus, ignoring religion as the moral basis of society may lead to a situation in which the development process, characterized by goals generated outside the country's value system, alienates people and makes them reject the whole development process."[37]

CHURCH AND DEVELOPMENT

Following World War II, most Western governments and development agencies considered religions as part of the problem, not as a potential solution to development. "Religion was widely regarded as being concerned with 'mere' spirituality, perceived by most Western academics, governments and development practitioners as irrelevant or antipathetic to the achievement of development goals, primarily understood as being concerned with material improvements."[38] However, the current perception has changed. Secularism has failed and this failure gave rise to the resurgence of religion in the West. Some governments and agencies realize the futility of the marginalization or exclusion of religion in development. Religion infuses all aspects of life for its adherents. Development actors need to take on religious leaders and communities and team up with them in development work. "Development . . . agencies need to have a basic understanding of this religious context if their partnership with religious communities is to be successful."[39] In this way, religion becomes not just an instrument of these governments and agencies but a partner or companion in development. Development as an intervention requires networking of different state and nonstate actors, churches, and governments, formal and informal players that can effectively implement the programs.[40] "Development is the outcome of how different political actors interact with each other in the public sphere."[41] Churches as political actors aiming for change can contribute to the development effort. "As a result, the emphasis of development thinking has shifted to include various religious expressions that are now widely seen as potentially important components of achieving development gains."[42] This partnership has strengthened development cooperation among state and nonstate actors in development. "Overall there is now widespread acceptance that desired development outcomes can more likely be achieved if the energies and abilities of various nonstate actors—including faith-based organizations—can be tapped into."[43]

We need to examine the way we define religion. Accordingly, religion can be defined in two ways, namely, as a static belief and as a dynamic tradition. In either case, this definition has some important consequences for development.

> Seeing religion as a set of static beliefs in the individual conscience means that the role of development is to analyze the consequences of these beliefs for the functioning of the various social spheres. . . . In contrast, seeing religion as tradition means that the task for development is to understand how the religion's fundamental agreement and teachings are embodied in certain social practices, how certain social and historical processes have led to that particular embodiment and how the religion itself redefines this embodiment in the light of the new social context.[44]

Thus religion is not just a given fact that people just receive, but an ongoing construction and negotiation of people in their search for meaningful existence.[45] As a dynamic tradition, people invent their religion in response to emerging contexts as they confront new situations in society. Religion generates social capital and social trust by building networks between people and fostering trust among its members. It can mobilize people and rally for social reforms.[46]

LIBERATIONIST DEVELOPMENT

Development is usually confined to development assistance and aid to the developing countries from the developed world. This arrangement only fosters a relation of dependency of the developing to the developed countries. In this dependency, the developing countries are hooked up with the dictates and policies of the developed countries imposed on them such as the notorious structural adjustment programs.[47] Realizing the danger of dependency, some developing countries have opted for delinkage as the alternative toward independence. Moreover, churches have been affected by this turn of events and are s plit on this eventual move: either they continue with this dependency or break from it. In effect, we have to look at the churches not as homogenous but heterogeneous entities. This heterogeneity is manifested in their leaning as they politically engage with the people. The political engagements of churches and Christians are extremely varied. In a political spectrum, there are conservatives who continue the traditional way of charity such as assistance and aid to the poor. Then there are the liberals who operate within the system by joining political parties or civil societies in helping the poor. There are also progressives who endeavor to change the system by participating in social movements or advocacies against neoliberal policies and social injustices that perpetuate poverty and dependency.[48] Unsatisfied with development as usual, some church people have embarked into a radical option for the poor. Inspired by liberation theology, they work for the poor in slums and squatters among the urban poor in the cities. They have struggled against economic injustice.

This poverty is mostly felt in the case of Latin America where underdevelopment is realized as the product of dependency because of the unequal distribution of wealth in the world. This realization paves the way for the formation or emergence of the theology of liberation or liberation theology that directly confronts this poverty and injustice. Liberation theology gets its inspiration from the dual sources of the Bible and Marxism in a dialectical relationship. Liberation theologians try to bring the good news of the reign of God to the poor proclaimed by the historical Jesus with the use of Marxist analysis in interpreting and transforming the world.[49] Church people who have embraced liberation theology have struggled for justice and have suffered the consequences of their radical option. They are not just labeled as communists or atheists; they are silenced, ostracized, and persecuted by the official churches. They have disappeared, have been tortured and murdered by oppressive governments. Although liberation theology has waned, it remains relevant in developing countries and among the poor in many societies.

Thus some church people have transcended the neoliberal development model because they realize that poverty remains widespread among the people. This model neither eradicates nor even reduces poverty. In fact, poverty has worsened since the number of those in poverty has increased exponentially despite assistance and aid or the jobs and wages given to them. The widespread problem of poverty is not just the material lack of the developing world in comparison to the plenty of the developed world. It is not lack in the sense of unfortunate tragedy but a structure of injustice that robs the people of their labor. The structure of injustice in the economic system that favors the developed world at the expense of the developing world has kept the poor in everlasting and worsening poverty. The rich cannot afford to share their wealth and to redistribute their wealth. If this unjust global structure remains unchecked, poverty continues to aggravate. The global structure is underpinned by greedy capitalists who amass the wealth of production and deprive the masses of profit. There can be no poverty alleviation or reduction without engaging in social justice.[50]

POSTCOLONIAL PROPOSAL

The poor in Latin America have been fractured or metamorphosed into different faces and situations around the world. Aside from being simply materially impoverished, the poor take the forms of the excluded indigenous peoples, the subordinated women, the discriminated colored people, the victimized migrant workers, to name a few, in this pervasive "white supremacist capitalist patriarchy."[51] This white supremacist capitalist patriarchy intertwines the multiple forms of oppressions such as racism, classism, and sexism. This ideology must be criticized and disrupted by employing interdisciplinary methods and postcolonial studies in understanding the complex situations of the developing world. This interdisciplinary research and postcolonial discourse can equip development workers and church people in thoughtfully attending to the specific conditions of their context. It can really empower people in helping them craft their own history and transform their own situation.

Scholars have linked postcoloniality and development in their theories. Assistance and aid given by foreign donors can only "mask [their] institutional biases and economic and geopolitical interests, while silencing the subaltern (marginalized groups), on whose behalf [they] purportedly work."[52] Thus development workers must interrogate their intentions because it may be the case that instead of helping people, they merely perpetuate paternalism and dependency. Discussion and contestation are necessary in checking our hidden interests. Postcoloniality must in the end decolonize the people from dependency and paternalism. People need to stand and make decisions on their own. Moreover, instead of inwardly looking into the colonized condition, postcolonialism outwardly examines the colonizers by criticizing the representations and images that only imprison the colonized and perpetuate their dependency. Knowing those representations and images, the colonized return the gaze and break the mirror so that the colonized can come out and speak out of their own situation. The colonized must represent themselves and not be represented by the colonizers for their liberation from the bondage of bigotry and distortion.

Linked with postcolonialism is what is called *postmodernity*. Postmodernity heeds the appeal or call of the marginalized and excluded others in development. The ordinary people have been treated as mere recipients and beneficiaries of development assistance and aid. Postmodernity attends to the singularity or particularity of the people in contrast to the universality and uniformity of modernity in development. Postmodern scholars treat the ability of planners and experts of development in designing development for the people with suspicion. Instead, they involve the local people in their ability and knowledge in transforming their situation and carrying out their plan for development. The ordinary people are not helpless and powerless in development; they are equipped with power and, when they are organized, they can wield their power in development. In that case, they can intervene and negotiate in development for their own benefit.[53]

Informed by these theories of development in postcolonialism and postmodernity, churches can be open and critical to the new conditions and devise new responses to challenges. As church people, we work with people, not to dictate them or plan for them, but to engage with them and trust their knowledge in making changes in their own situation. When they are involved, they are empowered to make decisions and choices for their own good. We need to be proactive actors by continuously analyzing these conditions. We do so reflecting on our faith and by challenging our mission. We can no longer just rely on development as it was done in the past like charitable works, social services, or projects and programs made exclusively by church people. They only work temporarily and in a limited way. Ordinary people must learn to lead and use their resources for development. Together with the people, we need to shift to social justice and global solidarity and endeavor for a structural transformation of the economic system that will benefit the people and alleviate their poverty. We have to keep in mind that poverty is an injustice done to the people who should share the fruits of the earth and live an abundant life in the world.[54]

CONCLUSION

In our discussion, we have covered in a general view the role of the Christian religion in development in an Asian context. We have asserted that both the churches as nonstate actors and the governments as state actors can work together in development. Development agencies and practitioners can no longer ignore the churches and their development programs to the poor. They need to work together as partners in development. We have therefore linked the relationship between religion and development. In fact, religion predates the development efforts of the governments. People trust their religious leaders and communities more than the secular development agencies. Churches have engaged in different charity works in history and continue that engagement as an integral part of their mission and identity.

However, the discussion ended with a critique of the forms of development that are usually practiced by the developed countries in their use of the defective model of neoliberalism. This paradigm has failed the developing countries. In fact, it has just exacerbated poverty among the poor. We have discussed the alternative paradigm of liberation theology employed in Latin America in advocating social justice among the poor. This social justice aims to rectify the structural order of the global system and advocates for redistribution of wealth to the poor. If we really aim for genuine change, the elite need to sacrifice a little of their wealth in order to lift the poor out of debilitating poverty. If they are unwilling to share their wealth, poverty will remain in our midst. We have proposed a postcolonial development paradigm because it opens a space for liberating development on behalf of the many others in our society, not just the materially poor, but also indigenous people, women, colonized peoples, colored people, and migrant workers.

Development must be based on democracy as inclusive, participatory, and responsible governance. Western liberal democracy is not the exemplary model of governance since it is based on individual rights and freedom. This individuality is historically embodied in the bourgeois class who installed itself as the political and entrepreneurial leader. Moreover, liberal democracy relies on representative government that in theory should protect the rights, freedom, and dignity of the people but in practice only protects the life, liberty, and property of the elite class. Democracy is the rule of the people but, unfortunately, the people have been neglected by their supposed leaders. Democracy as the government of the people, by the people, and for the people is merely a rhetoric of the demagogues. This elite democracy that marginalizes and excludes the majority of the ordinary people must end to give way for a real democracy to come.[55] The democracy that we have is imperfect and inadequate for the needs and clamors of the ordinary people who are fed up with empty promises and who are only exploited during election by politicians. We need a genuine change that would lift people out of poverty and make them beneficiaries of the bounty of democracy. We need to democratize this democracy as we have it.

This democratization challenges the governments and churches alike. If there are tyrannical elements in some governments, churches may have tyrannical tendencies too. Churches have to examine their bureaucracies in the way they craft policies and in the making of decisions. Do they involve the ordinary people and respect the clamors of these people? It may appear hypocritical and preposterous if churches would clamor for democracy and democratization in our governments if they themselves resist or reject the summons for democracy and democratization in our offices and practices. We cannot also opt for the suggestion that the churches should democratize first and then criticize the undemocratic practices of the governments. Democratization works in a mutual and simultaneous way. We have to work for the direction of democratization while criticizing undemocratic practices present in our societies. The democratization that we envision is still to come and we have to prepare the way for that coming. There are prophets in our society who work within the churches and governments. Christians have to support and encourage them and not reject or persecute them as the authorities did to the biblical prophets and to Jesus himself. We have to learn from our history. Churches have to be witnesses and need to testify to the coming reign of God by becoming sacraments to that democracy to come.

BIBLIOGRAPHY

Asad, Talal. *Genealogies of Religion: Discipline and Reasons of Power in Christianity and Islam.* Baltimore, MD: John Hopkins University Press, 1993.

Bautista, Julius, and Francis Khek Gee Lim. "Introduction: Christianity and the State in Asia: Complicity and Conflict." *Christianity and the State in Asia: Complicity and Conflict,* Julius Bautista and Francis Khek Gee Lim, eds. London: Routledge, 2009.

Buonomo, Vincenzo. "Final Report: Ethics and Economics: The Challenge of Asian Development and the Contribution of the Catholic Communities." *Ethics and Economics: Religions Development and Liberation in Asia,* Roberto Papini and Vincenzo Buonomo, eds. Rome: Jacques Maritain International Institute, 1993.

Bush, Robin, Philip Fountain, and R. Michael Feener. "Introduction." In *Religion and the Politics of Development,* edited by Philip Fountain, Robin Bush and R. Michael Feener. New York: Palgrave Macmillan, 2015.

Calderisi, Robert. *Earthly Mission: The Catholic Church and World Development.* New Haven, CT: Yale University Press, 2013.

Cockcroft, James D., Andre Gunder Frank, and Dale L. Johnson, eds. *Dependence and Underdevelopment: Latin America's Political Economy.* New York: Anchor Books, 1972.

Deneuline, Severine with Masooda Bano. *Religion in Development: Rewriting the Secular Script.* London: Zed Books, 2009.

Derrida, Jacques. *Specters of Marx: The State of the Debt, the Work of Mourning and the New International.* London: Routledge, 1994.

Fukuyama, Francis. *The End of History and the Last Man.* New York: Free Press, 1992.

Giddens, Anthony. "Introduction." In Max Weber, *The Protestant Ethic and the Spirit of Capitalism.* London: George Allen and Unwin, 1976.

———. *Sociology,* 4th ed. Cambridge: Polity Press, 2001.

Gutierrez, Gustavo. *A Theology of Liberation: History, Politics and Salvation,* 15th ed. New York: Orbis, 1988.

Guzman, Rorasio Bella. "Establishing the Links between Wealth Creation, Poverty and Ecological Devastation: The Asian Experience." In *Poverty, Wealth and Ecology in Asia and the Pacific: Ecumenical Perspectives,* edited by Athena Peralta. Chiang Mai: Wanida, 2010.

Hasan, Rumy. *Religion and Development in the Global South.* Brinton, UK: Palgrave Macmillan, 2017.

Haynes, Jeffrey. *Religion and Development: Conflict or Cooperation?* Hampshire: Palgrave Macmillan, 2007.

hooks, bell. *Cultural Criticism and Transformation.* Northampton, MA: Media Education Foundation, 1997.

Kapoor, Ilan. *The Postcolonial Politics of Development.* London: Routledge, 2008.

Martin, Daniel D., and Janelle L. Wilson. "Role Theory." *Encyclopedia of Social Theory,* Vol. 2, edited by George Ritzer. Thousand Oaks, CA: Sage, 2005.

Mason, Colin. *A Short History of Asia,* 2nd ed. New York: Palgrave Macmillan, 2005.

McEwan, Cheryl. *Postcolonialism and Development.* New York: Routledge, 2009.

Moberg, David O. *Church as a Social Institution: The Sociology of American Religion,* 2nd ed. Grand Rapids, MI: Baker Book House, 1984.

Negri, Vera Zamagni. "Toward a One World Development Strategy: Outstanding Lessons of the Last 40 Years in Asia." In *Poverty and Development: The Call of the Catholic Church in Asia,* edited by Loreta N. Castro and Arij A. Roest Crollius, SJ. Rome: International Jacques Maritain Institute, 1995.

Parfitt, Trevor. *The End of Development? Modernity, Postmodernity and Development.* London: Pluto, 2002.

Pew Research Center. "The Global Religious Landscape." In *Religion,* December 18, 2012. Accessed February 14, 2018, from http://www.pewforum.org/2012/12/18/global-religious-landscape-exec/.

Pollard, Jan, Cheryl McEwan, and Alex Hughs, eds. *Postcolonial Economies.* London: Zed, 2011.

Rotra, Santosh Meh, and Mario Biggeri. *Asian Informal Workers: Global Risk, Local Protection*. London: Routledge, 2007.
Said, Edward. *Orientalism*. New York: Routledge & Kegan Paul, 1978.
Sen, Amartya. *Development as Freedom*. Oxford: Oxford University Press, 1999.
Tornquist, Olle. *Politics and Development: A Critical Introduction*. London: Sage, 2001.
United Nations Development Programmes (UNDP), *Human Development Report 1996*. Oxford: Oxford University Press.
Wong, Tai-Chee, and Jonathan Riggs, eds. *Asian Cities, Migrant Labor and Contested Spaces*. London and New York: Routledge, 2011.

NOTES

1. Quoted in Jeffrey Haynes, *Religion and Development: Conflict or Cooperation?* (Hampshire: Palgrave Macmillan, 2007), 53.
2. Robin Bush, Philip Fountain, and R. Michael Feener, "Introduction," in *Religion and the Politics of Development*, eds. Philip Fountain, Robin Bush and R. Michael Feener (New York: Palgrave Macmillan, 2015), 2.
3. Severine Deneuline with Masooda Bano, *Religion in Development: Rewriting the Secular Script* (London: Zed Books, 2009), 48.
4. For the complex relationship between the church and state (government) in Asia, see Julius Bautista and Francis Khek Gee Lim, "Introduction: Christianity and the State in Asia: Complicity and Conflict," in *Christianity and the State in Asia: Complicity and Conflict*, eds. Julius Bautista and Francis Khek Gee Lim (London: Routledge, 2009), 1–18.
5. In the literature, different terms are used to refer to the same thing such as *church*, *religion*, and *faith-based organization*. I use interchangeably or synonymously *church* and *religion* in my discussion.
6. Deneuline with Bano, *Religion in Development*, 4–5.
7. For the discussion on the relationship between religion and development in the global south, see Rumy Hasan, *Religion and Development in the Global South* (Brinton, UK: Palgrave Macmillan, 2017), 1–40.
8. Bush, Fountain, and Feener, "Introduction," 12.
9. Daniel D. Martin and Janelle L. Wilson, "Role Theory," in *Encyclopedia of Social Theory*, Volume II, ed. George Ritzer (Thousand Oaks, CA: Sage, 2005), 651–54.
10. Haynes, *Religion and Development: Conflict or Cooperation?*, 8.
11. See Francis Fukuyama, *The End of History and the Last Man* (New York: Free Press, 1992).
12. See David O. Moberg, *Church as a Social Institution: The Sociology of American Religion* (Grand Rapids, MI: Baker Book House, 1984).
13. Anthony Giddens, *Sociology, 4th Edition* (Cambridge: Polity Press, 2001), 531.
14. Amartya Sen, *Development as Freedom* (Oxford: Oxford University Press, 1999).
15. See United Nations Development Programmes (UNDP), *Human Development Report 1996* (Oxford: Oxford University Press, 1996), 5.
16. Bush, Fountain, Feener, "Introduction," 3.
17. See Edward Said, *Orientalism* (New York: Routledge and Kegan Paul, 1978).
18. Tai-Chee Wong and Jonathan Rigg, eds., *Asian Cities, Migrant Labor and Contested Spaces* (London and New York: Routledge, 2011); Santosh Meh Rotra and Mario Biggeri, *Asian Informal Workers: Global Risk, Local Protection* (London: Routledge, 2007).
19. Rorasio Bella Guzman, "Establishing the Links between Wealth Creation, Poverty and Ecological Devastation: The Asian Experience," in *Poverty, Wealth and Ecology in Asia and the Pacific: Ecumenical Perspectives*, ed. Athena Peralta (Chiang Mai: Wanida Press, 2010), 28–85.
20. Colin Mason, *A Short History of Asia*, 2nd ed. (New York: Palgrave Macmillan, 2005), 4.
21. Bush, Fountain, and Feener, "Introduction," 16–18.
22. Mason, *A Short History of Asia*, 306.

23. Robert Calderisi, *Earthly Mission: The Catholic Church and World Development* (New Haven, CT: Yale University Press, 2013), 69–94. See also Vera Zamagni Negri, "Toward a One World Development Strategy: Outstanding Lessons of the Last 40 Years in Asia," in *Poverty and Development: The Call of the Catholic Church in Asia*, eds. Loreta N. Castro and Arij A. Roest Crollius, SJ (Rome: International Jacques Maritain Institute, 1995), 141–66; Vincenzo Buonomo, "Final Report: Ethics and Economics: The Challenge of Asian Development and the Contribution of the Catholic Communities," in *Ethics and Economics: Religions Development and Liberation in Asia*, eds. Roberto Papini and Vincenzo Buonomo (Rome: Jacques Maritain International Institute, 1993), 245–57.

24. Pew Research Center, "The Global Religious Landscape," in *Religion*, December 18, 2012. Accessed February 14, 2018, from http://www.pewforum.org/2012/12/18/global-religious-landscape-exec/.

25. Bush, Fountain, and Feener, "Introduction," 20.

26. Deneuline with Bano, *Religion in Development*, 15.

27. Bush, Fountain, and Feener, "Introduction," 22.

28. Deneuline with Bano, *Religion in Development*, 6.

29. Deneuline with Bano, *Religion in Development*, 26.

30. Haynes, *Religion and Development*, 13.

31. Bush, Fountain, and Feener, "Introduction," 37.

32. The work of Max Weber titled *Protestant Ethic and the Spirit of Capitalism* is exceptional in linking Calvinist religion and capitalist ideology. But it is also controversial not just because of its causal linkage between Calvinism and capitalism but also lamping and reducing other religions into hindrance to development. See Anthony Giddens, "Introduction," in *The Protestant Ethic and the Spirit of Capitalism*, Max Weber (London: George Allen and Unwin, 1976).

33. Deneuline with Bano, *Religion in Development*, 38.

34. Deneuline with Bano, *Religion in Development*, 73–84.

35. Bush, Fountain, and Feener, "Introduction," 22.

36. Bush, Fountain, and Feener, "Introduction," 44.

37. Deneuline with Bano, *Religion in Development*, 38–39.

38. Haynes, *Religion and Development*, 1–2.

39. Deneuline with Bano, *Religion in Development*, 6.

40. Bush, Fountain, and Feener, "Introduction," 14.

41. Deneuline with Bano, *Religion in Development*, 46.

42. Haynes, *Religion and Development*, 1.

43. Haynes, *Religion and Development*, 3.

44. Deneuline with Bano, *Religion in Development*, 63.

45. See Talal Asad, *Genealogies of Religion: Discipline and Reasons of Power in Christianity and Islam* (Baltimore, MD: John Hopkins University Press, 1993).

46. Deneuline with Bano, *Religion in Development*, 47.

47. Olle Tornquist, *Politics and Development: A Critical Introduction* (London: Sage, 2001).

48. Deneuline with Bano, *Religion in Development*, 86.

49. See Gustavo Gutierrez, *A Theology of Liberation: History, Politics and Salvation*, 15th ed. (New York: Orbis Books, 1988).

50. See James D. Cockcroft, Andre Gunder Frank, and Dale L. Johnson, eds. *Dependence and Underdevelopment: Latin America's Political Economy* (New York: Anchor Books, 1972).

51. bell hooks, *Cultural Criticism and Transformation* (Northampton, MA: Media Education Foundation, 1997), 7.

52. Ilan Kapoor, *The Postcolonial Politics of Development* (London and New York: Routledge, 2008), xiii. See also Cheryl McEwan, *Postcolonialism and Development* (New York: Routledge, 2009).

53. Trevor Parfitt, *The End of Development? Modernity, Postmodernity and Development* (London: Pluto Press, 2002), 1–11.

54. Jane Pollard, Cheryl McEwan, and Alex Hughs, eds., *Postcolonial Economies* (London: Zed, 2011.

55. See Jacques Derrida, *Specters of Marx: The State of the Debt, the Work of Mourning and the New International* (London: Routledge, 1994).

Part Three

Ecclesiastical Perspectives

Chapter 6

Church and Development in Nigerian Context

Theological Foundation, Practical Appraisal, and Prophetic Call to Action

Ibrahim Bitrus

In this chapter, I explore the contributions of the Church in Nigeria to development. I start off by asking whether the participation of the Church in development process is a distraction. I argue that in spite of its huge capital demand and worldliness, development is not a distraction to the church from its from primary job of preaching the Word and serving the sacraments. Rather, it is a call for the Church to penetrate the social and political structures of the world with its prophetic Word and a faith that is active in love. I will then highlight the social, economic, and political issues plaguing the nation, which are actually opportunities for development in Nigeria that Nigerian churches have used to engage in sustainable development. I round off the chapter with discussing the profound contributions Nigerian churches have made to the development of the country in the fields of education, healthcare, political participation, and economic empowerment.

THE CHURCH'S PARTICIPATION IN DEVELOPMENT: CALL OR DISTRACTION?

To begin, the word *church* denotes the community of believers gathered up in the world by the Holy Spirit to celebrate the gift of new life in Christ with an eschatological horizon. As an embodiment of Jesus Christ, the Church is the true body of Christ in its faith, unity, holiness, and universality. The image of the Church as the body of Christ bears an unambiguous testimony to the interconnectedness and interdependence of each member of the Church not only on one another, but ultimately on Jesus Christ for a rich, fulfilling, and healthy Christian life on earth. Thus Christ is the one and only true head of the Church, which is a spiritual community constituted by his own believers. The Church is not just a human institution with its human leaders, structures, and plans. It is a divine institution established by God in the world. Word and Sacrament are God-given, true distinguishing marks of the church. Where the Word is faithfully preached and sacrament rightly served in the world, there is the Church. Hence, God's mission for the Church is to preach the good news, administer the sacrament, and make disciples in the world through word and deed.

As for the word *development*, what it means, in many ways, is ambiguous and elusive. The word seems to defy all manner of definition because it means a monumental improvement, which impacts every aspect of human life. Thus development is a deliberate multidimensional process of improving and changing the social, political, economic, and environmental quality of human lives without doing any substantial damage to the environment. As Jan Marie Fritz sees it, development is "a planned and comprehensive economic, social, cultural and political process, in a defined geographic area, that is rights-based and ecologically oriented and aims to continually improve the well-being of the entire population and all of its individuals."[1] For Idris Ahmed Jamo, development is a "continuous process of positive change in the quality of life of an individual or a society, [in terms of] reduction of poverty, unemployment and inequality."[2] In other words, development is a multifaceted process that alleviates poverty and accords individuals and communities the opportunity to actualize their God-given potentials through unproblematic access to education, employment, good health care, participatory democracy, and information. But development comprises more than just dynamic improvements in the living conditions and quality of life of the people. It also involves change in peoples' culture, values, attitudes, and mindsets that leads to willingness to embrace new means and ways of producing, distributing, and consuming goods and services. For example, invention of a new technique of farming is counterproductive unless it is accompanied by a corresponding change in the traditional attitude of the people, which would block them from accepting and using it on their farms.

True development must be a sustainable process; otherwise such a development will prove short-lived and short-sighted. Development is sustainable when it is capable of satisfying on the long-term the contemporary human needs without jeopardizing the needs of the upcoming generations. As the United Nations defines it, "development that meets the needs of the present without compromising the ability of future generations to meet their own needs."[3] Because the focus of sustainable development is on meeting needs, proponents of sustainable development repudiate any undue exploitation of material and natural resources to satisfy human wants. Human development, which is placed at the heart of sustainable development, seeks to empower the poor who, in their quest of survival, often h ave no other viable option of livelihood but to destroy the natural environment. According to the United Nations Development Programme,

> Human development is a process of enlarging people's choices. The most critical ones are to lead a long and healthy life, to be educated and to enjoy a decent standard of living. Additional choices include political freedom, guaranteed human rights and self-respect.[4]

However, expanding people's choices does not necessarily enhance their power to afford these choices, especially when that expansion is guided by a sole desire to make profit at the expense of the people as a human-centered enterprise. Sustainable development addresses critical issues essential to people bordering among other things on food, security, education, medical care, sanitation, clean water, justice, and shelter for everybody. Development is also sustainable when people are empowered to be self-reliant, to possess the capacity to develop themselves and their communities without foreign or outside support. Empowering individuals and communities to be self-reliant is key to any sustainable development. Unless it bears the trademark "homegrown," it is not an authentic development. It is unviable, and hence it is doomed to crumble! This is a crucial point that must not be pushed to the background for any development to be sustainable. Homegrown development creativity gives back into the hands of the people the power to take control of their destiny and to harness their resources for viable development and self-determination. Sustainable human development is not unrelated to the development of the Church. The two are intertwined. A church that initiates and engages in the sustainable human development of its members and their communities engages and sustains its own development. It is self-destructive for any church that declines to engage in sustainable human development.

Since development is a capital-extensive and this-worldly process, one is compelled to ask whether the Church's engagement in development is a call or distraction. As a charity and spiritual institution, Church and development appear to be in conflict. The two are often perceived as incompatible. This is because one deals with spiritual matters, while the other concerns itself with temporal issues. As such, many scholars strongly feel that the Church has no business in development and vice versa. They contend that government and society rather than the Church should carry out development work. Consequently, the involvement of the Church in any development process is seen as a distraction, a deviation from its primary call. C. A. Jansen, F. J. Pretorius, and E. J. van Niekerk have noted,

> The essence of the Church as a societal institution is tied to its role of preaching the Word of God, serving the sacraments and disciplining members who deviate from Biblical prescriptions. . . . The church thus has a specific function in the world, and should not be distracted from its calling by taking over the roles of other societal structures or aligning itself to a state that promotes secularism.[5]

In other words, the Church should not abandon its task of ministering the word and breaking the bread to serve the tables, as the saying goes. Mark Mattes argues that the Church cannot effectively change the world through either emphasizing personal piety or engaging in social and political action. Mattes sees focusing on the ministry of the Word as the most effective way by which the Church can make sufficient impact in the world. He suggests, "The Church can make the most difference in the world when it tends to the Word. It tends to the Word in catechesis and proclamation. The church is most authentic when it makes truth claims that deal with ultimate matters in distinction from penultimate matters."[6] Insisting that the Church must concentrate on its spiritual role in the world, the theology of the "two kingdoms" has been used to challenge the Church's participation in development. According to the two kingdoms framework, the state and the church are separate institutions, which God uses to rule the world. God works in the state to maintain law and order in society so that humans can enjoy peace, freedom, and prosperity. As a spiritual community, God uses the Church to offer grace, forgiveness, and new life in Christ. Given their distinct roles, it is argued that the Church not only derails from its primary call but most importantly, encroaches on the spheres of the state when it sees itself as an instrument of social and political transformation.

Mattes argues that the role of the Church is not to fix the world, but to make disciples who should fix the world, or at best the Church should leave that job of fixing the world in the hands of the secular government. He thinks that the Church's engagement in public moral deliberation on issues of health care, tertiary education, and businesses regrettably secularizes the Church more than spiritualizing the world. The Church has no special prerogative powers in moral discourse over other groups in civil society. Every human being has the natural capacity for moral deliberation and action. Hence, the Church's involvement in moral deliberation is countereffective; it does not often change the world. Instead, it undermines the authority of Scripture and pressures the church into embracing a partisan progressive social agenda of the world. He believes that only secular powers rather than the Church can most effectively fix the world through worldly measures.[7] Thus he advises that the church should invest its resources in doing that job, which no other agency can do in the world, namely the task of preaching the Word rather than taking measures to transform the world, which rightly belong to the secular government. He writes,

> If we truly care about the world, we are advised to let the church be the church—let it do what no agency in this world can do—bear witness to God's wonder and mystery, not least of which is the mystery of Christ's death and resurrection. There we need to trust that the Word of God can and will change the world as God sees fit.[8]

Although Mattes contends that his advice by no means reduces the Christian faith to a private sacred domain of life, his advice is but a step removed from it. In many ways, the advice amounts to retreatism, which means that the church should give up on the world. Put differently, the church should leave the world alone to fix itself without the irresponsible interference of the church! His proposal runs the risk of dichotomizing our life as Christians into sacred and secular spheres of human existence, which many Nigerian Christians have misused to lead a double standard life in the world. That is, it has given them the justification to live as "believers" in church while behaving as "unbelievers" in government. But there is no part of our life, whether sacred or secular, for which Jesus did not died to save. The victory of Christ's death and resurrection has impacted every aspect of human and nonhuman life. Thus the church cannot preach the mystery of Christ's death and resurrection only in a private sacred domain of life without engaging the world God so loved and saved. God calls the church to neither leave the world alone nor to live in isolation from it but to engage the world with the transforming power of the mystery of Christ's death and resurrection. As Ferdinand Nwaigbo argues,

> The mission of the Church is to penetrate the world, above all the most abandoned sectors of human life [with the Gospel]. This penetration requires a direct confrontation of the Church with the socioeconomic, and political problems of the world. The Church penetrates in the world, especially in [its] involvement in education, health-related ministry and combating with social problems. The Church's focus on integrated human development makes [its] mission in the world distinctive.[9]

The church that engages the socioeconomic and political structures of the world is dead to sin but alive in Christ. It is not to spiritualize the world but to make it a "better place" through the enabling power of God. A better world is one where all people, regardless of who they are, have fair and equal access to God's ongoing and comprehensive creative provision of daily bread in the world. Such a world includes good government.[10]

Moreover, the advice does not take into account the theory of divine-human cooperation as propounded by Martin Luther in his *Bondage of the*

Will. As Luther writes, "[God] does not work in us without us, because he has created and preserved us that he might work in us and we might cooperate with him, whether outside his Kingdom through his general omnipotence or inside his Kingdom by the special virtue of his Spirit."[11] Though God can use the Word to change the world, he cannot do it apart from us. God desires always to enlist our collaboration in impacting the world because his work is our hand, a mask behind which God hides to fix the world. While the ultimate transformation of the world awaits eschatological realization, this by no means provides, in the face of the world's resistance to change, a theological justification to leave fixing the world entirely to secular authority, or to God for that matter. As a matter of fact, it ought to generate the spiritual conviction based on which the church does not give up on the world but engages it. Trusting that God can fix the world as God deems fit is no excuse for retreating from the world; rather it is an empowerment for the church to engage it with the Word and a faith that is active in love.

But the involvement of the church in changing the world does not abrogate but rather affirms the principle of the two kingdoms, which are the masks behind which God hides to rule the world separately through the institutions of state and church. Although the purposes of both is to change the world as God sees fit, they accomplish this through distinct modus operandi. The one uses the law to effect change in the world, while the other uses the Word and a faith that is active in love for neighbor and world. They are never rival competitors but God's co-collaborators working together to promote and sustain the well-being of the world. As a nonpartisan institution, the church is not to embrace progressive social ideology nor is it to maintain conservative values in as much as they undermine the essence of the Gospel in its call to serve the world. The church must rather affirm and promote whatever values and ideas on both sides of the political spectrum that, in the opinion of the church, align themselves with the Gospel. The church is not the puppet of any political party. Neither should it see itself as such. The church is God's own public instrument of the mystery of Christ's death and resurrection in the world. What the Word of God teaches rather than any political ideology, whether left or right, must be the canon for the church's participation in the developmental task of transforming the world. The church compromises its public prophetic authority when it overtly or covertly identifies itself with a certain political ideology. Political neutrality must always be the absolute guiding policy for the church while engaging social issues affecting the world. The church's participation in moral deliberations must not be misconstrued as the church is laying a claim to higher moral authority (God) than any other people in the society, even though it does, so to speak. As a community of those who are sinners and saints simultaneously, the church simply collaborates with other communities of sinners in finding new ways to make the world that they share in common a better place. In other words, the church engages in public moral discourse not as a superior moral police but as a beggar collaborating with other co-beggars in the world to endorse only those moral resolutions that are true and consistent with its faith convictions. It is important to note that the church remains true sinner and saint simultaneously not by avoiding the world but by engaging the world with its all sinfulness in the fashion of the incarnate Word of God.

Therefore, the church's participation in developmental work consists of its faith active in love, thereby transforming people and unjust structures in our society and our world such that the Gospel, God's kingdom of forgiveness, justice, and mercy is able to tangibly impact the lives of all people and all of creation here and now. It is not simply what the church does, it is what God does in and through the church. As an act of faith rooted in God, development is the church's participation in the ongoing creative work of God in the world. This is a work that God started when God brought the world into being from the beginning. God is already ahead of us engaging in an enterprise of sustainable development. In many ways, creation itself, which is an overflow of God's abundant love, is God's act of developing humanity and the world. But God's creative work of development was not merely a one-time historical event. Nor was it perfect or complete. It is an unceasing divine act that takes place at this very moment as it did in the past. Although God continues to create everything every day, God does not do it alone without our involvement. God has always made a space in God's own ongoing creative development plan for human collaboration. As I have argued elsewhere,

> When the Triune God declares after creation that everything was "very good," this does not mean that what was created is "perfect" and hence does not require any further improvement. On the contrary, the world was not created "perfect," but "very good" so as to give ample room to humanity to constantly deploy its power and creativity to make it better than it was first created.[12]

Undoubtedly, the traditional mandate according to which God commanded humanity to "Be fruitful and multiply, and fill the earth and subdue it; and have dominion over" the earth (Gen 1:28) was accompanied with a greater responsibility to "till it and keep it" (Gen 2:15). As responsible steward, humanity is mandated not to leave the earth as God created it nor is it to destroy the earth through unwarranted exploitation. Its task is rather to constantly care, preserve, and develop the earth to its ultimate heights. Thus the church's industrious and groundbreaking improvement of the world and its inhabitants promotes and affirms the goodness of creation. Although God gave this traditional developmental mandate initially to all of humankind as part of the orders of creation, the church is exempted from the mandate. Through its developmental services, the church bears powerful witness to

God's love in Christ, thus fulfilling God's creative developmental mission in the world.

The church's participation in development comes in the form of grace rather than law. God's grace by which humanity and our world are saved is a free gift; hence the church's role in development work must be benevolent and unconditional. Whether God converts the recipients through it or not, it is a worthwhile work for the church to do because undoubtedly it is one of the most effective ways in which the church can bear an eloquent public witness to God's indescribable gift of love to the world. The overarching ministry of Jesus's proclamation of the Word was indistinguishable from his compassionate ministry of healing the sick, feeding the hungry, teaching the "unlettered," and liberating the oppressed. These formed the tangible embodiment of Christ's message of God's love to a broken and sick world. Responding to John's inquiry of whether or not he was the expected messiah, Jesus said, "Go and report to John what you hear and see: the blind receive sight and the lame walk, the lepers are cleansed and the deaf hear, the dead are raised up, and the poor have the gospel brought to them" (Lk 7:22 NRSV). Therefore, preaching the gospel without the concrete gift of love that liberates people from the bondage of disease, ignorance, poverty, and oppression is a mere abstract exercise. It is simply an insensitive gospel that lacks the transformative power of the Holy Spirit. In fact, the Church's preaching of the mystery of Christ's death and resurrection in the world is no good news at all to those who are ill in body, spirit, or mind when their suffering is ignored by the Church or when it simply leaves them at the mercy of the worldly government. The Church cannot ignore their needs and that of the world without endangering the very essence of the Gospel itself. In fact, the Church can never ever be guiltless.

DEVELOPMENT OPPORTUNITIES IN NIGERIA

The opportunities for the church to participate in sustainable development enterprises have always abounded in Nigeria. God has blessed Nigeria with abundant material and human resources, which the church has always harnessed for sustainable development. The country has a vast arable land with different types of vegetation, fertile soil, and climatic conditions suitable for a variety of agricultural purposes ranging from grain and livestock to tree and root-crop farming. God has also endowed the country with enormous reserves of solid minerals. These include, among others, columbite, iron ore, gypsum, lignite, coal, topaz, tin barite, talc, and bitumen. Nigeria is also the most densely populated black nation on earth. It has about 180 million people with diverse ethnic, cultural, and religious backgrounds. As the fastest growing church in Africa, Nigeria has an estimated eighty million Christians.

These Christians belong to either Catholic, Protestant, or African-initiated churches (AIC).

But in spite of its enormous rich natural resources and impressive economic growth, Nigeria is still a developing country that has one of the largest numbers of poor and unemployed people in Africa. According to the World Bank Data Team, the number of Nigerians living in extreme poverty has risen from 51 million in 1990 to 80 million in 2013.[13] The vast majority of the people live on less than $2 per day. The National Bureau of Statistics recently reported that about 112 million Nigerians, who represent 67.1 percent of the country's total population, live below the poverty line.[14] This means that poverty is a stark, ubiquitous reality in Nigeria. Such a painful reality is characterized by poor and inefficient basic infrastructures such as electricity supply, running water, healthcare delivery, good roads, and decent and affordable housing. As Chimobi Ucha rightly points out, "In Nigeria, widespread and severe poverty is a reality. It is a reality that depicts a lack of food, clothes, education and other basic amenities."[15] The adverse effects of poverty on the life and health of the people are glaringly disturbing. These include insecurity, poor standards of living, and bad health evidenced by the untimely death of both children and adults from preventable diseases.

Poverty, which is a multihydra monster in Nigeria, has continued to persist because of personal, but largely systemic problems. As Ucha argues, "unemployment, corruption, the nondiversification of Nigeria's economy, inequality, laziness, and a poor education system are some of the key determinants of poverty."[16] These systemic problems are intractable; they seem to defy virtually every solution. This is so largely because those invested with the state power to curb these structural problems are themselves the perpetrators that cause them to exist in the first place. These people have done much to enrich themselves through their actions or inactions instead of eradicating poverty. As Alex Addae-Korankye rightly argues,

> In Africa, programmes designed to fight poverty are not fully implemented because the funds end up in the hands of corrupt individuals, who pocket the majority. Again due to poor governance, those in authority have failed to apprehend the corrupt. This creates an imbalance in society and leads to more poverty because you end up with a few influential and powerful individuals oppressing the poor.[17]

The prevalence of the systemic problems has not only exacerbated the menace of poverty, but has also created and aggravated environmental degradation in Nigeria. God has blessed Nigeria with a rich and diverse group of ecosystems. The country is famous for its abundant agricultural land, its plant and animal life, and its diversity of species. Nevertheless, because of its needs as an agrarian and oil producing country, the human and industrial use of the land for growing crops and drilling oil is destroying its natural habitats and ecosystems. There is a close correlation between poverty and this environmental degradation. The poor who rely exclusively on the exploitation of natural resources for their livelihood have become agents of environmental destruction. Anijah-Obi argues, "Those who are poor and hungry will often destroy their immediate environments in order to survive. They are responsible for tilling tired soils and cutting down forests. They live in slums and throw waste into gutters and streams, because they lack the basic necessities of life."[18] The rate at which the poor destroy the environment through unwarranted cutting of trees for firewood, bush burning, indiscriminate hunting, and overgrazing has reaching an alarming proportion. Such unfettered human activities are the prime causes of the loss of biodiversity. For example, Philip Mfon Jr. claims that Nigeria has one of the world's highest rates of deforestation. He contends that the country has lost more than 50 percent of its primary forest. An even larger proportion of its fauna and flora species is either threatened, endangered, or at the verge of extinction.[19]

The ecological degradation has been intensified by the operations of multinational oil corporations in the Niger Delta region of Nigeria. The Niger Delta Ecosystem is being destroyed by acid rain caused by gas flaring and oil spills. Poor waste management and disposal by the oil companies has devastating ecological consequences for the indigenous peoples who reside in the areas that surround oil extraction sites. W. Corbett Dabbs has reported that Nigeria's export of twelve million barrels of oil a day comes from 12 percent of the country's land, yet indigenous minority communities where the oil is extracted receive no substantial economic benefits.[20] He claims that the oil production has not only socioeconomically underdeveloped and pauperized people amid the immense oil wealth but also has instigated and intensified bitter and bloody conflicts between emerging interest groups within and between communities. The environmental hazards of oil production include destruction of wildlife, loss of fertile soil, pollution of air and drinking water, degradation of farmland, and damage to aquatic ecosystems. This ecological degradation is not only a clear-cut violation of the fundamental ecological and human rights of the people but also a disruption of the balance between living and nonliving components of the environment, which the Triune God, the creator of the earth, has designed to exist and function in perfect harmony.

However, I contend that it is a misrepresentation to perceive these issues as problems. Rather they are opportunities for sustainable investment. The church has been taking advantage of these opportunities to jump-start development work and contribute its share to sustainable development in Nigeria.

CONTRIBUTIONS OF THE CHURCH IN NIGERIA TO DEVELOPMENT

The church has always played a critical role in the socioeconomic, political, and human development of Nigerian society since its inception in Nigeria. This includes changing lives and service delivery in the areas of education and health care. Christian missionaries pioneered the provision of Western education and medical care in Nigeria. They are precursors to the present church educators and healthcare providers. They established schools and healthcare centers alongside mission stations to proselytize the people, but also to give them all-inclusive spiritual and physical care. The missionaries preached the Gospel, taught literacy, cared for the sick, empowered the poor and liberated the oppressed. This holistic service, which cares for the whole person, brought about social and political transformation. Omotoye, Rotimi Williams, and Elisabeth DeCampos capture it succinctly: "Christian missions led the founding of the first schools that provided Western education to Nigerians. . . . The church contributed indirectly in producing elites who challenged white domination in both the Christian church and the political system and led the nationalist struggle for independence."[21]

Like their parent missionaries, almost all of the mainline Nigerian churches, including the AICs have continued with the church's legacy of human development. First and foremost, they have contributed enormously to the educational development of their immediate communities and Nigerian society as a whole. Virtually every denomination has established kindergarten, primary, secondary, and tertiary educational institutions. Prominent among them are Junior Lutheran secondary school, Loyola Jesuit College, Karl Kumm University, Bingham University, and Covenant University. These educational institutions have better professors and teaching and learning materials and facilities than public educational institutions of higher learning. Their learning environment is safer, more conducive and stable, and devoid of most of the problems that largely characterize public educational institutions such as secret cults, brain-drain syndrome, sexual harassment, deteriorated infrastructures, and incessant strikes. These Christian liberal arts institutions of higher learning have integrated the Christian faith and liberal arts education into a holistic curriculum to train well-rounded graduates who go into society with sound biblical values and a viewpoint of knowledge, life, and destiny. Consequently, they have produced capable and suitable human resources that serve the country in different capacities.

Similarly, Nigerian churches have played a substantial role in providing healthcare services to individuals, families, and communities through their primary, secondary, and tertiary health centers. Like their educational institutions, these church health centers have improved healthcare facilities, competent and compassionate health personnel, and essential equipment and drugs with which to provide quality healthcare services. As Christian, faith-based health centers, they are usually founded on the Christian conviction that healing and deliverance from diseases and mental illnesses ultimately come from God. The Christian spiritual maxim, which guides many of these Christian healthcare providers, is that "we treat, but God heals." In Nigeria, health problems are believed to have not only physical causes, but also spiritual roots such as evil spirits, witches, and sorcerers. As a result, spiritual care in the form of prayer constitutes an essential component of the diagnosis and treatment of the patients in both church and public healthcare centers. As Abiodun J. Oluwabamide and John O. Umo claim,

> In African societies, a number of ill-health problems have spiritual origins. In a situation whereby necessary medical tests were carried out yet no disease was discovered, but the patient concerned was still terribly sick, there would be the need, to adopt the spiritual/prayer (religious) approach. . . . Nurses often arrange for priests (male and female) to come into the hospital wards and pray for patients.[22]

Because of the superior quality of holistic healthcare services Christian healthcare centers provide to the public, they are often more prized and trusted by the members of the general public than government health centers. The Lutheran Church of Christ in Nigeria (LCCN) healthcare system, which is community-based, provides health education and empowers communities to assume responsibility for their healthcare facilities. The community-based healthcare system has brought basic healthcare to the community level through community healthcare workers, by empowering the people to own their health, and by improvising basic healthcare practices such as sleeping under bed nets, drinking clean water, exclusive breast feeding, and basic nutrition, as well as local treatment of diarrhea, pneumonia, and malaria.[23]

Corollary to the Nigerian churches' involvement in the provisions of education and healthcare services is that the educational and healthcare institutions owned by them have created job opportunities for the teeming unemployed youth in the country. These churches have employed young men and women to work for their educational and healthcare institutions as professors, teaching and nonteaching staff, doctors, nurses, and community health workers. The employment has empowered them and their families financially, but has also reduced unemployment problems in Nigeria. The taxes paid by their employees have contributed to public revenue needed by the government for the provision of security and social services to the general public.

Negatively, the churches in Nigeria have come to be a huge political platform w here many political candidates regardless of their religion and party affiliation declare their intention to run for political office. Many politicians have taken advantage of the church's platform as a campaign trail where they not only mobilize political support for their election, but also sell their manifesto to the church. They have usually done this under the pretense of seeking prayer during worship service and other church gatherings. In many ways, the act of declaring their intention to run for elective public positions in the church, including on campgrounds, is a direct way of seeking the church's endorsement. Osamolu Titilayo Fehintolu and Atuluku John write about presidential candidates who visited the campgrounds of the Redeemed Christian Church of God during the 2011 presidential campaign for prayers.

> In preparation for the 2011 General elections, Muhammad Buhari, a Muslim also visited Adeboye at the camp. He was accompanied by his Vice-Presidential candidate, Pastor Tunde Bakare with the aim of soliciting for his cooperation and prayers. In fact, President Jonathan Goodluck kept a vigil at the Camp in 2010, so as to seek the blessing and prayer of Pastor Adeboye. The camp has become a regular prayer venue for seeking political victory for Nigerian politicians.[24]

Political aspirants view the church offering prayers for their victory as a sign of divine approval; not only the church but also God has endorsed their political ambition. This is based on their belief that only God alone can give political power to whoever he wills, albeit through the people.

In response to this political manipulation, Nigerian churches provide political education to their members. They educate them about their political rights to vote and to be voted for and encourage them to exercise these political rights and participate in the political process of government. Some of them even have trained electoral observers to monitor elections to ensure that elections are conducted freely and fairly in accordance with the electoral law.

Furthermore, the church has played an enviable role in the economic development of Nigeria. Many Nigerian churches have established microfinance banks, which disburse short- and long-term loans for small- and medium-scale businesses. Eric Emeka Anozie writes, "In the area of banking, the church is contributing immensely towards economic development. Many churches today establish a Community Bank . . . to encourage saving of funds which would be invested in business ventures, to provide the needed capital for development, to promote trading activities, and to provide short and long term loans to individuals and firms."[25] These banks have helped many people to set up and run successful businesses that have empowered them and their communities. They have also encouraged many Nigerians to save and invest their money in productive sectors of the economy such as poultry, arable farming, husbandry, and fishing.

Many of the churches have helped to alleviate poverty in Nigeria whether singlehandedly or in collaboration with other faith-based nongovernmental organizations. The LCCN Bonotem diocese has collaborated with the Youth and Women Development Association for Social Transformation to provide skill training in tailoring, driving, wood work, plumbing, knitting, bakery and decoration, hair dressing, computer operation and repairs, automobile mechanics, tricycle and motorcycle mechanics, laundry and dry cleaning, electrical work, peanut oil processing, and other skills. The training is provided on the job. The apprentices work with experienced master craftsmen to be trained on the job for a period of one to two years. The aim of the program is to combat poverty by empowering the beneficiaries to be self-reliant and self-supportive. The Evangelical Churches of West Africa (ECWA) has also helped to create jobs and has improved the lives of many people through its poultry and animal feed services. According to Joseph Antyo, "ECWA set up many rural farms that are known nationwide for the production of eggs, chickens, and animal feed. These farming centres are generally pilot projects and model farms that use improved seeds and also create avenues for people to learn improved farming methods."[26]

As laudable as the contributions of the church in Nigeria to human development are, its public prophetic engagement with social and political systems of injustice leaves much to be desired. Therefore, the church needs to be more proactive in challenging structural evils of patriarchy, the Big Man syndrome and nepotism, which inhibit monumental human development in Nigeria.[27] The preaching of the Word accompanied by the church's prophetic public action will accomplish it. Accordingly, the church should engage in a public prophetic subversive action against these systemic evils by demanding strict accountability, transparency, justice, rule of law in government, and, if necessary, should embark on public prophetic nonviolent action in collaboration with other groups in civil society.[28] As a dangerous prophetic enterprise, the church should enter into the public space with its Word and action as wise as serpents and as innocent as doves without compromising its primary task.

Second, poor environmental sanitation and practices is a public health crisis in Nigeria. In many ways, living with toxic human and animal waste has become part of the normal way of life for many people in both rural and urban areas in the country. As such, Nigerian churches need to teach the biblical view of environmental sustainability, expose dangers of a filthy environment, and inspire their members to cultivate environmentally friendly behavior. Most importantly, they should deliberately engage in a regular environmental sanitation exercise to clean, gather, and dispose public waste in their immediate communities, although without forgetting to mount pressure on public health officials to religiously enforce the legislations on environmental sanitation and protection. This is the most cost-effective way for the churches to contribute to a clean, safe, and healthy environment and the overall well-being for the society. Churches may set aside a day at least each month for this exercise.

Although Nigerian churches provide high-quality education and healthcare services to the public, these services are ridiculously costly. They are beyond the reach of the average of Nigerian. Many of their members who contribute generously toward funding these institutions cannot afford these services themselves. These services are largely luxuries reserved for privileged people who have sufficient financial resources to afford them. Hence there is an urgent need for church proprietors of educational and health institutions to make their education and healthcare services cost-effective without undermining the high quality so that more people can afford them. E. Ade Odumuyiwa suggests, "A situation in which churches establish private universities, charge exorbitant fees should be replaced with technical colleges that can be maintained within the resources of the church."[29] E. O. Opoola also proposes, "If these Universities are missionary endeavors they should have a human face to the extent that pastors laboring in such ministries should enjoy some benefits and scholarships for their children, because they labour side by side."[30]

CONCLUSION

What I argue for in this essay is not that the church should abandon its primary job of proclaiming the mystery of salvation to serve the tables, nor do we suggest it take over the role of the state and other agencies in the world. Rather the church should focus on preaching the mystery of Christ's death and resurrection without neglecting its public prophetic social and political vocation. The church should not retreat from the world and allow it to be fixed by God and secular government alone; rather, it should collaborate with them in developing it into a better world where all people have fair and equal opportunity and access to God's ongoing creative provision of God's all-inclusive daily bread. The Church should do this even though the full attainment of such a mission will take place at the eschaton. The contributions of the Nigerian churches to development in the fields of education, health care, political participation, and economic empowerment are commendable. Nonetheless, not only are their education and healthcare services too exorbitantly priced, their public prophetic engagement with social and political systemic evils, which hinder human development in Nigeria, is largely marginal. Hence the need for these churches to deliberately make their education and healthcare affordable, engage more actively in public prophetic social and political action, and carry out regular environmental sanitation exercises in their communities.

BIBLIOGRAPHY

Addae-Korankye, Alex. "Causes of Poverty in Africa: A Review of Literature." *American International Journal of Social Science* 3, no. 7 (2014): 147–53. Accessed September 11, 2017, from http://www.aijssnet.com/journals/Vol_3_No_7_December_2014/16.pdf.

Ahiuma, Victor. "Poverty: 112m Nigerians Live Below Poverty Line." *Vanguard*. Accessed September 5, 2017, from https://www.vanguardngr.com/2016/10/poverty-112m-nigerians-live-poverty-line/.

Anozie, Eric Emeka. "Christian Church: A Catalyst for Economic Development in Nigeria." *An International Multidisciplinary Journal, Ethiopia* 7, no. 31 (2013): 274–87.

Antyo, Joseph. "The Role of Churches in Government Poverty Eradication Program in Nigeria." NGTT *Nederduitse Gereformeerde Teologiese Tydskrif* 53, no. 1 (2012): 231–41.

Bitrus, Ibrahim S. *Community and Trinity in Africa*. New York: Routledge, 2017.

———. "Disturbing Unjust Peace in Nigeria through the Church and Legal Reforms: The Contribution of Luther's Critical Public Theology." In *On Secular Government: Lutheran Perspectives on Contemporary Legal Issues*, edited by R. W. Duty and M. A. Failinger. Grand Rapids, MI: Wm. B. Eerdmans Publishing Co., 2016.

Dabbs, W. Corbett. " Oil Production and Environment Damage." Accessed July 5, 2011, from http://environment-ecology.com/environment-writings/759-oil-production-and-environmental-damage.html.

Fehintolu, Osamolu Titilayo and Atuluku John. "An Appraisal of the Role of the Church of the in National Development: A Case of the Redeemed Christian Church of God in Nigeria." Accessed October 21, 2017, from http://globalacademicgroup.com/journals/nard/Osamolu.pdf.

Fritz, Jan Marie. "Social and Economic Development." *Socioeconomic Developmental Social Work* 1. Accessed October 12, 2017, from http://www.eolss.net/sample-chapters/c13/e1-20-01.pdf.

Jamo, Idris Ahmed. "Democracy and Development in Nigeria: Is There A Link?" *Arabian Journal of Business and Management Review (OMAN Chapter)* 3, no. 3 (2013): 85–94.

Jansen, C. A., F. J. Pretorius, and E. J. van Niekerk. "Education and the Role of the Church in Africa: Three Relevant Aspects." *Koers* 74, no. 1 and 2 (2009): 67–83.

Luther, Martin. "The Bondage of the Will." In *Luther's Works*, Vol. 33. Edited by Philip S. Watson and Hulmut Lehmann. Philadelphia, PA: Fortress Press, 1972.

———. "The Small Catechism." In *The Book of Concord: The Confessions of the Evangelical Lutheran Church*. Edited by Robert Kolb and Timothy Wengert. Minneapolis: Fortress Press, 2000.

Mattes, Mark. "Discipleship in Lutheran Perspective." *Lutheran Quarterly* 26 (2012): 143–63.

Mfon, Philip, et al. "Challenges of Deforestation in Nigeria and the Millennium Development Goals." *International Journal of Environment and Bioenergy* 9 no. 2 (2014): 76–94.

Nwagbara, Eucharia N., Raphael P. Abia, Francis A. Uyang, and Joy A. Ejeje. "Poverty, Environmental Degradation and Sustainable Development: A Discourse." *Global Journal of Human Social Science Sociology, Economics & Political Science* 12, no. 11 (2012). Accessed September 11, 2017, from https://globaljournals.org/GJHSS_Volume12/1-Poverty-Environmental-Degradation.pdf.

Nwaigbo, Ferdinand . " The Church and Repositioning The Maternal Care in Africa: A Project of th e Millennium Development Goals." *OGIRISI: A New Journal of African Studies* 6, no. 1 (2009): 105–25 .

Odumuyiwa, E. Ade. "Christianity, Governance and Development: A Case Study of Nigeria in the 21st Century." *Religion, Governance and Development in the 21st century* . Edited by R. A. Raji et al. Nigeria: Nigerian Association for the Study of Religions, 2006.

Oluwabamide, Abiodun J., and John O. Umo. "An Assessment of the Relevance of Religion to Health Care Delivery in Nigeria: Case of Akwa Ibom State." *Journal of Sociology and Social Anthropology* 2, no. 1 (2011): 47–52.

Omotoye, Rotimi Williams, and Elisabeth DeCampos. "The Role of the Christian Church in Building Civil Society in Nigeria." In *State Fragility, State Formation, and Human Security in Nigeria*. New York: Palgrave Macmillan, 2013.

Opoola, E. O. "The Living Faith Church and Sustainable Development in Nigeria." PhD Seminar Paper Presented at the Department of Religions, University of Ilorin, Nigeria, 2010.
Tokheim, Russell. "Lutherans to Focus on Nigerian Health Care in 2013." *Metro Lutheran: An Independent, Pan-Lutheran Newspaper Serving the Greater Twin Cities Area*, 2013. Accessed October 25, 2017, from http://metrolutheran.org/2013/01/lutherans-to-focus-on-nigerian-health-care-in-2013/.
Ucha, Chimobi. "Poverty in Nigeria: Some Dimensions and Contributing Factors." *Global Majority E-Journal* 1, no. 1 (2010): 47.
United Nations Development Programme. *Human Development Report: Concept and Measurement of Human Development*. New York: Oxford University Press, 1990.
United Nations General Assembly. *Report of the World Commission on Environment and Development: Our Common Future*. Oslo, Norway: United Nations General Assembly, Development and International Co-operation: Environment, 1987.
World Bank Data Team, "The 2017 Atlas of Sustainable Development Goals: A New Visual Guide to Data and Development." Accessed September 5, 2017, from http://blogs.worldbank.org/opendata/2017-atlas-sustainable-development-goals-new-visual-guide-data-and-development.

NOTES

1. Jan Marie Fritz, "Social and Economic Development," in *Socioeconomic Developmental Social Work* 1. Accessed October 12, 2017, from http://www.eolss.net/sample-chapters/c13/e1-20-01.pdf.
2. Idris Ahmed Jamo, "Democracy and Development in Nigeria: Is There a Link?" *Arabian Journal of Business and Management Review (OMAN Chapter)* 3, no. 3 (2013): 87.
3. United Nations General Assembly, *Report of the World Commission on Environment and Development: Our Common Future* (Oslo, Norway: United Nations General Assembly, Development and International Co-operation: Environment, 1987), 43.
4. United Nations Development Programme, *Human Development Report: Concept and Measurement of Human Development* (New York: Oxford University Press, 1990), 10.
5. C. A. Jansen, F.J. Pretorius, and E. J. van Niekerk, "Education and the Role of the Church in Africa: Three Relevant Aspects," *Koers* 74, no. 1 and 2 (2009), 70.
6. Mark Mattes, "Discipleship in Lutheran Perspective," *Lutheran Quarterly* 26 (2012): 143.
7. Ibid., 155–56.
8. Ibid., 157.
9. Ferdinand Nwaigbo, " The Church and Repositioning the Maternal Care in Africa: A Project of th e Millennium Development Goals," *OGIRISI: a New Journal of African Studies* 6, no. 1 (2009): 115 .
10. See Luther's interpretation of the Fourth Petition of the Lord's Prayer for an exhaustive list of daily bread. Martin Luther, "The Small Catechism," in *The Book of Concord: The Confessions of the Evangelical Lutheran Church*, eds. Robert Kolb and Timothy Wengert (Minneapolis: Fortress Press, 2000), 357.
11. Martin Luther, "The Bondage of the Will," in *Luther's Works*, Vol. 33, eds. Philip S. Watson and Hulmut Lehmann (Philadelphia, PA: Fortress Press, 1972), 243.
12. Ibrahim S. Bitrus, *Community and Trinity in Africa* (New York: Routledge, 2017), 159.
13. World Bank Data Team, "The 2017 Atlas of Sustainable Development Goals: A New Visual Guide to Data and Development." Accessed September 5, 2017, from http://blogs.worldbank.org/opendata/2017-atlas-sustainable-development-goals-new-visual-guide-data-and-development.
14. Victor Ahiuma, "Poverty: 112m Nigerians Live Below Poverty Line," *Vanguard*. Accessed September 5, 2017, from https://www.vanguardngr.com/2016/10/poverty-112m-nigerians-live-poverty-line/.
15. Chimobi Ucha, "Poverty in Nigeria: Some Dimensions and Contributing Factors," *Global Majority E-Journal* 1, no. 1 (2010): 47.

16. Ucha, "Poverty in Nigeria," 54.
17. Alex Addae-Korankye, "Causes of Poverty in Africa: A Review of Literature," *American International Journal of Social Science* 3, no. 7 (2014): 151. Accessed September 11, 2017, from http://www.aijssnet.com/journals/Vol_3_No_7_December_2014/16.pdf.
18. As cited in Eucharia N. Nwagbara, Raphael P. Abia, Francis A. Uyang, and Joy A. Ejeje, "Poverty, Environmental Degradation and Sustainable Development: A Discourse," *Global Journal of Human Social Science Sociology, Economics and Political Science* 12, no. 11 (2012). Accessed September 11, 2017, from https://globaljournals.org/GJHSS_Volume12/1-Poverty-Environmental-Degradation.pdf.
19. Philip Mfon Jr., et al., "Challenges of Deforestation in Nigeria and the Millennium Development Goals," *International Journal of Environment and Bioenergy* 9 no. 2 (2014): 77–78.
20. W. Corbett Dabbs, " Oil Production and Environment Damage." Accessed July 5, 2011, from http://environment-ecology.com/environment-writings/759-oil-production-and-environ-mental-damage.html.
21. Omotoye, Rotimi Williams, and Elisabeth DeCampos, "The Role of the Christian Church in Building Civil Society in Nigeria," in *State Fragility, State Formation, and Human Security in Nigeria* (New York: Palgrave Macmillan, 2013), 205.
22. Abiodun J. Oluwabamide and John O. Umo, "An Assessment of the Relevance of Religion to Health Care Delivery in Nigeria: Case of Akwa Ibom State," *Journal of Sociology and Social Anthropology* 2, no.1 (2011): 50.
23. Russell Tokheim, "Lutherans to Focus on Nigerian Health Care in 2013," *Metro Lutheran: An Independent, Pan-Lutheran Newspaper Serving the Greater Twin Cities Area*, 2013.Accesed October 25, 2017, from http://metrolutheran.org/2013/01/lutherans-to-focus-on-nigerian-health-care-in-2013/.
24. Osamolu Titilayo Fehintolu and Atuluku John, "An Appraisal of the Role of the Church of the in National Development: A Case of the Redeemed Christian Church of God in Nigeria." Accessed October 21, 2017, from http://globalacademicgroup.com/journals/nard/Osamolu.pdf.
25. Eric Emeka Anozie, "Christian Church: A Catalyst for Economic Development in Nigeria," *An International Multidisciplinary Journal, Ethiopia* 7, no. 31 (2013), 283.
26. Joseph Antyo, "The Role of Churches in Government Poverty Eradication Program in Nigeria," *Nederduitse Gereformeerde Teologiese Tydskrif* 53 no. 1 (2012): 235.
27. For a detailed analysis of these structural evils, see Bitrus, *Community and Trinity in Africa*.
28. See Ibrahim Bitrus, "Disturbing Unjust Peace in Nigeria through the Church and Legal Reforms: The Contribution of Luther's Critical Public Theology," in *On Secular Government: Lutheran Perspectives on Contemporary Legal Issues*, ed. R. W. Duty and M. A. Failinger (Grand Rapids: MI: Wm. B. Eerdmans, 2016).
29. E. Ade Odumuyiwa, "Christianity, Governance and Development: A Case Study of Nigeria in the 21st Century," in *Religion, Governance and Development in the 21st century*, eds. R. A. Raji, et al. (Nigerian: Nigerian Association for the Study of Religions, 2006), 211.
30. E. O. Opoola, "The Living Faith Church and Sustainable Development in Nigeria," A PhD seminar paper presented at the Department of Religions, University of Ilorin, Nigeria, 2010, 16.

Chapter 7

Hospitality and Social Responsibility

The Church in the Age of Globalization

Nestor M. Ravilas and Wilfredo A. Laceda

The Parable of the Talents found in the Gospel of Matthew (25:14–30) is fascinating in various ways. Leery and critical of people's handling of wealth, Jesus should not have used money to illustrate what it would be like on the great judgment day. Using financial growth as the baseline for divine approval or rejection scandalizes the story even more. Because of his failure to generate income out of the capital entrusted to him, the punished servant perplexes us as to what the story really wanted to convey. Such a conundrum has left its exegetical boundary so porous that hermeneutical adventurism may trespass and bring mayhem with it. Caution should be considered, but, within the range of the parable's probable meaning, it is hard to deny that it endorses the themes of investment, profits, and progress. And when used as a standard for the approval or disapproval of the servant, the primacy of those themes is immediately assumed. That is to say, economy is not detached from spirituality.

Having said this, it remains unclear how the church should behave in the midst of the pervasive race for progress and growth. The absence of any social encounter other than the assumed transactions the first two servants had engaged with that made them produce income does not tell us more as to how we should deal with other people other than through profit making. Do we have to care for the poor, the marginalized, and the unprivileged in general? Such social engagements for sure will cut our income and may wear us down to the original capital as happened to the third servant.

As predicted in the past, the interactions of various market players including labor forces indeed create an insurmountable wealth. Capitalism is far from dead. Instead, the new global order brings us into an unimaginable progress in all aspects of life. No one will follow the fate of the third servant in a society where the opportunity to earn is enormous. No one will be cast out into a place where there is gnashing of teeth. Nevertheless, it does not show the whole picture of the world, especially on this side of the planet (Philippines) where poverty is scattered almost everywhere. This is to say, development has failed to democratize itself; progress has not "trickled down," as they say in economic parlance. In view of this, the church is placed at a crossroad, baffled as to whether to slow down in order to walk with the weak majority or to accelerate its stride to be with swift progress. There are Christians, inspired by the earnings of servants in the parable coupled with the neoliberal individualist ideology, who espouse the latter. Some churches and individual Christians we know are in this chase, obviously motivated by the drive for personal success and growth. On the other hand, others are treading the hardest path. Reining their excitement to join the rat race, they choose rather to slow down in order for the weak, the hungry, and the poor to walk along with them toward social emancipation. This is the tension with which this paper wants to grapple. It wishes to engage the larger picture of the new global economy with its still-iffy ideology, neoliberalism. Nonetheless, we do not intend to enmesh ourselves in the technical side of the intricate web of the economics of globalization. That part must be left to economic experts. In the midst of intertwining forces, the goal of this endeavor is to locate the place of hospitality and human responsibility invoked by the biblical precept to love your neighbor. It wishes to help us see through the blinding smokescreen to locate our true identity as Christians, and to assist us to sift through these competing voices to see our supposed responsibility for the flourishing of human life.

As people of God, the Bible remains our standard and will be regarded as the final authority in all social issues discussed. We have sought out help from theologians and ethicists who either have worked directly on the effects of globalization in social relationship, or have ventured judgments on issues of ethics or social responsibility in general, such as Emmanuel Levinas, Zygmunt Bauman, William Leach, Lorenzo Bautista, and so on. We did so to assist us to deepen our (1) problematization of issues mentioned and (2) analysis of possible responses to them. Although excellent secondary materials on globalization and neoliberalization are available, such as books by Rachel Turner, David Harvey, and George Ritzer, we deemed it necessary and fair to consult the original proponents of the phenomenon such as Ludwig von Mises, Friedrich A. Hayek, and Milton Friedman. Social thinkers such as Max Weber and Charles Taylor were also included in the dialog to help us clarify the significant interface between society and religion. We hope that this project can contribute to the search for a life that is abundant and, at the same time, just.

THE RIDDLE OF GLOBALIZATION

Globalization, Zygmunt Bauman opines, is perhaps the most important change in human history.[1] Globalization has penetrated every conceivable area of modern life. Although its effects vary, we are all affected by it.[2] The technology that enables us to be connected globally at the touch of our fingertips has created distinct possibilities for human solidarity and development. A picture of the earth from outer space poignantly captures the once unimaginable idea of transforming us to a single global community. As seen through this prism, globalization thus brings together different peoples, classes, and cultures from all over the globe.[3] Its promise is cast in terms of a democratized access to the goods of this world, thus paving the way for equal development, which will then end the vicious cycle of injustice and poverty. Yet a quick glance at the world around us shows otherwise.

We have the moral imperative to make sense of this discrepancy between the ideal and the reality of globalization. Our entry point is to analyze the modes of its complex operations. At this juncture a caveat, however, is necessary. First, globalization is not a monolithic block. And because it encompasses several, if not all, areas of our present condition, its impacts are inherently ambiguous. Globalization, in other words, has adverse effects. The goal for the rest of this section is to untangle threads that make globalization such a complex tapestry. A significant step in this untangling is what Leslie Sklair calls the "untheorized" identification of globalization with capitalism, a suspicion particularly instigated by the surprising shift of discussion over the positive and negative effects of capitalism into the pros and cons of globalization. In a similar vein, William I. Robinson, a staunch critic of globalization, directly identified globalization as the "new epoch in the continuing evolution of capitalism."[4] If globalization is indeed capitalism hidden under some alluring camouflage, we are then in big trouble since, in simple terms, capitalism is understood as an insatiable accumulation of wealth and a translation of everything into private properties.

If this understanding is correct, and the process is irreversible, the propertied class has finally trapped us into an iron cage akin to what Max Weber warned in his genealogy of capitalism and the rise of modern society.[5] However, Sklair's nuanced analysis of the global order tempers this gloomy picture. For Sklair, globalization's complexity resists a singular explanation. Rather, it is ramified in various expressions, of which "capitalist globalization" is just one. Such a taxonomy of globalization provides an idea that not all expressions are ominous, and not all, at the same time, are irreversible. Sinklair employs different categories to describe globalization, one of which is "generic globalization," which for him is irreversible. "Capitalist globalization," on the other hand, Sinklair is confident can be reversed.[6]

Another point of view from which globalization can be examined is its transformation of the material foundation: space and time. Globalization's effectiveness can be attributed to "time/space compression," which is directly linked to the great chasm in wealth and poverty.[7] The unprecedented lightness by which capital and a select few or the "mobile elite" travel exacerbates the already unequal class and economic disparity. Thus, instead of development for all, it tends to polarize or create an unequal development. Globalization, simply put, fails to deliver on its promise. For a select few, globalization is a blessing because it unburdens an elite minority from the shackles of a locality. This extraterritorial reality is a new form of freedom: a freedom of movement or what Bauman calls the "new weightlessness of power."[8] For the vast majority, however, this configuration is the bane of their collective existence. "Being local in a globalized world," says Bauman, "is a sign of social deprivation and degradation."[9]

GLOBALIZATION, NEOLIBERALIZATION, AND FREEDOM: CONNECTING THE DOTS

Milton Friedman, a major influence in the globalizing movement, says that political freedom came along with the free market and the development of capitalist institutions.[10] He understood political freedom to be a free exercise of individual liberty apart from the coercion of other people. Hayek accentuated the same thing earlier in his book, but he added that the individual must also be spared from infringement.[11] The two are almost the same, with a small but significant difference. In a nutshell, Friedman and Hayek assert that political freedom is realized when the individual is neither infringed in his pursuant of his goal in life, nor coerced to accomplish other people's interest. Globalization, with its ideology and practices, stands and is reinforced by this revival of liberal philosophy.

In this phenomenon dubbed now as *neoliberalism*, freedom is being reimagined and cleverly turned into an environment in which capitalist globalization can grow and prosper. Social democracy, socialism, or any social arrangement that promotes cooperative order is seen as totalitarian in nature, since it interferes with individual freedom. As a consequence, it hampers the potential of the individual for growth and development by ensnaring him or her in what democracy called the common interest. Neoliberalism sees its mission as removing all these forms of control and coercion in order to allow the individual to reclaim one's freedom. In the words of Friedman, "As liberals, we take freedom of the individual, or perhaps the family, as our ultimate goal in judging social arrangements."[12]

THEY GAVE ME LIBERTY, AND BEHOLD, THERE WAS A MARKET!

In most of the literature produced by the proponents of neoliberalism, the concern over the decline of individual freedom is conspicuous. Among them, Hayek may be the most candid when he removes all qualifiers [13] by arbitrarily declaring the "individual end is supreme!"[14] Underneath this great release of the self is the subterfuge of a clandestine release of the market from state-controlled planning. The passionate clamor for the liberation of the individual has been dexterously utilized to pop the free market out of the magician's hat.

Consider a society where every citizen is free to pursue his personal goal and happiness. Any unitary economic plan is doomed to fail from the very start, because it presupposes that the happiness of every individual depends on what Hayek called "the infinite variety of needs," or in the language of Friedman, "the economic activities of the millions."[15] It is impossible to reduce all of these into a single end that could be addressed by one unitary plan. No centralized economic plan, however sophisticated, is able to comprehend and embrace this enormous number of needs, let alone address them equally and properly to the full satisfaction of all members of a given society. A chained market is anathema to a free society. It is necessary, therefore, for the market to be unfettered to efficiently allow every individual to progress through the infinite number of market approaches. What David Harvey, a staunch critic of neoliberalization, assumes is a bit amiss when he says that individual freedom is guaranteed by the freedom of the market.[16] The reverse is actually true. It is market freedom that is being guaranteed by the freedom of the individual.

THE RISE OF INDIVIDUALISM AND THE DEATH OF SOCIAL RESPONSIBILITY

George Ritzer indicted neoliberalism as radically individualistic.[17] The libertarians did not deny this, however. Hayek, for one, bragged that the essence of the individualist position is a recognition of the individual as the ultimate judge of his ends and the belief that as far as possible his own views ought to govern his actions.[18] A neoliberal man is a man for himself. He is free so long as his intention, goals, and happiness are pursued apart from any external infringement, dictation, or imposition from others. The slogan—the individual end is supreme—succinctly sums up this neoliberal drive for individualism.

Nevertheless, to emancipate the individual is a herculean task. The human being is not introduced to this world all by himself. He lives and survives within the context of a community, being dependent in one way or another on a web of social assistance. In our first community, the family, this mutual sense of dependency and responsibility are awakened and fostered. Hence, no one is born and lives without being initiated and nurtured in this reciprocity of hospitality. This implies that every human being is a creation of the infinite variety of relationships. One is a son or a daughter, a brother or a sister, a father, a mother, a husband or a wife, an aunt or an uncle, a cousin, a brother-in-law, a friend, a neighbor—and the list will go on and on. Asians are not the only people invariably attached to an infinite number of relationships. In the same way, Westerners are also inescapably enveloped in these multiple relationships. Every designation we claim for ourselves comes with the burden of relationships. Against this overwhelming myriad of relationships and responsibilities, neoliberalism is wheedling us to declare that the individual end is supreme!

In light of this, neoliberalism generally views responsibility and hospitality as inimical to human development. To demonstrate the point, see how Friedman inveighed against the debacle of most democratic societies in which political and economic freedom that should have been used to accelerate growth was saddled instead with the weight of a commitment to social welfare and other forms of social assistance. The response, as observed by Ritzer, is to reduce or, in some instances, to cancel state support for social welfare programs in societies where neoliberal policy is being implemented, in order for the state to propel growth by investing capital into more productive industries and income-generating undertakings. What is true in the macro applies too in the micro. Responsibilities hobble not only our personal freedom but impede our drive toward personal progress. The more a person is attached to a number of responsibilities and obligations, the smaller his chance to succeed in life. Wages and other income that should have been put into multiple investments, acquiring more properties and commodities, traveling abroad for business and leisure, or acquiring a convenient life in general, are rather rechanneled into the support of other people's existence. Neoliberalism is basically obligated to counter the biblical precept of love your neighbor in order to propel the individual into progress and development. Has the church been able to stand its ground against this enticement, or has it succumbed to this invitation for privatized utopia? This is a good question to consider.

On the Accusation of Selfishness

Eloquent rhetoric is not enough to pull the individual away from the pressure of hospitality and responsibility. People who turn their back to obligation and responsibility cannot just leave unscathed. This is even more the case for Christians who are supposed to love one another in the context of a cooperative community such as a church; they cannot just walk away untarnished. Hurled against them are accusations of ingratitude, greediness, and selfishness, and thus they will forever be haunted by guilt and remorse. This is exactly what makes people wary of responding to the call to bolt from the ethical demand of relationships and live a private life.

Hayek immediately comes to the rescue. In an astute way, he eliminates the sentinel guarding the door that separates cooperation and individualism. Aware of the problem, he claims from the outset that individualism should not be seen as motivated by selfishness or greed. Given the immensity of human needs and problems, Hayek says, we are capable, to the best of our capacity, of embracing and addressing only an "infinitesimal fraction." He assumes as an indisputable fact that the limits of our powers of imagination make it impossible to include in our scale of values more than a sector of the needs of the whole society. Added to this liability is the fact that this human scale of values is partial and subjective and therefore cannot be considered as a reliable standard. When all these are taken into consideration, Hayek concludes that individuals should be allowed, within defined limits, to follow their own values and preferences rather than somebody else's.[19] Selfishness is dismissed from the equation, and individualism has emerged triumphant.

This is the most publicized polemic of the neoliberals. We should maintain caution, however, not to swallow it hook, line, and sinker. There is a lot more to it than meets the eye. Here is another way of looking at the correlation of this simultaneous unfettering of the individual and of the market: is there an integral relation between the individual and the market, other than what has been offered so far, that means it must be kept unperturbed and hence, in seeking the freedom of both, intensifies their relation?

As already mentioned, neoliberals argue that the unfettering of the market is to serve the "infinite variety of needs" of free men. This misleads us regarding the true relation of the two, as to which really benefits from their interaction. Just as in the old days, in a neoliberal society the symbiotic relationship of consumers and vendors remains intact. The market is useless without consumers who buy and consume the products and commodities it sells. More than the market serving the infinite needs of people, the people as consumers serve the market's infinite craving for profit. And, since the entire world is almost saturated already by the market, the prospect of expanding its domain is now coming to an end. The best option left for the market players to keep the market alive and accelerate their income is therefore to intensify the people's desire to consume.

CONSUMERISM

The early gestation of individualism has become an all-pervasive order in our present condition, curiously dubbed by social critics as the *consumer society*. Globalization has created a new sociality wherein certain aspects of our lives have become powerful animating forces. To understand this new form of society we need to identify the substantive distinction between consumption and consumerism. Consumption is a basic fact of life.[20] Like production, consumption is a cultural universal necessary for sustaining life throughout human history.[21] Consumerism, on the other hand, is a way of life.[22] Consequently, consumption is an act of individuals, whereas consumerism is a societal trait. Therefore, our consumer society engages its members first and foremost in their roles as consumers.[23] Another distinctive feature of our consumer society is the central role of consumption previously held by production.[24] Consumerism, in other words, is the *"principal propelling and operating force* of [a consumer] society."[25] For others, consumerism is the dominant social ethos of a consumer society.[26] At any rate, consumerism functions as what Taylor calls a "social imaginary," that is, "the ways people imagine their social existence" using images and narratives.[27] A plethora of factors gave rise to consumer society.[28] The provenance of our global consumer culture can be traced back to America. In his book *Land of Desire*, William Leach catalogues the complex changes in American life:

> In the decades following the Civil War, American capitalism began to produce a distinct culture, unconnected to traditional family or community values, to religion in any conventional sense, or to political democracy. It was a secular business and market-oriented culture, with the exchange and circulation of money and goods at the foundation of its aesthetic life and of its moral sensibility. . . . The cardinal features of this culture were acquisition and consumption as the means of achieving happiness; the cult of the new; the democratization of desire; and monetary value as the predominant measure of all value in society. . . . By World War I, Americans were being enticed into consumer pleasure and indulgence rather than into work as the road to happiness.[29]

Crucial in this transformation is a change in formative values. This period falls in what Bauman calls the solid phase of modernity or the "society of producers" with its own social values such as prudence, long-term security, and durability;[30] along with the Protestants' *this-worldly* stance, which includes economic matters. Production and reinvesting capital in new ventures are celebrated in the society of producers. This overproduction creates an interesting conundrum. For the culture of consumption to capture the collective consciousness of Americans, a fundamental virtue of the producer society needs to take the back seat: thrift.[31] Taking its place is a new immaterial product never before manufactured en masse—the "mass production of desire."[32] To facilitate this change, new strategies are used to cultivate desire—for example, department stores—a harbinger of things to come. The effect is a radical change in social ethos.

A historical trajectory sees the globalization of consumer culture and lifestyle paving the way for the configuration of consumer society. The social fabric was ruptured once consumerism burst on the scene with its own attendant culture, ways of shaping sensibilities, and subtle forces of the formation.

Social Formation and the "Market-mediated Mode of Life"

Part of Leach's analysis of the transformation of American life is the increased role of the market. Instead of religious conviction influencing economic decisions, the market "caused a fundamental change in prevailing religious outlooks."[33] This turns Weber's thesis on its head. The increasing hegemonic role of the market is evident in the way it transforms not just religious convictions but also political discourse. Democracy, freedom, and autonomy have been translated into what Leach calls as the "market notion of democracy."[34] In our consumer society, the market's cooptation of society is complete. The market has colonized every meaningful area of our lives. Our consumer society "has been reshaped in the likeness of the marketplace."[35] The shopping mall is the architectural and symbolic image that best describes our contemporary condition. Consumer society has its own way of fashioning and controlling its members. Previous eras were policed by the Panopticon, a surveillance mechanism that imposes a "uniform pattern of behavior."[36] Consumer society employs a new technology of control that does not rely on coercion but on *spectacle* and encourages the many to watch the few, which Bauman calls as the synopticon.[37] The synopticon's tool for control is the mass media and new forms of it. The majority of the population thus is transformed from being watched and recast as watchers. Bauman summarizes their difference: "The Panopticon *forced* people into the position where they could be watched. The Synopticon needs no coercion—it *seduces* people into watching."[38] According to Roberta Sassatelli, consumer agency is one of the key issues in the study of consumption.[39] Consumers are neither sovereign nor mindless. To understand the dynamics of an individual's agency we have to include the matrix of social and material structures. This includes what Ritzer terms "cathedrals of consumption" which in a way restrict and at times predetermine a person's actions.[40]

Moreover, what are the consequences when a society is shaped by the insatiable desire to consume? The first problem occurs when life in its entirety is seen through the vectors of the market. The market works by putting an exchange value on commodities. Our consumer society "transforms everything—objects, experiences, time, and other people's lives into commodities."[41] The market as the paradigm for contemporary life is aptly called by Bauman a "market-mediated mode of life."[42] The commodification of the life-world includes the *"transformation of consumers into commodities."*[43] This transformation in many instances can be dehumanizing.[44] Thus a salient feature of consumer society is the interface between identity and consumerism.[45] The social landscape is redrawn. Consumer products now more than ever are embedded in social relationships. Sassatelli calls this "the purposive construction of identity through commodities."[46] Every product, however banal or mundane, can have "profound existential consequences."[47] Consumer society, in other words, is a "society of identities."[48]

Another angle by which we can analyze identity vis-à-vis consumerism is Charles Taylor's claim that the self always exists in a moral space. "Selfhood and the good, or in another way selfhood and morality, turn out to be inextricably intertwined themes," writes Taylor.[49] Here we come to terms with the ethical ramifications of consumerism and individualism. Taylor has been wary of the effects of individualism.[50] With consumerism as its conduit and riding the waves of the cultural revolutions since the 1960s, individualism gained a new impetus.[51] What has emerged is a distinct way by which the self is expressed through consumer products. For theologians like William Cavanaugh, consumerism has the power to form individuals, which he likens to "a spiritual disposition, a way of looking at the world around us that is deeply formative."[52] He suggests that it is a powerful system of moral formation, even more powerful than Christianity.[53] Bauman in a similar fashion calls consumerism the "cognitive and moral focus of life" in a consumer society.[54] It is therefore not uncommon for social thinkers to look at consumerism as a kind of "religion."[55] Part of the agenda of the church in the age of globalization needs to be the way consumer goods function as cultural symbols that shape our sensibilities, mediate identities, and animate social relations.

Worship at the Altar of Consumption

Religion does not exist in a vacuum. It is embedded in social and political structures. As the historical analyses of Weber and Leach have noted, religion and the market are entangled. The globalization of consumer culture redefines the relationship between the market and religion. At the heart of this relationship is a question of power. If we frame religion and the market in terms of "power relations," which of the two exercises power and influence over the other? Answering this question requires careful nuance and methodological acuity. Although consumer culture tends to homogenize, there are distinct configurations of religion in different localities. In the Philippines, for instance, the history of its double bind of colonization and Christianity has helped configure Filipino church and society. Filipino theologian Lorenzo Bautista's seminal essay on the Philippine church is a good starting point. Bautista, in a comprehensive yet concise manner, provides a history of the church in the Philippines and at the same time identifies the contours of emerging trends.[56] One of the emerging trends that Bautista notices is the phenomenon of the megachurch. In just two decades after Bautista's essay, the megachurch phenomenon has grown to the point that it has become virtually the dominant vision and expression of being "church." At first glance, the megachurch crystallizes the enmeshing of religion and the market. The suspicion of some scholars of religion that the market shapes the church in its image seems justified.[57] To put substance to the suspicion, we have to take note again how consumerism frames individuals and the mediating role of consumer goods in constructing identity. Megachurches in the Philippines are expanding in a way that, interestingly, is similar to how fast food restaurants are being franchised. The logic at work is perhaps the same: offering the same experience and providing an association with a brand or a product. In this sense, religious experience is homogenized, whether one is in the commercial districts of Manila or in the province. It thus changes the way religious communities are constructed. One consequence is that churches vie for "customer loyalty" and thus the need to always upgrade their services.[58] One can surmise that our consumer society produces a church fashioned through its symbolic economy of a transaction between the self and a consumer product. If this is true, we are perhaps worshipping at the altar of consumption.

Another lens by which we can refract the almost symbiotic relationship of the megachurch and the market is what one scholar calls as "substantial commodification."[59] This commodification goes beyond the church's formal use of marketing strategies. It gives us another avenue by which to scrutinize the way the church has allegedly embraced market logics and its ways of shaping our sensibilities, religious or otherwise. An accounting of the practices of churches, including the tacit assumptions behind them, provides a way forward. By scrutinizing the church's teachings instead of just the mechanism that it purportedly copied from the market, we can have a better grasp of the contemporary way the church has succumbed to the alluring power of the market. A step in this direction is the subtle transposition of the inequalities, economic or otherwise, under the aegis of globalization, to the church. The megachurch has its own target audience, middle and upper classes, which in a way re-creates the class divisions in society. The difference, however, is that the division lies between those who can consume and those who cannot. A church that is too enmeshed within the trappings of consumerism is hampered in its capacity to reflect critically on its own condition. Lastly, with religious beliefs and practices manufactured through the "good life" offered by consumerism, we need to provide the substantial basis of our faith—themes that are prominent in the Bible—like social justice. In this way we can set up these biblical themes as a benchmark by which to analyze the market co-optation of our faith.

BIBLICAL FAITH AND THE INNER CONTRADICTIONS OF CONSUMERISM

Self-Interest Negates Spontaneous Orders

The market left all by itself will do well, since people will voluntarily coordinate and cooperate their actions together for the good of the public. Proponents of the free market have generally drawn their justification for the abolition, or reduction, of market control and restriction from Adam Smith's idea of an "invisible hand."[60] Since Smith, the invisible hand has evolved into different versions within the discourses of libertarian philosophers and economists. Whether or not they remain faithful to the original usage of Smith is another question. Nonetheless, modern renditions such as the "spontaneous order" of Friedrich A. Hayek and Michael Polanyi[61] and the "mutual coordination" of Milton Friedman[62] all refer to the absence of coercion in economic transactions. Coercion is what characterizes market activities organized and monitored by the state. By removing government intervention, the market will naturally proceed into the spontaneous or mutual coordination of self-interests, resulting in progress that will benefit the public. Interference by the state only disrupts this innate harmony.

Such a line of argument breaks down when we recall that consumerist society is inhabited by various self-interests that are all claiming to be superior to each other. This observation exposes an inherent dissonance within the philosophy of neoliberalism. The allegedly free space is actually saturated with an infinite number of personal interests. We are talking of approximately 7.5 billion interests all asserting priority and thus vying to be served and satisfied first in this consumerist society. This image alone does not give us a picture of harmony and voluntary coordination. Even John Rawls, who affirmed the existence of "identical interests," was still bothered by the threat of "conflicting ones," and hence next pondered how to avert clashes among these interests.[63] Instead of proposing political systems that will adjudicate the conflicting interests, libertarians heighten the conflict by coaxing each individual to insist on the supreme priority of his interest. What most likely will follow is a fight for the survival of the fittest rather than voluntary coordination.

Did the libertarian proponents miss that point, or was it really part of their propaganda to accelerate the consumerist's habit? As one Peruvian economist says, "The problem with Milton Friedman and his fellow libertarians is they never took into consideration the importance of class. . . . They ignored the way elites were able to distort the policies they prescribed for their own benefit."[64] It was these conflicting interests and the desire to regard one's interest ahead of the rest that gave birth to what Vladimir Lenin called the "antagonism of classes."[65] The world was never, as the libertarians claimed, in a harmony that was disrupted by the invention of government. To the contrary, this animosity among classes created the state, in the hope that through its mediation the exploitation and oppression inflicted by the powerful on the weaker class would stop, and harmony would finally be achieved. In actual fact, the state, in some instances, failed to carry out this role. It only legitimized the subjugation of one class by another rather than resolving it. Nevertheless, to insinuate that the introduction of the state disturbed the previously harmonious society is malicious and harmful. Society was instead in complete chaos. The monarchs and the feudal lords of previous social arrangements had entrenched their supreme personal interests above the general public.

Jesus seemingly agrees with the idea that people left to pursue their personal interest result in a society highly stratified between the exploited and the exploiters, the oppressed and the oppressors, the consumers and the capitalists. On many occasions, the rich and the powerful endured the brunt of Jesus' indignation and disapproval. The kingdom of God was preached to the poor and to the outcasts. He warned the greedy (Luke 12:15), shamed those craving for money (Luke 16:14), rebuked those looking for honor and recognition (Matthew 23:6), castigated those who oppressed people, and rejected those who withdrew help and failed to redress the sufferings of the weak (Matthew 23:4). The Parable of the Rich Man and Lazarus poignantly underscores this sad reality (Luke 16:19–31). The slogan—the personal end is supreme—obviously was a factor in such a huge divide between the two protagonists in the parable. The rich man is guilty of intentional neglect and apathy toward Lazarus, whose misery, as highlighted in the story, the rich man was fully aware of. The torment the rich man experienced after the short stint in this life makes sense.

Freedom without Justice Is Chaos

Let us return again to the tension of individualism and responsibility we left for a while unchallenged. The procedure was intentional in order to provide space for the libertarian voice without abruptly suppressing it under counter-arguments. Unfortunately, the arguments for why individualism should not be identified with selfishness are flimsy and ludicrous. If humans can be affected and can sympathize only with an infinitesimal fraction of human needs and suffering, why should such a limit be used to drop them off peremptorily and proceed to the cloister of privatized utopia instead? As small as the fraction may be, it shows how our life is naturally entangled with human misery, as well as happiness. The latter we celebrate together, and together we look for ways to redress the former. We heard no demand to do what is impossible for a finite creature, to embrace the entire suffering world. Our limitation as humans manifests itself in all aspects of life and not only in our capacity to sympathize with others. An infinitesimal fraction of concern, then, is a good point from which to start, and it is better to keep and nurture it more. It is unthinkable to regress to *amour de soi*, where your obligations, sympathy, care, and love are all directed toward yourself alone. Is it not unimaginable in the same way to use freedom to extinguish the flickering fire of generosity rather than stoking it into a flame? This is the very thing Richard Rorty[66] and Judith Butler[67] are prodding us to do, to expand our circle of "we" from the parochial affinity to a much larger community by welcoming even people with whom we share no commonality.

Against the neoliberals, the Apostle Paul made an interesting point regarding how to deal with freedom. In the Book of Galatians he says, "For you were called to freedom, brothers. Only do not use your freedom as an opportunity for the flesh, but through love serve one another" (Galatians 5:13, ESV). This is a mind-blowing exhortation from the Apostle. Whether he was saying that the interest of the "other" is at par with or higher than one's personal end, he underscored that the church has to take a path different from what the consumerist society is coaxing us into. Stunned by the apostle's idea of freedom, it is good for us to mention that he was just echoing the voice of his master. Jesus did and said a lot of things that undergird the point Paul is making in Galatians. There is, however, one enigmatic parable that at times seems to escape sensible interpretation. We think it serves as an illustration of we are seeking.

The Parable of the Rich Fool in the Gospel of Luke dares to represent God in such an inappropriate manner—snapping out without warning and then threatening the rich man with death. Seeing God fuming and threatening death does not surprise us much because he did that on a few occasions in the Old Testament. Was it too much to ask for a justifiable reason from our parable, say a golden calf, that infuriated God enough to strike the rich man down? Nothing of such evil was committed by the rich man other than what if found in these lines of his monologue:

> Then he said, "I will do this: I will pull down my barns and build larger ones, and there I will store all my grain and my goods. And I will say to my soul, Soul, you have ample goods laid up for many years; relax, eat, drink, be merry" (Luke 12:18–19, NRSV)

The personal pronouns "I" and "myself" are so prevalent that they are hard to miss. All these indicate an individualist life: a deregulated self and a privatized happiness. He will build bigger barns to "store," or in the capitalist parlance, to hoard all the insurmountable produce of his field. "And I say to myself" suggests a preoccupation of the self, of a personal pursuit of comfort and security. It was a perfect picture of a person who pushes down the "others" and takes responsibility only for "himself." "You have plenty of good things laid out for many years, take life easy, eat, drink and be merry"—that is an insane preoccupation with the self. Living in comfort and luxury in the midst of a famished people, which was the social context of Jesus and of the parable, is inconceivable. It is enough to anger the divine and visit the rich man with death, and it threatens those who follow the steps of the rich fool to suffer the same predicament (Luke 12:21).

What the libertarians have failed to factor in to their explication of freedom is the idea of justice. As mentioned earlier, billions of personal interests are fighting to be served first. This infighting will definitely produce a multitude of casualties. The weak, the poor, the "others," the marginalized, the disenfranchised, the unprivileged, the nonpropertied, the oppressed, the exploited, all of them will be pressed down to the ground to form the very platform on which the rich, the strong, and the powerful are standing. As poignantly emphasized by Emmanuel Levinas, "to justify freedom is not to prove it but to render it just."[68] Jesus saw no justice in the rich man's exercise of freedom, so God indicted and slaughtered him right there. When freedom becomes arbitrary and violent rather than justifying itself, ethics begins, Levinas explained.[69] Ethics, understood both by Jesus and Levinas, is about the interhuman relationship, which infers the responsibility to use one's freedom by welcoming the "others" in hospitality and in generosity leading toward a cooperative existence and communal development.

CONCLUSION

Capitalism could be the shrewdest animal loosed on earth. It survives centuries of effort to slaughter it. Its ability to adapt to different and changing social conditions is the reason it remains with us, and significantly affects our way of life. Not yet factored here is the idea that humans are intrinsically predisposed to capitalist ideals, such as the accumulation of wealth and the pursuit of a privatized utopia. If this is correct, Jesus has all the more reason to be concerned when he warns his disciples, saying, "I am sending you out like sheep into the midst of wolves; so be wise as serpents and innocent as doves" (Matthew 10:16, NRSV). He was able to see how the world is deceiving and the disciples are susceptible; Jesus is fully aware that the church could easily be beguiled and ensnared. Its innocence at its softest point, capitalism, can easily be exploited. A dose of astuteness mixed with innocence will help the church remain honest and faithful to its calling and mission.

Capitalist globalization has so far been regarded as the best development in this unending evolution of capitalism. It no longer depends on the power of violence and coercion, but on a simple stimulation and intensification of desire. No ravaged victims are in view, as they were in the brutal age of direct imperialism. Global capitalism cleverly hides the emaciated majority who fell behind in this race for individualism behind the walls and gates of prominent villages and opulent cities. Unmindful of their tragedy, however, these modern outcasts are busy in the same way coping with their own awakened desire, and hence they make their way out to the market selling cheaper products to pay homage at the altar of consumerism. As we have underscored, the church is not safe from this pitfall. With most of our eschatological hope anchored in material gains in the paradise called heaven, we are awfully susceptible to the enticement of the market and of consumerism. Ignorant of the words of the prophets and of Jesus in the gospels, we immediately yield to the allurement of market players and promoters who have clandestinely entered the church, occupied the pulpits, and run the church's affairs like a market. They pride themselves on subscribing to the great commandment, but only to the half that says, "as you love yourself"—which echoes the individualist's motto, "one's personal end is supreme!"

The Parable of the Talents, which we mentioned in the introduction, does not talk about this kind of progress, however. The metaphor of the talents is explained in the concluding Parable of the Sheep and the Goats (Mathew 25:31–46) where apathy or hospitality toward the marginalized and the unprivileged is used as the criterion for either punishment or reward. When the talents are understood in light of the concluding parable, progress is not about increasing one's wealth, but about how we have tried to alleviate the lives of those who have been railroaded by this drive for individualism. To be wise as serpents, therefore, is to "love your neighbor." The basis of the entire Bible is this command. To be a Christian is to be in relation to others. It is to entangle yourself in a myriad of relationships. In the Gospel of John, Jesus asks Peter three consecutive times if Peter loves him (John 21:15–19, NRSV). And Peter affirmatively responded in all those instances. What amazes us is what Jesus demands from Peter as an empirical proof of his confessed love for him. Jesus never asked Peter for personal favor. Rather, on three occasions, Jesus asked Peter to feed and take care of his people. Christian faith is not supposed to celebrate with God in isolated worship, whether in a private cloister or in a luxurious auditorium, but to be experienced outside in the context of community. Egalitarian community, or a democratic space, is the context where freedom is utilized to promote social justice, where individuality is expressed in the embrace of hospitality and generosity, and where we intentionally create political and social conditions that will promote and support the flourishing of everyone's life.

BIBLIOGRAPHY

Bauman, Zygmunt. *Consuming Life*. Cambridge, UK: Polity Press, 2007.
———. *Globalization: The Human Consequences*. Cambridge, UK: Polity Press, 1998.

———. *Intimations of Postmodernity*. London: Routledge, 1992.
———. *Liquid Love: On the Frailty of Human Bonds*. Cambridge, UK: Polity Press, 2003.
———. *Work, Consumerism, and the New Poor*, 2nd ed. England: Open University Press, 2005.
Bautista, Lorenzo. "The Church in the Philippines." In *Church and Asia Today: Challenges and Opportunities*. Edited by Saphir Athyal. Singapore: Asia Lausanne Committee for World Evangelization, 1996.
Bladel, James. "Against Polanyi-centrism: Hayek and the Re-emergence of 'Spontaneous Order.'" *Quarterly Journal of Austrian Economics* 8, no. 4 (Winter 2005). Accessed March 7, 2018, from https://mises.org/library/against-polanyi-centrism-hayek-and-re-emergence-spontaneous-order.
Brewer, Talbot. "Reflections on the Cultural Commons." In *Being Human in a Consumer Society: Classical and Contemporary Social Theory*. Edited by Alejandro Nestor Garcia Martinez. Farnham, UK: Ashgate, 2015.
Butler, Judith. *Frames of War: When Is Life Grievable?* New York: Verso, 2009.
Cavanaugh, William T. *Being Consumed: Economics and Christian Desire*. Grand Rapids, MI: Wm. B. Eerdmans, 2008.
Dasgupta, Samir. "Introduction: A Reflection on Politics of Globalization and Textual Entrails." In *Politics of Globalization*. Edited by Samir Dasgupta and Jan Nederveen Pieterse. India: Sage, 2009.
Friedman, Milton. *Capitalism and Freedom*. Chicago: The University of Chicago Press, 1962.
Friedman, Milton, and Rose Friedman. *Free to Choose: A Personal Statement*. New York: Harcourt Brace Jovanovich, 1980, 1979.
Garcia-Ruiz, Pablo. "The Two Faces of Consumerism: When Things Make US (In)Human." In *Being Human in a Consumer Society*. Edited by Alejandro Nestor Garcia Martinez. Farnham, UK: Ashgate, 2015.
Gauthier, Francois Linda Woodhead, and Tuomas Martikainen. "Introduction: Consumerism and the Ethos of Consumer Society." In *Religion in Consumer Society: Brands, Consumers and Markets*. Edited by Francois Gauthier and Tuomas Martikainen. Farnham, UK: Ashgate, 2003.
Harvey, David. *A Brief History of Neoliberalism*. New York: Oxford University Press, 2005.
Hayek, Friedrich A. *The Constitution of Liberty*. Chicago: The University of Chicago Press, 1960.
———. *The Road to Serfdom*. New York: George Routledge and Sons, 1944.
Leach, William. *Land of Desire: Merchants, Power and the Rise of a New American Culture*. New York: Vintage Books, 1994.
Lenin, V. I. *State and Revolution*. Chicago, IL: Haymarket Books, 2014.
Levinas, Emmanuel. *Totality and Infinity: An Essay on Exteriority*. Translated by Alphonso Lingis. Pittsburgh, PA: Duquesne University Press, 1969.
Miles, Steven. *Consumerism as a Way of Life*. London: Sage, 1998.
Montemaggi, Francesca E. S. "Shopping for a Church? Choice and Commitment in Religious Behavior." In *Religion in Consumer Society: Brands, Consumers and Markets*. Edited by Francois Gauthier and Tuomas Martikainen. Farnham, UK: Ashgate, 2003.
Rawls, John. *A Theory of Justice*, rev. ed. Cambridge, MA: Belknap, 1999.
Ritzer, George. "The Dehumanized Consumer: Does the Prosumer Offer Some Hope?" In *Being Human in a Consumer Society: Classical and Contemporary Social Theory*. Edited by Alejandro Nestor Garcia Martinez. Farnham, UK: Ashgate, 2015.
———. *Globalization: The Essentials*. London: John Wiley and Sons, 2011.
Robinson, William I. "Global Capitalism Theory and the Emergence of Transnational Elites," UNU-WIDER (2009): 1. Accessed from http://wider-unu.edu/publications/working-papers/2010/en_GB/wp2010-02/.
Rorty, Richard. *Contingency, Irony, and Solidarity*. New York: Cambridge University Press, 1989.
Sassatelli, Roberta. *Consumer Culture: History, Theory and Politics*. London: Sage, 2007.

Sklair, Leslie. "The Transnational Capitalist Class and the Politics of Globalization." In *Politics of Globalization*. Edited by Samir Dasgupta and Jan Nederveen Pieterse. Newbury Park, CA: Sage, 2009.

Smart, Barry. *Consumer Society: Critical Issues and Environmental Consequences*. London, UK: Sage, 2010.

Taylor, Charles. *Modern Social Imaginaries*. Durham, NC: Duke University Press, 2004.

———. *Varieties of Religion Today: William James Revisited*. Cambridge, MA: Harvard University Press, 2002.

Turner, Bryan S. "Post-Secular Society: Consumerism and Democratization of Religion." In *The Post-Secular in Question*. Edited by Philip Gorski et al. New York: New York University Press, 2012.

Weber, Max. *The Protestant Ethic and the Spirit of Capitalism*. Translated by Talcott Parsons. Los Angeles, CA: Roxbury, 1996.

NOTES

1. Zygmunt Bauman, *Liquid Love: On the Frailty of Human Bonds* (Cambridge, UK: Polity Press, 2003), 156.
2. Zygmunt Bauman, *Globalization: The Human Consequences* (Cambridge, UK: Polity, 1998), 1.
3. Samir Dasgupta, "Introduction: A Reflection on Politics of Globalization and Textual Entrails," in *Politics of Globalization*, ed. Samir Dasgupta and Jan Nederveen Pieterse (India: Sage, 2009), 1.
4. William I. Robinson, "Global Capitalism Theory and the Emergence of Transnational Elites," UNU-WIDER (2009), 1. http://wider-unu.edu/publications/working-papers/2010/en_GB/wp2010-02/.
5. Max Weber, *The Protestant Ethic and the Spirit of Capitalism*, trans. Talcott Parsons (Los Angeles, California, Roxbury Publishing Company, 1996), 181.
6. Generic *globalization* according to Leslie Sklair is defined by four characteristics such as electronic revolution, postcolonial revolution, creation of transnational social space, and cosmopolitanism. See Leslie Sklair, "The Transnational Capitalist Class and the Politics of Globalization," in *Politics of Globalization*, ed. Samir Dasgupta and Jan Nederveen Pieterse (Newbury Park, CA: Sage), 82.
7. Bauman, *Globalization*, 2.
8. Bauman, *Globalization*, 19.
9. Bauman, *Globalization*, 2.
10. Milton Friedman, *Capitalism and Freedom* (Chicago: The University of Chicago Press, 1962), 9.
11. Friedrich A. Hayek, *The Constitution of Liberty* (Chicago: The University of Chicago Press, 1960), 16, 17.
12. Friedman, *Capitalism and Freedom*, 12.
13. We can notice in the earlier quotation from Milton Friedman that he included "the family" as a qualifier to potentially widen the range covered by freedom from the individual alone to the small unit of the family. But Hayek constrained this to the individual.
14. Friedrich A. Hayek, *The Road to Serfdom* (New York: George Routledge and Sons, 1944), 62, 63.
15. Friedman, *Capitalism and Freedom*, 13.
16. David Harvey, *A Brief History of Neoliberalism* (New York: Oxford University Press, 2005), 7.
17. George Ritzer, *Globalization: The Essentials* (London: John Wiley and Sons, 2011), 41.
18. Hayek, *Road to Serfdom*, 63.
19. Hayek, *Road to Serfdom*, 62, 63.
20. Zygmunt Bauman, *Consuming Life* (Cambridge: Polity Press, 2007), 25.
21. Barry Smart, *Consumer Society: Critical Issues and Environmental Consequences* (London: Sage, 2010), 4.

22. Steven Miles, *Consumerism as a Way of Life* (London: Sage Publication, 1998), 4; Smart, *Consumer Society*, 5.
23. Zygmunt Bauman, *Work, Consumerism, and the New Poor*, 2nd ed. (London: Open University Press, 2005), 24.
24. Bauman, *Consuming Life*, 28.
25. Italics in the original. Bauman, *Consuming Life*, 28.
26. Francois Gautheir, Linda Woodhead and Tuomas Martikainen, "Introduction: Consumerism and the Ethos of Consumer Society," in *Religion in Consumer Society: Brands, Consumers and Markets*, ed. Francois Gautheir and Tuomas Martikainen (Farnham: Ashgate, 2003), 4.
27. Charles Taylor, *Modern Social Imaginaries* (Durham, NC: Duke University Press, 2004), 23.
28. Roberta Sassatelli advocates a nuanced approach in constructing the historical emergence of consumer society. Instead of a linear historical development or tracing the various stages of development, she advocates "an imagery of *increasing but uneven stratification*, whereby a variety of ongoing processes, among different sections of the population in different places and times, are piled one on another, partly displacing previous trends, partly resuming them." Italics in the original. Roberta Sassatelli, *Consumer Culture: History, Theory and Politics* (London: Sage, 2007), 43.
29. William Leach, *Land of Desire: Merchants, Power and the Rise of a New American Culture* (New York: Vintage Books, 1994), 3–4.
30. Bauman, *Consuming Life*, 31.
31. Talbot Brewer, "Reflections on the Cultural Commons," in *Being Human in a Consumer Society*, ed. Alejandro Nestor Garcia Martinez (Farnham, UK: Ashgate, 2015), 132.
32. Brewer, Reflections on the Cultural Commons," 132.
33. Brewer, "Reflections on the Cultural Commons," 132.
34. Leach, *Land of Desire*, 7.
35. Bauman, *Consuming Life*, 57.
36. Bauman, *Globalization*, 50.
37. Bauman, *Globalization*, 51–52.
38. Bauman, *Globalization*, 52. Italics in the original.
39. Sassatelli, *Consumer Culture*, 91.
40. George Ritzer, "The Dehumanized Consumer: Does the Prosumer Offer Some Hope?," in *Being Human in a Consumer Society*, ed. Alejandro Nestor Garcia Martinez (Farnham, UK: Ashgate, 2015), 29–31.
41. Pablo Garcia-Ruiz, "The Two Faces of Consumerism: When Things Make US (In)Human," in *Being Human in a Consumer Society*, ed. Alejandro Nestor Garcia Martinez (Farnham, UK: Ashgate, 2015), 70.
42. Smart, *Consumer Society*, 40.
43. Bauman, *Consuming Life*, 12. Italics in the original.
44. George Ritzer, "The Dehumanized Consumer," 29–31.
45. Gautheir et al., "Introduction," 13; Zygmunt Bauman, *Intimations of Postmodernity* (London: Routledge, 1992), 223.
46. Sassatelli, *Consumer Culture*, 108.
47. Gautheir et al., "Introduction," 13
48. Gautheir et al., "Introduction," 14.
49. Taylor, *Sources of the Self*, 3.
50. Taylor, *Ethics of Authenticity*, 4.
51. Charles Taylor, *Varieties of Religion Today: William James Revisited* (Cambridge, MA: Harvard University Press, 2002), 79–80.
52. William T. Cavanaugh, *Being Consumed: Economics and Christian Desire* (Grand Rapids, MI: Wm. B. Eerdmans, 2008), 35.
53. Cavanaugh, *Being Consumed*, 47.
54. Bauman, *Intimations of Postmodernity*, 49.
55. Miles, *Consumerism*, 1.

56. Lorenzo Bautista, "The Church in the Philippines," in *Church and Asia Today: Challenges and Opportunities*, ed. Saphir Athyal (Singapore: Asia Lausanne Committee for World Evangelization, 1996), 175–202.

57. Bryan S. Turner, "Post-Secular Society: Consumerism and Democratization of Religion," in *The Post-Secular in Question*, ed. Philip Gorski et al. (New York: New York University Press), 143.

58. See Turner, "The Post-Secular Society," 143.

59. The distinction is made between "formal commodification" and "substantial commodification." The former is the process of marketing consumer goods to consumers, while the latter makes a value judgment, usually a decline, in religious life. Francesca E.S. Montemaggi, "Shopping for a Church? Choice and Commitment in Religious Behavior," in *Religion in Consumer Society*, ed. Gautheir et al. 110.

60. Milton Friedman and Rose Friedman, *Free to Choose: A Personal Statement* (New York: Harcourt Brace Jovanovich, 1980, 1979), 1, 2.

61. James Bladel, "Against Polanyi-centrism: Hayek and the Re-emergence of 'Spontaneous Order,'" *Quarterly Journal of Austrian Economics* 8, no. 4 (Winter 2005). Accessed March 7, 2018, from https://mises.org/library/against-polanyi-centrism-hayek-and-re-emergence-spontaneous-order.

62. Friedman, *Capitalism and Freedom*, 13.

63. John Rawls, *A Theory of Justice*, rev. ed. (Cambridge, MA: Belknap, 1999), 4.

64. Peter S. Goodman, *A Fresh Look at the Apostle of Free Markets*. New York Times, 13 April 2008, quoted in George Ritzer, *Globalization: The Essentials*, 40.

65. V. I. Lenin, *State and Revolution* (Chicago, IL: Haymarket, 2014), 41–43.

66. Richard Rorty, *Contingency, Irony, and Solidarity* (New York: Cambridge University Press, 1989), 189–98.

67. Judith Butler, *Frames of War: When Is Life Grievable?* (New York: Verso, 2009), 33–62.

68. Emmanuel Levinas, *Totality and Infinity: An Essay on Exteriority*, trans. Alphonso Lingis (Pittsburgh, PA: Duquesne University Press, 1969), 83.

69. Ibid., 84.

Chapter 8

On Not Answering the Public Cry for Justice

The Silence of the Ethiopian Evangelical Churches in the Context of National Crisis

Wondimu Legesse Sonessa

The silence of churches in the face of a political dispute that causes the loss of a countless number of irreplaceable lives and exposes thousands of citizens to oppression, injustice, and human rights violation must be interrupted because silence in the face of injustice is a speech act that speaks volumes. Silence in such situations is all too often evidence for a hidden integration of church and state, in which compliance with government policies requires the church to exist in society in its false version. This identity crisis gradually leads not only to a confusion of the purpose of existence, but also to a loss of moral integrity, missional identity, and spiritual authority as a divine institution. When this unofficial marriage makes the church a mere political power at the expense of its mission and reputation, a demand for divorce is justifiable. The church needs to break the silence and take action that leads to justice and peace. In this article, I will reflect on the importance of rediscovering the purpose of existence of a Christian church in a nation that suffers from a political instability characterized by injustice and human rights violation. In this paper, I will first present the church as the frontline of an army storming the gates of hell, after which I will discuss Christian presence in the context of religious nationalism and ethnic federalism, in order to, finally, reclaim the church's forfeited dynamic presence (as exemplified by twentieth-century martyrs) in society.

Chapter 8

THE CHURCH AS THE FRONTLINE OF AN ARMY SET OUT AGAINST THE GATES OF HELL

It may be useful to look at what Martin Luther thought about the church and society hand in hand with the biblical view of the church. The church is metaphorically described as the body of Christ (Ephesians 5:23) in the New Testament. The church is founded on the divine revelation that Christ is "the Son of the living God" (Mat 16:16); on the confession that he is the true God, the promised King, and the faithful High Priest "of the good things that have come"; who entered once for all into the Holy Place and obtained eternal redemption with the sacrifice of his own blood through which he purifies "our conscience from dead works to worship the living God" (Hebrews 9:11–14).

The church is not established on the knowledge of popular priests, bishops, theologians, and leaders with a perfectionist view and blameless personality. Neither can conventions nor the constitution they design be regarded as a foundation for the church. These all are humans who are always inclined to sin and make mistakes. As human beings born of flesh and blood, they are not immune to a guilty conscience from which they need to be healed through seeking genuine forgiveness. It is only faith, not reason, in the divine revelation, which Jesus confirms for Peter saying, "[F]lesh and blood has not revealed this to you, but my Father in heaven" (Mat 16:17) that leads them to understanding and new life. Thus Martin Luther stated, "And let such a person know that he possesses the revelation of the Father from heaven and that is truly a Christian, blessed and saved from sin, death, and hell."[1] In short, none of these people is the owner of the church, but called and appointed to serve on behalf of the church and in the name of Christ standing in the grace of the living God who justifies sinners. Outside God's gift of grace, all of them have the potential to turn back to their old weakness, ungodliness, and enmity against God.

Luther criticizes the Roman pontiffs for "leaping right over" Peter's faith and confession and seizing the keys, which they have distorted and misinterpreted with an intention to make themselves the successors of Peter. Alluding to 1 Timothy 1:5, he describes the true successors of Peter as those who "possess faith and the confession of the Christ, the Son of the living God, just as the Father in heaven reveals it, that is, in truth, as the Holy Spirit teaches through a faith unfeigned."[2]

Jesus promised, "I will build my church, and the gates of Hades will not prevail against it" (Mat 16:18). Luther understands Jesus's word, "My Church," as pointing to something beyond this temporal life. It is about the future life and the kingdom of heaven. Thus the church Jesus builds is not a temporal kingdom that contends with any earthly empire. It is rather a heavenly body contending with the gates of hell. This puts it in a continuous battle with the power of Satan and the kingdom of sin and death, which Luther describes as the "real enemies of the church."[3] However, the church should not be misunderstood as having no obligation to the present life. Luther describes the church as "the front line of an army" in a society's struggle against sin and evil. To put in his words,

> We must therefore take note here that Christ is using clear words in defining His Church: She is the front line of an army, a warrior heroine, arrayed [Song 6:4] against the very gates of hell, that is, against the trials of sin, death, and hell.... Therefore, the church fights, conquers, triumphs, and rules against sin, death, and the author and lord of them both, the devil, or against the gates of hell—just as Christ promises in this passage.[4]

Luther clearly indicates who the church must fight against. But medieval Christianity, not taking the boundary that exists between religion and politics seriously, went through challenging experiences characterized by the Crusades, the Inquisition, and general intolerance. The competition for political and religious power (to which social, cultural, and economic interests were attached) marked public life of the Middle Ages and Christian life of the Middle Ages (c. 500–1500). It is also important to note that as a result of many bishops becoming feudal lords in pursuit of wealth and political privileges, which involved them in constant and complicated intrigues and warfare, the church became a political power at the expense of its moral and spiritual authority.[5]

The identity crisis of the medieval church in which the political and the religious collapse into each other is a recurring problem. Commenting on the situation in South America in the late 1970s and early 1980s, Romero says "The church is not an opposition party. The church is a force of God in the people, a force of inspiration so that the people may forge their own destiny. The church does not want to impose political or social systems. It must not. That is not its field of competence. But the church calls for the freedom of peoples."[6] The church has to present itself to a society among which it is established as a light that shines in the darkness and the voice for the voiceless. It has to proclaim the gospel of freedom whereby it can resist the power of darkness and the forces of evil enslaving society. The church is not alone, but fights this battle alongside Christ who has already launched the war against the power of devil, when it faithfully resists the forces of evil, injustice, and violation of human rights. Either ignoring this battle or engaging in a selfish endeavor causes the church to have an identity crisis.

The church is neither a political system set by a state nor a mere national institution that begs its freedom from a state to do its work. Just as it is free to work with the government for the common good of the citizens, it can also resist any attempt of the state to get rid of faith and Christian values from the land. Christian love is one among the values the church extends to all people.

As Oscar Romero rightly argues, "Christian love goes beyond all categories of regimes and systems. The church is not identified with any political system. The church cannot identify itself with any political organization."[7] Just as the church finds itself in this world by the secret of Christ's incarnation, it also stands above all systems of the society by the power of mystery of His resurrection and ascension. This indicates the limits of the involvement of the church and state in each other's affairs.

Gudina Tumsa, Ethiopian theologian and church leader in the 1960s and 1970s, views the church from a functional standpoint rather than an institutional one. What makes a functional approach so significant is its motives, flexibility, and integrity. A functional approach to a society's development does not involve any lucrative engagement but focuses on ways to address people's needs and support their effort toward nation building. This approach safeguards the church against tainting the gospel with self-centeredness. A church with a functional outlook always revisits its decisions and ministry strategies to adjust to the changing sociopolitical situation, which Tumsa refers to as "the demand of the situation." What matters for this church is not preserving motives of prestige but persevering to labor alongside the needy members of the society out of Christian love to transform their life. Tumsa argues that it is against Christian integrity for the church to render any social service out of fear of the government.[8]

In summary, when the church exists among the society with its dynamic presence exhibiting its true missional goal, the power of faith will be felt in public spheres and the gates of hell of which Luther speaks will shake. For the church to be victorious over evil, the following three things are essential: maintaining and building on its foundation (faith), insisting on the proclamation of the gospel of freedom, and prioritizing its mission of spreading a genuine Christian love that exceeds all systems of the society. Let us proceed to the discussion of Christian presence in the midst of religious and political challenges.

CHRISTIAN PRESENCE IN THE CONTEXT OF RELIGIOUS NATIONALISM AND ETHNIC FEDERALISM

> [T]he Christian gospel is a two-way road. On the one hand it seeks to change the souls of men, and thereby unite them with God; on the other hand it seeks to change the environmental conditions of men so that the soul will have a chance after it is changed. Any religion that professes to be concerned with the souls of men and is not concerned with the slums that damn them, the economic conditions that strangle them, and the social conditions that cripple them is a dry-as-dust religion.[9]

Ethnic identity and religion were at the center of national issues challenging the church during the Reformation period. Speaking one language was wrongly considered as the major identification of ecclesial and national unity, which made translating the Bible into other languages unlawful. Luther's German translation of the New Testament was regarded as a big threat to the large Holy Roman Empire, for which Latin was the common language of the Bible. When the dispute over the unity of faith caused a serious division in Europe, Catholicism and Protestantism were defended by their respective adherents.[10] One thing we can learn from this is that, in general, when religion, language, and politics are handled with a lack of flexibility, they become the divisive factors that restrict the ecumenical and missional effort of the church.

Likewise, Ethiopia has gone through a long history of religious nationalism, which became a prevailing approach to the politics and citizenship for centuries. Of course, there has never been an organized movement in Ethiopia under the umbrella of religious nationalism like the ones currently taking place in some Asian countries including Myanmar, India, and Pakistan with one religious group campaigning to liberate the land from the adherents of other religions with or without a consent of the state. Nevertheless, religion and nationalism have been intertwined in Ethiopia for centuries and untangling them remains the goal to be achieved. This involves both identifying "the politicization of religion and the influence of religion on politics"[11] Although there is a significant number of citizens who are affiliated with Ethiopian traditional religions, Islam, and Protestant Christianity, most of the adherents of Ethiopian Orthodox Christianity believe and promote the view that the Ethiopian Orthodox Church (EOC) is an icon of national unity. This means that the adherents of other religions are seen as religious outsiders. Besides, given the oppressive attitude of the past imperial rulers toward Islam and other religions, it is not easy to distinguish the current political activism of some Muslims (whether living in country or abroad) from a mere religious aspiration.

The influence of religion on Ethiopian politics was more clearly seen in the way the Emperor and the clergy jointly responded to the arrival of the pioneering missionaries than was the case centuries ago. The arrival of the German missionary Petter Heyling (c. 1634) and the Swiss Samuel Gobat (c. 1830) as well as the German Johann Ludwig Krapf (c. 1837) with the intention of reviving the Ethiopian Orthodox Christianity was not successful because of the joint effort of the clergy and monarchs.[12] For example, Gustav Arén states, "Unable to move into Oromo territory proper without royal permission, Krapf submitted his plan to Sahle-Sillassé in September 1839. The monarch flatly turned him down. 'The Gallas will kill you,' he argued."[13] Birri reports that the clergy convinced King Sahle Sellassie of Shoa of the political and religious importance of preventing Europeans from proceeding to the central part of the country. As a result, in 1842, he gave orders at the coast to prevent missionaries, including Carl Wilhelm Isenberg and Johann Ludwig Krapf, from reentering the kingdom. As Birri states, "The king discouraged him [Krapf] by saying that the Oromo would kill him if he were granted permission to go. . . . The Orthodox priests influenced the people to rise in protest against the return of the missionaries."[14] This was a deliberate attempt to prevent mission to the Oromo people, which is a clear result of religious nationalism.

Later, modern Ethiopia came into existence with the victory over the Italians at the battle of Aduwa in 1896 under the rule of Emperor Menelik II (1889–1913), who integrated his mission of unification with the spreading of Ethiopian Orthodox Christianity. Emperor Haile Selassie (1892–1975) not only maintained Menelik's achievements until 1974, but also fostered the domination of the Amhara ethnic group under the umbrella of the Ethiopian Orthodox Christianity as a dominant religious force. Nation and religion were viewed as identical, as one had to be Amhara and the member of EOC to be recognized as a citizen. Obligatory use of Amharic, taking an Amharic name at baptism, and banning the public use of any other language were among the means of "Amaharization."[15] Although there was openness for missionaries during this period, the Protestant missions were considered a potential threat to the integrity of the EOC. As Hammerschidt, Uhlig, and Bonk testify, "Church and state have traditionally been closely intertwined in Christian Ethiopia, the ruler regarding himself as the defender of faith."[16] This way, religious nationalism exposed the people of the land to religious and political oppression.

Later, after the return of missionaries during the Italian invasion, the evangelical churches experienced a great revival movement. In the west, the Evangelical pioneers of the Ethiopian Evangelical Church Mekane Yesus (EECMY) could cross the barriers of ethnicity, status, regionalism, and denominationalism. Qes Gebre-Ewostateos (from Eritrea) and Qes Badma Yalew (from Gojjam in North Ethiopia) took the initiative to reach the people in their own language and started to learn Afaan Oromoo to use it in reading the Scripture for worship in Bojji Mariam Church (the then-Orthodox Church in west Wollega).[17] Wilfred and Eleanor Bockelman claim that it was the lay movement that took place in the west, which led to the beginning of the church, saying, "During the years 1946–1948 a wider spiritual awakening took place, and it resulted in the formation of congregations."[18] Staffan Grenstedt states in reference to the Kambata/Hadiya evangelical churches in the south that the reason for this revival could be the initiative the local evangelists had taken to witness for Christ in the people's local language. Ethnic identity was not seen as a divisive element, as the people were crossing the border to Walayita and achieving the conversion of many to Evangelical Christianity. Consequently, the formerly hostile ethnic groups started to worship together after receiving the gospel of reconciliation.[19] All this has caused a remarkable disruption to the influence of religious nationalism in society as people could boldly confess their Christian faith without any essential attachment to the EOC. These practices should be referred to as a model for addressing the imbalance between theology and ethnicity, even in the other Ethiopian Evangelical churches.

Political and cultural oppression continued during the time of the military government ruled by Mengistu Hailemariam (1974–1991). Religious nationalism continued as a recessive trait hibernating under the layer of new socialist ideology. The confiscation of the property of the Ethiopian Evangelical church Mekane Yesus (including the radio station known as Radio Voice of the Gospel, which was mainly sponsored by the Lutheran World Federation and serving millions in Africa and Southeast Asia from 1957–1977), signified a denial not only of religious freedom but also of the ecumenical presence in Ethiopia.[20] With the separation of church and state under the current Ethiopian government, the church has taken advantage of religious freedom and reclaimed most of its properties, continuing to render social services to society, although the goal of reclaiming its dynamic presence in the political life of the country remains to be achieved.

However, despite this legacy of the past, there is currently a tendency to be attracted toward regionalism at the expense of the longstanding sense of belonging and unity among believers. This unity, which continued to exist during imperial rule and the severe persecution by the communist regime, is being threatened today.[21] In order not to fall prey to disunity, the church needs to seek ways of maintaining the balance between the identity of believers as a spiritual community and their loyalty to their national heritage as good citizens before it is too late.

If there is a lesson to be learned from the centuries-long intertwined history of religion and nationalism in Ethiopia, the following three points are noteworthy. (1) The subordination of the church led to the imbalanced and egotistic use of both the religious and ethnopolitical powers under imperial rule. (2) The denial of religious freedom under the military regime caused the church to develop a passive attitude toward an unjust political system. (3) The church's forfeiting a significant dynamic presence in the society at present indicates that it is satisfied with freedom to gather for worship in disregard of its public theological existence. If theologians in Ethiopia continue to be irresponsive to this issue, we will fail to balance the present situation and right the past history of Christianity. Of course, the church had a clear statement in its constitution that allowed mutual recognition and respect for ethnic identity and cultural values even before the government started to do so. However, I believe that, in addition to having a right constitution, a Christian presence in contemporary Ethiopia needs to be expressed by the church through interpretive and integrative engagement in the practical life of society.

COMMITMENT TO THE WORD VERSUS OBLIGATION TO SOCIAL JUSTICE

To begin with the words of Henri J. M. Nouwen, who wrote the foreword to Oscar Romero's *The Church Is All of You*,

> A commitment to the word requires a commitment to history. Such a commitment challenges us to recognize, criticize, and change the unjust structures of a society that causes suffering. Such a commitment leads to conflicts and persecutions. Such a commitment can even ask of us that we give everything, even our life, for the cause of justice and peace.[22]

The religious freedom that has been exercised in Ethiopia for nearly three decades has not been able to affect the long-standing mentality of religious nationalism. In this section, I will analyze the Ethiopian evangelical churches' commitment to the Word and the wellbeing of the society in terms of the pattern of church-state relations under the Ethiopian People's Revolutionary Democratic Front, which claimed to establish a democratic government in 1991.

RELIGIOUS FREEDOM OR CONSTITUTIONALLY VESTED MUTUAL EXCLUSIVITY?

The remarkable political change following the downfall of the Dergue regime helped all Ethiopians to taste equal freedom and justice. The current federal government encourages the unity that recognizes diversity rather than enforcing it by weapons. Regarding religious matters, the government claims a liberal stand. This separation of state and religion, which is clearly recorded in the constitution under Article 11, is composed of three points: "[1] State and religion are separate. [2] There is no state religion. [3] The state shall not interfere in religious matters and religion shall not interfere in state affairs."[23] There was a glimpse of hope to eliminate the fabrics of religious nationalism from the land, which later proved to be unachievable because of its recessive gene that gradually revived in the current political system. The third point is often misunderstood as meaning there should be "a wall of separation between church and state,"[24] while what Ethiopians have been longing for was a proper relation between government and religion that allows a proper role of religion in public life of the society rather than a strict neutrality between faith and politics. Speaking of the separation of state and religion in Ethiopia based on the country's constitutional law often causes the tension between the need for institutional separation and the mutual exclusivity, which can be described as the tension between impartiality and noninvolvement.

In addition to the separation of church and state, freedom of worship, freedom of press (which currently seems questionable), and self-governance make the rule different from those before it. The human and democratic rights of the citizens are indicated under Article 10 of the constitution in unambiguous words, as follows: "[1] Human rights and freedoms, emanating from the nature of mankind, are inviolable and inalienable. [2] Human and democratic rights of citizens and peoples shall be respected."[25] The introduction of ethnic federalism has further modified the process of defining ethnic identity. This has enabled the regional states to work for the socioeconomic development of their region including conducting education in the language of their choice, which is a tremendous change in Ethiopian history.[26] However, because of the longstanding impact of religious nationalism, the Ethiopian evangelical churches are yet to recover from their passive attitude toward politics. They have exhibited a lack of commitment to the Word by not discharging their obligation to social justice. Consequently, they are too slow to use the existence of the seed of democracy (Constitution) and speak up in favor of democracy and human flourishing.

The church as an independent entity, has authority to hold the government accountable to its claims and promises to establish a democratic rule. When the government traumatizes its people in demand of uncritical submission to all decisions, it is the church's role to challenge the system by bringing to attention the significance of raising an assertive and visionary generation. Ethiopia needs a generation of pastors who, like Martin Luther King Jr., step forward to announce their indebtedness to history, saying, "I can't stop now. History has thrust upon me a responsibility from which I cannot turn away."[27]

In this regard, the Evangelical churches face sharp criticism for neglecting the question of social justice notwithstanding their full awareness of the government-led campaign on poverty, which includes human rights violations both in agricultural and industrial aspects. This effort has been criticized for exposing the country to a global land-grab. Recent research done by The Oakland Institute in the United States reveals that Ethiopia is one of the preferred destinations for agricultural investment in Africa, which transferred 3,619,509 hectares of land to domestic investors, state-owned enterprises, and foreign companies (including Indian agro-enterprise) between 2008 and 2011. Accordingly, the existing formal and informal rights to land are neither respected nor recognized, which is a huge obstacle to a progress toward democracy. As it is reported in this study, "Because there is no community consultation or independent media reporting, there is little knowledge of land deals at the local level, and communities often only find out that the land has been given to investors when the bulldozers or workers show up to clear the land."[28] The government claims that "these investments will allow for much[-]needed foreign currency to enter into the economy and will contribute to long-term food security through the transfer of technology to small-scale farmers."[29] However, in this process, the local farmers are forced to leave the area chosen for investment.

In her work on the conditions for flourishing human development, Martha Nussbaum has identified a number of "capabilities" that are the conditions of possibility for healthy human development. One of these is the capability to have control over one's material environment.[30] In this case the control of the land and moveable properties is compromised for the sake of the gross domestic product. The poor farmers do not have the same property rights as with the rich investors. Here is where the church misses the opportunity to be a voice for the voiceless in response to the Word of God, which commands to "[s]peak out for those who cannot speak, for the rights of all the destitute . . . defend the rights of the poor and needy" (Proverbs 31:8–9). God summons the faithful ones to "seek justice, rescue the oppressed, defend the orphan, [and] plead for the widow" (Isaiah 1:17).

Although the church-state relation doesn't allow the church to propose a better strategy toward the country's economic development, that cannot be a good excuse for the church to go with the flow. Instead, it must slow down to understand why members of the Oromo, one of the major ethnic groups in Ethiopia from all walks of life have been protesting unanimously since 2015. After a centuries-long tolerance, they now learn that it is their responsibility to lift themselves by their own bootstraps and have started to rally against the government's pseudo economic development policies. Their concern can be likened with King's description of African Americans' determination to boycott the Montgomery, Alabama, city bus system in 1955, saying, "[I]t is ultimately more honorable to walk the streets in dignity than to ride the buses in humiliation. . . . Our concern would not be to put the bus company out of business, but to put justice in business."[31] In a similar vein, the *Qeerroo* (Oromo youth) prefer to die in the streets of the Ethiopian cities and villages while protesting the abusive economic development project and speaking up for justice, equality, and human rights.

Gudina Tumsa set us a good example when he challenged even the Western donors of his time to take into account the values that make local people's lives meaningful as well as the socioeconomic situation in Ethiopia and its impact on the church before designing a project for the development of society. For him, "man is not only the suffering creature who needs help but . . . also the most important development agent."[32] Today, Ethiopia needs a joint effort of political analysts and theologians, who boldly exercise the freedom of critiquing the current government's economic-oriented ideology and the mentality of religious nationalism, which both promote injustice and ethnic inequality. There is a lot to reintegrate into the church's life and ministry from the legacy of Tumsa as well as another twentieth-century martyr, Dietrich Bonhoeffer, whose thought I will interact with later in this chapter.

Religious freedom entails so much more than only freedom to preach the gospel. As Pastor Martin Niemoeller argues, "The [German] church was separated from the state [under Adolph Hitler], not because of religious liberty but because the state wished to get rid of the church and Christian life."[33] Adolf Hitler didn't want to restrain the church from preaching the gospel as long as it recognized him as the master of life on this world. The same is true in many African countries, particularly Ethiopia today. The churches are free to preach the gospel as long as they keep silent in the face of injustice and violation of human rights inflicted by the government. The Ethiopian churches have a "negative liberty." They are free from interference by an external entity, including the state, but are not allowed to fully use their capacity to advocate for justice and human rights. This negative freedom is often justified with reference to the constitutional article establishing the separation of church and state, which serves as a tool for a systematic marginalization of the church and its dynamic presence from society. In other words, religious freedom in Ethiopia today is a constitutionally conferred mutual exclusivity of church and state, which allows for either a passive participation of the church in the political life of society or no participation at all.

When the church neglects its dynamic presence, what follows is an identity crisis. As Martin Luther King Jr. rightly argues, "Whenever the church, consciously or unconsciously, caters to one class, it loses the spiritual force of the 'whoever will, let him come' doctrine, and is in danger of becoming little more than a social club with a thin veneer of religiosity."[34] A route to democracy demands careful discernment between religious freedom and systematic restriction of the church's role in society. The Ethiopian church should heed King's admonishment to Christians who were not willing to commit themselves to social justice, saying, "If you haven't discovered something that you will die for, you aren't fit to live."[35] The dynamism with which the Ethiopian Evangelical churches should stand among the suppressed citizens emanates from the theology of the Cross regardless of the government's attitude toward the church. Equipping pastors and theologians to confess what they believe and to reject all forms of evil in the midst of sociopolitical crisis, requires that the church in Ethiopia as a whole reclaim the quality of their theological training.

Theological schools need to give particular attention to instilling in their students a sense of indebtedness to church and society. The same God that calls them to plant churches by setting people free from the bondage of sin by the power of the Word has commissioned them to challenge the unjust and oppressive sociopolitical structure. As Nouwen articulated, "A commitment to the word requires a commitment to history. Such a commitment challenges us to recognize, criticize, and change the unjust structures of a society that causes suffering. . . . Such a commitment can even ask of us that we give everything, even our life, for the cause of justice and peace."[36] One way for the church to express its commitment to the Word and social justice is to set itself free from a centralized interpretation of social justice. To be more explicit, theologians must not express their loyalty to the federal government by keeping silent in the face of arbitrary killing and suppression of citizens in other regional states only because their own region is unaffected. This would mean that we have a "centralized theology" while living in many autonomous regional states.

RECLAIMING THE FORFEITED DYNAMIC PRESENCE: REINTEGRATING THE LEGACY OF THE TWENTIETH-CENTURY MARTYRS INTO THE ECCLESIAL AND THEOLOGICAL REALITIES IN ETHIOPIA

In this section I will draw the attention of the Ethiopian evangelical churches to the legacy of two twentieth-century martyrs, Dietrich Bonhoeffer of Germany and Gudina Tumsa of Ethiopia, to inspire them reclaim their neglected dynamic presence in contemporary society.

DIETRICH BONHOEFFER OF THE GERMAN CHURCH

The life and death of Dietrich Bonhoeffer, a German pastor and theologian, shows that a response to the call to church leadership involves a risk-taking decision. When he went through the study programs of different levels, which qualified him for the ministry in the church as a theologian and pastor, he knew that he was committing himself for the task that others did not want to undertake because of the risk it entailed.[37] This shows clearly his preparedness to respond to his call to set himself free for serving those who were suffering persecution and marginalization by the Nazi government of Germany to the point of self-sacrifice. Bonhoeffer faced boldly the abrupt and tragic ending of his earthly life in the hands of the Nazi soldiers on April 9, 1945, whereby he followed in the suffering and death of Jesus Christ on the cross for the sin of the world. Edwin Robertson in his *Bonhoeffer's Legacy* rightly says, "God's people are to be a blessing, to bring light to a world of darkness, not by conquest, but by suffering."[38]

This legacy of Bonhoeffer was embodied again in the life of the late Reverend Gudina Tumsa of the EECMY in response to the atheist ideology of the socialist regime led by Mengistu Hailemariam (1974–1991). Tumsa challenged Mengistu's rule, which outlawed preaching the gospel, and his legacy exemplifies the dynamic presence of the church in the face of severe persecution. To reclaim this now-forfeited dynamic presence in society, the Ethiopian evangelical churches need to start afresh thinking how Bonhoeffer's and Tumsa's faithfulness to their respective callings can shape contemporary African pastors' commitment to the ecclesial and theological realities in their context.

The context for ethics of Bonhoeffer was marked by Hitler's naïve ambition to build a strong Germany by means of a superior German race, which could not be fulfilled without getting rid of the Jewish community that was considered as a national threat. Bonhoeffer, who interpreted the attack on the Jews as an attack on God, was very much disappointed by the church's failure to be a voice for the voiceless. He criticizes the church as becoming a "religious society," which was fighting for preserving itself rather than for the salvation of the world, whereby it ceased to be the church of God in the world.[39] As we can see later in this paper, Tumsa took similar steps in Ethiopia with the exception of participation in a plot to overthrow the government like Bonhoeffer did. Today, it is not the church but the *Qeerroo* (Oromo youth) and *Fanno* (the Amhara youth) who are publicly protesting a political system that endorses social injustice and arbitrary killings. When the *Fanno* of the Amhara regional state were attacked, the *Qeerroo* of the Oromia regional state said, "Your blood is our blood," and the *Fanno* responded likewise. However, the church failed to exhibit its dynamic presence by condemning the attack on the Amhara and Oromo as an attack on God. The silence of the Ethiopian Evangelical churches in times of national crisis puts into question the capability of the currently mushrooming theological colleges and seminaries to prepare assertive, critical, and risk-taking pastors and theologians. In the past, seminaries instilled in students of theology a commitment to the Word and a faith-based, self-giving involvement in the society. Today, it seems that theology is the safest field that one could study to avoid being contaminated with the things that one thinks to be purely secular, particularly politics. This misunderstanding has resulted in a decontextualized Christianity.

Piet Meiring, in his article "Bonhoeffer in South Africa," asserts that it is possible to argue that Dietrich Bonhoeffer played a greater role than any other European theologian in the struggle against apartheid. Bonhoeffer's thought, as can be summarized with the five basic principles in his teaching with regard to the public realm, namely, confessing Christ here and now; putting a spoke in the wheel of the systems of oppressive government; learning to see things from below, that is, from the perspective of the oppressed; acknowledging our guilt; and becoming a church for others; is very relevant to the churches in Africa and beyond.[40] This indicates that Bonhoeffer's legacy contains much that is worthy of imitation by African Christians and church leaders today. In the light of Bonhoeffer's basic principles of the church's involvement in a society, the voice of the Ethiopian evangelical churches is missing in Ethiopian society, except where the church participates in reduction of poverty and mediates reconciliation in times of conflicts. A passive interaction with the State is apparent from the silence of the church in the context of public cry for democracy and human development. Reclaiming the church's dynamic presence in society requires of Ethiopian theologians to pay attention to four aspects of Bonhoeffer's legacy as illustrated next with regard to Bonhoeffer's influence in the ecclesial and theological realities in South Africa.

Firstly, Bonhoeffer's call to the church in Germany to *confess its guilt and the guilt of the nation* is highly significant in the context of the churches in Africa. The South African Council of Churches has decided that the church should confess its guilt in regard to racism, apartheid and oppression.[41] John De Gruchy has written a paper that examines the meaning of confessing guilt in the Christian tradition and its significance in South Africa today, as well as whether it is needed, and what it should include. He found it important to study the experience of the Confessing Church in Germany whereby he reflected on Bonhoeffer's insights as someone for whom the confession of guilt was of vital importance.[42] If there is a corrective turn by Ethiopian theologians to the right source at this time of national crisis, it is to the legacy of Bonhoeffer and the Confessing Church in Germany, whose past experience gives an unfading lesson beyond its own contextual and historical boundaries. Noninvolvement does not make a church the innocent one.

Secondly, Bonhoeffer's *life, thought, and faithfulness to his vocation* has a strong positive influence on African theology as well. In his book, *Bonhoeffer and South Africa*, de Gruchy demonstrated that some South African theologians have discovered the relevance of the life and thought of Bonhoeffer in the context of Nazism to Christians' complicity in apartheid. He argues that the paradigm shift in Bonhoeffer's life as determined by his identification with those who are powerless (the Jews) and in neglect of his aristocratic heritage summons South African Christians to set themselves free for the victims of apartheid.[43] In his *Life Together*, Bonhoeffer argues that life together, which he describes as the gift of grace for Christian life, is important for Christians to strengthen each other and to embody Christ's presence in this world in the form of community.[44] Appropriating this for our context would help the African churches to be "the church for others." Bonhoeffer's concern for the future of the church and how the next generation ought to live as witnesses of the gospel of Jesus Christ is what Ethiopian theologians gain from his thought and faithfulness to his vocation. It is time for the church to start thinking about the most practical way in which the legacy of those who gave their life for the cause of the Gospel (Gudina Tumsa, Michael Qana'aa, and others) is to shape a beloved community.

Thirdly, Bonhoeffer's view of *the church as the responsible body placed by God in this world* plays an important role in envisioning God's acting in history, provided that African theologians properly grasp the political dimension of his thought. De Gruchy, interpreting his political dimension in the context of the church in South Africa, which he describes as standing at a turning point in history, states, "The church is the first to feel the disturbing tremors of God's work in history in order that it might be renewed and become a sign of hope for the world. If the church can discern the kingdom of God . . . then it may well begin to be an instrument of his justice and peace, and a sign of hope."[45] This implies that the church should not consider itself as otherworldly institution unaffected by sociopolitical disorder. Instead, feeling the pain of those who are being oppressed and challenging the government with questions of justice and truth would make the church the community that embodies Christ on earth. A church is alive only if it is a feeling and a responding church.

Finally, if the Ethiopian churches are to *reclaim their public theology*, they have to set themselves free from "state theology" and start acting in solidarity with those suffering injustice and violation of human rights. In this regard, there is a good lesson to learn from South African theologians and pastors in the context of apartheid. Walter Wink, during his April 1986 visit to South Africa, learned that the South African churches had not yet engaged in a thorough discussion of social justice.[46] However, since that time, they have shown commitment to producing a guiding document called *The Kairos Document* (submitted for publication by September of 1986) to call Christians to action in response to the challenge they were facing from the political crisis in the country. This document deals with the division of the church based on racial identity (black church and white church in the same denomination) and in doing so critiques "state theology" (theological justification of racism, capitalism, and totalitarianism) as well as a prevalent form of "church theology" (peace and reconciliation at the expense of justice—false peace and counterfeit reconciliation), the need for a prophetic theology (biblically founded—the KAIROS calls for a *return to the Bible*) and challenges the church into action (No to apartheid—God sides with the oppressed).[47] The document is ultimately a call to discover one's identity and responsibility as a church in an African nation where racism, injustice, and oppression are daily practiced. It has resulted in mobilizing the black and white Christians toward peaceful public protest. This example may inspire the Ethiopian evangelical churches to discern ways to act, with critical reflection on the meaning of their silence in the midst of massive protests and the public cry for democracy, peace, and justice.

In summary, since his death, Bonhoeffer's writings have been influential in the church worldwide. His works carry his insights and their relevance to the next generation.[48] Girma Bekele, in his book *The In-Between People*, effectively argues that Bonhoeffer has left us a legacy of love that extends beyond family, kin, ethnic group, nation, and social class; a love that loves the unlovable, embraces the despised, and forgives the unforgivable.[49] In this regard, the Ethiopian pastors and theologians may need to confess their guilt in preferring a strategy of noninvolvement with regard to the victims of social injustice. This is necessary if the church is to reclaim its reputation as a church for others. What these times require of church leaders is by far greater than mourning with or comforting those who lost their loved ones to the bullets fired by government security forces. We have an obligation to history to join hands and stand between the armed security forces and the unarmed young citizens to resist arbitrary killing. With this, let us proceed to Gudina Tumsa's influence on the ecclesial and theological realities in Ethiopia.

GUDINA TUMSA OF THE ETHIOPIAN EVANGELICAL CHURCH MEKANE YESUS

The Reverend Gudina Tumsa (1929–1979), the general secretary of the EEC-MY, was a visionary theologian during the military regime. His legacy is known to almost all members of the Mekane Yesus Church. Forums have been conducted at which papers focusing on Tumsa's contribution were presented by theologians, including expatriates who knew and worked with Tumsa. In this regard, the Gudina Tumsa Foundation has been adding a significant effort to integrate Tumsa's legacy with the life and ministry of the contemporary church. The question is whether this could lead Ethiopian Christians to self-awareness and solidarity with the victims of suppressive political system. It is time for Ethiopian evangelical Christianity to exhibit maturity through making a thoughtful and persuasive engagement in the life of Ethiopian society. However, the silence of churches in the face of the ongoing political dispute arising from oppression, injustice, and human rights violation is a clear evidence for a lack of engagement with the legacy of this twentieth-century martyr. The Evangelical churches are standing at the crossroads where they have to decide whether to break the silence and take action that leads the country to justice and peace or to maintain that silence in the midst of the current political instability at the expense of their theological and missional identity.

Tumsa's groundbreaking contribution, which has a far-reaching influence on the ecclesial and theological realities in Ethiopia, was exemplified in his early 1970s effort to integrate the church's mission of proclaiming the gospel with human development. He criticized the criteria set by donor agencies for designing projects that neglected "the question of man as an agent in the development process."[50] Those criteria limited the national church's involvement in the life of the Ethiopian nations in this regard, which was unacceptable to Tumsa, whose task, as stated by Darrell Jodock, "was to bring this young church to maturity."[51] Tumsa, therefore, argued that the EECMY was mature enough to discern its role in the land. He was of the opinion that its conscience and Christian conviction could not allow the church to accept anything less than a "maximum engagement" in the sociopolitical life of imperial Ethiopia.[52] For Tumsa, the church's full involvement would liberate all Ethiopians from "their living conditions" and create a just society only if it incorporated the preaching of the gospel of Jesus Christ with human development activities.[53] Improving the living condition of a society requires dealing simultaneously with the human situation and the problem of sinful human nature. Tumsa did not hesitate to give his life for this purpose. It is worth noting the wider and immediate contexts for his martyrdom for the cause of the gospel.

A pivotal point to the wider context was Tumsa's becoming a student at Luther Seminary from 1963–1966. This had given him access to theological resources, including the works of Dietrich Bonhoeffer, through which lens he could analyze the unjust sociopolitical structures that characterized his contemporary Ethiopian society.[54] While reflecting on the contemporary situation, Tumsa neither forgot to keep an eye on the past experience nor lost hold of the future of church and society.[55] Paul Wee states that both Dietrich Bonhoeffer and Gudina Tumsa have passed on a powerful legacy of faithfulness to the gospel of Christ to the next generation by willingly sacrificing their own lives for others. Through their resistance, they maintained a basic conviction that discipleship to Christ entails resistance to the powers of darkness. As Wee rightly argues, "Just as the witness of Dietrich Bonhoeffer remains a source of inspiration to the church today, so also does the witness of Gudina Tumsa continue to inspire and guide the church as it faces new challenges."[56]

Two years before Tumsa's last arrest on July 28, 1979,[57] Janani Jakaliya Luwum (c. 1922–1977), the archbishop of the Anglican church of Uganda from 1974 to 1977, criticized Idi Amin's regime and delivered a note of protest to him against the policies of arbitrary killings and unexplained disappearances. As a result Luwum and other church leaders were accused of treason.[58] Nevertheless, like Bonhoeffer in Germany, Archbishop Luwum did not hesitate to "put a spoke in the wheel" of the dictator Idi Amin who wanted to erase God from the history of the people of Uganda. For this he had to pay a costly sacrifice. The archbishop was arrested on February 16, 1977 and was falsely accused by the military government of planning to seize political power. He was shot through the mouth and also riddled with bullets in the chest.[59] Although Tumsa was fully aware of what it takes to challenge a military regime led by the dictators, like Idi Amin and Mengistu, he regarded it a part of responsible church ministry.

As he interpreted this in the Ethiopian church context, he wrote,

> It is true a contextual definition of a responsible church ministry is always a risky undertaking because in every situation and in every event both divine and demonic elements are at work, and, as has rightly been said, one can easily be carried away with the wind of the times and allow the church to become a tool of other powers than the Lord.[60]

Tumsa believes that a responsible engagement of the church in a given society requires interpreting the gospel into its cultural, social, and political situations. This entails preaching the gospel of salvation, rendering a service that restores mankind to liberty and wholeness, and advocating for social justice and human flourishing whenever there is need.[61] As Darrell Jodock, who shared a dormitory room with Tumsa at Luther Seminary in St. Paul, Minnesota, describes Tumsa's theological stand, "[H]e articulated a theology that was both deeply rooted in core Lutheran ideas and deeply contextual. It was a triune theology that gave attention to creation, redemption, and the work of the Spirit. It was a holistic theology that explored the implications of the gospel for all life, not just for individual spirituality (as important as that may be)."[62] This helped the EECMY to uphold its motto to "serve the whole person."

We now come to the immediate context to his martyrdom, Tumsa and the other EECMY leaders have shaped the church's response to the political changes in Ethiopia that took place in February 1974. The revolutionary changes that affected the life of the church from February 1974 included a new political order, a new social and economic policy, and a new religious policy. In those days the church was engaging in a stringent effort to create a just society in Ethiopia in which equality, democracy, and human dignity is secured. But what the government was doing both at the peripheries and at the central part of the society was the opposite. Thus the church found it important to make internal and external adjustments in response to the sociopolitical changes that took place.[63]

As Tumsa expressed the significance of the internal, theological, adjustment,

> A church may continue her activities as if nothing has happened in this country. However, this will be ignoring the complex social issues, a disservice to the cause of the gospel of Jesus Christ. . . . This is to say that there is a lack of theological reflection regarding the changes that affect all aspects of the life of our society. . . . Lack of a sound theological reflection in the present Ethiopian situation has, in my opinion, affected our work in a negative way, which if allowed to continue uncorrected, will be harmful to the life of this church to which we have committed ourselves for service.[64]

The Marxist ideology was taken so seriously that it became the agenda of the time on the church's meetings at different levels.[65] Another most important event was a two-day reflection organized at the invitation of the Reverend

Gudina Tumsa of lecturers and church leaders on the situation of the church in Ethiopia. As a result, in March 1975, the draft of a pastoral letter that describes the situation of the EECMY in the Ethiopian Revolution was presented to the church's executive committee. The advancement of the well-being of the people, the definition of the church, comments on economic policy, and the question of ideology were among contents of this EECMY's official statement on the revolution.[66]

Appeal for religious freedom was the external adjustment demanded. The church made a wise decision to work with the secular government since the well-being of citizens was considered to be central. On the other hand, the EECMY wrote a letter requesting more religious freedom. The continuing revision of the constitution of the country, which stated that complete religious freedom can be realized only by establishing a secular state that secures equal freedom to all religious groups, was the main concern of the letter.[67] By demanding the establishment of a secular state, the young Mekane Yesus was resisting the longstanding religious nationalism characterizing imperial rule. As Jodock describes Tumsa's role in the church's effort,

> Early on, he was one of the few willing to criticize the stratified society of the emperor, and later, one of the few willing to say "no" to the revolutionary government. His theology was not overtly political, but he did not back away from criticizing the policies of the emperor, and after the emperor was succeeded by a Marxist regime, he was able to give it only qualified support. He endorsed the new regime's economic reforms but objected to its overt materialism.[68]

This indicates that the separation of church and state (the EOC and the imperial rule) became an issue of big concern for the EECMY. Nevertheless, the marginalization had not hindered the church from contributing positively to the sociopolitical life of the society. As mentioned in the memorandum written and presented by Tumsa to the church's General Assembly in 1976, "The ECMY will continue to contribute her share to the economic development of Ethiopia, to improve the living conditions of the people, and to the political orientation of the people in being useful to society, in knowing their rights and obligations as citizens."[69] However, this was not an easy endeavor. Today, the evangelical churches are at a turning point, where putting the well-being of society first must be central to their relations with the state.

Eventually, the Reverend Gudina Tumsa was arrested by the revolutionary government of Ethiopia in June 1979.[70] Despite the efforts made to help him escape after he was released from prison, Tumsa preferred to remain faithful to his calling and boldly faced whatever challenge was ahead of him. As a result, he was abducted and strangled on July 28, 1979. Christian Krause, a representative of the Lutheran World Federation, reported, based on a conversation with Gudina after his release from his second arrest, "Guddinaa Tumsaa drew all his motivation from Scripture. In my opinion he is only comparable to Bonhoeffer!"[71] It is with good reason that Tumsa is often referred to as the "Bonhoeffer of Africa." Suzanne Hequet articulates the unfading significance of Tumsa's legacy to the global churches well.

> The words, teaching, and life of Gudina Tumsa reach out to us from his grave. His strong confessional stance was inextricably linked to the gospel message of love and justice. His theology was holistic in the best sense of the word, calling for unity in the midst of a church divided, for justice in the midst of social and economic inequities.[72]

The current church leaders and theologians need to pay attention to Tumsa's concern for unity, justice, and equality. In response to those who neglect the role of religion, Peterson argues, "The most successful social movements do not reject religion and "disenchant" the world but rather enlarge religious worldviews and values to confront contemporary political challenges."[73] Bekele has intended to call both the Orthodox and Evangelical churches of Ethiopia "to be God's in-between people, taking risks, giving up claims to exclusivity, and taking up themselves the form of the servant of servants," which involves turning away from their institutional self-preservation toward fulfilling their calling. According to Bekele, Krause refers to Tumsa's death for the cause of the gospel of Jesus Christ in recognition of the symbol of hope it is for many among the poor and the disenfranchised.[74] Tumsa's life, ministry, and death in Ethiopia is the most reliable witness to help shape the ecclesial and theological realities in Africa and beyond.

CONCLUSION

Not all Ethiopian evangelical churches think about the church's involvement in politics as part of its spiritual responsibility in the same way. Those who speak up for justice and human dignity are often regarded as a threat for national and Christian unity. However, the legacy of the twentieth-century martyrs testifies to the fact that the Christian church does not use weapons that harm peace and unity in a given society. Rather, their witness encourages believers to live up to the theological and ethical convictions drawn from Scripture, which is sufficient for challenging the dominant ideology that promotes injustice and inequality. Telling the truth in a respectful way is more powerful and effective than any modern weapon in bringing peace and stability. Bonhoeffer and Tumsa gave their life to maintain the church's dynamic presence in the socioeconomic and political life of their respective societies. Under their leadership, the church demanded that the state should incorporate justice, equality, and human rights in a new political system. Even when it became obvious that the church's presence was considered either as a threat or unnecessary, the church, rather than being intimidated by the death of its martyrs, celebrated them as the ones with a victorious faith.

Finally, one may ask how Tumsa's legacy can be reclaimed almost four decades after his martyrdom. Tumsa was not only a theological thinker, but also a visionary church leader. Christian ministry is like a relay race, where one person starts, all team members take turns to complete their parts, and one team member finally brings the race to the finishing line. Similarly, Tumsa started thinking theologically and critically, gave his life leaving behind the church with a dynamic public theological stand, and many others have since taken their turn to complete their respective contribution to the race. It is our duty to maintain the existence of a vibrant Evangelical church in Ethiopian society through critical theological thinking until, finally, someone else will take their turn and bring the vision to completion. This requires religious commitments and a determination to closely analyze the political struggle of a society from a religious perspective instead of making appeals for revolutionary action from a distance. The EECMY has already brought Tumsa's particular vision of a self-supportive Ethiopian evangelical church into accomplishment, but his concern for social justice, democracy, and human development still needs to be retrieved.

BIBLIOGRAPHY

Arén, Gustav. *Envoys of the Gospel in Ethiopia: In the Steps of the Evangelical Pioneers.* Stockholm: EFS Förlaget, 1999.

———. *Evangelical Pioneers in Ethiopia: Origins of the Evangelical Church Mekane Yesus.* Stockholm: EFS Forlaget, 1978.

Bekele, Girma. *The In-between People: A Reading of David Bosch through the Lens of Mission History and Contemporary Challenge in Ethiopia.* Eugene, OR: Pickwick, 2011.

Birri, Debela. *Divine Plan Unfolding: The Story of Ethiopian Evangelical Church Bethel.* Minneapolis: Lutheran University Press, 2014.

Bockelman, Wilfred, and Eleanor Bockelman. *Ethiopia: Where Lutheran Is Spelled "Mekane Yesus."* Minneapolis: Augsburg, 1972.

Bonhoeffer, Dietrich. *The Cost of Discipleship.* New York: Touchstone, 1995.

———. *Dietrich Bonhoeffer Works,* Vol. 6, *Ethics.* Edited by Ilse Todt, Heinz E. Todt, Ernst Feil, and Clifford J. Green. Minneapolis: Fortress, 2005.

———. *Life Together: Prayerbook of the Bible.* Minneapolis: Fortress, 1996.

Church and Society: Lectures and Responses: Second Missiological Semminar 2003, on the Life and Ministry of Gudina Tumsa, General Secretary of the Ethiopian Evangelical Church Mekane Yesus (Eecmy) (1966–1979). Hamburg: WDL, 2010.

De Gruchy, John W. "Confessing Guilt in South Africa Today in Dialogue with Dietrich Bonhoeffer." *Journal of Theology for South Africa* (1988).

———. *John W. De Gruchy, Bonhoeffer and South Africa: Theology in Dialogue.* Grand Rapids, MI: Eerdmans, 1984.

Deressa, Samuel Yonas, and Sarah Hinlicky Wilson, eds. *The Life, Works, and Witness of Tsehay Tolessa and Gudina Tumsa, the Ethiopian Bonhoeffer.* Minneapolis: Fortress, 2017.

Eide, Øyvind M. *Revolution and Religion in Ethiopia.* Stavanger: Misjonshøgskolens Forlag, 1996.

Flores, Luis. "Engineering Ethnic Conflict: The Toll of Ethiopia's Plantation Development on the Suri People." The Oakland Institute, Accessed February 10, 2015, from http://

www.oaklandinstitute.org/sites/oaklandinstitute.org/files/Report_EngineeringEthnicConflict.pdf.

Gidada, Negaso. "Constitution of the Federal Democratic Republic of Ethiopia: Proclamation." *Federal Negarit Gazeta*. Accessed February 22, 2015, from http://www1.umn.edu/humanrts/research/Proclamation%20no.1-1995.pdf.

Gonzalez, Justo L. *Church History: An Essential Guide*. Nashville: Abingdon, 1996.

Grenstedt, Staffan. *Ambaricho and Shonkolla*. Sweden: Uppsala University, 2000.

Hammerschidt, Ernst, Siegbert Uhlig, and Jonathan J. Bonk. "Ethiopian Orthodox Church." In *The Encyclopedia of Christianity*, edited by Geoffrey W. Bromiley. Vol. 2. Grand Rapids, MI: Wm. B. Eerdmans, 2001.

Hasselblatt, Gunnar, and Jonathan J. Bonk. "Ethiopia." In *The Encyclopedia of Christianity*. Edited by Geoffrey W. Bromiley. Vol. 2. Grand Rapids, MI: Wm. B. Eerdmans Publishing Company, 2001.

The Kairos Document: Challenge to the Church. Grand Rapids, MI: Eerdmans, 1986.

Kelly, Geffrey B., and F. Burton Nelson. *The Cost of Moral Leadership: The Spirituality of Dietrich Bonhoeffer*. Grand Rapids, MI: Eerdmans, 2003.

King Jr., Martin Luther. *The Papers of Martin Luther King, Jr.* edited by Clayborne Carson. Vol. 6. Berkeley, CA: University of California Press, 2007.

———. *Stride toward Freedom: The Montgomery Story*. New York: Harper and Row, 1958.

Luther, Martin. *Luther's Works*. Edited by Christopher Boyd Brown. Annotations on Matthew Chapters 1–18. Vol. 67. Saint Louis: Concordia, 2015.

Meiring, Piet. "Bonhoeffer in South Africa: Role Model and Prophet." *Verbum et Ecclesia* (2007): 150–64.

Niebuhr, Reinhold. "The Death of a Martyr." *Christianity and Crisis*, 1945.

Niemoeller, Martin. "What Is the Church." *The Princeton Seminary Bulletin* XL (1947).

Nussbaum, Martha O. *Creating Capabilities: The Human Development Approach*. Cambridge, MA: Belknap, 2011.

Oates, Stephen B. *Let the Trumpet Sound: The Life of Martin Luther King, Jr.* New York: Harper and Row, 1982.

Orlowska, Izabela. "Ethiopia, Modern: Society and Culture." In *New Encyclopedia of Africa*. Edited by John Middelton and Joseph C. Miller. Vol. 2. Detroit: Thomson/Gale, 2008.

Peterson, Anna L. *Martyrdom and the Politics of Religion: Progressive Catholicism in El Salvador's Civil War*. Albany, NY: State University of New York Press, 1997.

"Religious Nationalism." *Wikipedia*. Accessed April 2, 2018, from https://en.wikipedia.org/wiki/Religious_nationalism.

Robertson, Edwin. *Bonhoeffer's Legacy: The Christian Way in a World without Religion*. New York: Macmillan, 1989.

Romero, Oscar A., and James R. Brockman. *The Church Is All of You: Thoughts of Archbishop Oscar Romero*. Minneapolis: Winston, 1984.

Thiemann, Ronald F. *Religion in Public Life: A Dialemma for Democracy*. Washington, DC: Georgetown University Press, 1996.

"Today in History: Archbishop Janan Luwum Is Shot Dead." *Daily Monitor*, February 16, 2015. Accessed May 10, 2018, from http://www.monitor.co.ug/News/Insight/Today-in-History--Archbishop-Luwum-is-shot-dead/-/688338/2625040/-/1hkwx4/-/index.html.

"Understanding Land Investment Deals in Africa: Ethiopia." The Oakland Institute. Accessed August 16, 2018, from http://www.oaklandinstitute.org/understanding-land-investment-deals-africa-ethiopia.

Wink, Walter. *Violence and Nonviolence in South Africa: Jesus's Third Way*. Philadelphia: New Society, 1987.

NOTES

1. Martin Luther, *Luther's Works*, ed. Christopher Boyd Brown, vol. 67, Annotations on Matthew Chapters 1–18 (Saint Louis: Concordia Publishing House, 2015), 273.

2. Ibid., 275. Luther further stated, "[I]t is necessary that the Church, founded and built up and victorious over hell, should stand up on a living, eternal foundation, upon the Rock that will abide with her until the end of the world. But the apostle Peter, beyond the fact that he is a sinful man and dead, has himself also been, just like all the other saints, built upon this Rock together with the Church" (278).

3. Ibid., 282–83.

4. Ibid., 283.

5. Justo L. Gonzalez, *Church History: An Essential Guide* (Nashville: Abingdon Press, 1996), 47–48.

6. Oscar A. Romero and James R. Brockman, *The Church Is All of You: Thoughts of Archbishop Oscar Romero* (Minneapolis: Winston, 1984), 85.

7. Ibid., 72.

8. Samuel Yonas Deressa and Sarah Hinlicky Wilson, eds., *The Life, Works, and Witness of Tsehay Tolessa and Gudina Tumsa, the Ethiopian Bonhoeffer* (Minneapolis: Fortress, 2017), 78–79. Gudina argues, "This is the guiding principle for all forms of Christian ministry and service. It should be clear to all, therefore, that Christian integrity does not allow us to do Christian social service out of fear. What is not done out of faith is sin." As to the position of the church, Gudina asserted, "As the church by nature is not interested in making profit, those who do not desire to serve in such an uncertain situation should decide for themselves" (84). Gudina further stated, "It should be understood that the ECMY has been able to maintain her integrity and credibility before those with whom we are working in this country, as well as before international organizations of all sorts" (81).

9. Martin Luther King, *Stride toward Freedom: The Montgomery Story* (New York: Harper and Row Publishers, 1958), 21.

10. Cairns, *Christianity*, 280–87.

11. "Religious Nationalism," *Wikipedia*. Accessed April 2, 2018, from https://en.wikipedia.org/wiki/Religious_nationalism.

12. Debela Birri, *Divine Plan Unfolding: The Story of Ethiopian Evangelical Church Bethel* (Minneapolis: Lutheran University Press, 2014), 24–31.

13. Gustav Arén, *Evangelical Pioneers in Ethiopia: Origins of the Evangelical Church Mekane Yesus* (Stockholm: EFS Forlaget, 1978), 74.

14. Birri, *Divine Plan*, 27–29. Gustav Aren, in *Evangelical Pioneers*, reports, "The clergy argued with the monarch: 'Their ethos is not like ours and their sacred book is different from that which is accepted in our country. If they are allowed to return, people will fall away from the faith of the fathers'" (81). Sahle Selassie's response to this shows his firm stand to act according to the request of the clergy. He said, "By the death of Wasen-Seged, neither Isenberg nor Krapf shall ever enter my kingdom again" (82).

15. Izabella Orlowska writes, "The Amharic language, which is the national language of Ethiopia, is also an important source of identity. In the conquered regions, unless individuals adopted these traits, they were stigmatized and exposed to harsh forms of economic exploitation." Orlowska rightly states that being Amhara has been nearly synonymous with being an Orthodox Christian in Ethiopian history. Orlowska further explains: "Fluency in Amharic provided some ability to engage in the litigation that was necessary to claim rights to land within the new system." Izabela Orlowska, "Ethiopia, Modern: Society and Culture," in *New Encyclopedia of Africa*, ed. John Middleton and Joseph C. Miller, 2nd ed., vol. 2 (Detroit: Thomson/Gale, 2008), 299.

16. Ernst Hammerschidt, Siegbert Uhlig, and Jonathan J. Bonk, "Ethiopian Orthodox Church," in *The Encyclopedia of Christianity*, ed. Geoffrey W. Bromiley, vol. 2 (Grand Rapids, MI: Wm. B. Eerdmans, 2001), 160.

17. Staffan Grenstedt, *Ambaricho and Shonkolla* (Sweden: Uppsala University, 2000), 70–71.

18. Wilfred Bockelman and Eleanor Bockelman, *Ethiopia: Where Lutheran Is Spelled "Mekane Yesus"* (Minneapolis: Augsburg, 1972), 46. Wilfred and Eleanor Bockelman stated that some Orthodox priests, who could see the spiritual awakening, joined the evangelical movement. They continued, "[B]ut the Orthodox Church soon put pressure on them and accused them of leaving the faith of their fathers. Local authorities used imprisonment and various

kinds of persecution to try to reclaim former priests and members of the Orthodox Church" (46).

19. Grenstedt, *Ambaricho and Shonkolla*, 65. As Gustav Arén articulates, "This incident aptly illustrated the deep fellowship that might arise from the rediscovery and the personal experience of the core of the Gospel: salvation through faith in the atoning death, resurrection and glorification of our Lord Jesus Christ. This fellowship bridged social and ethnic gaps. In these years it united Amara, Eritreans, and Oromo in a common concern for spiritual renewal through the dissemination and the study of the vernacular Holy Scripture." Gustav Arén, *Envoys of the Gospel in Ethiopia: In the Steps of the Evangelical Pioneers* (Stockholm: EFS Förlaget, 1999), 96.

20. Gunnar Hasselblatt and Jonathan J. Bonk, "Ethiopia," in *The Encyclopedia of Christianity*, ed. Geoffrey W. Bromiley, vol. 2 (Grand Rapids, MI: Wm. B. Eerdmans, 2001), 157–58. As included in the work of Hasselblatt and Bonk, "With assistance from the former Soviet Union, the military regime pursued a Marxist-Leninist policy while at the same time continuing the Amharicizing and centralizing policy of the emperors" (157).

21. The misperception of the political and religious freedom, coupled with the longstanding mentality of religious nationalism, has its own negative impacts on the life of the community. First, just as nationality and religion were too closely identified in the past, ethnic identity is being confused with one's religious identity to the extent of compromising the core values of our identity in Christ for secular practices. This is apparent from the tendency to be engrossed by the revival of traditional religions without questioning how they affect one's spiritual life. The church seems to be unprepared for bridging the gap between traditional religions and Christianity, which may cause an identity crisis arising from toleration of syncretism. Secondly, the solidarity of the nations is challenged because of the lack of clear understanding of federalism and the long-standing impact of religious nationalism.

22. Romero and Brockman, *The Church Is All of You*, ix.

23. Negaso Gidada, "Constitution of the Federal Democratic Republic of Ethiopia: Proclamation," *Federal Negarit Gazeta*. Accessed February 22, 2015, from http://www1.umn.edu/humanrts/research/Proclamation%20no.1-1995.pdf.

24. Ronald F. Thiemann, *Religion in Public Life: A Dilemma for Democracy* (Washington, DC: Georgetown University Press, 1996), 42. Thiemann describes the advantage and disadvantage of introducing the principle called *the separation of church and state*, which is derived from the metaphor "a wall of separation between church and state" that first appeared in Roger Williams's letter to John Cotton and then in Thomas Jefferson's letter to the Baptist Association of Danbury, Connecticut, into the legal tradition of the United States of America. The advantage, as Thiemann states, is that "this principle has come to shape our nation's understanding of the relation between the political and religious spheres in the United States. Not only has it guided constitutional interpretation of the first amendment; it has also molded the American public's understanding of the proper relation between government and religion" (42). As he points out the disadvantage, "At a time when our nation is struggling to define the proper role of religion and religiously based moral convictions within public life, the phrase 'separation of church and state' and its standard metaphor 'a wall of separation between church and state' serve not to clarify but to confuse. . . . By confusing on religious and governmental institutions they obscure the essential concern for individual freedom and equality that undergirds both the 'no establishment' and the 'free exercise' clause" (42–43).

25. Gidada, "Constitution."

26. Seeing the change from a different angle, Orlowska says, "This system has given rise to debates over the authenticity of ethnic identity that serve to critique the system of ethnic federalism as a whole, or to question the rights of particular groups or individuals." Orlowska, "Ethiopia, Modern," 301.

27. Stephen B. Oates, *Let the Trumpet Sound: The Life of Martin Luther King, Jr.* (New York: Harper and Row, 1982), 146.

28. "Understanding Land Investment Deals in Africa: Ethiopia," The Oakland Institute. Accessed August 16, 2018, from http://www.oaklandinstitute.org/understanding-land-investment-deals-africa-ethiopia. As it is documented in the recent publication of the Oakland Institute, "Implementation of this strategy involves human rights violations including coerced dis-

placement, political repression, and neglect of local livelihoods, and places foreign and political interests above the rights and needs of local populations, especially ethnic groups who have historically been marginalized and neglected by the government." Luis Flores, "Engineering Ethnic Conflict: The Toll of Ethiopia's Plantation Development on the Suri People," The Oakland Institute. Accessed February 10, 2015, from http://www.oaklandinstitute.org/sites/oaklandinstitute.org/files/Report_EngineeringEthnicConflict.pdf.

29. "Understanding Land Investment," 1, 5, 20. It is also reported that "many of the larger lease areas include [land] traditionally inhabited by the Gumuz, Anuak, Oromo and other peoples."

30. Martha O. Nussbaum, *Creating Capabilities: The Human Development Approach* (Cambridge, MA: Belknap, 2011), 34. Nussbaum believes that the capabilities approach to social justice has to ask what a life worthy of human dignity requires. She provides a threshold level of ten central capabilities a government should secure to all citizens, namely, (1) life; (2) bodily health; (3) bodily integrity; (4) senses, imagination, and thought; (5) emotions; (6) practical reason; (7) affiliation; (8) other species; (9) play; and (10) control over one's environment. She argues that the removal of these constitutes robbing a life of its human dignity (30–34).

31. King, *Stride toward Freedom*, 27, 36.

32. Deressa and Wilson, *The Life, Works, and Witness*, 38. Tumsa furthers elaborates, "Looking at the so-called development societies, we realize that in the midst of their affluence, man is still suffering from all kinds of evil. The values that make life meaningful seem to be in danger of being lost in this societies."

33. Martin Niemoeller, "What Is the Church," *The Princeton Seminary Bulletin* XL (1947): 10. To accomplish his mission of making the church the follower of National Socialism, Hitler had reorganized the churches as a mere institution under the name "German Christian Church," with the word *German* coming before the word *Christian* with an intention to take control of the entire life of the church. Pastors who denounced this attempt to reduce the church into a national institution that preaches Hitler as a savior for life on earth explicitly declared that they proclaim "Christ crucified" (1 Cor 1:23) as the only Savior for this life and the life to come. Niemoeller considers this as the emerging of a new church, "not an institution, not an organization, just a voice preaching that all people are like grass and like flower of the field, and that only one thing stands forever, the word of God, the word that became flesh in Jesus Christ." Niemoeller further asserted, "'We preach Christ crucified,' to whom is given all the power not only in heaven but also on earth, for he is not only in heaven but here on earth and in our midst, even under the eyes and within the ears of government under the reign of Adolf Hitler" (11).

34. King, *Stride toward Freedom*, 10. This is where the prosperity gospel preachers are leading their followers. When I see the dramatic flourishing of the so-called prophets and apostles who plant their income-generating tents adjacent to the church buildings, I am less optimistic that we are not far away from seeing the emergence of critical pastors with compassion for the marginalized and the voiceless.

35. Martin Luther King Jr., *The Papers of Martin Luther King Jr.*, vol. 6, ed. Clayborne Carson (Berkeley, CA: University of California Press, 2007), 445.

36. Romero and Brockman, *The Church Is All of You*, ix.

37. Dietrich Bonhoeffer, *The Cost of Discipleship* (New York: Touchstone, 1995), 14. Bonhoeffer led a purpose-driven life as a pastor fixing his eyes on Christ, the perfecter of faith, and on His cross, the depiction of God's self-giving love. From his book *The Cost of Discipleship*, one can see that faith and love of God were the guiding forces in his life, which encouraged him to resist National Socialism, which aimed at destruction of Germany as Christian country. Kelly and Nelson state, "Bonhoeffer lived what he wrote." Geffrey B. Kelly and F. Burton Nelson, *The Cost of Moral Leadership: The Spirituality of Dietrich Bonhoeffer* (Grand Rapids, MI: Eerdmans, 2003), 2. Besides understanding his call to discipleship as inseparable from interpreting and applying the Word of God to his daily life, Bonhoeffer put emphasis on the Lutheran view of costly grace and the need of a single-minded obedience for the life of discipleship. The "call to follow Jesus" is a core theme that guides his life and thought in unpromising situations. For him, the call of Jesus is the Word of God himself, which can

remove the barriers and create a single-minded obedience in the one who is called. It is only in this obedience that one enjoys fellowship with Jesus as promised (22, 28, 79–80).

38. Edwin Robertson, *Bonhoeffer's Legacy: The Christian Way in a World without Religion* (New York: Macmillan, 1989), 56. Robertson has written his book according to the "Outline" Bonhoeffer had sent with his letter to his friend Eberhard Bethge from Tegel Prison. He refers to this letter as describing the environment in which Bonhoeffer was working and telling the reader his sense of guilt for involvement in conspiracy. Nevertheless, Reinhold Niebuhr, who referred to Bonhoeffer's martyrdom as belonging "to the modern acts of the Apostles," argues that Bonhoeffer's life and death will become "one of the sources of grace for the new church in a new Germany." Reinhold Niebuhr, "The Death of a Martyr," *Christianity and Crisis* (1945), 6.

39. Dietrich Bonhoeffer, *Dietrich Bonhoeffer Works*, Vol. 6, *Ethics*, ed. Ilse Todt et al. (Minneapolis: Fortress, 2005), 64. Bonhoeffer's criticism was not confined to the church compound, but resisted Hitler through direct confrontation of the political cadres in writings that give evidence of the incompatibility of the church and National Socialism, and leading the conspirators' movement.

40. Piet Meiring, "Bonhoeffer in South Africa: Role Model and Prophet," *Verbum et Ecclesia* (2007): 150–64. Because of his influence in the theological and ethical debates in the country, Bonhoeffer is considered as a role model by many South African theologians. Meiring argues that Bonhoeffer's message for the church does not fade away with time and circumstances. Most of all, his joy during those dark moments is what helped African Christians to see Christ working in and through his life.

41. The National conference of the South African Council of Churches had resolved in 1987 "to plan and convene a conference on the subject matter of the responsibility of the churches in relation to the crisis in South Africa and the evils of the apartheid system, and whether Christian people can write a Confession of Guilt for the past and of commitment for the future." John W. De Gruchy, "Confessing Guilt in South Africa Today in Dialogue with Dietrich Bonhoeffer," *Journal of Theology for South Africa* (1988): 37.

42. Ibid., 37–45. De Gruchy based his research on Bonhoeffer's poem from Tegel prison, in which Bonhoeffer confesses that the evil within Nazi Germany had forced the innocent (conspirators against Hitler) to become guilty, and his *Santorum Communion* (written before the Nazis came to power), in which the church was called to confess vicariously a guilt of rejecting Christ by keeping silent in the persecution of the Jews. De Gruchy applies this to the church in South Africa and calls the church to both the concrete and specific confession of the guilt of apartheid at the right moment. The Ethiopian evangelical churches have responsibility in relation to the ongoing sociopolitical crisis in the land. They have to confess the guilt of noninvolvement in the political life of their contemporary society instead of lending their ears to the sermons and teachings that urge them to repent the sins of the imperial era. To reject the evil in the country's political system, the churches should not wait until the ethnopolitical exclusivity escalates into a bitter hatred and a holocaust. It is time to confess the guilt of keeping silent in the face of persecution of the citizens who are either suffering in jail or exiled because they spoke up for their rights.

43. John W. De Gruchy, *John W. De Gruchy, Bonhoeffer and South Africa: Theology in Dialogue* (Grand Rapids, MI: Eerdmans, 1984), 74. De Gruchy further explains, "God's grace in Jesus Christ has set us free both individually and corporately for other people, but this grace is experienced concretely only in relationships. In this way Christian freedom and liberation are rescued from abstraction. They are no longer a concept or an ideological program but a commitment to other people."

44. Dietrich Bonhoeffer, *Life Together: Prayerbook of the Bible* (Minneapolis: Fortress, 1996), 29–31. As Bonhoeffer stated, "Christian community means community through Jesus Christ and in Jesus Christ" (31). In the life together, the self-centered emotional love, both in individuals and in the community, leaves the way for the spiritual love that transforms the relationship between people. Because the spiritual love creates freedom of Christians under the Word in which service is conducted by the truth, it is not a movement but part of the Christian church. Faith is what holds the Christian community together. The presence of Christ among the community allows them access to one another, joy in one another, and community with one another. Accordingly, communion among Christians is possible only through Jesus Christ. This

implies that other claims, for example, ethnic identity, should come second or be totally omitted. However, even in the global church today, this is the most vulnerable aspect of life together as the enemy always attacks the identity of the Christian community by attacking what signifies Christ's presence among his followers (40–47).

45. De Gruchy, *Bonhoeffer and South Africa*, 51.

46. Walter Wink, *Violence and Nonviolence in South Africa: Jesus's Third Way* (Philadelphia, PA: New Society, 1987), vii. Wink reports what he heard from Beyers Naude, general secretary of South African Council of Churches, as follows: "In South Africa we have never yet had a thorough discussion of the issue of violence or nonviolence. It is vitally important to form a legitimate theological position regarding that question."

47. *The Kairos Document: Challenge to the Church* (Grand Rapids, MI: Eerdmans, 1986), 3–28. The South African pastors described the obligation of their *kairos* as a biblically founded prophetic response to what South Africans were experiencing. It is the role of prophetic theology to interpret the Word of God and appropriate it to the critical situation that the church and society are going through (17).

48. Robertson, *Bonhoeffer's Legacy*, 1, 12. In his analysis of Bonhoeffer's statement, "The church is the church only when it exists for others," Robertson states that it has a far-reaching implication for the future of the church in different contexts beyond Germany. Robertson argues that especially the consequence of Bonhoeffer's view that the church should be deeply concerned with justice, peace, and integrity of creation was being felt by Christians living among those who were suffering. Robertson further explains what it takes for the church to be the one that "exists for others": "The church must serve, not dominate. It must tell men of all kinds what it means to live in Christ, to exist for others. But far more important than what it 'tells' is its example. It is not abstract argument, but human example which gives the abstract argument, but human example which gives the church credibility. It must fight against the vices of *hubris*, the worship of power, envy and humbug within the church itself. It must speak of course, but of 'moderation, purity, trust, loyalty, constancy, patience, discipline, humility, contentment, and modesty'" (11–12).

49. Girma Bekele, *The In-between People: A Reading of David Bosch through the Lens of Mission History and Contemporary Challenge in Ethiopia* (Eugene, OR: Pickwick, 2011), 119.

50. Deressa and Wilson, *The Life, Works, and Witness*, 40. In Gudina's words, "The basic question that is asked is: How many will benefit from this project? The community that the project is supposed to serve is seen more as an object than as an agent for betterment."

51. Ibid., xix.

52. Ibid., 61–63. In Gudina's words, "Are we mature enough not only to take care of our own business but also mature enough to contribute to international efforts in finding solutions to the problems of our day?" (56).

53. Ibid., 56–59.

54. Bekele states that Bishop Dr. Christian Krause, the then–General Secretary of the German Lutheran Church, witnessed that Tumsa had read extensively and made reference to Bonhoeffer's works. Bekele, *The In-between People*, 362.

55. Paul Wee, who refers to Tumsa as "the Bonhoeffer of Ethiopia," further stated that in addition to theological resources and the people, both Tumsa and Bonhoeffer were brought face to face with the burning issue of racial discrimination and economic and political injustice during their studies in the United States. *Church and Society: Lectures and Responses: Second Missiological Seminar 2003, on the Life and Ministry of Gudina Tumsa, General Secretary of the Ethiopian Evangelical Church Mekane Yesus (EECMY) (1966–1979)* (Hamburg: WDL, 2010), 15–17. This implies not only that both Tumsa and Bonhoeffer were effective learners who could use classroom interaction and available literature, but they were also ready to learn from their challenges and to make adjustments that the church benefited from it.

56. Ibid., 15.

57. "Gudina Tumsa was arrested for the first time on October 11, 1978, and released on November 7. He was detained a second time from June 1 to 23, 1979." Deressa and Wilson, *The Life, Works, and Witness*, 121.

58. A wife of an American expatriate business man living in Uganda from 1972–1975, who testified that her husband was the only expatriate business man living in the country during this

time, had contributed an article under the title "The Terror of Idi Amin" to the *New York Times*. She reported, "While living in Uganda in 1975, I witnessed firsthand the rape by Idi Amin of this stunningly beautiful country. Uganda had no food, limited water, no supplies and great fear resulting from his torture and murder of hundreds of thousands of locals and foreigners." "Today in History: Archbishop Janan Luwum Is Shot Dead," *Daily Monitor*, February 16, 2015. Accessed May 10, 2018, from http://www.monitor.co.ug/News/Insight/Today-in-History--Archbishop-Luwum-is-shot-dead/-/688338/2625040/-/1hkwx4/-/index.html.

59. Ibid. As it was reported, "Bishop Luwum made it his business to confront the injustices and atrocities of Amin. He took his criticism public in a radio address in 1976 at Christmas. His sermon felt the power of censorship before he even finished. The Bishop then threatened a public demonstration, and for a time worked to bring his Anglicans, other Protestant groups, and the Catholics together in opposition to Amin." The Church of England and the Anglican Communion recognize Archbishop Luwum as one among the twentieth-century martyrs.

60. Deressa and Wilson, *The Life, Works, and Witness*, 64–65.

61. Ibid., 65–67.

62. Ibid., xviii.

63. Øyvind M. Eide, *Revolution and Religion in Ethiopia* (Stavanger: Misjonshøgskolens Forlag, 1996), 145–47.

64. Deressa and Wilson, *The Life, Works, and Witness*, 76–77.

65. Eide, *Revolution and Religion*, 145–47. The outcome of the discussion involved preparing the believers for the challenges ahead of them through seminars, lectures, trainings, official statements, and research papers regarding the relation between the scientific socialism and Christianity. Tumsa, together with other church leaders, played a significant role in giving the believers a clear and biblically based direction in this situation.

66. Ibid., 148. To put the position of the church in Tumsa's words, "On the question of ideology the letter first affirms that it (the church) 'aspires to justice, respect for human right and the rule of law,' but it guards itself with the words: 'Ideologies cannot be considered as absolute. Complete allegiance is due to God and God alone.'"

67. Ibid., 148–70. With regard to the church and state relations, all religions were denied freedom lest the socialist ideology and the government policy on war be compromised. The harassment of the church members by the EOC, the resistance of the patriarch to recognize the EECMY as an Ethiopian church, imprisonment of the ministers (Emanuel Abraham was imprisoned on April 30, 1974, and was released on January 27, 1975), and the confiscation of the church's property by the government were among the problems that prompted the church's reaction. As Eide rightly asserted, "From now on the EOC was the vehicle of the regime. Its role was one of unconditional loyalty to the state and its policies. When the regime applied its harsh measures against denominational groups, labeled as foreign, the EOC supported it, as it had the previous regime" (207).

68. Deressa and Wilson, *The Life, Works, and Witness*, xx.

69. Ibid., 85.

70. Eide, *Revolution and Religion*, 220. President Nyerere of Tanzania approached the military government led by dictator Mengistu Hailemariam to get the Reverend Tumsa released as per the request of the representatives of the LWF. Although Nyerere managed to get him released from prison and offered him a possibility of escape, Tumsa didn't accept the request to escape. He said, "Here is my church and my congregation. How can I, as a church leader, leave my flock at this moment of trial? I have again and again pleaded with my pastors to stay on." He then quoted 2 Corinthians 5:15: "'Christ died for all that those who live should no longer live for themselves but for him who died for them and was raised again.' Never ever will I escape."

71. Ibid., 220–22.

72. This note is taken from Suzanne Hequet's appreciation of Deressa and Wilson's *The Life, Works, and Witness of Tsehay Tolessa and Gudina Tumsa, the Ethiopian Bonhoeffer*, which appears in the frontmatter of the book.

73. Anna L. Peterson, *Martyrdom and the Politics of Religion: Progressive Catholicism in El Salvador's Civil War* (Albany, NY: State University of New York Press, 1997), 179. A good illustration for this is Martin Luther King Jr.'s effort as a pastor of a congregation in Montgom-

ery, Alabama. King expressed his concern with the social injustice African Americans were going through and formed a social and political action committee "to keep the congregation intelligently informed on the social, political, and economic situations." King, *Stride toward Freedom*, 15. In commitment to this responsibility, the committee published a biweekly newsletter with an intention to help the church members become aware of the social and political issues. As a result, a remarkable achievement was registered with regard to African American's right to equality in the sociopolitical arena. Similar commitment is expected of the Ethiopian evangelical church leaders.

74. Bekele, *The In-between People*, xii, 362.

Part Four

Theological Perspectives

Chapter 9

The Roles of Religions in Public Theology

An Asian Perspective on the Paradoxes of Religious Violence and Peace

David Thang Moe

Sri Lankan theologian Aloysius Pieris sums up the context of Asia into a twofold reality: "religious diversity (in which Christianity is a minority religion) and mass poverty/suffering (both Christians and people of other religions suffer together)."[1] It is hard to argue against his summary. Asia's uniqueness lies precisely in this twofold reality. From the religious perspective, Asia is home to the world religions, such as Buddhism, Hinduism, and Confucianism, on the one hand, and to a primal religion[2] of spirit worship on the other. While Pieris's use of religious diversity is an accurate depiction of Asia's religious context, his use of poverty is not a complete expression of Asia's suffering. When Pieris uses the word *suffering*, he refers to human suffering. What he misses is the problem of natural or ecological suffering. The aim of this paper, therefore, is to examine two kinds of suffering in Asia. From the sociopolitical perspective, Christians and other faiths suffer together in the face of sociopolitical oppression. I call this "anthropocentric suffering." From the ecological perspective, the Asian world suffers in the face of the human exploitation of nature. I call this "ecological suffering." I argue that Asian public theology must address the problems of these two kinds of suffering.

Using religious diversity and anthropological and ecological suffering as a twofold context, the aim of this paper is to explore the roles of religious pilgrims and citizens in public theology. I will first explore the role of Asia's world religions with regard to human rights and human development and then the role of Asia's primal religion in relation to the rights of nature and ecological healing. I use the phrase "the roles of religions in pubic theology from an Asian perspective" as the title for this chapter deliberately. By the phrase "the role of religions in public theology," I do not mean the roles of other religions in public theology, thereby excluding the role of the church. Since Christianity is one of religions in Asia, the phrase "the roles of religions" embraces the role of the church as well. The church has to affirm the contributions of other faiths for what Brant Meyers calls the "transformational development."[3] Myers uses the term "transformational development" to seek a holistic transformation of humanity and society materially, socially, spiritually, and ecologically.[4] Of course, other belief systems do not make a contribution to the spiritual dimension of Christian evangelism, but they do play a role in socioecological development.

To affirm the roles of other religions in a public theology of human development and rights of nature, we need to reconsider God's first commandment seriously. This commandment is recorded on the first page of the first book of the Bible. As Genesis 1:27–28 records, God created human beings to be His stewards for creation. The vocation of human beings is to care for the world and the people in it. However, the entry of sin (Gen. 3) and the redemption wrought by Jesus change everything. We see Jesus's last commission to His disciples (Matt. 28:16–20) as the first concern of the church's mission. History tells us that Jesus's final commission became the primary model for the modern Protestant mission.[5] While I deeply believe the crucial importance of Jesus's commission to His disciples for an evangelism of calling people of other faiths to Christ, I am dissatisfied with our misuse of it as a singular colonial approach of doing mission *to* people of other faiths rather than a "two-way" approach of doing mission *with* people of other faiths without ceasing to evangelize them in love.

In this chapter, I propose that the goal for a transformational development of society in Asia is to "rediscover our common identity as human beings created in the image of God, and to rediscover our human vocation as faithful and public stewards for the world and for all people in it."[6] All human beings of different religions are created truly in the image of God for public stewardship (Gen. 1:28), but not all human beings belong to the body of Christ (1 Cor. 12:27), the spiritual community of worship and praise. My goal is not to separate the image of God from the body of Christ, but to embrace their significance for the common good of human and nature justice and peace within a larger Asian framework of *missio Dei*. It is in terms of the relation between the *image of God* (human vocation) and the *body of Christ* (ecclesial vocation) that I explore the roles of Christianity and other religions in public theology from an Asian perspective.

This chapter will proceed as follows. First, I will begin by exploring some convergences and divergences between public theology and political theology. I will then offer a methodological proposal for a public theology in Asia as a prophetic relationship between being church-centered and being world-engaged and a hermeneutical proposal for a public theology as a dialectical relationship between a personal confession of Christ and a public commitment to God's kingdom of human and nature flourishing. Second, I will explore the paradoxes of religions—the problems of religions for a public theology and the prospective roles of religions in public theology of justice and peace—shalom with God, with humans, and with nature. I will then explore the ethical roles of the Christian community and other religious communities in a public theology of human rights and the rights of nature. Finally, I will explore the problems of the exploitation of nature, and will investigate the role of primal religion in the care of creation and ecological healing.

PUBLIC THEOLOGY AND POLITICAL THEOLOGY AS PARTNERS IN PRAXIS FOR HUMAN AND NATURE FLOURISHING

What is the difference between public theology and political theology? In answer to this question, I will briefly explore the convergence and divergence between public and political theology. I will argue that political theology and public theology share convergences in their hermeneutics, but they diverge in both their origin and scope. Both disciplines have a theological interest not only in how the church and the state should be dialectically related for the common good (Rom. 13:4),[7] but also in the relation between God's authority over the world and political authority, and in how the Christian community and other religious communities should stand against the unjust state.[8]

Political theology is older than public theology. Political theology was born in Germany in the 1920s, and the term was developed by a German scholar, Carl Schmitt.[9] Public theology was born in the United States in the 1960s, and the term was coined by an American theologian, Martin Marty.[10] Although the idea of political theology was introduced in the time of St. Augustine and was developed in the times of Martin Luther and John Calvin, the modern use of the term was developed by Schmitt in the 1920s. Karl Barth popularized a new political theology with the focus on the church's critical and prophetic engagement with the world or state in Europe throughout the Nazi period (1933–1945), and World War II (1939–1945) and its aftermath.[11] Jürgen Moltmann, through the influence of Karl Barth, and Johann Baptist Metz, through the influence of Karl Rahner, developed a contemporary political theology in the 1960s, after Auschwitz and its aftermath, at the same time when public theology was born in the United States.[12]

A critical question we must ask in a postcolonial age is: was a political theology shifted from the West to the non-Western world? Asian feminist postcolonial theologian Kwok Pui-lan argues against what she considers a colonial claim that political theology shifted to Asia. She argues that, while the German scholar Schmitt may have come up with the term and its modern usage, political theology was at the same time forming along different trajectories elsewhere in the world, as was the case in Asia. In China, for instance, Protestant Wu Yaozong advocated in the 1930s that a social revolution was necessary to save both China and the world.[13] Pui-lan's proposal is that an academic discourse on political theology may have been born in Germany in the 1920s, but its Western mode of development did not necessarily shift to Asia and other non-Western areas. In the non-Western world, there has been the idea of a political theology with its own version of Christian resistance against the monopoly of the oppressive government.[14]

While the question of whether political theology was shifted to Asia from the West is important, my interest is more in how political theology is related to and distinct from its younger and more popular sibling, public theology. What I am saying is that, although political theology is older, public theology is more popular in the global contexts.[15] While political theology is directed more toward the state with the question of whether the state is ruling justly, public theology is directed more toward civil society and its larger community, not just the state, with the question of how to achieve the common good.[16]

By using "civil society" as a framework for a public theology, a Korean theologian, Sebastian Kim, helpfully identifies a six-fold "publicness" of theology. For Kim, public theology prophetically engages not only the political issues of injustice in the first public realm (human rights), but also with other five public spheres—markets (economic exploitations), media (freedom of speech), academic institutions (promoting education), religious communities (interreligious interactions for a common good), and civil society and nongovernmental organizations (advocating for human and ecological development).[17] While political theology and public theology share a common interest in political engagement on behalf of human rights as a major concern, the latter (public theology) embraces the issue of natural rights and addresses the need for ecological liberation. Because of its wider scope of advocacy, I choose "public theology" but without excluding "political theology."[18] I see political theology and public theology as two hands in the praxis of Christians and other religious communities against their common enemies, the oppressors, as they work for a common goal of human-nature flourishing in Asia. In their advocacy for and solidarity with the oppressed humanity and nature and in their resistance against the oppressors, political theology and public theology use liberation theology as their instrument.

Public theology in Asia must be concerned with three central questions. First, what is the role of Christian community in a public theology of the common good? Second, what is the role of other religious communities in the common good? Third, how should Christians and non-Christians as citizens and pilgrims achieve the common good? In response to these questions, I offer a methodological proposal of public theology as a church-centered and world-engaged discipline. Some Asian public theologians argue against a church-centered model of public theology and propose a world-centered model.[19] But I propose a church-centered public theology. By *church-centered*, I do not mean an exclusive way of seeing the church as separate from the world nor do I see the world as an object for the church. Richard Magnus states two options for Asian churches. One is escape or separation and the other is engagement. By *escape*, he means Asian churches' turning their backs on the government and their fellow citizens and remaining silent in the face of injustice. By *engagement*, he means Christians' turning their faces toward their government, fellow pilgrims, and citizens of other faiths by appreciating their good works while also criticizing their unjust works, for the common good.[20]

I choose the term *engagement* as a way to describe the ethical and missiological responsibility of the Christian community in Asia. This is a Christian response to the divine commission and the voice of God who calls His people into the world to live faithfully, work prophetically, and engage critically, as did Jesus.[21] If we see public theology as a church-centered discipline, we rediscover the significance of the immanent Trinity (an inner communion among the Trinity) for the church as a gathered community of faith, prayer, and worship and rediscover the significance of the economic Trinity for the church as a scattered community of public engagement with the world for the common good of both Christians and other religions in Asia.[22] The former expresses Christian identity (personal confession of Christ), while the latter describes Christian vocation (public commitment). Our identity and vocation must be grounded in the triune God, who calls us out of the world for doxology and calls us into the world for witnessing to Christ's act of shalom. Public theology in Asia must be grounded in both what we believe (confession of Christ) and how we are to live for God's kingdom by engaging with the world (commitment).

I emphasize that public theology in Asia must take the church as its ground for the love of God through spiritual engagement in an intra-Christian community of faith and prayer, and for the love of neighbors and nature[23] through social engagement in an interreligious community. As we gather, we worship God by reading and meditating on the Bible and praying for the state's rulers (1 Tim. 2:2). But we cannot know the contemporary issues by reading the Bible alone. To know the public issues of what is happening in our daily world, we also need to read the newspaper. Swiss reformed theologian Barth famously said, "Take the Bible in one hand, and the newspaper in the other, and read both."[24] Barth does not merely urge Christians to read the Bible and the newspaper, but he asks them "to interpret the newspaper from the Bible."[25] I find Barth's dictum of reading the Bible and the newspaper a persuasive starting point for developing a public theology in Asia. Reading the Bible informs us of God's historical act of salvation and shapes our spiritual growth in righteousness (2 Tim. 3:16b), whereas reading the newspaper informs us of what is happening in Asia and calls for our response to the public issues of injustice by engaging with neighbors for the common good of all.

WORLD RELIGIONS AND A PUBLIC THEOLOGY OF HUMAN RIGHTS AND FLOURISHING

The Problems of Religions for Public Theology: Religious Violence and Injustice

I begin with the paradoxical statement. "Religions are alive today—for good and for ill," observed the celebrated public theologian Miroslav Volf correctly.[26] Religions are the cause of violence and injustice but also the source for peace and justice. These are the problems of religions for public theology and the prospective roles of religions in public theology. Religious violence, whether caused by one dominant religious group against the state or against another minority religious group, is a sociopolitical reality in Asia. I will describe two Asian countries as the examples for how religions cause violence. I will then propose some prescriptive roles for religions in a public theology of human rights and development.

The first country is China, the world's largest country. It has been ruled by the Chinese Communist Party for more than six decades. As a communist country, the authoritarian state exercises a hierarchical and colonial level of restrictive control over a wide range of human rights, such as freedom of expression (media rights), freedom of worship (religious rights), and restrictions on the leadership of women (women's rights). It would be helpful to call these aspects of the dictatorial control an internal colonization. Moreover China's Communist Party exercises what I call an external colonialism over Tibetans. Tibet is not a province of China, but China's government has extended its control (i.e., its geographical colonization over Tibet) by violating the land and the human rights of Tibetans since 1959.[27] The Chinese colonization of Tibet has resulted in the deaths of about one million Tibetans (about one-sixth of the population) from both direct causes (torture, executions, labor camps) and indirect causes (famine resulting from Chinese agriculture policies). These are among the most serious accusations regarding human rights violations in Tibet.[28]

Religiously, China is a country of three world religions, Confucianism (with its moral and social focus), Taoism (with its mysticism and immortality cult), and Buddhism (with its meditative focus). All of the adherents of these religions widely practice ancestral worship as well, which is marked by its spirituality and respect for the spirit of the dead.[29] Because of this religious mixture, it is difficult to differentiate Chinese cultures from Chinese religions. In this paper, however, I affirm the central role of Confucianism in a Chinese public theology, not necessarily because it is more important than the other religions, but because Confucianism is not only a truly native religion of China when compared to Buddhism, but is also a morally oriented religion that, more directly than the other two religions, shapes the moral and social transformation of the private sphere of the family and the public sphere of the state.

If China's government is religiously rooted in the moral and social teaching of Confucianism, then why do the state rulers unethically violate human and religious rights? As I said earlier, these are the problems of religion for public theology. But if religion—let us stay with Confucianism—teaches ethics, then what might be the ethical and prospective role of Confucianism in transforming the problematic and evil acts of Confucian state rulers? Are the state rulers misusing Confucianism (religion)? What is the prophetic role of Christianity in promoting a Chinese public theology of human rights and development? I will answer these questions later in the section on prescribing the roles of religion in public theology. Let me first describe the second problematic country, Myanmar.

Myanmar is a country with a Theravada Buddhist majority. The Burmans[30] make up two-thirds of the population. They are part of a Buddhist majority that includes 89 percent of the people. Burman Buddhist nationalism leads us to the ethnic minorities. A majority of the ethnic minorities is Christian. They make up 6.2 percent of the population.[31] Of course, not all the ethnic minorities have a Christian majority. Three ethnic groups, however, the Kachins, Karens, and Chins, do have a Christian majority. Christianity is the majority religion among these three ethnic minorities in Myanmar.[32]

In Myanmar, religious violence and conflict can be divided into two related types. One is what I would call the intersection of the military and violence. This violence is carried out by the Burman Buddhist ruling class. The other is the intersection of religions and politics. This form of violence is perpetrated by ordinary Buddhist nationalists who support the ruling class. The first group has its roots in 1962, when the military junta took power by force. The latter group began in the 2000s. The goal of this group is to promote a threefold nationalist slogan begun in 1962; *amyo* (only the Burman race), *barthar* (only the language of the Burmese), and *thathanar* (only the religion of Buddhism). The first (*amyo*) and second (*bartha*) support the idea of Burmanization (nationalism) and the third motivates Buddhistization (religious resurgence).[33] Burmanization and Buddhistization are the causes for religious violence and ethnic discrimination, whereas militarism is the cause of the religious violence, responsible for rejecting the rights of ethnic minorities, as well as ignoring the economic poverty of masses of people.[34]

In her widely read book *Freedom from Fear*,[35] Aung San Suu Kyi, the Noble Peace laureate, rightly notes that the economic suffering of people—both the ordinary Burmans and the ethnic minorities—results from the unjust rule of the military government. In fact, Myanmar is a rich country blessed with natural resources, such as timber and jewelry. Yet people are economically poor. Myanmar was once the most energetic country in Southeast Asia in terms of economic flourishing and education. But since the regime took power in 1962, Myanmar has become one of the poorest countries in the world.[36]

The question we have to ask is: if a religion, such as Buddhism, causes violence and poverty, shall we eliminate religion to achieve peace and human flourishing? The answer is no because it is better for world religions, including Buddhism, to increase.[37] In the context of religious violence, economic poverty, political oppression, and the growth of Buddhism, what should Christians do? Do all the Burman Buddhists support Buddhist nationalism, religious violence, and ethnic discrimination? What are the roles of the Christian community and the Burmese Buddhist community with regard to a Burmese public theology? In answer to these and other questions, I will now turn my attention to exploring the prescriptive and ethical roles of Christianity and Buddhism in Myanmar.

The Prospective Roles of Religions in Public Theology: Religious Ethics and Human Flourishing in Two Asian Cases

The Roles of Religions in a Burmese Public Theology of Human Rights

I will first explore the role of religion (singular) or the role of the Christian community in a public theology. I will then propose the roles of religions (plural)—the roles of both the Christian community and other religious communities or civil society in a public theology. What should the Christian community do in the face of sociopolitical oppression, economic poverty, and conflict? I would propose that the Christian community in Myanmar in particular and Asia in general should participate in at least three roles. The first is the Christian responsibility of prayer. First Timothy 2:2–10 identifies the importance of prayer. Paul wrote the letter to Timothy who was an overseer for a number of churches, which were going through sociopolitical challenges. Howard Marshall observes that in this passage, Paul develops two reasons for prayer. First, the Christians should pray for everybody, especially those who suffer from injustice. Second, Paul encourages the Christian community to pray for the state rulers so that they may live peaceful lives and that the rulers may rule the country with sociopolitical justice (2:2).[38]

Since Christian identity is deeply rooted in a gathered community of faith that engages in worship, preaching, and prayer, Christians should pray for the rulers and for those who suffer from injustice, poverty, and violence. We may pray for them both communally and individually, but I will focus more on the communal practice of prayer. Having said this, the aim of the ecclesial gathering is to pray for what is happening not only within the Christian community, but also in the larger society. It is important that we should bring public concerns into the church for reflection in communal prayer and preaching. I am not suggesting that we should politicize the church. Rather I am suggesting the role of the Christian community is to relate their faith to public issues.

To connect the spiritual responsibilities of the church with public issues, Christians must read not only the Bible but also the newspaper. As I said, Barth righty urges Christians to take the Bible in one hand and the newspaper in the other and read both for the church and the world.[39] I find Barth's dictum compelling for seeing public theology not only as a priestly discipline (mediating between God and the voice of the oppressed in terms of meditating on the Bible, preaching, and prayer), but also as a prophetic discipline (hearing the voice of God and advocating for justice in society: "Thus says the Lord" is a prophetic slogan [Jer. 9:23]). As a priestly community, the church hears the voices of people and tells God. As a prophetic community, the church hears God's voice and advocates for justice. The role of the Christian community must be rooted in this dialectic. I will now elaborate on the prophetic role.

The second is the prophetic role of Christians in a public theology. A priestly role of prayer is not enough in the sociopolitical context of nationalism, poverty, and discrimination. Christians must affirm the prophetic and defensive roles in the context of injustice and nationalism. Here I would first like to focus on ethnic justice in the face of nationalism in Asia. I will then return to the broader aspect of social justice and human flourishing. The reason is that Christianity is a majority religion among the ethnic minorities in Southeast Asia, and their struggle for their ethnic Christian identities in the face of nationalism should not be ignored. The Asian macro liberative hermeneutics of *Minjung* theology, for instance, ignores the micro liberation of the minority ethnic Christians. This ignoring goes unnoticed among Asian liberation theologians.

An often-quoted work by Ahn Byung-Mu, "Jesus and the *Minjung* in the Gospel of Mark,"[40] gives Ahn's rereading of Mark use of *ochlos* from the *Minjung* perspective. Ahn is one of the fathers of *Minjung* theology. In his notable article, "Jesus and the *Minjung* in the Gospel of Mark," Ahn makes a famous distinction between Mark's use of *ochlos* and *laos*. Using the historical method, Ahn argues that the former connotes the ordinary people or mass, whereas the latter connotes the chosen ones or the disciples of Christ. Adopting Mark's preference for *ochlos* rather than *laos*, Ahn proposes to identify *ochlos* with the *Minjung* in Korea who suffered at the hands of dictatorship.[41] When reading Asian *Minjung* theology through the lens of minority ethnic Christianity in Myanmar, I argue that it has both strengths and weaknesses. The strength is to see *ochlos* as the paradigm of the collective oppressed in Asia, regardless of religions or ethnicity and to struggle for their collective and macro liberation. Yet the weakness is its methodological ignorance of *laos* and its paradigmatic implication for the micro liberation of the ethnic Christians who resort under the paradigm of Jesus' disciples.

Ethnic Christians suffer a double oppression through experiencing both a collective poverty and ethnic discrimination. As I said earlier, the Chin, Kachin, and Karen ethnic groups together represent the country's highest percentage of Christians in Myanmar. The Chinese ethnic and indigenous groups in Malaysia as well as the indigenous Pataks and some Chinese in Indonesia represent those nations' highest percentage of Christians.[42] The ethnic groups in Myanmar, in particular, experience a collective poverty and marginalization. While the slogan of liberation theology is that God has preferential option for the poor or marginalized, in those particular Southeast Asian contexts, privileges go to the ethnic and religious majorities. It is even more painful to see how ethnic Christian minorities are assimilated to the dominant cultures.

In those challenging contexts, ethnic Christians face two options. One is to change one's religion by becoming Buddhists, Muslims, or Hindus so that they get equal opportunities just like the other ethnic majorities in their country. I call this the option of *opportunism*. The other is for Christians to remain faithful to who they are by defending themselves against any assimilative form of religious nationalism and by prophesizing against any ethnic monopoly's injustice and discrimination. I call this the option of *bold faithfulness*. I choose the latter. My proposal is that a tendency toward the defensive model of self-determination is an option for the ethnic identities, along with a prophetic model of criticizing the unjust systems and structures of the ruling class and criticizing discrimination by the majority classes. In short, a well-balanced emphasis on both the defensive and prophetic models of ethnic Christians would lead to achieving true ethnic liberation and rights in Asia.[43]

The third role of Christian community is prophetic in cooperation with Buddhists who hate religious violence. This does not mean that Christians in Myanmar are to take the initiative of cooperative resistance against the oppressive rulers. Rather Christians are called to join Buddhists who resist the unjust rulers and religious violence. In fact, in 1988, Buddhists, led by Suu Kyi, took the initiative of a nonviolent resistance against the Buddhist regime, and in 2007, the Buddhist supporters of Suu Kyi, led by the monks, resisted the Buddhist regime in a peaceful way, calling for democracy. The latter resistance movement is known as the *Saffron Revolution* (named after the colors of Buddhist monastics' robes). While the engaged Buddhists resisted the unjust rulers and soldiers, Christians remained silent. According to Chin Christian scholar Pum Za Mang, Christian silence arises from the problem of the separation of church and state.[44] Mang is right, but I will further argue that Christian silence in the face of military violence also arises from fear. It is natural for people to fear those who have guns, but as a prophetic community, Christians, like engaged Buddhists, ought to be courageous in resisting the regime. In short, resistance is central to both religions. Engaged Buddhism is a resisting type of religion,[45] and prophetic Christianity is likewise a resisting type of religion.[46]

To many people in the West, Buddhism is a nonresisting religion of private withdrawal from the public issues regarding sociopolitical injustice. The reality of Buddhism in Asia in general and contemporary Myanmar in particular, however, shows us a Buddhism in energetic engagement with the public issues of sociopolitical and ecological injustice without neglect of a spiritual practice of meditation. Western scholars Christopher Queen and Sallie King have helpfully provided an excellent resource for reconsidering Buddhism as a socially engaged and a spiritually practiced religion in the role of liberation movement.[47] I consider the Buddhist dialectical practice of social engagement and spiritual meditation analogous to what I have described and prescribed for Christianity as a dialectical community of priestly prayer and prophetic advocacy in its public role in support of social and ethnic justice.

In pursuing human rights and justice, I ask the following question. If Buddhism is a democratic religion by nature, why is Myanmar not a democratic country? In answer to this question, I suggest that we see "religious ethics" as a point of contact between Christianity and Buddhism in their ethical response to the undemocratic problems of human discrimination, religious violence, and political oppression. There are theological differences between Christianity and Buddhism over the doctrines of God and theodicy. While the Christian faith affirms the doctrine of God as the creator, judge, and sustainer of the world, Buddhists reject the doctrine of God because of the existence of evil. For them, the goodness and power of God cannot be reconciled with the existence of evil.[48] As a nontheistic religion, Buddhism teaches the doctrine of dependent origination. According to this doctrine, *karma* (the link between act and consequence), not God, is the impersonal judge from the beginning to the end of the world. Yet, despite major theological differences, Christianity and Buddhism have some convergences in their ethical teachings.

Using their ethical teachings as a point of contact, I will address two goals of Christian and Buddhist dialogue and cooperation. First, religious peace in

Asia cannot be promoted if directed against engaged Buddhists who hate religious violence. In the wake of the religious violence and conflict supported by the Burman nationalist Buddhists, Christian dialogue with Buddhists who hate such religious violence is imperative. Hans Küng was right when he said, "There can be no peace among nations without peace among religions."[49] In line with Küng, I argue that Myanmar's national peace depends on the success of interreligious dialogue with ordinary Buddhists. Only through dialogue with them can religious peace and social harmony in Myanmar be promoted.

In their interreligious dialogue, Christians and Buddhists have to be prophetic by speaking religious truth against the deceptions of the nationalist Buddhist misuse of religious violence and by criticizing the unjust systems that violate human dignity and human rights. By religious truth, I mean the fundamental religious doctrine of humanity. Christianity's doctrine of humanity is grounded in the image of God (Gen. 1:27). God created humankind with egalitarian dignity, equal rights and different gifts and cultures. Nicholas Wolterstorff argues, "Human rights are grounded in the value and dignity of human beings."[50] He prioritizes dignity over rights without separating them. Likewise, Moltmann too prioritizes human dignity over human rights. Moltmann argues that "human rights are plural, but human dignity exists only in the singular, and so the dignity of human beings takes precedence over the many rights."[51] Whether we totally agree with their priority of dignity over rights or not, we must agree that human dignity and rights are inseparable in the doctrine of humanity.

While there are some convergences between Buddhism and Christianity over the doctrine of humanity, there are also some divergences. The divergence is that the Christian view of human rights and humanity is grounded in the image of God from a monotheistic perspective, while the Buddhist view of human rights and human dignity is grounded in the inherent value of humanity from an ethical perspective. We are talking about one doctrine of humanity from two different points of view. To bridge their convergences and divergences, we must use bilinguality[52] as our method. By bilinguality, I mean we must look at the doctrine of humanity through the double lenses of Christianity and Buddhism. Christians should not impose their Christianized concept of humanity on Buddhists without borrowing their own concept. God does not impose His divinity on humans without incarnation (Jn. 1:14), nor does God speak to us through divine languages. God communicates with humans through the incarnation of Jesus, and the Spirit speaks to people in their native language on the day of Pentecostal (Acts 2:8).

Building on this framework, it is right to use bilinguality as a method for Christian dialogue with Buddhism on the shared views of human rights and human dignity. According to noted Buddhist scholar, Sallie King, the Buddhist doctrine of human rights and dignity are deeply grounded in the five principles of humanity: "(1) the preciousness of human birth; (2) human enlightenability; (3) human freedom, (4) human equality, and (5) non-violence."[53] I would like to comment on these five principles.

First, King is right that Buddhism accords a high and precious value to human birth. Of all births, a human birth is considered the most precious. No human being is born by accident; all human beings are born with a precious purpose. Second, since a human being is so precious, he or she has a capacity to become enlightened.

Third, the Buddha taught that every human being has his or her own freedom and his or her decision and effort to become enlightened. This third principle is grounded in the Buddhist doctrine of enlightenment or self-salvation. No one should rely on anyone or anything external for his or her knowledge. Human freedom is the essence of Buddhism. The Buddha advises, "Be islands into yourselves, be a refuge to yourselves, do not take any other refuge—work out your own salvation with diligence."[54] This third principle has a negative and a positive implication for a Burmese public theology. The negative implication comes from a soteriological perspective, while the positive implication comes from an ethical perspective. Soteriologically, this principle contradicts Christ's salvation that is external to our human effort. However, its ethical implication is that the Burman domination over the ethnic autonomy of Christian freedom is not only immoral, but also un-Buddhist.

Fourth, Buddhism teaches that every human being is born with an inherent dignity and equal rights, though his or her future destiny of life or rebirth may be different, based on what one has done in this life. The Buddhist idea of inherent dignity and equal rights contradicts the Hindu concept of a caste system in which one's fate in life is determined by one's birth. In contrast to Hinduism, Buddhism teaches that a person's role in society must be determined by his or her actions, not by the class assigned at his or her birth.[55] The Buddhist doctrine of human equality contradicts the Burman Buddhists' unequal treatment of the ethnic-minority Christians in Myanmar. For the Buddhist nationalists, the status of ethnic Christians is lower; they are considered less civilized. Because of such a discriminatory mindset, the ethnic minorities have no access to equal opportunities, nor can they play equal roles in society even if they are more capable than some Burman Buddhists.

Fifth, human rights and human dignity are best grounded in the fundamental Buddhist value of nonviolence. Nonviolence in grounded in the Buddhist Five Lay Ethics. The Five Lay Moral Codes are the most basic of all the Buddhist moral codes. They instruct all Buddhists "not to kill, steal, lie, commit sexual misconduct, and ingest intoxicants."[56] A bilingual method allows us to find analogies to the five Buddhist precepts analogous in the fifth, sixth, seventh, eighth, and ninth moral codes of the Jewish-Christian Ten Commandments (Ex. 20:13–17). The moral codes of both religious traditions demand right and nonharmful relationships between fellow humans. Buddhism sees "non-violence as calling for a respect for the autonomy of each person, demanding in effect a minimal use of coercion in human affairs."[57] In violation of the doctrine of nonviolence, the Burman Buddhist nationalists violently harm their fellow human being. When human rights are violated, it is imperative for Buddhists and Christians to be dialogical in prophetic responses to religious violence. In both individual and communal ethics, Christian and Buddhist concepts of human rights and responsibilities are related.

An important point I would like to emphasize here is the relationship between human rights and human responsibilities in public theology. In the early 1990s, two prominent Asian politicians, the late Lee Kuan Yew of Singapore (Confucian-Buddhist) and Mahathir Mohammad of Malaysia (Muslim), argued that human rights are part of Western individualistic culture and therefore cannot fit into the Asian communal culture.[58] While their claim is partly right because rights are individual-centered and defensive, the claim ultimately fails because it does not equate human rights to human responsibilities. When we relate human rights to human responsibilities, rights are not simply individualistic, but incorporated in community with other human beings, and thus part of the ethical response to social injustice in favor of the common good. I do not suggest that rights and responsibilities are overlapping, nor do I attempt to replace the former with the latter. Rather my suggestion is that when our rights are unethically violated, our responsibilities become ethical and incorporate responses to those who violate ours and the rights of others.[59]

Finally, the corporate roles of the Christian community and the Buddhist community should see "human suffering" (the first truth of Buddhism) as a point of contact for their ethical roles in a public theology of human flourishing and economic development. A public theology of human liberation must address the relationship between sin and suffering. The economic suffering of people in Myanmar is not the result of the sufferer's desires (the second truth of the Buddhist four noble truths), but the result of the unjust rulers' sin. Yet there is no clear doctrine of sin in Buddhism, and it is difficult for Buddhists to understand what it means to sin.[60] There are two different ways of perceiving sin in Asia in general and Myanmar in particular. An evangelist sees sin more as a state from a soteriological perspective (Rom. 5:12–21), whereas a liberationist see sin more as an immoral act of domination (Eph. 1:21; Col. 2:15). While the former approach has an important role in evangelism with its emphasis on Christ's forgiveness of sinners, its weakness is to promote the oppressors' immoral act. To achieve social justice, public theology must adopt a liberationist way of seeing sin as a sociocultural domination and see the oppressors as the greater sinners from an ethical perspective.

Although an evangelist way of seeing sin as a state does not make sense to Buddhism, a liberationist way of seeing sin is analogous to their own concept of immoral act. In response to the regime's immoral corruption, we must see sin as an immoral act, which causes suffering (Rom. 8) without ceasing to see sin as a state. According to Buddhism, the role of government is to rule the country justly and to promote human flourishing in terms of economics, education, and other aspects of public life.

Suu Kyi provides ten duties of the government for the people. They include:

> First liberality, which demands that the rulers should contribute generously to the welfare of people; second morality, which demands that the ruler should commit themselves to moral act and win the respect of people; third sacrifice, which demands the rulers' high commitment for the sake of people and the nation at the cost their lives; fourth, integrity, which demands the rulers' willingness to speak truth; fifth, kindness, which demands the rulers or people's concern for the other in need; sixth, austerity, which demands the rulers' simple lives and spiritual disciplines, seventh, non-anger, which demands the rulers self-control of anger, eighth, non-violence, which demands the rulers and people's peaceful behaviors, ninth forbearance, which demands the rulers' patience, and non-opposition, which demands the rulers' acceptance of the criticisms from the people.[61]

These ten precepts of Buddhism are grounded on the principle of democracy not only in terms of right relationship between the government and the ordinary people, but also in terms of promoting human flourishing and economic development. All religions, including Christianity and Buddhism, have a common vision of human development. Their vision of human development includes economic growth, intellectual growth, sociopolitical justice, and well-being. In their book *Religion in Development*,[62] Severine Deneulin and Masood Bana rightly argue that "Religions have the crucial components of people's well-being."[63] The authors provide five dominant roles of religions in development:

> First, religions are instrumental to development goal (economic growth); second, religions form people's value and rights and what count as legitimate development (social justice); third, religious freedom is grounded in religious doctrine of human rights and free choice (religious liberty); fourth, religion is a constitutive part of people' health; fifth, religions are the political forces that shape and change the society's socio-political structures.[64]

These five roles of religions and the previously discussed ten duties of Buddhism reveal the fact that it is important to conceive of religions as the moral keys for people's well-being and society's development. If this is the case, it is necessary to use the ethical values of religions as tools for correcting the unethical behaviors of religions in society. Using ten ethical duties, Christians and Buddhists in Myanmar are to resist and correct the unjust structures and the unethical behavior of the government. The goal of resisting and correcting the unjust government is to transform or liberate their unethical behavior into ethical behavior for the common good of human flourishing and development. Human flourishing is not just for one particular group, but for the whole nation. Myanmar needs a comprehensive sense of human flourishing. To achieve this goal, Christians and Buddhists must use religious ethics as a necessary and corrective tool for the unethical behavior of religions, which causes human suffering.

The Role of Religion in a Tibetan Public Theology of Human Rights

In spite of three decades of religious revival and economic transformation, Chinese authorities continue to view both religions and human rights in narrow terms and have not yet generated a robust commitment to human rights and human dignity on Chinese soil.[65] As I have said, the unethical violation by the Chinese of Tibetan human rights in their native land calls for a questioning of the role of the Tibetan Buddhists in contemporary Asian public theology. Being sandwiched between two great Asian nations—China on the east and India on the west—Tibet is not widely known to the world. However, its story of marginalization and colonization plays a crucial role in Asian public theology today. A Tibetan public theology of human liberation has recently become known to the world through the Dalai Lama, Tibet's exiled God-king and an engaged and spiritual Buddhist.[66]

The aim of this chapter is to focus exclusively on how the Dalai Lama and Tibetan Buddhists serve as examples for the role of religion in an Asian public theology of human liberation. China invaded Tibet in 1949 and its effort to completely erase the Tibetan autonomy intensified in 1959. This continued until the Dalai Lama's safety was threatened. When Chinese troops suppressed an armed uprising, the Dalai Lama, together with one hundred thousand Tibetan Buddhist refugees fled to India where he established a Tibetan government in exile in Dharamsala.[67] Did the Dalai Lama simply flee to India for his own safety? If not, how does he serve as role model for the Tibetan liberation movement? Although the Dalai Lama fled to India for his own safety, he continues to work as a liberating and empowering advocate for his fellow Tibetans who live in his native land.

Under his empowerment and guidance, there have been several instances of Tibetan ethical resistance against the Chinese regime. In 1987, there was a demonstration against the Chinese regime in Lhasa, led mainly by the Tibetan monks. A similar protest against the Chinese regime occurred in March of 1988, and again on March 5, 1989—this time in commemoration of the thirtieth anniversary of the 1959 revolt—the year Dalai Lama fled to India for his safety. A number of Tibetan demonstrators were killed.[68] On March 7, 1989, the government imposed martial law in Lhasa, not lifting it until May 1990. Further demonstrations occurred in 1990. A March 2008 demonstration was the most recent protest against the Chinese regime. The case of Tibetan liberation has become known to the world through the visits of the Dalai Lama to the West since the 1990s. He has delivered public speeches at important venues, such as the United Nations and the European Parliament at Strasbourg, accusing the Chinese government of cultural genocide and demanding Tibetan autonomy and respect for human rights and dignity.[69]

The goal of the Dalai Lama and the Tibetans' struggle against the Chinese government is for both independence and liberation. Unlike Asian nations who struggle for human liberation in a postcolonial context after an external colonization by the West, the Tibetan struggle is for an internal liberation and a sociopolitical independence from the Chinese regime.[70] Dalai Lama formulated the Fivefold Peace Plan, which calls for:

> First, the transformation of the whole of Tibet into a zone of peace; second, abandonment of China's population transfer policy that threatens the very existence of the Tibetans as a people; third, respect for the Tibetan people's fundamental rights and democratic freedoms; fourth, restoration and protection of Tibetan's natural environment and the abandonment of China's use of Tibet for the production of nuclear weapons and dumping of nuclear wastes; and fifth, commencement of earnest negotiations on the future of Tibet and of relations between the Tibetans and Chinese peoples.[71]

This five-point peace plan indicates that the Dalai Lama's method of resistance against the Chinese regime is defensive and dialogical, loving and nonretaliatory. It is defensive, asking for respect of distinct Tibetan culture and identity. It is also dialogical, as it deals with the Chinese government on the grounds of truth-speaking and justice-seeking. As a true Buddhist, the Dalai Lama never uses violence as a means for achieving Tibetan independence. He also considers Tibetan independence to not involve a complete break in diplomatic relationship with Chinese, but envisioning Tibetan an autonomous region. Because of his nonviolent struggle for Tibetan independence, the Dalai Lama was awarded the Noble Peace Prize in 1989. In his Noble acceptance speech, he emphasized the necessity of making Tibet a zone of peace through the demilitarizing of the Tibetan plateau, and protecting its natural environment by ending the testing of nuclear weapons.[72]

Most importantly, the Dalai Lama sees love as a motivating power for the unceasing Tibetans struggle against their enemies, the Chinese rulers. According to the Dalai Lama, Chinese rulers are their enemies, but the Tibetans are not necessarily their enemies. Thus he proposes that the Tibetan love for the Chinese rulers and a nonviolent practice of demonstration against Chinese domination should go hand in hand.[73]

Chapter 9

WORLD RELIGIONS AND A PUBLIC THEOLOGY OF HUMAN RECIPROCAL LIBERATION

I have explored some descriptive and unethical ways in which world religions have caused public and political violence, nationalism, and conflict, and have explored some prescriptive and ethical ways in which world religions have a role to play in Burmese and Tibetan public theologies of human rights and democracy. The main goal of the ethical roles of Christianity, Burmese Buddhism, and Tibetan Buddhism is a sociopolitical liberation of the oppressed. Is there any necessity to liberate the oppressors as well? My answer is yes! When it comes to a theology of liberation, we tend to focus only on the liberation of the oppressed. I call this an exclusive liberation of the oppressed.[74] I do not have anything against an exclusive liberation of the oppressed, not only because God chooses to stand in solidarity with the oppressed from the Exodus story through the prophetic writings to the Gospels, but also because God calls His prophets and disciples to be in solidarity with the oppressed for their liberation (Ex. 3:7–11; Micah 6:8; Matt. 25:40; Lk. 4:18–19).[75]

Why is God so partial to the oppressed and the people on the margins if God loves everyone? There are two main reasons for this. First, because God is compassionate to them. The basis of God's preference for the oppressed and those on the margins is found in God's very essence of compassion. According to Gustavo Gutiérrez, the father of Latin American liberation theology, "the oppressed and the marginalized are privileged, not because they are morally superior, but because God is fundamentally compassionate and prefers the least and the last."[76] Secondly, while I concur with Gutiérrez, I would further argue that Jesus prefers and identifies with the least and the last partly because they are His humiliated image (Phil. 2:7). Jesus came into the world not simply as a member of humanity in general, but as one marginalized from the center (heaven). Kosuke Koyama rightly says, "Jesus the center-person came to us in the form of a margin-person and chose to be crucified at the periphery place outside Jerusalem (Heb. 13:12)."[77] Since Jesus was once on the margin, He does not merely understand the suffering of the marginalized, but He chooses to be identified with them as their empowerer and liberator.[78] Jesus is just because He sides with the oppressed and restores their rights, which are violated by the oppressors.

According to Jürgen Moltmann, the highest form of divine justice in the biblical tradition is the "justice of compassion."[79] It is through the advocating and prophetic act of God's justice of compassion that those without rights receive restorative justice and the oppressors are also converted to justice.[80] This means that God's solidarity with the oppressed and God's prophetic resistance against the oppressors are for the common goal of what I call a *reciprocal liberation* of the two groups. While God's solidarity with the oppressed expresses God's advocacy for and with them for their liberation from their oppressors, God's resistance against the oppressors creates the space for their liberation from the immoral behavior of their oppression. This is how God executes what I call a "double justice" in the biblical tradition; yet many liberation theologians never pause to think that God's justice is inclusive of the oppressors. Within the framework of a double justice, I use the term *inclusive liberation* of the oppressed and oppressors[81] interchangeably with a *reciprocal liberation* of two conflicting groups.

How about Buddhism? Does Buddhism teach the idea of a reciprocal liberation of the oppressed and the oppressors? The answer is yes! Its concept of reciprocal liberation is grounded in a twofold practice of spiritual meditation and social engagement. While spiritual meditation tends to focus on the self's internal liberation from immoral thoughts, social engagement tends to focus on the civil community's external sociopolitical liberation from the rulers' unethical behavior, including social injustice, economic exploitation, and discrimination. Two prominent Asian Buddhist spiritual and liberating leaders, the Dalai Lama and Suu Kyi, affirm this twofold task in the struggle for people's liberation in their respective countries. A spiritual practice of meditation not only reveals one's liberation from immoral thoughts but also gives one (the true meditator) the strength to forgive the unjust rulers or the immoral actors. It is not easy for victims like Suu Kyi and the Dalai Lama to forgive the perpetrators, but it is through the spiritual act of meditation that they are able to offer their forgiveness to the perpetrators.

This twofold liberation is best grounded in the summary of the Buddhist threefold command: "the command to cease committing evil, the command to do good, and the command to meditate the mind."[82] Buddhists emphasize that the third command makes the other two possible. Analogously, Paul said, "hold on to the good and avoid every kind of evil (1 Thess. 5:21–22) and renew the attitudes of your minds" (Eph. 4:23). When we meditate, we are called not only to realize what is ethically good and right and what is evil and immoral, but also to renew or transform the attitudes of our minds. I call this "psychological or ethical liberation" and this liberation is for the oppressors who commit evils. Liberationists who focus exclusively on the liberation of the oppressed never think of the need for the liberation of the oppressors. I argue, however, that liberation has to be done on both sides because "oppression," as Moltmann rightly says, "is on both sides of the oppressed and oppressors."[83] Says Moltmann,

> Oppression has two sides. On the one side stands the oppressors; on the other side lies the oppressed. On the one side is the arrogant-self elevation of the exploiters, on the other side the suffering of their victims. Oppression destroys humanity on both sides. The oppressors act inhumanely, the victims are dehumanized.[84]

Since oppression has two sides, Moltmann argues that liberation has to proceed on both sides as well. He calls the liberation of the oppressed "political liberation," the liberation of the oppressors "psychological liberation."[85] He proposes that "the liberation of the oppressed from their suffering must lead to the liberation of the oppressors from the evil of the injustice they commit."[86] I respectfully disagree with his reversal of the process of liberation. By contrast, I argue that liberation of the oppressors must lead to the liberation of the oppressed. My point is simple: to liberate the oppressed from oppressive suffering, the oppressors must first be liberated psychologically and ethically from their oppressive acts of evil, which is the cause of suffering of the oppressed. Since the oppressors are not liberated automatically, the oppressed must resist their behavior until they come to be liberated and pursue the liberation of the oppressed. The goal of such reciprocal liberation is to build a democratic community in which the oppressors live side by side with the oppressed as new human beings, rather than to nurture an exclusive vision of winners and losers that promotes hatred. The ultimate goal of reciprocal liberation is not just about liberation *from* (the oppressed's liberation from oppression and the oppressors' liberation from immoral acts), but about liberation *for* reconciliation (telos)—true reconciliation between the oppressed and oppressors.[87]

PRIMAL RELIGION AND A PUBLIC THEOLOGY OF NATURE RIGHTS

As I have said, the people who hold power are the oppressors. But in this section, I will argue that both the oppressors and the oppressed are the anthropological oppressors of nature in Asia. I mean the natural resources are mercilessly exploited and thus oppressed by human beings. This exploitation occurs in terms of both technology-power and grassroots human power, or deforestation. I am tempted to call this *anthropocentric oppression* or *ecological crisis*. "Our ecological issue should be seen as a justice issue in Asia,"[88] writes K. C. Abraham, one of the pioneer Asian theologians to advocate for liberating nature from human oppression. In line with Abraham, I ask three central questions. Is there any role for a primal religion in the public theology of nature rights? If yes, what role is there for a primal religion in nature rights? And how should a primal religion play a role in a public theology of nature rights and environmental issues?

First, a primal religion plays a role in rethinking an Asian perspective on a holistic worldview and a holistic dimension of healing. When it comes to an Asian perspective on public theology, it is customary to compare Western and Asian ways of thinking,[89] in part because Asian Christianity was introduced by Western missionaries with their enlightenment worldviews of the private-public dichotomy and, in part because Asian Christians uncritically adopted Western modes of thinking. It is said that the Western way of thinking is metaphysically dualistic in terms of a spiritual-material and a God-creation dichotomy and is epistemologically dualistic in terms of a subject-object dichotomy,[90] while the Asian way is nondualistic and holistic.[91] However, not all Asian religions are nondualistic. For example, Buddhism is a dualistic religion in terms of its separation between this cosmic world (*lokka*) and the meta-cosmic world (*lokkutra*).[92] I argue that only a primal religion is nondualistic in terms of seeing the world as an unending unity.

One of the pressing issues facing the field of Asian public theology is how to overcome the uncritical reception by Asian Christians of a Western dualistic worldview of a sacred-secular dichotomy and an anthropos-cosmos dichotomy with regard to liberation. Following Western Reformation theology, which emphasizes the redemption of Christ with the slogan of *sola Christus*, we often disconnect God's salvation in Christ from God's creation (Gen. 1). God's salvation or "new creation" in Paul's words (2 Cor. 5:17) is a fulfillment of God's creation rather than a replacement of it. Liberation is not one way—humans first, then nature—but an interconnected liberation of anthropos and cosmos.[93] This holistic concept of the liberation of both anthropos and cosmos is found in Romans 8:19–22 and Colossians 1:20.[94] The nondualistic worldview of primal religion could enrich a holistic view of liberation in Asia.[95] By holistic liberation, I mean not only a spiritual and physical salvation of humanity, but also a holistic peace with God that includes with human beings and nature.

Second, a holistic liberation offers the church a fresh insight regarding our starting point in missions and helps us understand the nature of God's mission activity. Kim argues that the concept of *missio Dei* in Asia should begin with creation as a starting point of God's mission to the world.[96] In line with Kim, I argue that the triune God is involved in one mission of creation and new creation from Genesis to Revelation.[97] This affirms the threefold relation of God-human-nature,[98] and calls for defining the role of God as creating and sustaining the creation. It also defines the stewardship role of human beings as participating in God's continual mission not as rulers over nature, but as duty-bound to protect it.[99] We see God's role as a sustainer of nature not only through the vocation of the church, but through the ethical vocation of other religions.[100] This leads me to my third point.

Third, public theology in Asia should take seriously the ethical role of a primal religion.[101] The Asian primal religion with its spirit worship has two positive points with regard to nature rights and eco-liberation. First, a primal religion with its spirit worship is an eco-ethical religion in terms of its recognition and veneration of nature rights. Since nature-spirits are powerful in their jurisdiction, they do not tolerate human trespass.[102] Neither shooting animals nor cutting trees is permissible in the vicinity of a nature-spirit's abode. Hunters and farmers must first give an offering to the spirits, asking permission for their undertakings. The failure to appease the nature-spirits brings misfortune to those who trespass. Even after asking permission from the spirits to use natural resources, no one is allowed to take more than necessary. This is relevant to those who cut trees for farming in Asia.[103] It is always a challenge to tell the farmers about the issues of creation care. They often think all of nature is God's gift to be used or abused at any time for any purpose related to farming. To convince them, we need to discern their cultural practice of spirit worship. They believe that the spirits are the guardians of nature. This is analogous to the purpose of God's creation of human beings as the guardians of nature rather than as the destroyers of nature (Gen. 1:28).

As I have said in the introduction, public theology in Asia ought to hold in tension the first mandate of creation care (Gen. 1:28) and the last commission of evangelism (Matt. 28:16–20). In light of this tension, it is not right for the church to see the adherents of primal religion as the mere objects for evangelism and conversion, but to see them as co-workers in stewardship for creation care without ceasing to evangelize them. This means that the primal religious ethics of nature rights can continue to play a stewardship role in a public theology of creation care and nature healing, even after practitioners become the followers of Christ. Too often, Christians confine the scope of mission to an anthropos emphasis. If God's intended purpose for creating human beings is for them to be stewards of His creation, Christians in Asia should expand the scope of anthropos-focused mission into the larger scope of nature care mission. But if God created humans a little lower than angels and a little higher than nature (Ps. 8:5), Christians may prioritize anthropos-focused mission over nature-focused mission without separating the two.

Why do we need to take care of nature? The answer is simple. It is because nature first takes care of us. So, in turn, we have to take care of natures. If there were no trees around us, it would not be safe to live. Nature takes care of us by providing safety, so we must take care of nature by planting more trees. However, I am not suggesting that we should worship nature or nature-spirits or practice what we may call *naturalism*. Rather, my suggestion is to love nature as God's creation. Therefore, Asian Christians ought to see the ethics of primal religion as a source for preserving nature. If we did so, Asia would be covered with green forests, wild animals would multiply, and fish would increase. Nature spirits have no power to create the world, but they are somehow complementary to the Spirit's continued work of healing a groaning nature (Rom. 8:21). Of course, the Holy Spirit is not a nature spirit, but the analogy lies in the latter's mysterious presence in nature where it serves as a guardian for a suffering nature.

Of course, a primal religion is not without its weaknesses. While we appreciate its ethical role in a public theology of nature rights and creation care, we must also acknowledge its weaknesses. There are two weaknesses in the cultural spirit worship.[104] The first weakness is that that spirits do not give people hope or future security. People worship spirits for the security of their present lives. While a primal religion of spirit worship tends to focus on a concern for this world, the Asian world religions, such as Buddhism, tend to focus on a concern for the worldly.[105] In a sense, Asian people, especially Buddhists, have two gods—the Buddha and the spirits. They worship the Buddha as the moral guide for their future lives, on the one hand, and worship the spirits, on the other. They worship the Buddha by following his moral teachings and worship the spirits by appeasing them.[106] The other weakness is that people worship spirits out of fear. If people did not appease them with sacrificial rites, the malevolent spirits would bring them misfortune. A public theology in Asia should grapple with and transform the challenge of spiritual principalities that combat God's kingdom of love, peace, and justice without ceasing to appreciate their moral contributions to the Asian need for creation care.

In short, Asian Christians should rethink the ethical roles of other religions in human rights and nature rights. If Christianity, Buddhism, and Confucianism play a role in promoting a democratic vision of human rights and human flourishing, primal religion plays a role in promoting a cosmological vision of nature rights and flourishing. Primal religion makes a contribution not only to nature rights, but also to land rights. Land rights are the crucial issue for the native people in Asia. Their lands are their identity markers. When struggling for nature flourishing, we also struggle for preserving the lands for the rights of the native people. Public issues of human flourishing, nature flourishing, and land preservation cannot be effectively addressed by a minority of Asian Christianity alone (9 percent); they can be addressed in cooperation with people of other religions.

CONCLUSION

I have explored the paradoxes of religious violence and peace in Asia. Using Tibet and Myanmar as two Asian contexts, I have shown the problems of religious violence, conflict, and injustice for public theology. I have examined the sociopolitical causes and consequences of religious violence as collective suffering and poverty. On the other hand, I have explored the roles of world religions, such as Buddhism and Christianity, in a public theology of pursuing human justice, fostering economic flourishing, and adding human development. For Christianity and Buddhism to share a common vision for a public theology of human justice and peace, I have proposed to see their respective religious ethics as the point of contact for their joint moral responses to the problems of violence and injustice. I have stressed that public theology in Asia must use the ethical doctrines of religions as the tool for criticizing and correcting the unethical behavior of religious nationalists and state rulers. The goal of these cooperative ethical responses is to achieve a mutual liberation of the oppressed and the oppressors.

I have also argued that the Christian liberative doctrine of human rights and human dignity is grounded in the image of God, while the Buddhist doctrine of human rights and dignity is grounded in the doctrine of humanity as a precious creature. To make a connection between the Buddhist and the Christian convergent and divergent doctrines of human rights and dignity, I have proposed to use bilinguality as a methodological key for an Asian public theology. Finally, I have explored the role of a primal religion in a public theology of nature flourishing. It is my strong suggestion that public theology in Asia should no longer separate human liberation and salvation from nature liberation and salvation. This is because God's act of salvation is one, not two. What God has joined together, the church must stop separating. Rather, the role of the Christian community is to witness to the one gospel of anthropos and cosmos flourishing and liberation in and with the other religious communities.

BIBLIOGRAPHY

Abe, Masao. "The Problem of Evil in Christianity and Buddhism." In *Buddhist-Christian Dialogue: Mutual Renewal and Transformation*, edited by Paul Ingram and Frederick Streng, 140–55. Honolulu: University of Hawaii Press, 1986.

Abraham, K. C. "A Theological Response to the Ecological Crisis." In *Ecotheology: Voices from South and North*, edited by David Hallman 65–78. Geneva: WCC, 1994.

Anderson, Christian J. "Beginning at the Beginning: Reading *Missio Dei* from the Start of the Bible." *Missiology: An International Review* 45, no. 4 (October 2017): 414–25.

Ahn, Byung Mu. "Jesus and Minjung in the Gospel of Mark." In *Minjung Theology: People as The Subject of History*, edited by Kim Young Bock, 136–54. Singapore: CCA, 1981.

Barth, Karl. *Community, State, and Church: Three Essays.* Eugene, OR: Wipf and Stock, 2004.

Cabezon, Jose Ignacio. "Buddhist Principles in the Tibetan Liberation Movement." In *Engaged Buddhism: Buddhist Liberation Movements in Asia*, edited by Christopher S. Queen and Sallie B. King, 295–320. Albany: State University of New York Press, 1996.

Carey, William. *An Enquiry into the Obligation of Christians to Use Means for the Conversion of the Heathen.* Greenwood: Attic, 1972.

Chan, Simon. *Asian Grassroots Theology: Thinking the Faith from the Ground Up.* Downers Grove, IL: IVP, 2014.

"China: Events of 2015." *Human Rights Watch.* Accessed March 22, 2018, from https://www.hrw.org/world-report/2016/country-chapters/china-and-tibet.

Ching, Julia. *Chinese Religions*. Maryknoll, NY: Orbis, 1993.

Dalai Lama. "Noble Lecture by the His Holiness Tenzing Gyatso, The Fourteenth Dalai Lama." *News Tibet* 23, no. 2 (1989).

De Gruchy, John W. "From Political Theology to Public Theologies: The Role of Theology in Public Life." In *Public Theology for the 21st Century: Essays in Honour of Duncan B. Forrester*, edited by William R. Storrar and Andrew R. Morton, 45–62. London: T and T Clark, 2004.

Deneulin, Severine, and Masood Bana. *Religion in Development: Rewriting the Secular Script.* London: Zed, 2009.

En, Simon Pau Khan. "Nat-Worship: A Paradigm for Doing Ecumenical Theology in Myanmar." *Asia Journal of Theology* 8, no. 1 (April 1994): 42–53.

Gaventa, Beverly Robert, ed. *Apocalyptic Paul: Anthropos and Cosmos in Romans 5–8*. Waco, TX: Baylor University Press, 2013.
Gutiérrez, Gustavo. *On Job: God-Talk and the Suffering of the Innocent*. Maryknoll, NY: Orbis, 1987.
Hackett, See William D. "Christian Response to Animistic Peoples." *Southeast Asia Journal of Theology* 10, no. 1 (1969): 50–60.
Haire, James. "Stories in Animism and Christian Pneumatology." In *Doing Theology with the Spirit's Movement*, edited by John C. England and Alan T. Torrance, 120–30. Singapore, ATESEA, 1991.
Harasata, Eva. "Karl Barth, a Public Theologian? The One Word and Theological Bilinguality." *International Journal of Public Theology* 3, no. 2 (2009): 188–203.
Horsley, Richard R, ed. *In The Shadow of Empire: Reclaiming the Bible as a History of Faithful Resistance*. Louisville, KY: Westminster John Knox Press, 2008.
Keys, Charles. "Buddhism, Human Rights and Non-Buddhist Minorities." In *Theology in the Public Sphere: Public Theology as a Catalyst for Open Debate*, edited by Sebastian Thomas Kim. London: SCM Press, 2011.
Kim, Sebastian. *Theology in the Public Sphere: Public Theology as a Catalyst for Open Debate* London: SCM Press, 2011.
Kim, Sebastian, and Kirsteen Kim. *Christianity as a World Religion*, 2nd ed. London: Bloomsbury Academic, 2016.
King, Sallie B. "Buddhism and Human Rights." In *Religion and Human Rights: An Introduction*, edited by John Witte and M. Christian Green, 103–118, 2nd ed. New York: Oxford University Press, 2012.
Koyama, Kosuke. "Extend Hospitality to Strangers: A Missiology of Theologia Crucis." *Journal of Currents in Theology and Mission* 20, no. 3 (June 1993): 165–76.
Kung, Huns. *Global Responsibility: In Search For a New Ethics*, translated by John Bowden. New York: Continuum, 1993.
Kung, Lap Yan. "Love Your Enemies: A Theology for Aliens in Their Native Land: The Chin Myanmar." *Studies in World Christianity* 15, no. 1 (2009): 81–99.
Lee, Jung Young. "The Yin-Yang Way of Thinking." In *Asian Christian Theology: Emerging Themes*, edited by Douglas J. Elwood, rev. ed., 81–88. Louisville, KY: Westminster John Knox Press, 1980.
Magnus, Richard. "The Christian Roles in a Pluralistic Society, with Special Reference to Singapore." In *Pilgrims and Citizens: Christian Social Engagement in East Asia Today*, edited by Michael Nai-Chiu Poon, 169–178. Singapore: ATF Press, 2006.
Mang, Pum Za. "Separation of Church and State: A Case Study of Myanmar (Burma)." *Asia Journal of Theology* 25, no. 1 (April 2011): 42–58.
Marshall, I. Howard. "Biblical Patterns for Public Theology." *European Journal of Theology* 14, no. 1 (2005): 73–86.
Marty, Martin E. "Reinhold Niebuhr: Public Theology and the American Experience." *Journal of Religion* 54, no. 4 (October 1974): 332–59.
Moe, David Thang. "Burman Domination and Ethnic Discrimination: Toward a Postcolonial Theology of Resistance and Reconciliation in Myanmar." *Exchange: Contemporary Christianities in Context* 47, no. 2 (2018): 57–88.
———. "The Church as the Image of the Trinity: Toward a Trinitarian Public Theology of Justice and Peace in Asia." *Asia Journal of Theology* 32, no. 2 (October 2018).
———. "Constructing a Theology of Mission." *Currents in Theology and Mission* 44, no. 2 (April 2017): 23–25.
———. "Nat-Worship and Paul Tillich: Contextualizing a Correlational Theology of Religion and Culture in Myanmar." *Toronto Journal of Theology* 31, no. 1 (Spring 2015): 123–36.
———. "Reading Romans 13:1–7 as a Hidden Transcript of Postcolonial Theology in Myanmar." *Journal of Theology for Southern Africa* 157 (March 2017): 71–98.
———. "Sin and Evil in Christian and Buddhist Perspectives: A Quest for Theodicy." *Asia Journal of Theology* 29, no. 1 (April 2015): 22–46.
———. "Trends and Issues in Asian Christianity: The Challenge to Intercultural Dialogue." *Journal of Asian Mission* 18, no. 1 (May 2017): 71–102.

Moltmann, Jürgen. *The Crucified God: The Cross of Christ as the Foundation and Criticism of Christian Theology*, translated by R. A. Wilson and John Bowden. Minneapolis: Fortress, 1993.
———. *The Crucified God*, 40th anniversary ed. Minneapolis: Fortress, 2015.
———. *Experiences in Theology: Ways and Forms of Christian Theology,*. translated by Margaret Kohl. Minneapolis: Fortress, 2000.
———. *God for a Secular Society: The Public Relevance of Theology*, translated by Margaret Kohl. Minneapolis: Fortress, 1999.
———. *On Human Dignity: Political Theology and Ethics*, translated by M. Douglas Meeks. Minneapolis: Fortress, 2007.
———. "Political Theology and the Ethics of Peace." In *Theology, Politics, and Peace*, edited by Theodore Runyon, 31–42. Maryknoll, NY: Orbis, 1989.
———. "Political Theology in Europe after Auschwitz." In *Public Theology for the 21st Century: Essays in Honour of Duncan B. Forrester*, edited by William R. Storrar and Andrew R. Morton, 37–44. London: T and T Clark, 2004.
"Myanmar's Christian Population Grows to 6.2 Percent." *World Watch Monitor*. Accessed April 6, 2018, from https://www.worldwatchmonitor.org/2016/08/myanmars-christian-population-grows-to-6-2-per-cent/.
Myers, Bryant L. *Walking with the Poor: The Principles and Practices of Transformational Development*, rev. ed. Maryknoll, NY: Orbis, 2011.
Nash, June C. *Practicing Ethnography in a Globalizing World: An Anthropological Odyssey*, 2nd ed. Lanham, MD: Altamira, 2007.
Nirmal, Irvind O. "Ecology, Ecumenics in Relation: A New Theological Paradigm." In *Ecology and Development: Theological Perspectives*, edited by Daniel D. Chettied, 3–25. Madras, India: Gurukul, 1991.
Ownby, David. "Religion, State Power, and Human Rights in China." In *Religion and the Global Politics of Human Rights*, edited by Thomas Banchoff and Robert Wuthnow, 213–45. New York: Oxford University Press, 2011.
Panikkar, Raimundo. *The Trinity and the Religious Experience of Man: Icon-Person Mystery*. Maryknoll, NY: Orbis, 1973.
Pieris, Aloysius. *An Asian Theology of Liberation*. London: T and T Clark, 1988.
———. "Political Theology in Asia." In *Blackwell Companion to Political Theology*, edited by Peter Scott and William T. Cavanaugh, 256–70. Malden, MA: Blackwell, 2006.
Pui-lan, Kwok. "Postcolonial Intervention in Political Theology." *Political Theology* 17, no. 3 (2016): 223–25.
———. "Introduction: The Shapes and Sources of Engaged Buddhism." In *Engaged Buddhism: Buddhist Liberation Movements in Asia*, edited by Christopher S. Queen and Sallie B. King, 1–44. Albany: State University of New York Press, 1996.
Queen, Christopher S., and Sallie B. King, eds. *Engaged Buddhism: Buddhist Liberation Movements in Asia*. Albany: State University of New York Press, 1996.
Ramachandra, Vinoth. *Subverting Global Myths: Theology and Public Issues Shaping the World*. Downers Grove, IL: InterVarsity Press, 2008.
Sakhong, Lian H. *In Search of Chin Identity: A Study in Religion, Politics and Ethnic Identity in Burma*. Copenhagen: NIAS Press, 2008.
Schmitt, Carl. *Politische Theologie*. Auflage: Duncker and Humblot, 1922.
Smith, Wilfred J. *The Faith of Other Men*. New York: New American Library, 1963.
Song, C. S. *Third–Eye Theology: Theology in Formation in Asian Settings*. Maryknoll, NY: Orbis, 1979.
Spiro, Melford E. *Burmese Supernaturalism*. Eaglewood Cliffs, NJ: Prentice Hall, 1967.
Steinberg, David I. *Burma/Myanmar: What Everyone Needs to Know*. New York: Oxford University Press, 2013.
Sunquist, Scott W. *The Unexpected Christian Century: Reversal and Transformation of Global Christianity 1900–2010*. Grand Rapids, MI: Baker Academic, 2015.
Suu Kyi, Aung San. *Freedom from Fear*. New York: Penguin Books, 1991.
Tibetan Center for Human Rights and Democracy. Accessed March 22, 2018, from http://tchrd.org/.

Volf, Miroslav. "Faith, Pluralism and Public Engagement." *Political Theology* 14, no. 6 (2013): 813–34.
———. *Flourishing: Why We Need Religion in a Globalized World*. New Haven, CT: Yale University Press, 2015.
Wilfred, Felix. *Asian Public Theology: Critical Concerns in Challenging Times*. New Delhi: ISPCK, 2010.
Willmer, Haddon. "Karl Barth." In *The Blackwell Companion to Political Theology*, edited by Peter Scott and William T. Cavanaugh, 123–49. Malden, MA: Blackwell, 2006.
Wolterstorff, Nicholas P. "Christianity and Human Rights." In *Religion and Human Rights: An Introduction*, edited by John Witte and M. Christian Green, 2nd ed., 42–55. New York: Oxford University Press, 2012.
———. *Journey Personal Encounters in the Global South Toward Justice*. Grand Rapids, MI: Baker Academic, 2013.
———. *The Mighty and Almighty: An Essay in Political Theology*. New York: Cambridge University Press, 2012.
Wright, Christopher J. H. *The Mission of God: Unlocking the Bible's Grand Narrative*. Downers Grove, IL: IVP, 2006.
World Rights Monitor. "Myanmar's Christian Populations Grows to 6.2 Percent." Accessed April 6, 2018, from https://www.worldwatchmonitor.org/2016/08/myanmars-christian-population-grows-to-6-2-per-cent/.

NOTES

1. Aloysius Pieris, *An Asian Theology of Liberation* (London: T and T Clark, 1988), 217. Pieris made this statement thirty years ago. Whether the collective suffering in terms of economic poverty can still be applicable to the five Asian tigers, such as South Korea, Hong Kong, Japan, Taiwan, and Singapore, is debatable. However, it remains true to a larger Asian community. For the updated population of Asian Christianity, see also Scott W. Sunquist, *The Unexpected Christian Century: Reversal and Transformation of Global Christianity 1900–2010* (Grand Rapids, MI: Baker Academic, 2015), xvii. According to the census in 2010, about 9 percent of the Asian population practices Christianity.

2. We should not see primal religion as a synonym to primitive religion. While primal religion indicates local religion, primitive religion refers to a colonial version of outdated religion.

3. Bryant L. Myers, *Walking with the Poor: The Principles and Practices of Transformational Development*, rev. ed. (Maryknoll, NY: Orbis, 2011), 3–5.

4. Ibid., 3.

5. William Carey, *An Enquiry into the Obligation of Christians to Use Means for the Conversion of the Heathen* (Greenwood: Attic, 1972).

6. Myers, *Walking with the Poor*, 3–4.

7. When I say the church and the state should be dialectically related, I mean the church should see the state as its partner in praxis for the common good of all, but the former has to resist when the latter misuses its power. See David Thang Moe, "Reading Romans 13:1–7 as a Hidden Transcript of Postcolonial Theology in Myanmar," *Journal of Theology for Southern Africa*, 157 (March 2017): 71–98.

8. Nicholas P. Wolterstorff, *The Mighty and Almighty: An Essay in Political Theology* (New York: Cambridge University Press, 2012), i.

9. Carl Schmitt, *Politische Theologie* (Auflage: Duncker and Humblot, 1922).

10. Martin E. Marty, "Reinhold Niebuhr: Public Theology and the American Experience," *Journal of Religion* 54, no. 4 (October 1974): 332–59.

11. For an excellent collection of Barth's political theology, see Karl Barth, *Community, State, and Church: Three Essays* (Eugene, OR: Wipf and Stock, 2004).

12. Jürgen Moltmann, "Political Theology in Europe after Auschwitz," in *Public Theology for the 21st Century: Essays in Honour of Duncan B. Forrester*, ed. William R. Storrar and Andrew R. Morton (London: T and T Clark, 2004), 37–44.

13. Kwok Pui-lan, "Postcolonial Intervention in Political Theology," *Political Theology* 17, no. 3. (2016): 223–25.

14. Ibid., 223–25.

15. See John W. de Gruchy, "From Political Theology to Public Theologies: The Role of Theology in Public Life," *Public Theology for the 21st Century: Essays in Honour of Duncan B. Forrester*, ed. William R. Storrar and Andrew R. Morton (London: T and T Clark, 2004), 47–61.

16. Ibid., 47–49.

17. Sebastian Kim, *Theology in the Public Sphere: Public Theology as a Catalyst for Open Debate* (London: SCM Press, 2011), 13.

18. Aloysius Pieris, "Political Theology in Asia," in *Blackwell Companion to Political Theology*, eds. Peter Scott and William T. Cavanaugh (Malden, MA: Blackwell, 2006), 256–70. Pieris's Asian political theology does not embrace the public issue of eco-liberation in Asia.

19. Felix Wilfred argues against public theology as church-centered. See Felix Wilfred, *Asian Public Theology: Critical Concerns in Challenging Times* (New Delhi: ISPCK, 2010), xv–xix.

20. Richard Magnus, "The Christian Roles in a Pluralistic Society with Special Reference to Singapore," in *Pilgrims and Citizens: Christian Social Engagement in East Asia Today*, ed. Michael Nai-Chiu Poon (Singapore: ATF, 2006), 170–171.

21. Jürgen Moltmann, *God for a Secular Society: The Public Relevance of Theology*, trans. Margaret Kohl (Minneapolis: Fortress, 1999), 1.

22. For full discussion of the Trinitarian doctrine as the model for public theology in Asia, see David Thang Moe, "The Church as the Image of the Trinity: Toward a Trinitarian Public Theology of Justice and Peace in Asia," *Asia Journal of Theology* 32, no. 2 (October 2018).

23. Miroslav Volf, "Faith, Pluralism and Public Engagement," *Political Theology* 14, no. 6 (2013): 823.

24. Quoted in Haddon Willmer, "Karl Barth," in *The Blackwell Companion to Political Theology*, eds. Peter Scott and William T. Cavanaugh (Malden, MA: Blackwell, 2006), 123. Barth commented this dictum to his students in the 1920s at the time when Hitler came to power in Germany in particular and Europe in general.

25. Ibid., 123.

26. Miroslav Volf, *Flourishing: Why We Need Religion in a Globalized World* (New Haven, CT: Yale University Press, 2015), 59.

27. "China: Events of 2015," *Human Rights Watch*. Accessed March 22, 2018, from https://www.hrw.org/world-report/2016/country-chapters/china-and-tibet. See also for example, Tibetan Center for Human Rights and Democracy. Accessed March 22, 2018, from http://tchrd.org/.

28. Ibid. See also Sallie B. King, "Buddhism and Human Rights," in *Religion and Human Rights: An Introduction*, eds. John Witte and M. Christian Green, 2nd ed. (New York: Oxford University Press, 2012), 103–104.

29. Julia Ching, *Chinese Religions* (Maryknoll, NY: Orbis, 1993), 15–152.

30. Some terminologies need clarifications. When I use the term *Burman*, I refer exclusively to it as the ethnic majority group that represents the Buddhist majority. I use the term *Burmese* to inclusively describe the language and the entire people regardless of ethnic minorities (Chins, Kachins, Karens, Kayahs, Mons, Shans, Rakhines) and ethnic majorities of Burmans. See David I. Steinberg, *Burma/Myanmar: What Everyone Needs to Know* (New York: Oxford University Press, 2013), 10.

31. For the Christian population in Myanmar, see "Myanmar's Christian Population Grows to 6.2 Percent," *World Watch Monitor*. Accessed April 6, 2018, from https://www.worldwatchmonitor.org/2016/08/myanmars-christian-population-grows-to-6-2-per-cent/.

32. See Lian H. Sakhong, *In Search of Chin Identity: A Study in Religion, Politics and Ethnic Identity in Burma* (Copenhagen, NIAS Press, 2008). See also Charles Keys, "Buddhism, Human Rights and Non-Buddhist Minorities," in *Religion and the Global Politics of Human Rights*, eds. Thomas Banchoff and Robert Wuthnow (New York: Oxford University Press, 2011), 165.

33. Sakhong, *In Search of Chin Identity*, 127

34. Steinberg, *Burma/Myanmar*, 185–280.
35. Aung San Suu Kyi, *Freedom from Fear* (New York: Penguin Books, 1991), 168.
36. Ibid., 168.
37. Volf, *Flourishing*, 61–62.
38. I. Howard Marshall, "Biblical Patterns for Public Theology," *European Journal of Theology* 14, no. 1 (2005): 80–81.
39. Quoted in Willmer, "Karl Barth," 123.
40. Ahn Byung Mu, "Jesus and Minjung in the Gospel of Mark," in *Minjung Theology: People as the Subject of History*, ed. Kim Young Bock (Singapore: CCA, 1981), 136–54.
41. Ibid., 136–154.
42. See Sebastian Kim and Kirsteen Kim, *Christianity as a World Religion*, 2nd edition (London: Bloomsbury Academic, 2016), 62–72. See also David Thang Moe, "Trends and Issues in Asian Christianity: The Challenge to Intercultural Dialogue," *Journal of Asian Mission* 18, no. 1 (May 2017): 71–102.
43. See David Thang Moe, "Burman Domination and Ethnic Discrimination: Toward a Postcolonial Theology of Resistance and Reconciliation in Myanmar," *Exchange: Contemporary Christianities in Context* 47 no. 2 (2018): 57–88. For the particular case of the ethnic Chins, see Lap Yan Kung, "Love Your Enemies: A Theology for Aliens in Their Native Land: The Chin Myanmar," *Studies in World Christianity* 15, no. 1 (2009): 81–99.
44. Pum Za Mang, "Separation of Church and State: A Case Study of Myanmar (Burma)," *Asia Journal of Theology* 25, no. 1 (April 2011): 42–58.
45. Christopher S. Queen, "Introduction: The Shapes and Sources of Engaged Buddhism," in *Engaged Buddhism: Buddhist Liberation Movements in Asia*, eds. Christopher S. Queen and Sallie B. King (Albany: State University of New York Press, 1996), 1–44. The term "engaged Buddhism" was first coined by a Vietnamese Buddhist activist Thich Nhat Hanh in 1963. See also C. S. Song, *Third-Eye Theology: Theology in Formation in Asian Settings* (Maryknoll, NY: Orbis, 1979), 11–113.
46. Richard R. Horsley, ed., *In The Shadow of Empire: Reclaiming the Bible as a History of Faithful Resistance* (Louisville, KY: Westminster John Knox Press, 2008).
47. See Christopher S. Queen and Sallie B. King, eds., *Engaged Buddhism: Buddhist Liberation Movements in Asia* (Albany: State University of New York Press, 1996), ix. The term "engaged Buddhism" was first coined by a Vietnamese Buddhist activist Thich Nhat Hanh in 1963. The prominent examples of engaged Buddhists in Asia include Dr. Ambedkar who struggled for Dalit liberation in India, Thich Nhat Hanh who struggles for Vietnamese liberation, Dalai Lama who struggles for Tibetan liberation.
48. Along these lines, see David Thang Moe, "Sin and Evil in Christian and Buddhist Perspectives: A Quest for Theodicy," *Asia Journal of Theology* 29, no. 1 (April 2015): 22–46.
49. Huns Kung, *Global Responsibility: In Search for a New Ethics*, trans. John Bowden (New York: Continuum, 1993), 76.
50. Nicholas P. Wolterstorff, *Journey Personal Encounters in the Global South toward Justice* (Grand Rapids, MI: Baker Academic, 2013), 47. See also Nicholas P. Wolterstorff, "Christianity and Human Rights," in *Religion and Human Rights: An Introduction*, eds., John Witte and M. Christian Green, 2nd ed. (New York: Oxford University Press, 2012), 42–55.
51. Jürgen Moltmann, *On Human Dignity: Political Theology and Ethics*, trans. M. Douglas Meeks (Minneapolis: Fortress, 2007), 9.
52. See Eva Harasta, "Karl Barth, a Public Theologian? The One Word and Theological Bilinguality," *International Journal of Public Theology* 3, no. 2. (2009): 188–203.
53. King, "Buddhism and Human Rights," 107–109.
54. Ibid., 108.
55. Ibid., 108.
56. King, "Buddhism and Human Rights," 107.
57. Ibid., 107.
58. Quoted in King, "Buddhism and Human Rights," 103.
59. Ibid., 111–113. See also Vinoth Ramachandra, *Subverting Global Myths: Theology and Public Issues Shaping the World* (Downers Grove, IL: InterVarsity Press, 2008), 92–93.
60. Moe, "Sin and Evil in Christian and Buddhist Perspectives," 22–46.

61. Suu Kyi, *Freedom from Fear*, 172–173.
62. Severine Deneulin and Masood Bana, *Religion in Development: Rewriting the Secular Script* (London: Zed, 2009), 48.
63. Ibid., 48.
64. Ibid., 28.
65. David Ownby, "Religion, State Power, and Human Rights in China," in *Religion and the Global Politics of Human Rights*, eds. Thomas Banchoff and Robert Wuthnow (New York: Oxford University Press, 2011), 213–14.
66. Ibid., 225.
67. Ibid., 225. See also Jose Ignacio Cabezon, "Buddhist Principles in the Tibetan Liberation Movement," in *Engaged Buddhism: Buddhist Liberation Movements in Asia*, eds. Christopher S. Queen and Sallie B. King (Albany: State University of New York Press, 1996): 296.
68. Ownby, "Religion, State Power, and Human Rights in China," 226.
69. Ibid., 227.
70. Cabezon, "Buddhist Principles in the Tibetan Liberation Movement," 298.
71. Quoted in Cabezon, "Buddhist Principles in the Tibetan Liberation Movement," 298.
72. Dalai Lama, "Noble Lecture by the His Holiness Tenzing Gyatso, The Fourteenth Dalai Lama," *News Tibet* 23, no. 2 (1989).
73. Ibid., 304.
74. Moe, "Sin and Evil," 214–16.
75. Ibid., 215.
76. Gustavo Gutiérrez, *On Job: God-Talk and the Suffering of the Innocent* (Maryknoll, NY: Orbis, 1987), 94.
77. Kosuke Koyama, "Extend Hospitality to Strangers: A Missiology of Theologia Crucis," *Journal of Currents in Theology and Mission* 20, no. 3 (June 1993): 167.
78. Jürgen Moltmann, *The Crucified God: The Cross of Christ as the Foundation and Criticism of Christian Theology*, trans. R. A. Wilson and John Bowden (Minneapolis: Fortress, 1993), 205.
79. Jürgen Moltmann, "Political Theology and the Ethics of Peace," in *Theology, Politics and Peace*, ed. Theodore Runyon (Maryknoll, NY: Orbis, 1989): 38.
80. Ibid., 38.
81. For this concept, see Moe, "Sin and Evil," 218–223.
82. Quoted in Masao Abe, "The Problem of Evil in Christianity and Buddhism," in *Buddhist-Christian Dialogue: Mutual Renewal and Transformation*, eds. Paul Ingram and Frederick Streng (Honolulu: University of Hawaii Press, 1986), 141.
83. Jürgen Moltmann, *Experiences in Theology: Ways and Forms of Christian Theology*, trans. Margaret Kohl (Minneapolis: Fortress, 2000), 185.
84. Ibid., 185.
85. Jürgen Moltmann, *The Crucified God*, 40th anniversary ed. (Minneapolis: Fortress, 2015), 419–494.
86. Moltmann, *Experiences in Theology*, 186.
87. Moe, "Sin and Evil," 223.
88. K. C. Abraham, "A Theological Response to the Ecological Crisis," in *Ecotheology: Voices from South and North*, ed. David Hallman (Geneva: WCC, 1994), 67.
89. Simon Chan, *Asian Grassroots Theology: Thinking the Faith from the Ground Up* (Downers Grove, IL: IVP, 2014), 9.
90. Wilfred J. Smith, *The Faith of Other Men* (New York: New American Library, 1963), 74. Smith acknowledges that "we in the west presume that an intelligent must choose either this or that."
91. Ibid., 9. See also Jung Young Lee, "The Yin-Yang Way of Thinking," in *Asian Christian Theology: Emerging Themes*, rev. ed., ed. Douglas J. Elwood (Louisville, KY: Westminster John Knox Press, 1980), 81–88.
92. Pieris, *An Asian Theology of Liberation*, 71–81.
93. Kim, *Theology in the Public Sphere*, 65.

94. Ibid. For a theological interpretation of Paul's anthropos and cosmos salvation, see also Beverly Robert Gaventa, ed., *Apocalyptic Paul: Anthropos and Cosmos in Romans 5–8* (Waco, TX: Baylor University Press, 2013).

95. Ching, *Chinese Religions*, 35. See William D. Hackett, "Christian Response to Animistic Peoples," *Southeast Asia Journal of Theology* 10, no. 1 (1969): 50. See also David Thang Moe, "Nat-Worship and Paul Tillich: Contextualizing a Correlational Theology of Religion and Culture in Myanmar," *Toronto Journal of Theology* 31, no. 1 (Spring 2015): 123–36.

96. Kim, *Theology in the Public Sphere*, 67. Along these lines, see also Christian J. Anderson, "Beginning at the Beginning: Reading *Missio Dei* from the Start of the Bible," *Missiology: An International Review* 45, no. 4 (October 2017): 414–25.

97. Ibid., 66–67. See Christopher J. H. Wright, *The Mission of God: Unlocking the Bible's Grand Narrative* (Downers Grove, IL: IVP, 2006), 393–530. In my article, I argued that the triune God is involved in one mission of creation and new creation from Genesis to Revelation. See David Thang Moe, "Constructing a Theology of Mission," *Currents in Theology and Mission* 44, no. 2 (April 2017): 23–25.

98. By this "threefold relation of God-human-nature," I do not follow Raimundo Panikkar's cosmotheandiric view of threefold relativism; see Raimundo Panikkar, *The Trinity and the Religious Experience of Man: Icon-Person Mystery* (Maryknoll, NY: Orbis, 1973), 74.

99. Kim, *Theology in the Public Sphere*, 64.

100. Ibid., 64. Irvind O. Nirmal, "Ecology, Ecumenics in Relation: A New Theological Paradigm," in *Ecology and Development: Theological Perspectives*, ed. Daniel D. Chetti (Madras, Gurukul, 1991), 22. See also Wilfred, *Asian Public Theology*, xiv–xix.

101. For the contours of Asian ancestral spirit-worship, see James Haire, "Stories in Animism and Christian Pneumatology," in *Doing Theology with the Spirit's Movement*, eds. John C. England and Alan T. Torrance (Singapore: ATESEA, 1991), 120–30.

102. Melford E. Spiro, *Burmese Supernaturalism* (Eaglewood Cliffs, NJ: Prentice Hall, 1967), 42.

103. Ibid., 47.

104. Simon Pau Khan En, "Nat-Worship: A Paradigm for Doing Ecumenical Theology in Myanmar," *Asia Journal of Theology* 8, no. 1 (April 1994): 42–53.

105. Moe, "Nat-Worship and Paul Tillich," 123–136.

106. June C. Nash, *Practicing Ethnography in a Globalizing World: An Anthropological Odyssey*, 2nd ed. (Lanham, MD: Altamira, 2007), 86.

Chapter 10

Justice and Peace Kiss Each Other (Psalm 85:10b)

Integrating the Ethics of Justice and Peace in the World of Injustice and Violence

David Thang Moe

One of the most distinctive passages in the Bible that emphasizes the need of an integral relationship between justice and peace is Psalm 85:10b—"righteousness/justice and peace kiss each other." Some scholars distinguish between "justice" (*dikaios* in Greek) and "righteousness"—the former signifies action, while the latter denotes virtue or moral quality of life that states the action of justice.[1] The aim of this chapter is not to separate and judge between the two, but to see their complementary relations in a way such that the latter demands Christians' virtue or morality of righteousness (being) and justice demands Christians' acts of justice (act) in their relationship with people and the world.

To see how righteousness, justice, and peace are related to each other in God's mission of holiness and shalom and His calling of people in participating in the mission of holiness and shalom, we first need to understand the meaning of Psalm 85:10b, especially its second section, verses 8–13. Walter Brueggemann calls Psalm 85:8–13 "the prophetic message" that speaks God's shalom.[2] Brueggemann goes on to suggest that Psalm 85 should be read as the "prophetic voice of shalom that reveals God's rule of shalom and as a welcome one to a community that has petitioned for restoration and salvation."[3] For the Psalmist, justice and peace are integrated in God's rule of shalom. According to Brueggemann, Psalm 85:8–13 states the primary nature and act of God and His demand for the prophetic Christians' secondary participation in God's mission of justice and peace.

Christian missionaries, however, have separated the two by focusing on evangelism of personal conversion. In response to the mission neglect of justice, peace, and the integrity of creation (JPIC), the Seoul Convocation of the World Council of Churches, held in South Korea on March 5–12, 1990, deliberately chose justice, peace, and the integrity of creation as the conference theme. This conference ranks as one of the most important ecumenical conferences that meditated on the ethics of justice, peace, and the integrity of creation.[4] The convocation made ten affirmations on JPIC:

> (1) We affirm that all exercise of power is accountable to God. (2) We affirm God's option for the poor. (3) We affirm the equal value of all races and peoples. (4) We affirm that male and female are created in God's image. (5) We affirm that truth is the foundation of a community of free people. (6) We affirm the peace of Jesus Christ. (7) We affirm the creation as beloved of God. (8) We affirm that the earth is the Lord's. (9) We affirm the dignity and commitment of younger generation. (10) We affirm that human rights are given by God.[5]

Put together, the whole world is the scope of God's mission; justice and peace are the foundation of God's salvation. The aim of this chapter is to explore the theological concept and implication of justice and peace in a broken and violent world corrupted by human sin. My aim is to explore the ethics of justice, peace, and the integrity of creation. I argue that God's creation and salvation are not just past events, but the continuous sense of transformative acts of God. The chapter is divided into two parts. First, I speak about the missional ethics of God's justice and peace described in the Old and New Testaments. Second, I explore how the missional ethics of God's justice and peace shapes the missional ethics of the church. I explore several roles of the church—mission as liturgical practice of justice and peace and mission as the church's witness of justice, peace, and the integrity of creation in a broken and violent world.

THE MISSION OF GOD: DIVINE JUSTICE, PEACE, AND THE INTEGRATION OF CREATION

Most Christians would agree that the Bible provides a basis for the mission of the church. However, Christopher Wright, in his famous book *The Mission of God*,[6] claims that we need to see the bigger drama of God's mission in a way such that we should understand the grand narrative of the Bible in the light of God's big mission. Wright suggests that we should understand the two—"Christian mission in the light of the Bible—and the Bible in the light of God's mission." Although the two are closely intertwined, Wright prioritizes the latter over the former without separating the two.

If so, the Bible is to be understood as the grand narrative of God's big mission and mission is to be understood as the grand movement of God's involvement in the biblical drama of "creation out of nothing" (Gen. 1), "new creation or redemption out of the old" (2 Cor. 5:17), and "re-creation out of the old" (Rev. 21:1–8)[7] and God's calling of the people to participate in His mission. Mission is, therefore, not primarily a matter of our activity. Mission is the committed participation of God's people in the purpose of God for the redemption of the whole creation—integrity of creation, justice, and peace.[8]

If mission begins and ends with the triune God, a good starting point for mission is God's creation.[9] Genesis 1–2 tells us about the mission of God's creation. At the prologue of the fourth Gospel, John in the New Testament also tells us about the mission of God's creation (Jn. 1:3). In delineating the various metaphors associated with God as Creator, Ronald Simkins distinguishes between internal metaphors associated with birth and external metaphors associated with design. God is the creator and designer of creation.[10]

In looking upon all of creation, "God saw that all of it was very good" (Gen. 1:31). According to the imagery of Genesis, human beings (Adam and Eve) in the beginning found themselves within the harmonious Garden of Eden, but with their free will they succumbed to evil and forfeited the fullness of life that God intended for them. God's intention of creation of humankinds is to preserve God's created order. But after the Fall, Adam and Eve dominated over the other and polluted the created world (Gen. 3). The story of Cain and Abel (Gen. 4) indicates that people did not recognize and respect the image of God in one another. The world became a place with full of sinfulness and violence.[11]

However, God did not abandon sinful humanity and condemn the world. After the Fall, God through Noah renewed His promise to creation and human beings were again set under God's blessings to multiply and fill the earth (Gen. 9:1).[12] "The pivotal nature of God's mission for the world is made through Abraham. Gen. 12:1–3 ('all nations will be blessed through you') is a pivotal text of mission in the Bible,"[13] said Chris Wright. Through faith-filled people like Isaac, Moses, Aaron, David, Isaiah, Amos, and other prophets, god maintained a relationship with Jewish peoples. This relationship or covenant with the chosen Jews was intended as part of God's plan to draw all nations to God.

God elected Israel to be the light to all the nations (Is. 46:9). It must be stressed that God's call of Israel is not for their exclusive privilege, but for an inclusive and embracing mission for God and for the world. Through the Jewish prophets, God reveals His holiness, justice, and peace in the world.[14] The Ten Commandments sum up God's moral character of justice, peace, and God's declared will for the integrity of creation. It is commonly noted that the centrality of the Ten Commandments lies in two sections: the first four commandments reflect God's character of justice and holiness, while the rest speak about God's declared will that should be expressed in our relationship with God, with humans, and with other creatures. God's declared will is peace with God, peace with fellow humans, and peace with other creatures.[15]

However, Israel failed to fulfill God's purpose and declared will of justice, peace, and the integrity of creation. Instead, they turned away from God by committing sin. According to Patrick Miller, the sin most commonly condemned in the Hebrew world is "idolatry and unfaithfulness" within Israel's relationship with God."[16] Since God so loved the sinful world, He sent His begotten Son to redeem the world (Jn. 3:16). At the heart of Christian faith lies the claim that God became flesh in Jesus (Jn. 1) and died on the cross for the unjust world (1 Cor. 15:3). In taking upon Himself the sin of the world (Jn. 1:29), God restored justice in an unjust world.[17] By suffering violence as an innocent victim, Jesus reestablished God's reign of justice, peace, forgiveness, and reconciliation.

By virtue of self-giving love, God overcame human enmity. The cross is God's embrace of the perpetrators. As Ernst Käsemann put it, it is through the crucified and risen Christ that God transformed the unrighteous into the righteous and the old into the new (Rom. 6–8). For Käsemann, God's restorative justice or righteousness (*dikaiosyne* in Greek) refers to God's reestablishing His reign of justice and peace.[18] Transformation of the world of violence into the world of peace and of the world of injustice into the world of justice is the aim of the Messiah's first coming. Although Jesus's second coming may entail violence, His first coming is nonviolent and humiliated. Miroslav Volf rightly notes that in His first incarnational coming, "Jesus did not come into the world of violence in order to conquer evildoers or the violent perpetrators through an act of violence, but to die for them in self-giving love and thereby reconcile them to God" (Lk. 23:34).[19]

The self-giving love and receiving arms of the crucified and resurrected Christ defined the whole of God's trinitarian mission. God's mission in the crucified Christ by the Spirit did not consist merely in passively receiving violence on the cross. "If Jesus had done nothing but suffer violence only as an innocent, His first coming into the world of violence was in vain and we would have forgotten Him as we have forgotten many other innocent victims in today's world of violence," Volf rightly said.[20] It is through His resurrection that Jesus defeated the Satanic power and reestablished God's universal reign of justice, peace, and reconciliation.[21] Jesus' re-creating act of justice and shalom is defined by Paul as a new creation (2 Cor. 5:17) and cosmic reconciliation (Col. 1:19–20).

I understand Pauline doctrine of new creation as Jesus's redemptive activity of transforming an old world into a new world of justice and peace. We are now in an apocalyptic and a reconciled world—a new world in the midst of the old that evil persists. We are called to criticize the individualistic perception of justification and to adopt a cosmic salvation without being confused with a universal salvation.[22] Salvation has to be understood as God's cosmic reconciliation in an anthropological and a cosmological scope.[23] Simon Chan observes that Western theology of salvation as an individual justification tends to be rooted in soteriological motifs located in Romans and Galatians, while non-Western or Asian theology of soteriology as a cosmic nature of salvation tends to be rooted in soteriological motifs found in Colossians and Hebrews.[24] Chan is right is some ways, but the notion of soteriology in Romans is not just individual but also cosmic (Rom. 8:18–25).

Not only in Romans 8, but also in Colossians 1:20, Paul indicates salvation in a cosmic and holistic manner. He said, "through Christ, God reconciled all things on earth and in heaven to Himself by making peace by blood" (Col. 1:20). Salvation as peace has to be understood as a vertical reconciliation between God and humans on the one hand, a horizontal reconciliation among humans and other creatures (Col. 1:21; Eph. 2:13–21), on the other. Here I am not interpreting Paul's conception of cosmic reconciliation in a dualistic way, but rather in a holistic or integrative way. Paul's integrative view of justice and peace is rightly described by Rudolf Bultmann as the dialectics of *indicative* and *imperative*. For Bultmann, "indicative states what one now is in Christ (salvation is already a reality), while imperative summons Christians to actualize what God has accomplished and is doing (participating in God's continual act of justice and peace)."[25] From this dialectical framework, I will now explore the role of the church.

THE MISSION OF CHURCH: THE ETHICS OF CHURCH IN THE WORLD OF INJUSTICE, VIOLENCE, AND PLURALITY

The central thesis of this section is that the *God of mission* calls the church for the *mission of God*. God calls the church out of the world to be a gathered community of faith, worship, justice, and peace and sends it back to the world to become a scattered and missionary community to proclaim and practice the gospel of justice and peace in word and work. The dialectics of God's calling and commissioning is what forms the identity of the church as the missional and missionary community of faith, justice, and peace. It is in this sense that I will explore how the mission of the church should participate in the God of mission (the life of missionary God) and in the mission of God (the act of God).

Mission as Worship: Practicing Justice and Peace

As central to Christian life as worship is, it cannot be an end in itself. Protestant Christians do not normally think of worship as act of mission because they see only activism outside the church as mission. But Orthodox

Christians describe mission as worship or the liturgy before the liturgy.[26] Matthew 5:23 provides such a model. Jesus said to His disciples, "bring your gift to the altar and first be reconciled to your brother, and then come and offer your altar." As we gather as an apostolic community for worship, the practice of God's healing, justice, peace, and reconciliation should first be reflected in our right relationship with one another as brothers and sisters in Christ.

Chan states in his book *Liturgical Theology*,[27] "The church is not merely the agent to accomplish God's purpose, the church is the very embodiment of God's ultimate purposes itself."[28] While the instrumental role of the church is important, what is often missing is the importance of the ontological identity of the church in her spiritual relation with God and with fellow Christians. The result is the failure to see worship as an act of mission. As central to Christian life as liturgy is, it cannot be an end in itself. Worship should be understood as an act of mission. While Protestants do not normally see worship as mission, Orthodox Christians see worship as mission.[29] Mission is not just from inside (church) to the world (outside), but also from outside to inside. By the latter, I mean bringing the world issue into liturgy and reflect them in our prayer and preaching.

As we bring them into liturgy and worship, we pray for the victims of injustice and violence. In our liturgy, we also celebrate the power of Christ's resurrection in the midst of death; we celebrate the Spiritual presence of the Lord's peace in the midst of violence; we celebrate the imminent presence of God's justice in the midst of oppression; we celebrate Christ's comfort and the Spirit's healing in the midst of decay and wounds; and we celebrate the promise of Christ's hope in the midst of hopelessness and despairs.

We understand mission to be primarily about going outside of the church and being involved in society. But in reality, not all church members are involved in society. Yet by bringing the public issues into our liturgy, everyone is involved.[30] To stress the liturgical community as an embodiment of what I prefer to call the "internal Trinity" or the immanent Trinity in the language of traditional theology, I argue that mission does not merely come to us from God in terms of what I call "His external relation" or the economic Trinity in the language of traditional theology, but mission may also go to God by way of our doxology. Here I am not talking about two kinds of mission. Mission is always one and God is the originator and we are participating in that one mission.[31] Rather I am talking about a mutual participation in one mission of the triune God.

Mission as Witness to God's Reign of Justice, Peace, and the Integration of Creation

The worshipping community needs to look beyond itself. The dismissal prayer at church, "Go in peace to love and serve God," is sending the missional church into the world as a boundary-crossing mission agent of God. Orthodox Christians describe this as the "liturgy after the liturgy." We are to witness to God's justice and peace to the world.

Since Christian faith is not only a personal confession but also a public commitment to following Christ as universal Lord, our faith is to be practiced not only within the life of the church but also in public spheres. God does not only call the church to gather for worship, but He also sends it to the world for witnessing to mission as the church breathing: "we inhale in worship, and exhale in witness."[32] God sends the church to the world to pursue work for justice and peace and care for God's gift of creation. Since God is involved in the mission of justice, peace, and integrity of creation care, the church must also participate in such an integrative mission of justice and peace.[33]

As we participate in God's continuing act of sustaining and saving the broken world, our task is to pursue work for justice, peace, and care for creation. It is noted that justice and peace are the wide concepts of shalom—ranging from sociopolitical and economic justice to peace activism to working for environmental sustainability.[34] Because the earth is the Lord's (Ps. 24:1), the responsibility of the church toward the entire the earth is a crucial part of the church's mission.[35] Justice and peace are intimately linked together, but I discuss them separately. In describing justice, I discern two kinds of justice: charitable and social-political justice and eco-justice. I will first study charitable justice, followed by social justice, eco-justice, and peace.

The Church as Apostolic Justice-Doer: Charitable Justice

Caring for the poor and those in need has always been part and parcel of the apostolic church's mission. The apostles sold their possessions and distributed the money to the poor (Acts 2:42ff), early Christian communities cared for the victims of the plagues, East Syrian monasteries were places for medical care, and Mother Teresa reached out to the poor.[36] We think above all of the Good Samaritan who cared for the wounded victim regardless of his social identity (Lk. 10:25–37). New Testament scholars confess that no one knows the social identity of the victim for whom the Samaritan cared. While the Gospel of Luke provides the ethnic identity of the Samaritan, no clue for the ethnic identity of the victim is provided.[37] This creates the room for scholars to debate. I consider the anonymity of the wounded victim's ethnic identity to be a good opportunity for the contemporary church to extend its charitable justice and love to all those who are poor and marginalized regardless of their sociocultural and religioethnic identities.[38]

The 1980 World Conference on Mission and Evangelism, held by the World Council of Churches in Melbourne, Australia, from May 12–2, proposed the marginalized as the objects of mission and the locus of missiological reflections. "Your Kingdom Come" was the theme chosen for the conference and its focus was on the ethics of the church's compassionate response to the voices of the margins and poor.[39] Two years after the ecumenical and progressive Melbourne meeting was held, the Lausanne Committee on World Evangelization and World Evangelical Fellowship (a more evangelical wing) also held a meeting in Grand Rapids, Michigan, on June 19–25, 1982, that called for the relation of social justice and charity with evangelism. Both meetings see the margins and poor as the prime sites for the mission of the church.[40] I will later develop the need of social justice.

At this point, I would like to focus on the mission of charity justice. Matthew 25:35–45 provides the missional locus for charitable justice. In this text, central to Jesus's word for charitable justice is that whatever we do for "the least," we do for Him (25:40). The meaning of Jesus's word is that our right relation to the least, the last, and the lost determines our relation to Jesus. I must emphasize that compassion should be taken as the first step for our relation to the least, the last, and the lost, and for doing charitable justice for them. Just as compassion is the motivating power of Jesus's ministry, so compassion must be the motivating power of the church's mission of charitable justice.[41] The mission of the triune God flows from the compassionate heart. Likewise, the mission of the church's charitable justice must also flow from the heart so that the church embodies the orthopathic mission of the triune God not only for social charity, but for social justice.

The Church as Prophetic Justice-Doer: Social Justice

In the struggle for social justice, "the poor and the oppressed are not merely the objects of mission, they become the subjects of mission,"[42] said David Bosch. While charitable justice remains essential, the church is called not only to take care of those in need, but also to address the structural evil that put them in that situation. The church needs to accompany and empower the marginalized in fining their own voice and choosing their action against injustice.[43] The biblical concept of social justice is grounded in three theological perspectives: "(1) Exodus as a model for God's restorative justice for the oppressed; (2) prophetic writings as the critiques of the structural evil; (3) Jesus' prophetic praxis against injustice and His resurrection as hope for the oppressed."[44]

When Israel were oppressed in Egypt, God liberated them through the prophet Moses (Ex. 3:7; Deut. 11:2); when their own people of wealth oppressed the poor, God spoke truthful words of condemnation through the prophet Amos; when God's people of Israel were in exile, God spoke words of comfort through the prophets in Second and Third Isaiah. And God's Spirit is fully manifested in Jesus's prophetic ministry of inaugurating God's kingdom in the words of Third Isaiah, of bringing good news of justice and peace to the oppressed and the poor.[45] According to Karl Barth, the first coming of Jesus is to inaugurate a universal Lordship of justice and peace. The question of who is our Lord becomes a missional and ethical question for Barth. He said, "Christian ethics is not centered in knowing what is good, but in knowing who is our Lord."[46]

Barth says this because he knows that there are two Lords—the Jesus who rules the world with justice and peace, and the other lord, which Paul calls "principality" (Eph. 6:12; Col. 2:15). But this does not mean that Jesus and the devil rule apart. As Barth suggests, Jesus defeated the devil through His resurrection and we realize His universal Lordship of justice and peace through the presence of the Spirit. Since we are still in the time between the "already" and "not yet reign of Christ," the devil combats Christ's universal Lordship of justice and peace. As a prophetic community of Christ, the church's task is to witness to Christ's Lordship of justice and peace by speaking truth and resisting any imperial forms of injustice, oppression, and discrimination.[47]

Martin Luther once called the church "the mouth house of God,"[48] that is, God's prophetic word spoken in the world through the church. Along the same lines with Luther, Barth called the church the "proclaimed word." Barth used the threefold word: "incarnate Word (Jesus), written Word (the Bible) and proclaimed Word (church)."[49] The three are linked together in the prophetic mission of the church. "Proclamation and witness are used interchangeably."[50] Both deal with the mission of God in word and work. Traditionally, Protestants focused more on preaching and focused less on practices.

Liberation theology emerged as a correction of such imbalance with the praxis model. Liberation theology was born at a time when theology was done only with words.[51] It puts orthodoxy (right belief) alongside orthopraxy (right practice). While I appreciate liberation hermeneutics of the combination of orthodoxy and orthopraxis, such hermeneutics fail to recognize orthopathy (feeling). I would argue that orthopathy is the ground for orthodoxy and orthopraxy. In the context of sociopolitical oppression, our compassionate feeling should be the ground for our prophetic action. Ecclesial orthopathy is an embodiment of the God who feels compassionate to the oppressed. In light of this, I would suggest that the trilogy of "orthopathy, orthodoxy, and orthopraxy" should play a crucial role in liberation theology. The church should embrace social justice and social charity as partners in response to sociopolitical oppression and economic exploitation.

While social charity is the church's immediate response to the poverty of the poor, social justice tends to be the church's long-term commitment. The latter form of justice takes time to change social structures and systems, which puts the poor in the unjust situations. I will call social justice "hard liberation theology" because it uses a radical action as a liberating tool for transforming social structures and systems. On the other hand, I will call social charity "soft liberation theology" because it uses a compassionate and pastoral concern as a liberating tool for transforming the lives of the poor without challenging systems. The two are interrelated. We must therefore bridge social justice (hard liberation) and social charity (soft liberation) for a holistic mission of God.[52] I emphasize the need of connecting social justice and social charity as the manifestation of justice and peace in a broken world corrupted by human sin.

In short, living in the world of what Bosch called "creative tensions," the identity and task of the church are dialectical.[53] God calls the church from the world to be an apostolic community of faith, worship, and love, and commissions it back to the world of injustice and violence to be a prophetic community of witnessing to God's justice and peace in solidarity with those who suffer regardless of the ethnic-religious differences.

The Church as Missional Witness of Peace and Reconciliation

The church's mission is a witness of God's act of peace and reconciliation in the world. Politically, peace (the presence of justice)[54] and political reconciliation (reconciliation can take place only after justice is restored) can be separable, but missionally, I will use them interchangeably. The relation of peace and reconciliation is understandable in the context of seeing salvation as communion with God, with fellow humans, and other creatures. Paul reminds us that God has given us a "ministry of reconciliation" and we are the ambassadors for Christ (2 Cor. 5:19–21). If we are the ambassadors for Christ, our mission task is to bridge the gap between the church and the world and between Christians and non-Christians. I will speak of mission as witness of peace and reconciliation from two perspectives. One is dialogical and the other is prophetic.

In their book, *Constants in Context*, Stephen Bevans and Roger Schroeder famously propose and summarize "mission as prophetic dialogue."[55] I agree with them, but I prefer to speak of mission as "dialogical and prophetic witness."

First, the church's missional witness of reconciliation must be dialogical. In contrast to monologue, that is, speaking without listening, teaching without learning, dialogue is conversation between people of different religions. With the stress on the church's mission as witness of peace and reconciliation in the world of religious plurality, I argue that crossing boundaries and reconciling with people of other faiths should go together. This I call "religious reconciliation." In crossing the heaven-earth boundary, God has reconciled us to Himself in Christ (2 Cor. 5:18). If Jesus, who crosses the heaven-earth and divine-human boundaries, is the model, our task is to witness to Jesus's act of peace, reconciliation, and shalom among people of other faiths by crossing, not crushing, their religiocultural boundaries.[56] Kosuke Koyama rightly reminds us to have the "crucified mind of Christ" (Phil. 2:5) that builds the bridge of love and embraces the other in light of the claim that all are created in the image of God (Gen. 1:26–27), not to have the "crusading mind" that builds the wall against and rejects the otherness of the other.[57]

The primary aim of the boundary-crossing mission is not simply to see other faiths as the objects of conversion, but to see them as neighbors to whom the conversation of hospitality must be extended and received. Our dialogical task is not only to open our mouth to speak to the other, but also to open our ears to hear them speak.[58] The result of such dialogue is mutual conversion. The example can be drawn from the mutual conversation and conversion between Peter and Cornelius (Acts 10). Cornelius was turned to God from his earlier belief, and Peter was turned from his earlier way to a new way of believing and behaving.[59] While Cornelius represents the paradigm of a non-Christian, Peter represents the paradigm of a Christian in our contemporary world.

More importantly, conversion is not just an event, it is a process. The church needs to continually be transformed and renewed by new cultures. By this, we do not mean that the church is to be conformed to the other religions (Rom. 12:2). Rather the church needs to be transformed by the ethical teachings of other faiths without ceasing to transform the immoral religious cultures. This is because communicating the gospel is no longer a one-way traffic light; it is a two-way traffic light. Thereby both groups have to experience the mystery of God anew through mutual interactions. Other faiths are to be seen not as mere objects for conversion, but as neighbors to whom the moral insights must be both given and received for mutual conversion. Durrell Guder rightly said,

> The church is always in need of continual conversion. The Holy Spirit began the conversion of the church at Pentecost and has continued that conversion through the pilgrimage of God's people from the first century up to now. The version of the church will be the continuing work of God's Spirit until God completes the good work began in Jesus Christ.[60]

Another aim of dialogue with people of other faiths is to address some common human issues, such as universal justice and peace. Violence and tension among religions following September 11, 2001, points to the urgent need for this dialogue. If we call the earlier type of dialogue a "dialogue of reconciliation," we may call the latter type of dialogue a "dialogue of action."[61] The latter is the result of the former. We need both in the world of violence. Huns Kung is one of those who developed the idea that world peace cannot be promoted against other religions, but with them.[62] For him, "there can be no peace among nations without peace among religions."[63] World peace depends on the success of interreligious dialogue. This leads us to the next level of reconciliation—political reconciliation.

Second, the church's missional witness of political reconciliation must be prophetic. Political reconciliation calls for the prophetic efforts of Christians against violence. As compared to religious reconciliation, political reconciliation is more risky and costly. Not all Christians are successfully involved in the latter. Successful prophetic Christians who represent political reconciliation include Nelson Mandela and Archbishop Desmond Tutu with the Truth and Reconciliation Commission in South Africa, Martin Luther King Jr. with the nonviolent resistance to racism in the United States, and similar efforts of resistance to oppression by others in Chile and the Philippines.[64] Overcoming violence nonviolently is possible. But it may require martyrdom. We can think of and King and Oscar Romero. We think above all of Christ. In order for reconciliation, Jesus refused to be sucked into the revenge, but sought to triumph over evil by doing good at the cost of His life.

"The first and the final reconciliation is not the work of human beings, but of the triune God,"[65] says Moltmann. Similarly, Robert Schreiter argues that it is God alone who brings about reconciliation in people's heart, but also that Christians are to be bride-builders and mediators in the process of final reconciliation.[66] In the process of reconciliation and peace, God plays His part, and we play our part in prophetic resistance to oppression and opening our arms to embracing the oppressors. God's self-giving love overcame human enmity, and His receiving arm welcomes the oppressors to come into a communion of peace and love. The hope for such reconciliation is possible only by love.

The Church as Ecumenical Steward: Toward Eco-Justice, Peace, and the Integration of Creation

Although the issue of ecology is integrally connected to the mission of God's creation and salvation, there has not been much reflection on how the preservation of the integrity of creation is linked to the mission of the church.[67] If God's salvation is holistic not only at the spiritual-physical level but also the anthropological-cosmic level of the integrity of creation (Col. 1:19–20), the identity of the church must be an ecumenical steward of God's mission. God's aim of creation of the first man and woman is to be the steward and preserver of God's creation (Gen. 1:28). But as a consequence of the Fall, humankinds instead tend to be the destroyers of nonhuman creatures.

Sins of injustice and greed, according to Walter Brueggemann, not only cause violence to human beings but also to the earth and all the earth's creatures. Politically, the powerful are the oppressors, but ecologically, the powerless and marginalized and the powerful are both the oppressors of the earth's creatures. As a result, the world is groaning in labor pains (Rom. 8:20–23).[68] As Brueggemann suggests, the call of the church to repentance and new vision is, therefore, the call to ecological responsibility. Repentance is not simply feeling bad about destroying nonhuman creatures, but seriously thinking about difference with a new vision. A new way of thinking about the church's mission as stewardship of God's created order is imperative. In light of this, Christian theologians need to retranslate Genesis 1:28 afresh. In this passage, God's word to the first man and women, "have dominion over the earth's creatures," has been misread.

God's use of "dominion" should not be translated as "domination," but rather as stewardship and preservation of the earth's creatures.[69] The earth is not ours to be destroyed, but it is the Lord's (Ps. 24:1) to be preserved. Since humankinds are created to be the stewards of the earth's creatures, the missional vocation of the church is to be nature lovers rather than to be nature destroyers. It is sometimes argued that a ministry of eco-justice and peace is only the concern of first-world countries that can afford the luxury of protecting their natural resources. People in Latin America, Africa, and Asia may need to cut trees and hunt animals to survive. While this is true, third-world peoples should somewhat minimize the waste of unwise exploitation of the natures.[70]

On the other hand, spirit worship being practiced in third-world countries, especially in Asia and Africa, paves the way for the possibility of eco-justice and peace. According to spirit-worship, spirits are considered to occupy every object—the trees, mountains, and rivers—and those places are sacred. Using profanity and destroying those sacred places are thus prohibited. If we want to use them for good purpose, we have to ask permission from the spirits. Suffice to show that spirit worship venerates natures and thus ecological concern is inherent in it. Spirit worship entails a new awareness of stewardship and eco-justice and peace. To promote awareness of ecology, Christians in the third world should interact with spirit worship and apply it as a source for cosmological healing.[71]

CONCLUSION

Three themes are discussed in conclusion. First, based on the Psalmist's integrative conception of justice and peace as the ethics of shalom ("justice and peace kiss each other"), I have explored that justice and peace are intimately related to the moral and personal characters of God. Justice and peace are primarily the personal characters of God and are secondarily the missional actions of God's shalom. The natures and actions of God are integrated to God's trinitarian mission of justice and peace. Second, since God is the God of justice and peace, God demands the church's ethical mission of justice and peace in the world. I have called on the church to redefine salvation not merely as an anthropological concern of divine-human just union but also as a cosmological concern. This demands the church's ethical engagement in the struggle for a just communion with God and with fellow humans, as well as with nonhuman creatures as a whole (Col. 1:19–20).

Third, the struggle for justice and peace and the integrity of creation is the hope for a new heaven and a new earth (Is. 66:22; Rev. 21:1). In this respect, we need to see "mission as faith in action, love in action and hope in action."[72] By faith and hope we live in Christ, in love we live with neighbors and created order. Justice and peace are the ethics of Christian mission, and the whole world is the scope of God's mission. If this is so, Lesslie Newbigin's words remain true to us: "The church's mission is to participate in God's mission to restore the whole creation. If the scope of salvation is as broad as creation, our participation in God's mission of justice and peace must also be equally broad."[73] Since the Psalmist does not say "justice and peace kill each other," but rather the "two kiss each other," I propose that we should not separate the ethics of justice and peace, but rather we should integrate them as a holistic dimension of salvation in the world of injustice and violence so that we embody both the natures and actions of the triune God.

BIBLIOGRAPHY

Barth, Karl. *Church Dogmatics: The Doctrine of the Word of God*, Vol. 1.1. Edinburgh: T and T Clark, 1936.

———. *Church Dogmatics: The Doctrine of Reconciliation*, Vol. 4.2. Edinburgh: T and T Clark, 1958.

Bevans, Stephen B., and Roger P. Schroeder. *Constants in Context: A Theology of Mission for Today*. Maryknoll, NY: Orbis, 2009.

———. *Models of Contextual Theology*. Maryknoll, NY: Orbis, 2002.

Bosch, David J. *Transforming Mission: Paradigm Shifts in Theology of Mission*, 20th anniversary ed.. Maryknoll, NY: Orbis, 2011.

Brueggemann, Walter. *Psalms*. New York: Cambridge University Press, 2014.

———. "The Uninflected Therefore of Hosea 4:1–3." In *Reading from this Place, Vol. I: Social Location and Biblical Interpretation in the United States*, edited by Fernando F. Segovia and Mary A. Tolbert, 231–249. Minneapolis: Fortress, 1995.

Chan, Simon. *Grassroots Asian Theology: Thinking the Faith from the Ground Up*. Downers Grove, IL: IVP, 2014.

———. *Liturgical Theology: The Church as Worshiping Community*. Downers Grove, IL: IVP, 2006.

Coorilos, Geeverghese Mor. "Mission as Liturgy before Liturgy." In *Orthodox Perspectives on Mission*, edited by Petros Vassiliadis, 175–178. Oxford: Regnum, 2013.

Fretheim, Terrence E. *God and World in the Old Testament: A Relational Theology of Creation*. Nashville, TN: Abingdon, 2005.

Fullenwieder, Jann E. Boyd. "Proclamation: Mercy for the World." In *Inside Out: Worship in an Age of Mission*, edited by Thomas H. Schattauer, 20–28. Minneapolis: Fortress, 1990.

Furnish, Victor Paul. *Theology and Ethics in Paul.* Louisville, KY: Westminster John Knox Press, 2009.
Galtung, John. *Peace by Peaceful Means: Development and Civilisation.* Oslo: PRIO, 1996.
Gaventa, Beverly R. *The Acts of the Apostles.* Nashville, TN: Abingdon, 2003.
———, ed. *Apocalyptic Paul: Cosmos and Anthropos in Romans 5–8.* Waco, TX: Baylor University Press, 2013.
Goheen, Michael W. *Introducing Christian Mission Theology: Scripture, History, and Issues.* Downers Grove, IL: IVP, 2014.
Green, Joel B. *The Gospel of Luke.* Grand Rapids, MI: Eerdmans, 1997.
Guder, Darrell L. *The Continuing Conversion of the Church.* Grand Rapids, MI: Eerdmans, 2000.
Kasemann, Ernst. "The Righteousness of God in Paul." In *New Testament Questions of Today*, 168–182. Philadelphia: Fortress, 1969.
Koyama, Kosuke. *Three Mile an Hour God.* Maryknoll, NY: Orbis, 1980.
Kung, Hans. *Global Responsibility: In Search for a New World Ethic*, translated by John Bowden. New York: Continuum, 1993.
Marshall, I. Howard. *Commentary on Luke.* Grand Rapids, MI: Eerdmans, 1978.
Miller, Patrick D. *Sin and Judgment in Prophets: Stylistic and Theological Analysis.* Chico, CA: Scholars, 1982.
Moe, David Thang. "Constructing a Theology of Mission." In *Currents in Theology and Mission* 44, no. 2 (March 2017): 23–25.
———. "A Cross-Cultural and Liberative Hermeneutics of Luke 10:25–37 in Asian and Asian-American Perspective: Reading One Text through the Two Lenses." *The Expository Times: International Journal of Biblical Studies, Theology and Ministry* 130, no. 10 (July 2019): 439–49.
———. "Exclusion and Embrace: A Theology of Breaking Boundaries and Building Bridges between Christianity and Buddhism in Myanmar." *Exchange: Journal of Contemporary Christianities in Context* 46, no. 2 (March 2017): 103–28.
———. "Nat-Worship and Paul Tillich: Contextualizing a Correlational Theology of Religion and Culture in Myanmar." *Toronto Journal of Theology* 31, no. 1 (2015): 123–36.
———. "A Synthetic Theology of Soft and Hard Liberation: Bridging Social Justice and Social Charity for a Holistic Missiology." *Dharma Deepika: South Indian Journal of Missiology* 21, no. 2 (2017): 60–72.
Moltmann, Jürgen. *The Coming of God: Christian Eschatology.* Minneapolis: Fortress, 1996.
Newbigin, Lesslie. *The Open Secret: An Introduction to a Christian Theology of Mission*, rev. ed. Grand Rapids, MI: Eerdmans, 1995.
Phan, Peter C. *In Our Own Tongues: Perspectives from Asia on Inculturation and Mission.* Maryknoll, NY: Orbis, 2003.
Rasmussen, Larry. "Global Eco-justice: The Church's Mission in Urban Society." *Mission Studies* 16, no. 1 (1999): 111–21.
Schattauer, Thomas H., ed. *Inside Out: Worship in an Age of Mission.* Minneapolis: Fortress, 1999.
Scherer, James A., and Stephen B. Bevans. *New Directions in Mission and Evangelization I.* Maryknoll, NY: Orbis, 1992.
Schreiter, Robert. *Reconciliation: Mission and Ministry in a Changing Social Order.* Maryknoll, NY: Orbis, 1992.
Schroeder, Roger P. *What Is the Mission of the Church?* Maryknoll, NY: Orbis, 2008.
Simkins, Ronald A. *Creator and Creation: Natures in the Worldview of Ancient Israel.* Peabody, MA: Hendrickson, 1994.
Sugirtharajah, R. S. *Postcolonial Criticism and Biblical Interpretation.* Oxford: Oxford University Press, 2009.
Schwartz, Regina M. *The Curse of Cain: The Violent Legacy of Monotheism.* Chicago, IL: University of Chicago Press, 1998.
Vassiliadis, Petros. *Orthodox Perspectives on Mission.* Oxford: Regnum, 2013.

Volf, Miroslav. "Christianity and Violence." In *War and the Bible and Terrorism in the Twenty-First Century*, edited by Richard S. Hess and Elmer A. Martens, 1–18. Winona Lake, IN: Eisenbruans, 2008.

———. *Exclusion and Embrace: A Theological Exploration of Identity, Otherness and Reconciliation*, rev. ed. Nashville, TN: Abingdon, 2019.

Wilkinson, Loren. *Earth Keeping in the 90s: Stewardship of Creation*. Grand Rapids, MI: Eerdmans, 1991.

Wilson, Frederick R. *The San Antonio Report: Your Will be Done, Mission in Christ's Way*. Geneva: WCC, 1990.

Wright, Christopher J. H. *The Mission of God: Unlocking the Bible's Grand Narrative*. Downer Groves, IL: IVP, 2006.

Wright, N. T. *Evil and the Justice of God*. Downer Groves, IL: IVP, 2013.

———. *Justification: God's Plan and Paul's Vision*. Downers Grove, IL: IVP, 2009.

NOTES

1. N. T. Wright, *Justification: God's Plan and Paul's Vision* (Downers Grove, IL: IVP, 2009), 88–92.
2. Walter Brueggemann, *Psalms* (New York: Cambridge University Press, 2014), 370.
3. Ibid., 370.
4. James A. Scherer and Stephen B. Bevans, *New Directions in Mission and Evangelization I* (Maryknoll, NY: Orbis, 1992), 82.
5. Ibid., 82–83.
6. Christopher J. H. Wright, *The Mission of God: Unlocking the Bible's Grand Narrative* (Downers Grove, IL: InterVarsity, 2006), 17.
7. Ibid., 62–68.
8. Ibid., 67.
9. Along these lines, see David Thang Moe, "Constructing a Theology of Mission," in *Currents in Theology and Mission* 44, no. 2. (March 2017): 23–25.
10. Ronald A. Simkins, *Creator and Creation: Natures in the Worldview of Ancient Israel* (Peabody, MA: Hendrickson, 1994), 91.
11. See Regina M. Schwartz, *The Curse of Cain: The Violent Legacy of Monotheism* (Chicago: University of Chicago Press, 1998), 1–3.
12. Wright, *The Mission of God*, 196.
13. Ibid.
14. Ibid., 189–392.
15. Ibid.
16. Patrick D. Miller, *Sin and Judgment in Prophets: Stylistic and Theological Analysis* (Chico, CA: Scholars, 1982), 22.
17. Miroslav Volf, *Exclusion and Embrace: A Theological Exploration of Identity, Otherness and Reconciliation*, revised and updated (Nashville, TN: Abingdon Press, 2019), 288–296.
18. Ernst Kasemann, "The Righteousness of God in Paul," *in New Testament Questions of Today* (Philadelphia, PA: Fortress Press, 1969), 168–182, pp. 176–180.
19. Miroslav Volf, "Christianity and Violence," in Richard S. Hess and Elmer A. Martens, *War and the Bible and Terrorism in the Twenty-First Century* (Winona Lake, IN: Eisenbruans, 2008): 12.
20. Volf, *Exclusion and Embrace*, 288.
21. Wright, *Evil and the Justice of God*, 83–87, 135–145.
22. N. T. Wright, *Justification: God's Plan and Paul's Vision* (Downers Grove, IL: IVP, 2009), 79–110.
23. See Beverly Roberts Gaventa, *Apocalyptic Paul: Cosmos and Anthropos in Romans 5–8* (Waco, TX: Baylor University Press, 2013).
24. Simon Chan, *Grassroots Asian Theology: Thinking the Faith from the Ground Up* (Downers Grove, IL: IVP, 2014), 126.

25. Victor Paul Furnish, *Theology and Ethics in Paul* (Louisville, KY: Westminster John Knox Press, 2009), 225.

26. Geeverghese Mor Coorilos, "Mission as Liturgy before Liturgy," in *Orthodox Perspectives on Mission*, ed. Petros Vassiliadis (Oxford: Regnum, 2013): 175–78.

27. Simon Chan, *Liturgical Theology: The Church as Worshiping Community* (Downers, IL: IVP, 2006).

28. Ibid., 21.

29. Petros Vassiliadis, ed, *Orthodox Perspectives on Mission* (Oxford: Regnum, 2013).

30. Thomas A. Schattauer, *Inside Out: Worship in an Age of Mission* (Minneapolis: Fortress, 1999), 1–21.

31. See Moe, "Constructing a Theology of Mission," 23–25.

32. Coorilos, "Mission as Liturgy before Liturgy," 175.

33. Stephen B. Bevans and Roger P. Schroeder, *Constants in Context: A Theology of Mission for Today* (Maryknoll, NY: Orbis, 2009), 369.

34. Ibid., 369.

35. Frederick R. Wilson, *The San Antonio Report: Your Will be Done, Mission in Christ's Way* (Geneva: WCC, 1990), 54.

36. Bevans, *Constants in Context*, 369–70.

37. I. Howard Marshall, *Commentary on Luke* (Grand Rapids, MI: Eerdmans, 1978), 444–45. See also Joel B. Green, *The Gospel of Luke* (Grand Rapids, MI: Eerdmans, 1997), 427.

38. For an extensive interpretation and implication of the Parable of the Good Samaritan, see David Thang Moe, "A Cross-Cultural and Liberative Hermeneutics of Luke 10:25–37 in Asian and Asian-American Perspective: Reading One Text through the Two Lenses," *The Expository Times: International Journal of Biblical Studies, Theology and Ministry* 130, no. 10 (July 2019): 439–49.

39. Scherer and Bevans, *New Directions in Mission and Evangelization I*, 27–35.

40. Ibid., 276–280.

41. David J. Bosch, *Transforming Mission: Paradigm Shifts in Theology of Mission*, 20th anniversary ed. (Maryknoll, NY: Orbis, 2011), 446.

42. Ibid.

43. Ibid.

44. R. S. Sugirtharajah, *Postcolonial Criticism and Biblical Interpretation*, reprinted (New York: Oxford University Press, 2009), 66.

45. Bevans, *Constants in Context*, 271.

46. Karl Barth, *Church Dogmatics: The Doctrine of Reconciliation*, vol. 4.2 (Edinburgh: T and T Clark, 1958), 86.

47. Bevans, *Constants in Context*, 348.

48. Quoted in Jann E. Boyd Fullenwieder, "Proclamation: Mercy for the World," in *Inside Out: Worship in an Age of Mission*, ed. Thomas H. Schattauer (Minneapolis, MN: Fortress, 1990), 24.

49. Karl Barth, *Church Dogmatics: The Doctrine of Reconciliation*, vol. 1.1 (Edinburgh: T and T Clark, 1958), 88–119.

50. Bevans, *Constants in Context*, 352.

51. Stephen B. Bevans, SVD, *Models of Contextual Theology* (Maryknoll, NY: Orbis, 2002), 70–79.

52. For bridging soft liberation and hard liberation, see my article, David Thang Moe, "A Synthetic Theology of Soft and Hard Liberation: Bridging Social Justice and Social Charity for a Holistic Missiology," *Dharma Deepika: South Indian Journal of Missiology* 21, no. 2 (2017): 60–72.

53. Bosch, *Transforming Mission*, 540, 542.

54. Johan Galtung, *Peace by Peaceful Means: Development and Civilisation* (Oslo: PRIO, 1996), 72.

55. Bevans, *Constants in Context*, 348.

56. Peter C. Phan, *In Our Own Tongues: Perspectives from Asia on Inculturation and Mission* (Maryknoll, NY: Orbis, 2003), 136–52. Along the same lines of thought, see also, David Thang Moe, "Exclusion and Embrace: A Theology of Breaking Boundaries and Building

Bridges between Christianity and Buddhism in Myanmar," *Exchange: Journal of Contemporary Christianities in Context* 46, no. 2. (March 2017): 103–28.

57. Kosuke Koyama, *Three Mile an Hour God* (Maryknoll, NY: Orbis Books, 1980), 54.

58. Moe, "Exclusion and Embrace," 103–28.

59. Ibid., 87. See also Beverly R. Gaventa, *The Acts of the Apostles* (Nashville, TN: Abingdon, 2003), 172.

60. Darrell L. Guder, *The Continuing Conversion of the Church* (Grand Rapids, MI: Eerdmans, 2000), 206.

61. Roger P. Schroeder, *What Is the Mission of the Church?* (Maryknoll, NY: Orbis, 2008), 120.

62. Hans Kung, *Global Responsibility: In Search for a New World Ethic*, trans. John Bowden (New York, Continuum, 1993), 89.

63. Ibid., 76.

64. Schroeder, *What Is the Mission of the Church?* 124.

65. Jürgen Moltmann, *The Coming of God: Christian Eschatology* (Minneapolis, Fortress, 1996), 11ff.

66. Robert Schreiter, *Reconciliation: Mission and Ministry in a Changing Social Order* (Maryknoll, NY: Orbis, 1992), 41–62.

67. Larry Rasmussen, "Global Ecojustice: The Church's Mission in Urban Society," *Mission Studies* 16, no. 1 (1999): 111–21.

68. Walter Brueggemann, "The Uninflected Therefore of Hosea 4:1–3," in *Reading from this Place, Vol. I: Social Location and Biblical Interpretation in the United States*, eds. Fernando F. Segovia and Mary A. Tolbert (Minneapolis, MN: Fortress, 1995): 231–49.

69. Loren Wilkinson, *Earth Keeping in the 90s: Stewardship of Creation* (Grand Rapids, MI: Eerdmans, 1991), 150–51.

70. Bevans, *Constants in Context*, 376.

71. David Thang Moe, "Nat-Worship and Paul Tillich: Contextualizing a Correlational Theology of Religion and Culture in Myanmar," *Toronto Journal of Theology* 31, no. 1 (2006): 130–131.

72. Lesslie Newbigin, *The Open Secret: An Introduction to a Christian Theology of Mission*, rev. ed. (Grand Rapids, MI: Eerdmans, 1995), 30–65.

73. Quoted in Michael W. Goheen, *Introducing Christian Mission Theology: Scripture, History, and Issues* (Downers Grove, IL: IVP, 2014), 248.

Chapter 11

To Be Like Christ

Decolonizing Theology for an Incarnational Church

Josh de Keijzer

When we talk about the relationship between the Church and the world we find a plurality of positions that range from a sectarian, world-eschewing attitude to a radical and porous openness that virtually obliterates the distinction between the two. Some believe the essence of the Church is to focus on the spiritual while others reduce the task of the body of Christ to the political. That these two options virtually coincide with conservative and liberal positions is no coincidence. Conservative churches tend to emphasize right doctrine and entertain various strategies of personal sanctification. Progressive liberal churches, on the other hand, are much more anthropocentric in their orientation and as such see as their primary task to translate the vertical relationship with God into the horizontal relationships between people, typically at the expense of not only a living relationship with God but also right doctrine. In this paper I propose a middle position, which harmonizes both the vertical and horizontal dimensions of the Christian faith where the emphasis on the vertical dimension of faith expresses itself in a radical horizontality that I will describe as "incarnational faith."

Our starting question is why the non-Western Church still too often operates within this binary, dualistic understanding of the Christian faith. The answer is well-known: the thoroughly Western dichotomy between conservative and liberal was dutifully transmitted by missionaries who operated on the basis of either paradigm. Non-Western churches were socialized into and received their formation exclusively within these paradigms, even though these paradigms were responses to developments in Western culture and had little or nothing to with African, Latin American, or Asian contexts. The situation was aggravated by the fact that missionaries often considered themselves emissaries of a superior culture and simply assumed that their own Western theological paradigm constituted a universally true and value-free theology. Kwami Bediako, whose work is one grand argument that the Gospel actually comes home in the African context, insists, on the contrary, that "the Western traditions did not enshrine universal norms."[1]

It is with this dichotomous legacy in mind that we now turn to the theme of Church and development. This is not simply a matter of practical theology. It is also a systematic question. It must be done in conscious acknowledgement of the paradigmatic binary that the Western Church bequeathed to non-Western Christianity. Part of this task of acknowledgement is a willingness to ponder whether that binary is helping or hindering the non-Western Church to assess and formulate its task in the world. I believe the latter is the case. This essay attempts to argue why this is so. The argument is not simply for the Church to function well. Managers, system analysts, and cultural anthropologists can do that much better than a theologian. The task here is to call the Church to its calling to be a truly incarnational Church, since it is the Church's task to be like Christ in the world.

However, simply arguing for a shedding of unnecessary Western baggage is not enough. I would in that case also not be up to the task, being a Western theologian myself, albeit one with extensive experience in non-Western contexts. Moreover, a simple argument in favor of a given church's involvement in the development of the nation it belongs to may simply fail to convince because church leaders may not see the need to adjust their strategies. The argument is therefore broader, that is, deeply theological and biblical. What I, as a Western theologian, am able to offer my non-Western readers is not *how* they should deconstruct non-Western theology or tell them *what* their theology ought to look like. What I can do, however, is to share how the binary of conservative versus liberal has hindered the Church in the West to be truly the Church of Christ. It has led in various ways to the Church's marginal status in society. I therefore offer a critique of that binary, exposing its pitfalls. My critique concerns mostly the conservative part of the binary for two reasons: (1) space does not allow a thorough analysis of both and (2) it is the conservative paradigm that most seems to hinder an effective involvement of the Church in society, while that paradigm is generally most widespread in the non-Western world.

The non-Western Church must become an incarnational church and this Church can only become that by becoming not only decolonialized in liturgical and cultural praxis but in theological thought as well. This is so important because the Church has a theological origin, that is to say—as Christians believe—the Church is a revelatory creation created by God in Christ such that, by implication, the true nature, or essence if you will, of the Church must be understood through theological reflection in dialogue with Scripture leading to praxis.

We see the scriptural injunction clearly in at least two places. Paul admonishes the believers in Philippi to have the mind of Christ. What this means is explained by Paul by reference to the kenotic nature of the incarnation: Christ did not consider his co-equality with God's glory something to be held onto. Taking on the mind of Christ means to live out such humility and lowliness as is evidenced in the humility of Christ.[2] This pertains not just to the character of the individual Christian. John's gospel is bookended by two important passages. In the one we read about the Word becoming flesh[3] and dwelling among us; in the other, Christ sends his followers as he himself was sent.[4] It only makes sense to interpret this in terms of the Church being sent in the manner of the Word becoming flesh. That is to say, the vocation of the Church is to live out the incarnation; this living out is characterized by participatory praxis and humble self-giving love.

BONHOEFFER AND THE INCARNATIONAL CHURCH

To get an appreciation for this, let's turn our attention to Bonhoeffer, who takes the idea of an incarnational Church one step further by linking it with the question of revelation and the theology of the cross. Dietrich Bonhoeffer was a German theologian who worked and wrote before and during World War II. In his second doctoral dissertation, Act and Being, Bonhoeffer addresses a problem that is typical for early twentieth-century Western theology: Does God reveal Godself and, if so, how and what can we know? It so happened that when Bonhoeffer started his work on this question, there had already been several answers. Ever since the Enlightenment philosophers had begun to cast doubt on the possibility of revelation or the notion of certain knowledge about God, theologians had tried to come up with formulae that eclipsed the challenges of philosophy and the doubts created by critical historical research. One way was to become entrenched in old positions and simply ignore what was happening in the world. This is, roughly, the conservative option. Another consisted of the route Schleiermacher took in making the human experience the starting point for theology. This was the liberal option. But at the time Bonhoeffer entered the academic world, a third option had just created a revolution in Western theology. This was the dialectical theology of Karl Barth and some of his colleagues.

Some readers may wonder how early twentieth-century German theology, with all its modernist trappings—including its attendant colonialist outlook on the world—could be relevant for the call for a postcolonial incarnational church. But it is precisely in the formulation of his response that Bonhoeffer eclipses modernity and creates a new approach that both inspires and brings us to the heart of the idea of an incarnational Church. To articulate a new way of thinking that avoids the pitfalls of both liberalism and conservatism and escapes the traps of revelation based in human experience or founded on epistemologies of certainty (e.g., apostolic succession and inerrancy), he focuses on the way one becomes a Christian and thereby a member of the community of faith. God is available, says Bonhoeffer; one can in fact have an encounter with the revealing God. But this revelation is neither located in the field of pure cognition (i.e., a body of knowledge external to the human being), nor is it something one discovers as a function of one's own emotions, nor is it the realization that God is indeed unavailable (Barth). No, for Bonhoeffer one comes to know and acknowledge revelation only in the encounter with Christ and then only through surrender of one's self. The Bible says that one who believes is in Christ.[5] Consequently, for Bonhoeffer, one can only know Christ by being in Christ.[6] And since Christ, and nothing else, is God's self-revelation, there is nothing else to know but Christ. Would we know any revelation outside of faith in Christ, we would possess that revelation thus rendering it moot as revelation.

But there is more. If Christ is the one self-revelation of God, then where is this Christ and how does the encounter take place? In his first dissertation, Sanctorum Communio, Bonhoeffer had stated that the Church is nothing but Christ existing as community.[7] Bonhoeffer thus brings Christ, revelation, and the Church together; they coincide. If Christ is the self-revelation of God then he is also at the same time manifest in the Church as his body on earth. Coming to know revelation is in Bonhoeffer's eyes a process of interpretation, participation, and self-discovery. It is participation in and with Christ, because the believer is in Christ, but since Christ is manifested as the Church, this entails participation in the Church. The believer is not simply in Christ and also in the Church but is in fact part of the Church by virtue of being in Christ. As such, it is self-discovery: who am I as part of the Church and with the Church as the community in which Christ is manifest? The answer to these questions about participation and self-discovery constitute what revelation is: the being of Christ as a being for others in and through the Church. What this is must be experienced, discovered experientially, and lived out. Revelation is an event of self-giving of the community of Christ.

Such a concept of revelation is dynamic, hard to nail, something that can't be objectified or mastered. Only by "doing it" can one know what divine revelation in Jesus Christ actually means. We get an idea of how Bonhoeffer's concept of revelation gives new meaning to the notion of incarnational Church. The Church does for Bonhoeffer not just emulate Christ and doesn't just represent Christ, but is, in a real and tangible sense, Christ. It is in and through the life of the Church that one ought to be able to recognize that the Word became flesh and that the cross brings reconciliation. The Church is the very thing that Christ was when he was born in a stable; lived a humble life of preaching, teaching, and healing; and died crucified as a criminal. This way of looking at revelation and Church is potentially very disruptive because it subverts the status quo of both individual and church community. Again and again.

It becomes clear, now, that incarnation and cross are inseparably linked. The Word that became flesh was rejected and the manner of existence the incarnated one takes on is that of a servant. The servant is rejected by those he serves and a cross awaits as throne. The Church of Jesus Christ cannot expect to be exempt from the ultimate consequences of emulating, no living out, the reality, of the incarnation. The cross is, if not the goal, a logical outcome of the, in the eyes of the world repulsive, nature of the radical self-giving that manifests itself in human flesh. Incarnation and theology of the cross go together.

DECOLONIZING THEOLOGY FOR AN INCARNATIONAL CHURCH

The disruptive nature of such a radical understanding of the incarnation is perhaps nowhere felt more concretely than in the interaction between colonizer and colonized in the past, and—by extension—between West and non-West today. Historically, the Church, at the dawn of modernity, moved from the West to the South and the East. It did so facilitated by and in accordance with the programs of colonization and imperialism. Paul Chung describes colonialism as "the historical process for the West to systematically exclude the cultural uniqueness and value of the non-West."[8] More often than not, the Church was an accomplice rather than a critic of the colonial powers. Of course this is not a uniform narrative. From the beginning efforts were made to translate the gospel; first linguistically (as early as William Carey) but later also culturally. Hudson Taylor's China Inland Mission comes to mind. Taylor at one point decided to adapt to the Chinese lifestyle so as to communicate the gospel without the cultural baggage of the English empire. Later, in the same nation, the Three-Self movement, initiated by Henry Venn of the Church Missionary Society, in the late nineteenth century promoted self-governance, self-support, and self-propagation. This has been extensively analyzed in missiological literature, of course, and I don't need to add to this. On the whole, however, the missionary enterprise's collusion with the colonial powers amounted to the very opposite of incarnation. Where the Word took on human flesh and dwelled among humanity in humility and self-giving love, the cumulative effect of the missionary enterprise was to depreciate indigenous cultures.

Churches in the non-Western world are generally all too aware of the colonialist influence and the damage it has caused, and have made great strides to become culturally, economically, and liturgically autonomous. Today we live in a situation where the roles are slowly being reversed: the

Western Church is fledgling and in need of help from the world Christian movement, the majority of which is located in the non-Western world.

Yet certain vestiges of the old colonial period remain and nowhere are stronger than in certain tacit and implicit theological commitments that are seen as axiomatic and therefore beyond scrutiny. The colonial period was one in which the missionary typically came down from his heavenly abode, the colonial empire, without, however, assuming the form of the world he intended to reach with the gospel. What does the theology look like that accompanies such a nonincarnational process? It has to be a theology that circumvents the uneasy confrontation with the fact that it preaches an incarnational savior by nonincarnational means. A sense of superiority and a lack of cultural awareness leads to the export of the missionary's own theology, which was designed within the context of the empire. It is now planted in foreign soil unhinged from its original context and presented as a neutral, universal, unbiased truth. There it is received as superior knowledge that belongs to the superior empire that dominates it. In this way, a nonincarnational missionary movement (despite its sincere effort to be incarnational in some respects) hands over a body of nonincarnational theology that is ill equipped to help the non-Western Church to be the Church for its own people. This is how the conservative-liberal split, a genuinely Western development in the wake of the Enlightenment, plays itself out across the globe. It is a legacy of colonial thought.

It is precisely this theology that is often accepted uncritically by non-Western theologians as the only possible theology for the Church. I wish to identify this theology as limiting and hindering the non-Western Church to become genuinely and fully incarnational. I suggest that there are theological assumptions and commitments that, though they are understood to be true and biblical, are nonetheless a continuation of the nonincarnational theological paradigm of the former colonial power. This is nowhere more true than with regard to the relationship between the non-Western Church and its own culture—precisely where it ought to be homegrown, indigenous, and authentic. As nonincarnational as the missionary enterprise often was (exceptions exist of course) so nonincarnational is the theology (bequeathed by the West) that regulates Church-state relations in non-Western contexts. And it is particularly the conservative paradigm that hinders incarnational involvement in the development of non-Western nations.

NEGATIVELY: POSTCOLONIAL DECONSTRUCTION

An antidote is, of course, not found in me as a Western theologian telling the non-Western Church what the right theology is by providing yet another (albeit updated) Western paradigm. Rather, I would like to argue, with a sharp and critical eye toward my own Western theological heritage, for a return toward a more biblical theology. One such return we have already discussed in Bonhoeffer whose incarnational theology eclipses the conservative-liberal paradigm out of sheer theological and spiritual necessity. Non-Western theologians need to formulate similar responses away from colonial vestiges and toward true incarnational theology.

An example of such theological innovation is discussed by R. S. Wafula in an essay in The Postcolonial Church: Bible, Theology, and Mission. He writes about biblical scholar Justin S. Ukpong who pioneered biblical scholarship in an African context.[9] Ukpong, a Nigerian biblical scholar who lived from 1940 to 2011, worked for the deconstruction of colonial theology at both an institutional and scholarly level. According to Wafula, Ukpong "broke the hegemonic hold that Euro-American 'contextless' biblical scholarship had on much of the African continent, declaring that African contexts must become the subject of biblical interpretation."[10] Ukpong discovered affinities between the biblical narratives and African values that actually contradicted what missionaries had taught.[11] What is valid for biblical hermeneutics is valid for theology. Only through such contextualization can theology point out a path for the Church to become truly incarnational. Another example is the theology of Paul Chung. His theological program entails "use [of] the term postcolonial as a critical and analytical epistemology that enables us to overcome limitations of the Western project of Enlightenment embedded within the nexus between knowledge and power."[12] Of course this is more or less a general description of the postcolonial project. However, he adds an important dimension to postcolonial public theology by saying that "God's kingdom, which has proleptically broken in [and] through the life of Jesus, finds its analytical reality in our midst through God's act of speech transpiring through the life of the subaltern."[13] Chung believes that by listening critically and in open dialogue to the marginalized cultures that make up the non-Western context, we stand to discern the voice of God's spirit. This is a radically different approach that gives bone and flesh to the demand for incarnational theology.

The return to a biblical, and thus incarnational, theology has both negative and positive aspects. The former will remove obstacles and the latter will help to construct a more incarnational engagement with society and state. Negatively, then, I observe the following harmful theological assumptions. One is the tendency to see spirituality mainly as a vertically oriented dynamic that solely concerns the believer and God above. As such it is individualistic rather than communal. This spirituality is not done in community nor is it done with the well-being of the community in view. It is directed away from society toward God; the further away one is from society and the closer one gets to God, the holier one becomes. A more biblical spirituality turns the spiritual bond with God into a horizontal spirituality that expresses itself in love, humility, and service toward other and community.

The direction away from the world leads us to another characteristic: that of apocalyptic expectation. An apocalyptic vision we find in the book of Revelation came into existence among the oppressed Christians in the Roman empire of the first century CE who yearned for God's deliverance. A modernist colonial apocalyptic has no need for deliverance since all power is already in the hands of the benevolent empire. It merely needs to eschew worldly involvement on the part of the colonial church and instruct the believers to wait for Jesus who one day will appear from heaven. The true thrust of biblical apocalypse was thus subverted, rendering the Church uncritical toward the colonial powers.

A third problem concerns the absolutist epistemology that was part and parcel of the missionary toolbox from the beginning of the nineteenth century well into the twentieth. Under the influence of and in response to the increased emphasis on human reason as arbiter of both worldly and religious matters, conservatives, who compose the largest percentage of the Western missionary force, developed modernist absolutist epistemologies, both in philosophical discourse and biblical studies. They did so under the guise of faithfulness to the Word of God. While this renders a faith community certain of its own convictions, it makes it less pliable and less open to dialogue. It tends to erect a wall of doctrine inside of which one believes the right things and outside of which one is lost. The world out there, the non-Christian society with its vices and sins, belongs to that which is lost. Also considered of no use or even inimical to the gospel are indigenous values and cultural traditions, as well as religious and spiritual wisdom of indigenous religions. The biblical tension between the world and the people of God is thus transformed into a rejection of the non-Western culture.

These three things combined—verticalized individualized spirituality, spiritualized eschatology, and modernist epistemologies—then, led to an ethics that is both largely world-eschewing and unable to value, affirm, or address the world in a positive sense. The ethics that is developed pertains to the individual and entails preserving oneself for the coming judgment, and to do so as a Church that is separate from and antithetical to the world. Such an ethics has very little to say about the actual cultural and political context of a particular church. It also finds itself at a loss to build communicative bridges between the biblical gospel and cultural truth (see again Chung).

While it is true that the so-called "non-Western" world is not one place but rather comprises a vast array of cultures, political ideologies, languages, and histories, many non-Western theologians from all continents will no doubt recognize one or more of these theological characteristics that have rendered the Church in a non-Western setting ill-equipped to be a Church for the world. The problems that I identified here are the conservative expressions of an issue that plagues all colonial theology, namely the separation of church and state. This separation is the product of a complex development in Western civilization in response to historical power dynamics that go back to the rift between the medieval world and the Reformation of the sixteenth century. However, in its colonial expression this separation of powers has served only two purposes: (1) render the non-Western Church uncritical of the colonial powers and (2) bequeath to the non-Western Church a model of political noninvolvement that is alien to the non-Western contexts. The result is an obstacle for the Church to become truly incarnational.

POSITIVELY: INCARNATIONAL RECONSTRUCTION

Thus far we have looked at the negative side of our task of developing a more biblical theology. If biblical theology means a theology that points to the person of Christ and clarifies his reality—which it should—then it speaks for itself that a more biblical theology will lead to an incarnational praxis by an incarnational Church. And so, positively, the following points delineate what a more biblical theology will look like in terms of an incarnational praxis of the Church. First it must be understood that incarnational praxis is more than cultural adaptation. Rather, for the non-Western Church, precisely because of its colonial inheritance in faith and praxis, there must be a strong resolve to shed colonial thought patterns as they form the source for theology, ethics, ecclesiology, and praxis. It is only when one engages this process consciously that one will be able to discover, under the guidance of the Spirit, what needs to change and how things can be different. As Chung says, critical epistemologies must be developed that expose Western bias and open up to God's voice among the subaltern. With Upkong we say that the non-Western context must become a resource to critique, contradict, and upend Western thought patterns.

A second important point that needs to be made is that being incarnational amounts to an affirmation—rather than condemnation—of the world one lives in. Even if Christ called people to a radical discipleship, he is still the Word that became flesh. He came to that world, took on the form of that world, and dwelled in it. All this because "God so loved the world." In much Christian theology, and especially the kind that that has been bequeathed to the non-Western Church, there is often a rejection of and a turn away from the world, leading to noninvolvement and abandonment of the world. An incarnational Church will first and foremost say Yes to the world it is part of in the spirit of the love of God. Chung goes even so far as to dialectically locate the voice of the incarnate Christ in precisely those myriad indigenous cultures.

The third observation derives from the second: An incarnational Church is one that involves itself in its own world. The Word became flesh and its light shines in the darkness. Its presence is such that the grace and truth are manifest and for all to see. This outward orientation toward the world the Word became part of points to a participation and self-involvement that goes well beyond activities like evangelism, which are often designed to snatch people away from an evil world to become part of an otherworldly community where everything is different. Rather than rendering people useless for the world, an incarnational Church ought to equip people to express God's love toward and for the world. Bonhoeffer's ecclesiology speaks volumes here. Thinking along Bonhoeffer, we can say that an incarnational Church is actually involved in politics, economy, and culture. Just as Christ became fully human, so the Church needs to participate fully in all aspects of the human culture it is part of.

Lastly, being incarnational is to practice self-giving. This is so because the love of God for the world, which was source and motivation for the incarnation, had to be carried to its ultimate consequence of being rejected and exterminated. As such, incarnation as the expression of love and the cross as the ultimate consequence of love are deeply intertwined. Here too we return to the theology of Bonhoeffer. An incarnational Church, then, is one that not only preaches the cross but embodies it through the giving of its life, that is, the self-less giving presence of its members. The living-out of such a radical lifestyle is ultimately more subversive for one's culture than the imposition of a foreign Christianity aligned with the colonial empire was for the colony. The latter was illegitimate as it was inauthentically imposed from without, whereas the former is genuine as it transforms a culture from within, thus bringing it to authenticity.

A WORLD-AFFIRMING INCARNATIONAL CHURCH

We find in conclusion that one of the important processes non-Western churches have to pass through to become incarnational in the sense Bonhoeffer understands this in his Act and Being, as we saw previously, is the deconstruction of the remnants of colonial theology. The non-Western Church is incarnational only when it becomes postcolonial. It must be noted that such a critical examination of one's inheritance is always necessary for any church in any country. It should be evident to the reader that my injunctions are the result not of a belittling attitude expressed by just another Westerner but a reassessment of my own (conservative) Western theology within a Western context. Even the Western Church needs to critically examine its theological heritage to become (and become anew in every era again) truly incarnational. But in the non-Western context, it very specifically means decolonizing the theology dominated by Western thought patterns.

Bonhoeffer's theology too represents such a critical move of renewal within a Western context. We let him speak once more. We find in Bonhoeffer's later works a further elaboration of his thoughts on the incarnational church. There is much supporting material in Bonhoeffer's Ethics, for instance, for the emphasis on the need to embrace and affirm one's particular context. Since Bonhoeffer brings the theology of the cross and the concept of the incarnational Church together, we will specifically make some remarks about that. Bonhoeffer observes that "it [is] not enough to say that God embraces human beings. This affirmation rests on an infinitely deeper one, a sentence with a more impenetrable meaning, that God, in the conception and birth of Jesus Christ, has taken on humanity bodily."[14] The word incarnation can easily become part of theological jargon and make us forget to what extend God in Christ affirms and partakes in the reality of human life and community. Bonhoeffer says: "God overrules every reproach of untruth, doubt, and uncertainty raised against God's love by entering as a human being into human life, by taking on and bearing bodily the nature, essence, guilt, and suffering of human beings."[15]

For Bonhoeffer, the Church is Christ existing as community (Act and Being), which is modeled after the incarnation. This incarnation is understood as a radical affirmation of the world in all its embodied reality, guilt, and suffering. The radical nature of the affirmation of the world is as radical as the participation in it. The Church is likewise called to fully participate in the world of human community, human reality, human life, human politics, and so on, with an equally radical self-giving love. In this love, incarnation and self-giving love are united. Instead of admonishing the Church to turn away from the world, Bonhoeffer calls the Church to be "worldly": "there is genuine worldliness only and precisely because of the proclamation of the cross of Jesus Christ."[16] This is not an autonomous worldliness that sets up its law apart from God, but a worldliness of a world that has come to its own in the reconciliation wrought by Christ. The Church is the minister of this reconciliation in word and deed.

CONCLUSION

The Church ought to desire to be an incarnational Church. For the non-Western Church this means decolonizing its theology for a space to open in which new theology may emerge that will be at once creatively original and solidly biblical. While it will depend on this new theology what content the term "incarnational" will acquire, certain things can be agreed upon by all theologians, Christian leaders, churches, and institutes: the incarnational church will be both world-affirming and self-giving. Thereby the two-fold thrust of the incarnation is respected: (1) the Word became flesh, thereby saying Yes to the world in all its fleshly reality and social intricacy; (2) the Word become flesh invested its earthly life for the well-being of that world. I assert these things not as universals but rather as radical particulars. It is only in the encounter with the particular person, Jesus Christ, who is God's self-revelation and whose reality is manifested in the Church, that we know these things to be true. It is also in that encounter that both the Western and the non-Western churches will recognize and acknowledge what particular form this world-affirmation and self-giving need to take.

The beautiful and interesting irony here is that decolonization is not just a necessary step toward incarnational theology, but that the two overlap. The process of decolonization means an opening up toward one's cultural context, by declaring this context relevant for theology (Upkong) and by recognizing its voice as a dialectical part of God's address to humanity (Chung). In other words, postcolonial thought has the potential of not just being a critical tool but genuinely being, in and of itself, a step toward incarnationality. And it is along this two-step process of decolonization and incarnation that non-Western theologians need to help the non-Western Church to rethink its role vis-à-vis the culture it is part of. That is one of the important tasks of non-Western theology. After all, no church can embody and practice the self-giving love of Jesus Christ without affirming the world and becoming part of the world it is sent to reach.

BIBLIOGRAPHY

Bediako, Kwame. *Jesus and the Gospel in Africa: History and Experience*. Maryknoll, NY: Orbis, 2004. Kindle.
Bonhoeffer, Dietrich. Sanctorum Communio: A Theological Study of the Sociology of the Church. Vol. 1 of *Dietrich Bonhoeffer Works*. Minneapolis: Fortress, 2009.
———. Act and Being: Transcendental Philosophy and Ontology in Systematic Theology. Vol. 2 of *Dietrich Bonhoeffer Works*. Minneapolis: Fortress, 2009. Kindle.
———. Ethics. Vol. 6 of *Dietrich Bonhoeffer Works*. Minneapolis: Fortress, 2009. Kindle.
Chung, Paul S. Postcolonial Public Theology: Faith, Scientific Rationality, and Prophetic Dialogue. Eugene, OR: Cascade, 2016. Kindle.
Wafula, R. S., Esther Mombo, and Joseph Wandera, eds. The Postcolonial Church: Bible, Theology, and Mission. Alameda, CA: Borderless, 2016. Kindle.

NOTES

1. The remark from Bedakio deserves to be quoted in context as it shows how in his view the universality of the Gospel message is universal precisely because of its deep affinity with the African religious context. He says: "Consequently, the task of African theology, came to consist, not in 'indigenising' Christianity, or theology as such, but in letting the Christian Gospel encounter, as well as be shaped by, the African experience. This task could proceed without anxiety about its possibility, but also without apology to Western traditions of Christianity, since the Western traditions did not enshrine universal norms. The overall goal of African theology was to show that there were genuinely and specifically African contributions—derived from the twin heritage of African Christianity, namely, the African primal

tradition and the African experience of the Christian Gospel—to be made to the theology of the universal Church. See Kwame Bediako, *Jesus and the Gospel in Africa: History and Experience* (Maryknoll NY: Orbis, 2004), 55–56, Kindle.

2. Cf. Philippians 2:5–8.
3. Cf. John 1:1–14.
4. Cf. John 20:21–23.
5. See, e.g., John 15:1–15.
6. See Dietrich Bonhoeffer, Act and Being: Transcendental Philosophy and Ontology in Systematic Theology , Vol. 2 of *Dietrich Bonhoeffer Works* (Minneapolis: Fortress, 2009), Kindle locations 403, 999, 1006.
7. Dietrich Bonhoeffer, Sanctorum Communio: A Theological Study of the Sociology of the Church , Vol. 1 of *Dietrich Bonhoeffer Works* (Minneapolis: Fortress, 2009), 121, 138fn29, 141.
8. Paul S. Chung, Postcolonial Public Theology: Faith, Scientific Rationality, and Prophetic Dialogue (Eugene, OR: Cascade, 2016), 1, Kindle.
9. R. S. Wafula, Esther Mombo, Joseph Wandera, eds. The Postcolonial Church: Bible, Theology, and Mission (Alameda, CA: Borderless, 2016). 93–108, Kindle.
10. Ibid., 105.
11. Ibid., 105.
12. Paul S. Chung, Postcolonial Public Theology: Faith, Scientific Rationality, and Prophetic Dialogue (Eugene, OR: Cascade, 2016), 5.
13. Ibid., 189.
14. Dietrich Bonhoeffer, Ethics , Vol. 6 of *Dietrich Bonhoeffer Works* (Minneapolis: Fortress, 2009), 83.
15. Ibid.
16. Ibid., 400.

Chapter 12

Capitalism as Divine Necessity

Toward a Political Theology of the Cross

Josh de Keijzer

One meaningful way to engage the current political-economic order of Western capitalism is to describe it in religious terms. The task of political theology is to bring theological thought and analysis to bear on the current structures of power. The underlying assumption in this endeavor is that the world can best be described in theological categories because human reality is ultimately religious before it is anything else.[1] What exactly this means is best left for another time. The basic idea, however, is that the way humans interact with each other on an individual and a corporate level is infused with a religious imagination. That is to say, gods, divine revelation, liturgy, and worship play a central role even in the Western world today, albeit in a demythologized and secularized form. As the West transformed from a deeply Christian civilization to a secular one, religion merely took another form; religiosity morphed into another domain, that of economy.

In his *Desiring the Kingdom*, James K. A. Smith describes the modern suburban mall as a religious site where liturgical enactment takes place.[2] Similarly, Harvey Cox recently published a book with the telling title *The Market as God*.[3] A simple analogical transference of concepts from organized religion to the secular realm is not sufficient to adequately assess and critique the divine status of the capitalist system. Such an approach tends to look exclusively at superficial characteristics that both forms of Western culture, the religious and the secular, have in common. A question that remains unanswered in all of this is why there was a transformation from a religious imagination to a secular one in the first place, or how it is that the secular realm operates according to the parameters of a religious imagination, resulting in a "deified market" that as a "system, which tends to devour everything which stands in the way of increased profits," rules in "absolute autonomy."[4] While such analogies express a deep intuition that something has gone horribly wrong, they do not satisfy, in that the deeper structures of the Western mind have not been examined. Who is god here and why? In what way does analogy denote identity? While Cox and Smith offer their own analyses, I will follow a different trajectory here.

In his philosophy, Italian philosopher Giorgio Agamben seeks to understand politics by way of ontology and, more specifically, the concept of potentiality. At one point he writes, discussing the work of fellow philosopher Negri: "in the final perspective it opens insofar as it shows how constituting power, when conceived in all its radicality, ceases to be a strictly political concept and necessarily presents itself as a category of ontology. The problem of constituting power then becomes the problem of the 'constitution of potentiality.'"[5] For Agamben, power is not merely to be viewed under the perspective of the political. It has deeper roots. Its origin is ontological (i.e., related to being). Drawing on Aristotle's theory of potentiality, Agamben claims that power is ontological insofar it is related to the realization of potentiality present in being. Power is realized or actualized potential. But before potentiality is actualized it also has the potentiality not to be actualized; otherwise it wouldn't be potentiality. However, in its state of potentiality that can be either actualized or not actualized, the potentiality is greater than its actualization. "In this sense all potentiality is impotentiality"[6] and impotentiality (i.e., not-yet-realized potentiality) is greater than potentiality.

In this essay, I will not interact deeply with Agamben's philosophy. I do, however, take his ideas of power as realized potentiality and of impotentiality being greater than potentiality as my departure point for my claim that the cross of Christ represents, in its weakness and impotentiality, a greater power than that of the political and economic power that rules the world. When Jesus of Nazareth was arrested, he claimed that if he wanted he could have invoked twelve legions of angels (Matt 26:53). But he didn't do so, because his kingdom is not of this world (John 18:36).[7] Whether Jesus has such powers is not the point. What matters is that Jesus presents and executes his program under the category of powerlessness, that is, *withheld* power; in other words, unrealized potential, what Agamben calls *impotentiality*.

In this essay I sketch the contours of a political theology of the cross. To connect Luther's sixteenth-century theology of the cross with today's political and economic situation, I claim that the medieval scholastic ordering of God and world along the concepts of potentiality and necessity has, in spite of the breakdown of the medieval unity of grace and nature, and in spite of the widespread secular abandonment of the god of Christianity, transformed into what today is the capitalist neoliberal order. After that, I will offer a critique of this semireligious order based on the same theological paradigm that stood at the basis of the Reformation and the deconstruction of the scholastic theological system of the late medieval period: Luther's theology of the cross.

Obviously Agamben's concept of potentiality and the medieval understanding of it are linked by the indebtedness of both to Aristotle. When I discuss the medieval understanding of potentiality, I link it with another concept, necessity, as an important foundation for the maintenance of political and economic power. Necessity, too, is an ontological concept. Agambian and medieval understandings of potentiality also meet in my understanding of Christ who is the epitome of impotentiality (Agamben) and the antithesis to necessity.

NECESSITY AND POTENTIALITY IN AQUINAS

In the thirteenth century, Aquinas achieved a grand synthesis between Neoplatonic Christianity and the newly discovered works of Aristotle. Conclusions in Aristotle's work seemed to contradict the Neoplatonic ordering of the world. Was Aristotle's more world-oriented philosophy going to cause a rift between nature and grace? A new understanding of nature and the world seemed to be in tension with the entrenched inheritance of Neoplatonic thinking that was fully integrated with Christian theology. To overcome the tension, Aquinas brought the two philosophical paradigms together in one grand theological understanding of God and world.

Part of this understanding was how God and God's being were related to the being of the world and the things in it. We find a concise understanding of how Aquinas saw this in one of his proofs for the existence of God. The proofs do not concern us at the moment. Of interest is that in his third proof, based on contingency, Aquinas made an ontological distinction between God and non-god beings. A world full of potential beings needs a necessary being to account for its existence.[8] We generally understand this necessary being to be God, said Aquinas. God is the necessary being while all other beings are merely possible beings. To start with the latter, you and I are possible beings. We come into existence and pass out of existence. We once were not and once will not be (at least not in the world and not physically). In other words, you and I exist possibly. We are the kind of beings that could or could not exist and the world would not be better or worse off because of it. In short, a necessary being needs to exist to function as the ground or cause of our contingent or possible being. God, therefore, must exist.

The argument from contingency, it appears, is closely linked to the argument from cause and effect. Thinking about cause and effect, wondering where we come from, we realize that our being was caused by other beings. Those beings, let's say our parents, in turn were themselves effects of other causes. You could go on and on, but eventually, there needs to be an originating cause, a being that is itself uncaused. The chain of cause and effect needs to come to rest; it must have a beginning point. If it doesn't, our minds, or at least Aristotle's and Aquinas's minds, would blow up. And thus there needs to be one being that is the original cause, as Aristotle would say, the prime mover, of the whole thing called the world with everything in it. That being must necessarily exist. It is a necessary being. And Aquinas was sure that this is what we usually mean when we talk about God.

Necessity, Virtue Ethics, and Salvation

In the medieval schema, beings are ordered according to a Neoplatonic hierarchy that places God as the originating—and therefore necessary—being on top of a pyramidal structure. The world flows forth, emanates from God into higher and lower forms of existence. The world is also drawn back into the divine being. For human beings, this ascendancy toward God, at the end of which we experience the beatific vision of God, consists of both grace and nature. Yes, God saves, but this saving is predicated on human beings doing the very best that is in themselves, within their own nature.[9] It is here that our potentiality as nonnecessary beings turns out to be something we must develop toward salvation and toward God. Our potentiality is moral in nature.

Potentiality was connected with virtue ethics in a peculiar way. Though God, the prime mover, was responsible for the existence of things and beings as their original cause, the coming into existence of beings was not of a static nature. Aristotelian causation theory had it that beings are not just caused by an external causation, they also have a causative effect built into their own structure and being. We would say, they have the ability to develop their potential. Aristotle called it *final cause*. So the God who caused beings caused them to be with a potential that they needed to develop on their own accord. All beings have their own kind of potential. The specific potentiality given to human beings, however, was to develop into virtuous human beings, which, incidentally, was the first step into the direction of moral perfection in the eyes of God. Inner potentiality (final cause) drew, as it were, people back to God, but it was something that was one's own responsibility. Hence the virtues. Character building is something you have to train for.

By integrating Aristotle's causation theory into his theology, Aquinas had integrated soteriology (salvation) with Aristotelian virtue ethics. There is nothing wrong with virtue ethics per se—what's wrong with trying to develop a good character? In scholastic theology, however, virtue ethics provided a path of purification and sanctification that prepared the way for grace. Salvation meant to proceed along a path of sanctification through the exercise of the (Christianized Aristotelian) virtues toward God. The final goal was, after having ascended up to the divine through virtue, to attain the beatific vision, to behold God in moral perfection.

It is highly significant to note that the notion of divine necessity, initially conceived as a proof for the existence of God, leads, by means of a hierarchical ordering of entities in the world, to a deep organic connection between ontology, ethics, and soteriology (salvation). Necessity is not incidental to the theological imagination; it drives everything from thought to praxis. It identifies the location of power and determines who are the intermediaries, who represent this power on earth, and who determine the path one needs to take to get to God, the highest good.

Necessity and Power

There are two ways the medieval ordering of God and world can be visualized: three-dimensionally hierarchically, on the one hand, and spatially concentrically, on the other. The first sees God residing on the top of a pyramid, with all created beings deriving their being from God and returning back to God. The second sees God residing in a center, with beings ordered in relative distances from the center. In both cases, God reigns supreme. In the first, the higher you are, the closer you are to God, the more you represent the being and qualities of God and share in God's radiance and power. In the latter, it is all about the center, from which all power emanates and to which everything is drawn. It is important to locate things with regard to their relative proximity to the center. The closer you are to the center, the closer you are to the center of power, with a corresponding access to power.

The lower a being is in the hierarchy, the lower the importance attached to it is. A rabbit is a lower life form than a human being, while a virtuous human being is a higher life form than an unvirtuous one. In more than a few cases, lower forms of being might well want to regret their potentiality of being. In fact, according to Dante's *Inferno*, there are many forms of being that will live out their eternal immortal existence in hell. Those beings wish they did not have the potentiality of being and regret not having developed their potentiality for virtuosity. Similarly, looking at the two-dimensional model, those living at the edge of the circle are absolutely removed from the center and have no access whatsoever to power, since their function is not to exercise power (indeed, there is nothing beyond the periphery). They merely exist to indicate the outer realm over which power extends itself. They are utterly used for the benefit of the entire realm, from center to margin, without themselves having any intrinsically meaningful role to play.

There is undoubtedly a strong correlation between the ontological and ethical ordering of the world in Aquinas's theological imagination and the feudal structure of society in the medieval era. While I do not further explore that correlation here, it provides probably one of the best arguments for connecting the medieval order with that of the capitalist society that would emerge later.

Necessity and power are correlated in an absolute way. The necessary being of God has absolute power, since of necessity it provides the chain of being with its initial causation and ground and, as such, continues to be necessary to uphold reality with its power. Inasmuch as there is a chain of cause and effect, there is also a chain of mediation of power, as some potential beings stand closer to the necessary being of the divine than others on the basis of their mediating function as priest, bishop, or cardinal, or on the basis of their presumed progress on the scale of virtue and sanctification (saints, relics, sacraments).

The two models of the hierarchical pyramid and the concentric circles need to be understood as existing in different modes. There is an ontological sense in which certain beings stand closer than other beings to the necessary divine being with regard to the status of their being. But there is also a moral-soteriological level. That is to say, the lower one is, the further one is from the qualities that characterize the divine necessary being. The political and economic are two additional perspectives under which the models can be examined and understood.

As we consider the integration into this necessity-potentiality dialectic of the hierarchical structures of power and the ethics of ascendancy, we can easily be struck by how the idea of a necessary being is very unlike the Hebrew or early Christian concept of God who is known as the One who is present to save. No wonder, then, that for Luther, this whole theological system, with its attendant idea of the sovereignty of God and the way this divine power is hierarchically disseminated to human power (pope, Holy Roman Empire), is no more than an idol. During his intense study of Scripture he discovered a God who justifies not based on merit but solely based on the promise of forgiveness in Jesus Christ. This God was radically different than the sovereign deity of the scholastic hierarchy.

It is my suggestion that this idol has simply been transplanted to our secular age. It is the same idol. It has merely exchanged a religious mask for a secular one while the victims remain the same: the peasants, serfs, the slaves, the workers, the blue-collar laborers, nonwhites, the colonized. Necessity has subconsciously been inscribed into the ordering of our modern civilization and has as its corollaries power, hierarchy, domination, being versus nonbeing, justification of injustice by means of the idol of necessity, and so on.

THE DIVINE NECESSARY BEING OF THE FREE MARKET

I have described how potentiality and necessity came to be attached by Aquinas to the theological apparatus of medieval scholastic thought. Created beings are potential beings, but the Creator is the necessary being. How was this transformed into the free market of capitalism? This story takes us from the failed synthesis of Aristotelian and Platonic thought through the Reformation to the Enlightenment and beyond.

The Collapse of the Religious Order of Nature and Grace

In the late Middle Ages, there were already signs that Aquinas's integration of Aristotle into the Neoplatonic ordering of the world was not going to hold. Nominalists like William of Ockham were busy creating a distance between God and the world. Their thinking about God made grace more dependent on the uncertainty that came with an absolutely free God. The distance grew into a fissure between grace and nature.

It was especially Luther who exacerbated the situation by positioning the cross of Christ, that eminent symbol of divine (dis)grace, as the antidote against human systems of thought, especially human thinking about God. The systematizing theology of the scholastics was no longer able to keep grace and nature together. For Luther, these two were each other's opposites. Moreover, Luther's insistence on one's conscientious interpretation of the Bible, as opposed to the required obedience to state and church authority, had tremendous consequences for the way God was conceived. Divine necessity was now justified, not on the basis of the official teaching and tradition of the Church in a world were Church and states vied for political dominance, but on the Scriptures. God's beginning was in Scripture and from there God's influence permeated the world.

This was a weak basis on which to maintain the medieval ontological ordering of the world, especially since Luther was extremely effective in subverting that ordering with his new theology of freedom in Christ. New discourses could and did emerge that eventually displaced the discourse based on Scripture. They undermined the notion of divine necessity of the God of Scripture. Bacon experimented with the newly developed scientific method, while Descartes partly located the justification for God in human reason (or at least, that's the direction where his dictum *Cogito ergo sum* was taken). Inductive knowledge and skeptical thinking were the new way to go. It did not take long for philosophers to think the world outside of Scripture and otherwise than Scripture. Apparently, the world worked just fine without the divine necessity posited by medieval scholasticism.

However, divine necessity was not going to go away. The ordering of the world in a hierarchy under a supreme authority on which the entire world depended for its existence, and to which all of the world was on its way in a quest for fulfillment, continued under another name. Divine necessity was immanentized and transferred to another domain that was to be imbued with all or most of the characteristics of the Neoplatonic-Aristotelian God of scholastic thought and granted all the absolute necessity of radiant unavoidability. In the first place, divine necessity was made immanent. In other words, it was no longer ascribed to a postulated invisible divine being in a supernatural world but was applied subconsciously and in nonreligious terms to something in the here and now. Secondly, it was transferred to another domain. Immanentizing it automatically implied a transference, since Enlightenment and modernity brought about displacement and eventual erasure of the supernatural world and any metaphysical speculation regarding it.

In the secular age, all notions of a divine being who rules the world have been discarded. Yet the necessary being continues to play a role. It has, detached from its theological origins, been identified with a new immanent and impersonal entity, the free market of capitalism. This turned out to be a logical transformation. If God is rejected as the highest authority, no power is left to prop up the claims to power of earthly rulers. The French Revolution broke the world open to a new horizon in which the old hierarchical order of feudal system, nobility, and clerical hierarchy was replaced by the new era of the bourgeoisie. The colonial efforts of the European nation states and the Industrial Revolution opened up to a vast horizon of economic expansion and profit making.

One could wonder why the French Revolution ideals of *egalité*, *fraternité*, and *liberté*, proposed as a grand alternative to the feudal system and absolute monarchism, were so quickly replaced by a new hierarchy, a division of society into a new class system that produced the enslavement of the masses during the Industrial Revolution. Was it merely greed? Was it the technological progress that brought the machine? Or did the new ordering of society merely copy the old one? I believe the latter is the case. Just as Luther provided a protest against the scholastic system and the exploitation of the common people by the medieval Roman Catholic Church, Marx raised his banner against the capitalist system in aid of the new class of poor laborers. This link between Luther and Marx is not often explored. The analogy is valid not only between Luther and Marx but also between the Holy Roman Empire and scholasticism, on the one hand, and capitalism and modernity, on the other.

Before digging deeper into the nature of the subconscious reappropriation of divine necessity, I want to briefly touch on how different theological concepts that were part of the scholastic system can be mapped onto the free market of capitalism. In addition to the assignment of necessity to the free market as a dominant, all-encompassing system regulating all aspects of life, potentiality was assigned as a morally neutral attribute to the human agent within that system: the consumer. The consumer is called into being by the system and is fully dependent on it. The consumer, having been granted life by the system, possesses the potential for upward mobility. Progressing through the "virtues" of consumerism, from need to greed to self-aggrandizement, the consumer may attain the beatific vision that consists of the conflation of being the ultimate consumer and ultimate producer. The CEO is the true demigod. The downtrodden, destitute, and exploited of this world are assigned the shadowy status of nonbeing and function as the raw material from which being is exacted for the system. As such, capitalism is the ultimate perversion of Western Christianity and is the secularized continuation of it.

The Idol

In the capitalist society, necessity, potentiality, virtue ethics, soteriology, and beatific vision, those all-determining concepts of scholastic theology, are secularized. To facilitate the immanentization of the necessary being and to make the transference to another domain possible, the necessary being needs to be desacralized. That is to say, the concept of necessary being needs to be divested of its religious character. This is not an active and conscious process in which a culture says: we want to retain the concept of divine necessary being, but without heaven. Rather, God is rejected and made irrelevant. And with the "irrelevantization" of God, the notion of divine necessity is obscured and forgotten. This is precisely how it is retained. It continues to dominate the collective consciousness of the culture and functions as ideology: in other words, it determines the boundaries of and conditions under which we imagine the world.

Just as this happens for the divine necessary being, so it happens with the other interlocking concepts. Human beings in the secular age, too, are told to develop their potential. In the secular age, to be virtuous means to be good consumers. Beginning as a virtuous consumer, one ascends a ladder of salvation and sanctification of sorts. If one is successful, one experiences the beatific vision of the *Wirtschaftswunder* or the American Dream. One then occupies the highest tier of the hierarchical pyramid around which our Western civilization is ordered. One is transformed into the image one worships. The jet set consists of those who have undergone a form of deification, which comes with a certain divine authority that stipulates that one is above the law and shall live in perpetual luxury at the expense of nonbeings (i.e., those who do not participate in the divine cycle of divine emanation and ascendancy, i.e., the chain of supply and demand). The narrow path of virtue to be traveled runs between career and consumption. Excess will be the final reward, which one has to purchase with one's soul.

My argument is that in the West we are incapable of envisioning a world in which divine necessity does not emerge in some shape or form. While it is up for debate whether the emergence of market capitalism is dependent on the grafting of divine necessity into scholasticism, or both are exemplars of a systemic function of human sociality, bringing medieval world order and capitalism together in our thinking is necessary, I believe, for an analysis of our Western culture to open it up to transformation.

Providing a redescription of the free market as the divine being in capitalist culture highlights the dangers involved for human self-destruction, survival of animal species, and the ecological state of our planet in the near future. For it is to the idol that we will sacrifice anything it demands. Such a redescription helps uncover the religious nature of our secular age. It is precisely through its implicit necessity that the free market is never exposed as harmful or called to account. We cannot live without the free market, which is why that form of state capitalism that called itself communism was considered the archenemy of the *free* West. It is precisely in the invisibility of the religious dimension of this necessity that the idol sets itself up as a Moloch, able to devour millions of poor people while causing many animal species to go extinct. There simply is no alternative. The market is god. And we cannot live without god.

Religiosity as Ideological

One question remains: why? Why is it that medieval divine necessity still plays a role in our current Western secular society? Perhaps a reference to Žižek's critique of ideology can be helpful. In his *The Sublime Object of Ideology*,[10] he insists that the power of ideology is not in the masking of reality in thinking but in the praxis of reality, a praxis we cannot do without. There are certain structural features to the ideological that both are invisible and prevent us from envisioning the world otherwise. Žižek goes so far as to say that even where the cynical person has exposed the ideological for what it is, that same cynical person continues to enact those ideological features subconsciously and compulsively. We could easily apply this to the cynical rejection of religion by our culture at large. In spite of this rejection, the god, the idol, is enacted.

We could perhaps say, roughly and imprecisely speaking, that our modern world is constructed with religious symbols—or a religious structure—that we simply cannot do without. Even when in our thinking we have abandoned religion and religiosity in our secular age, excised them from public discourse, and banned religions from participating in the public sphere, we continue to enact religiosity subconsciously in our daily praxis, such that our world is still dominated by it. This is not some vague process that we struggle to identify by way of analogy or symbol. We have, in all concreteness, retained and reworked the being of divine necessity and its hierarchical ordering of society. We cannot do without divine necessity. We have to locate it somewhere, enshrine it as holy, worship it, and pay it homage—this, in spite of our adherence to the ideals of democracy and the classless society.

LUTHER AND DIVINE NECESSITY

This analysis is pointless if the hegemony of the being of divine necessity is not critiqued and challenged. As the necessary divine being, the free market has inflicted immensely more damage than the medieval Christian-Neoplatonic-Aristotelian god ever could. The Christian God was at least an entity that was morally bound (in principle) to its own rules and "knew" how to behave, so to speak. Economists, however, are at a loss how to predict the free market. It is indeed an impersonal entity that is out of our control, even when our very being and our society are completely dependent on it with regard to the actualization of their potentiality. The system controls us. Warnings of a dangerous future in which artificial intelligence will rule over us have already been fulfilled in the omnipotent being of the free market. We have created it and now it rules us. Those who are close to the top are relatively safe, but those at the bottom may face extinction, the threat of nonbeing, at any time.

I begin my critique with the thought of Luther for various reasons. The best location to critique and expose the ideological nature of religious ideology is to start with religion. There is no better deconstruction of theology than some good deconstructive theology, as Luther knew very well. If my thesis is correct that the scholastic welding together of Neoplatonism, Aristotelianism, and Christian theology is the origin of the current neoliberal order, Luther's thought, as the insightful and highly effective deconstruction of that political and theological ordering of society, stands to provide us with invaluable resources to do our work today. Luther's theology is helpful in uncovering the religious archetypes of neoliberalism. Theology may well prove to be the ideal location for an assault against the rampant consequences of our capitalist market economy.

The Hidden God

Luther's theology of the cross provides a rich and multifaceted metaphor. I will make use of two aspects of this theology as they appear in Luther's *Heidelberg Disputation*: (1) the *Deus Absconditus*, or the hidden God, and (2) Luther's concept of revelation as *revelatio sub contrario*, the insistence that God reveals Godself under God's opposite (or in antithesis to human expectations regarding God).[11]

Luther rejected the medieval ontological ordering of God and world, the division of beings into the categories of necessity and potentiality. He relegated the idea of the necessity of God to the realm of the *Deus Absconditus*. *Deus Absconditus*, Latin for "hidden God," marks that domain belonging to the divine that is hidden from sight. Is God almighty? Is God omniscient? And particularly important: does God elect people for salvation? Luther was adamant: It is not spoken about. Don't speculate on the unknown things of God because (1) we cannot know them, (2) such speculation can bring us to rather dark places (like hierarchies and the abuse of power), and (3) it misses the point of the Christian God. With Luther, the static, well-structured ordering of medieval society, so carefully crafted by Aquinas and the medieval realists, is replaced by a world in flux. Yes, there are kings and cardinals, emperors and popes, but they are confronted by God rather than upheld and supported. Luther's God is otherwise[12] and appears where we don't expect it: outside the center of power.

According to Luther's theology of the cross, God comes to humanity and becomes, in fact, a human person. The "I am who I am" is not the ontologically necessary being but the One present to save. Christ is God in the flesh, the incarnation. This may sound odd for nonreligious readers, but the consequences of insisting on the incarnation and virtually nothing beyond it, metaphysically speaking, are startlingly refreshing, even today. In Luther's thought, thinking about God is narrowed to the Christ-event (i.e., the incarnation, life, death, and resurrection of Christ).[13]

Remarkable things happen when the Hidden God—whatever God is or may be metaphysically speaking—is only referred to but not invoked or assimilated into a theological system. On the one hand, questions remain unanswered. For instance, the question of divine election (i.e., who is saved by God, a rather pernicious question in Luther's day since theologians reasoned that since God was omnipotent, absolutely free, and in control, salvation or damnation of the individual soul could not be left to chance or human agency). On the other hand, God cannot be invoked for power. Since God cannot be assimilated into a system, God cannot be imagined as sitting on the top of a hierarchical pyramid of being. God cannot be located anywhere, much less on a throne. Authorities, therefore, can no longer derive their power from a divine necessary being who stands in approval above them (but is in reality under them, because to speak on behalf of God is to let God speak your own words). In short, God and the worldly powers are untethered.

A New Ontology of Self-Giving

The Christ-event, furthermore, is marked, not by dissemination of being or causation of beings who need to actualize their potentiality, but by unconditional promise and radical forgiveness. This brings the freedom beyond freedom, which does not consist in unfettered realized potential but in being the gift. Christ is the gift beyond our means, beyond our human ordering of the world, and beyond the expectations and judgments to which human beings subject each other. Whoever is *in Christ* imagines the world otherwise, in a way that is not available within the current structures of human existence.

The Christ-event comes with a new ontology, a new form of being, that is structured as a gift, as self-giving. Briefly lingering within the conceptuality of scholastic thought, its potentiality and final cause is to give itself away. The maximization of its potentiality is precisely the opposite of the potentiality of being in Aquinas's thought. It is not a self-organizing being that draws from its own potentiality to actualize itself, its final cause. Rather, it gives; it gives itself away. Its diminishing is its realization. Its unfolding consists of its erasure. Christ is the divine gift that lives on behalf of others, expending its energy in the giving away of itself and thus maximizing its potential into nonbeing. The ontology of causation and effect, necessity and potentiality, is replaced by an arrival in the midst of time of that which is neither necessity (because it is free) nor potentiality (because it is gift).

When we turn to the believer who has faith in Christ, scholastic-Aristotelian nomenclature is no longer adequate. The way to God is no longer described in terms of ascent and actualizing the potentiality of virtue. Rather, salvation is gift, sheer gift. Ascent is replaced by grace, the gift of forgiveness. It is the lack of potentiality on the human side that God answers in Christ in terms of gift (i.e., justification by grace). It is Christ's potentiality—again, to linger with scholastic conceptuality—that supplies our lack. But, against all expectations, Christ supplies this lack not through actualized potentiality but by the maximization of his impotentiality, his suffering and death on the cross.

This invites relating the Christ-event to Agamben's concept of potentiality. Christ as the revelation of God is sheer potentiality. The moment that potentiality would become actualized, it would start to exert its influence by organizing bodies in categories and hierarchies. Yet Christ does not actualize his potentiality. By withholding his potentiality to the point of death on the cross, he becomes the example of utter impotentiality. Since in Agamben's thought impotentiality is more than potentiality, the impotentiality of the Christ is more than the actualized potentiality of the world powers. In his death, that sublimation of impotentiality, Christ conquers the powers of the world.

This gift of impotentiality is Christ's freedom: to lay down his life on behalf of those he loves. The announcement of this new being in the person of Christ provides a rupture in the system, in any system: the Jewish law, the Roman order, the scholastic hierarchical order, as well as the economic order that stands in service of the free market. Moreover, for Luther, God does not make God's Self known within the framework of abstract universal ontological categories. God's revelation speaks to the particular situation of power and oppression. God comes in the mode of impossibility: in weakness and powerlessness.[14]

Powerlessness instead of Hierarchy

By reserving a central place for the cross of Christ, Luther subverted the human system (in which God and world were welded together by means of Aristotelian categories) and showed us a God who is otherwise than power. Both necessity and potentiality are not categories through which the world is to be understood, since such abstract categories reduce human beings to ciphers and turn God into a Moloch who devours flesh despite the best intentions to let this God speak the language of grace. God is, in Christ, not necessity, but the gift of love, while the world is not potentiality, but the beloved.

This brings us to an important observation concerning the pyramidal structures of scholastic thought built on the dual concepts of necessity and potentiality. The pyramid is turned upside down, quite literally. The God of the divine being of necessity who sits on top of the structure that orders the world is replaced by the servant God who comes in the body of an infant and lives and dies to serve humanity. The weight of the world crushes God to death. Power, or more precisely, necessity in the form of omnipotence, is replaced by powerlessness. Christ is the weak power whose appearance is neither necessity nor potentiality.

His death is the result of the mechanical cause-and-effect process produced by the system. The system is based on power and dominance and uses the god-figure as the justification for the exertion of power, the extension of dominance, and the amassing of wealth. The god of the system has to enact the death of the Christ-figure. The disruption of the flow of power and wealth that the system produces in the interplay between necessity and potentiality cannot be interrupted by the radical gift of love and must be exterminated. Either Christ or the god of the system has to die.

Thus Christ is crucified. But in this crucifixion, the tables are turned and the pyramid is overturned. The defeat of the death of Christ is the ultimate vindication of the divine love that poured itself into Christ for the world. The God of Christ is revealed as the one who does not justify power, dominance, and greed, but justifies the sinner and brings justice to the sinned-against.[15] It is in the repeated enactment of crucifixion and annihilation that the system itself is subverted.

THEOLOGY AS DECONSTRUCTION OF CAPITALISM

Analyzing the political through the lens of the religious has the advantage of uncovering hidden traces of thought that originated from the religious imagination and have gone undercover, so to speak, during the process of secularization of Western civilization. It seems that although modernity does indeed constitute a major rupture in the Western mind, it was not so deep that it changed the basic orientation of our societies or the cultural imagination. While it is true that the process of secularization of our world has brought about almost limitless possibilities for human development, the basic patterns of freedom and bondage, power and subjugation, as well as our tendency to locate power in absolute necessity haven't really changed much. If, in the premodern era, the Christian God was set up as the idol, regulating the power structure of society in favor of the powerful and ordering bodies on a continuum of not-yet-realized potential and actualized potential, in the modern and late modern period, the role of the idol has been assigned to the free market. Thus the regulating and the ordering continue as before.

The question remains whether a theological analysis is any use, given the entrenched position of the free market; or, better, whether any theology has the wherewithal to take the idolatrous position of the free market to task. It is my conviction that Luther's theology of the cross, once effective enough to revolutionize the medieval world, could, when rearticulated for today and brought into conversation (or better, alliance) with other theologies that have originated from the margin and stand in solidarity with those to whom ontological status in the system has been denied, indeed has the capability to achieve this once more. More than that, I suspect that only such a theology will be able to accomplish this, since it is only in the theological realm that a truly different ordering of the world can be realized that gives way to possibilities that are simply nonexistent in the current system.

This will be a theology that does not properly belong in the category of "theologies." It is diametrically opposed to the scholastic ordering of the medieval world or any pyramidal model that inscribes God into a human system. Rather, it is in another category altogether. It has affinities with important moments of disruption in history, but is at the same time unlike all of them. As a theory, it simply bears that name because there is a theoretical component to it that articulates what it is about, so to speak. Other than that, it has little to do with theory, no matter how many books are written about it.

It is called *theology* simply because it refers to the appearance of God in human history but it is not religious in nature—no more religious, that is, than anything else human beings come up with or do. As such, it is not religiosity over against nonreligiosity, religious imagination over against a-religious imagination. It simply stands over against everything conceived by humanity inasmuch it stands outside the system of necessity and potentiality.

It addresses humanity from outside its framing, capabilities, imaginings, and doings. As theology, it describes the humanly nonpossible inasmuch as it originates from beyond ourselves. It imagines reality otherwise, and its arrival is not in power but in weakness. As weakness, it turns the world upside down.[16]

Two Gods

There are two basic uses of the word *god* under religion: one invokes God for power and the other invokes God for justice. When God is invoked for power, its use leads to systemization and hierarchy. When God is invoked for justice, its use leads to decentralization of power.[17] We see both functioning at the end of the medieval period: the former in the theological system of scholasticism, the latter in Luther's subversion of that system.

In the secular age, the first use of *God* has not receded, but has instead become secularized. The word *god* is no longer used, but the god still functions. When I say "god," I do not use the word here as metaphor or placeholder for the unnamable, but as the indicator of an invisible but real ontological power, an actual entity that reigns with demonic autonomy. The "god" is the location of justification for those who are in power. Its location is behind and above those who are in power in order to justify that particular ordering of the world that facilitates their power. Its ontological status is manifest in the reality of the system that it embodies. Its necessity is shown in humanity's inability to change it and in the indignation that surfaces should anyone dare challenge its hegemony. All beings in the world are dependent on it for the actualization of their potential while countless beings, individuals, tribes, ethnic groups, species, and ecosystems have to see their actuality reduced to less than potential; that is, they are annihilated; they become nonbeing. This god is rightly called the idol, whether it reigns as the biblical God or the secular god of the free market. Its proper name is *idol* and its power is real. That is why calling it *idol* is the beginning of truth and the beginning of its subversion.

The big problem we have created is that we allow the god of the system to operate invisibly. Precisely by not unmasking this god, we pay homage to its status as an idol. We allow the Moloch to devour the masses in the name of necessity, because, we think, this is not god but the system of necessity, the self-grounding, self-validating system of capitalism. By not invoking god-talk we simply allow the system to maintain its claim to necessity. We do not uncover the religious nature of the system, held in place by the thirst for wealth and power of the mighty. But when we call this god out and expose its necessity as fiction, we can begin to work for change. We have then taken away the powers of the worshipers of the idol: necessity and invisibility.

The second use of God, that of God as justice and mercy, has by and large retained all the characteristics of the very religiosity that secularity had gotten rid of. While the secular age created a new space that was, in its deep structure, every bit as religious, it was no longer recognized as such. It was called the *public realm* or *secularism*. The second use of God, the God of justice and mercy, was, in fact, kept alive in the secular age. Its only function, however, was to demarcate precisely that space that no longer played a role in the real world: religion. In that sense, the God of justice and mercy nicely played into the hands of the submerged God of power, the first use. The God of mercy was encouraged to be as merciful as possible as long as this mercy did not impinge on the secular realm or infringe on the realm of the idol. And Christianity, both in its conservative and liberal appearance, obliged. The liberal God of mercy succumbed to the bourgeois mentality of superficial decency while the conservative God of mercy busied himself with saving souls (and only souls) for paradise.

The Theology of the Cross

There is a third use, however. It rejects the use of God as justification for power and rejects the use of God as merely spiritual in its justification of sinners by faith. It takes the concept of justification back to the world. The justice of the love of God poured out for the world in the man Jesus Christ is a justice that is both gift and call. It is a gift in a two-fold sense. First, it is the gift of love that is willing to sacrifice all on behalf of the other. It is symbolized by the cross. It is also gift in a second sense, namely, that the love given is not a human possibility, that is, it comes from outside of the human system of necessity and potentiality. This love is neither necessary nor does it, because of its weakness and vulnerability, have any potential in this world of ours. And yet it subverts and conquers. It is the true rupture in the system of hierarchical power and suppression.

But this justice of God also constitutes a call. And this call is two-fold as well. First, because of its mere presence, it issues a *no* against the system and proves in its appearance that the world is not to be divided into the exclusive categories of necessity and potentiality. It claims that the only God one is to speak of stands outside this bifurcation and ordering of the world, outside its system. In this way, this justice implicitly exposes the God of the system, this God of free market capitalism, as a false god, an idol, thereby taking away the absolutism and necessity with which those in power justify the system and their position. It calls out the false idol and its sycophants.

Secondly, this justice is also a call to participate in that justice. Or in other words, it is the invitation to participate in the new ontology that is neither necessity nor potentiality but sheer gift, self-gift, self-giving. This brings justification and love together in the new ontology, the new being that is the gift of oneself to the other. All that is required to participate in this new being of Christ is to no longer participate in the ontological machinations of necessity and potentiality, supply and demand, consumption and consummation.

In either system, whether the religious one of scholasticism or the secular free market, the god is connected to the world in a scheme of necessity in which abuse and exploitation are enshrined from the top down as law. In the notion of God as gift, however, God is not linked to the world by necessity, causing (and thereby causally justifying) the chain of events that transpire. God is present but not as causation, not as controlling force, and therefore is not available to be controlled. As gift, God comes in weakness and occupies a specific location in the world vis-à-vis the hierarchical system and the center of power. That is to say, God is outside the system, underneath the bottom of the pyramid and outside the circle of power. This weak God is not connected with the center of power to influence the human system. Nor is this God allied with the powerful at the top of the hierarchical system disseminating order and power. This God is present where we find the nonbeings with nonpotentiality, who have no access to the system and only serve as the raw material for its functioning and are considered expendable, rubbish, the living dead. That is the location of God in Christ; that is the meaning of the manger and cross.

This is the theology of the cross. As has been said, however, the theology of the cross is all cross and little theology. Its analysis is purely for the sake of clarifying the otherness of the divine love in Christ and to point to the call that is constituted in the cross. It then gives way to embodiment and enactment, for this is the power of the weakness of the cross. Once one's life has been gripped by the transformative power of the cross, once the love of God in Christ has set one free from oneself, one understands the system for the idolatry it is and knows what it takes to take on the system, namely, passionate self-involvement. This does not imply that my solution to the problem presented by the system is merely individual transformation; that would be individualist fideism. Rather, that which subverts the system is a categorical denial of the system through an embodiment and enactment of the life of Christ, the new ontology of a new community of radical and determined love.

Just as the theology of the cross has a deconstructive, subversive moment, it also has a constructive, formative phase. By this, I do not mean a new system to replace the old, with the Jesus of love now acting as the Lord who executes judgment and orders bodies in a new earthly theocracy. On the contrary, the new ontology of Christ is diametrically opposed to the system of cause and effect and freely does the opposite of what cause and effect, necessity and potentiality, tell it to do: It gives and invests itself. This giving of oneself is rooted in the withholding of the actualization of the potentiality to power. As such, it is impotentiality, which is more than potentiality. This impotentiality announces a new form of being: that of Christ.

What this giving looks like is not part of this essay. A few brief remarks may help, however. Applying Luther's reconstruction: The poor in their nonbeing possess the potentiality of weakness, the power of the cross. The impossibility of nonbeing in the margin is the location of revelation. It is where God begins and becomes visible.

Beyond the Dichotomy of Religious versus Secular

The theology of the cross that I suggest as the deconstruction of the system of the free market is neither secular nor religious. It is not secular, in that it is a theology that employs the terminology of God and Jesus. But it is at the same time not religious, in the sense that it refuses to be locked up in the religious realm, nicely tucked away so as not to be harmful to the system. But it is also not religious in the sense that it doesn't require a religious outlook on life or a conversion experience. It simply is a new kind of ontology that refuses to be reduced to the categories of the old world of necessity and potentiality or actualized potentiality in power.

The theology of the cross merely recognizes that the systemic evil that emerges in free-market capitalism is of a religious nature, though dressed up in secular garb. The free market is the idol that is carried around in order to be invincible. The free market is the new location of divine necessity that enables the construction of a system in which power and wealth are distributed as rewards in terms of realized potential. The theology of the cross merely recognizes and exposes this and follows the logical conclusion: An alternative is not part of human imagination. A different way of living, a new ontology that escapes the conditions of necessity and potentiality, is not a human possibility.

What manifests as a new ontology comes from beyond and proves itself to be divine love poured out for a fractured world. In the religious imagination this was recognized as God: God in Jesus Christ, the Word become flesh, and so on. In our time, we use different language to express this, but we still cannot avoid the inescapable conclusion that a new way of existence is not possible for us on the basis of our own givenness, in which we seek to actualize potentiality into power. Humanity does not possess the resources for such transformation. Those resources are simply given with that figure of old, the Christ, in whom a love is manifest that inspires others to love similarly by investing their lives in their neighbor. Is that God? Does it matter? In Luther, God is the hidden God. There isn't very much to say about the "godness" of God. What we can say is that it is something we are decidedly not. Our closed loop of cause and effect, of necessity and potentiality, leaves no room for the love encountered in Christ. And yet it manifests among us, loves us, transforms us, simply is there. It calls us to resist the system and live out another ontology that we are made part of in Christ.[18]

CONCLUSION

I initially set out to describe how the medieval ordering of God and world within the Thomistic-Aristotelian ontology of necessity and potentiality re-emerged in the post-Enlightenment era as free-market capitalism, in which the free market takes on the qualities of necessity and dispenses potentiality to whom it wills. If correct, this means that the religious imagination of the medieval period has deeper roots and persisted longer than typically assumed. It continues to guide the secular imagination. The secular age is considerably more religious than we think. If this is true, we can also conclude that religiosity has the characteristics of ideology, in the Žižekian sense that ideology is not something we can unmask in order to see the world otherwise.

Ideology conditions the way we imagine the world and leaves us no other possibility to see it. As Žižek points out, even an ironic or cynical distancing from the ideological cannot prevent the ideological praxis of precisely those who are skeptical. That is to say, precisely in its cynical abandoning of religion, religiosity attached itself all the more strongly to the cultural imagination. The idol was set up (or, rather, emerged out of necessity) and homage was to be paid, regardless of the modernity of the moderns. The medieval religiosity of necessity and potentiality simply resurfaced, now invisibly, under secular terms, but with graver consequences. The medieval God, though perfectly free, at least operates according to a certain morality. The free market, however, is responsible to no one: It is a "self-regulating" mechanism that radiantly burns as a dark sun, demanding ever greater sacrifices. It has brought us the specter of ecological apocalypse, with rising sea levels, mass extinction of species, and widespread famine and water shortage. When will we kill the idol? When will we kill this god? I'm addressing my fellow Westerners here. When hordes of desperate people trying to escape their state of nonbeing caused by economic exploitation and climate change overrun our borders by the millions?

The necessity-potentiality continuum is but an exemplar of the tendency of human society to create systems that regulate beings, favor the powerful, and trample the poor. It is sad to see that the Western exemplar of the medieval god is, in fact, a product of the Christian religion. Capitalism, as has been suggested before,[19] is indeed the product of Christian theology and, more specifically, the theology of glory that seeks to actualize potentiality into power and inscribe that power into its dogmas, law, and ethics.

I then moved to the theology of the cross as the subversion of this system, the attack on the theology of glory, the exposure of the idol. Luther's theology of the cross fulfilled a subversive and reconstructive function vis-à-vis medieval scholastic theology. Since Luther's theology was highly effective in disrupting the political-religious order of his time by presenting revelation as something that is antithetical to the hierarchical ordering of necessity and potentiality, it stands to reason that his theology provides resources for analysis and subversion of capitalism. And indeed, it does. The theology of the cross places (or, rather, hears of) God outside the system of necessity and potentiality as an anomaly that presents itself as the epitome of weakness. To conceptually explain how weakness in the form of nonactualized potential (i.e., impotentiality) can be greater than the power of the world, I resorted to Agamben's notion of potentiality.

Even today, in an age where we no longer believe in God or gods, the relevance of the theology of the cross remains. In the Christ-figure we see a form of being breaking through that has not been heard of, that stands outside of both the religious and the secular imagination. Christ represents a new ontology of impotentiality that expresses itself as self-giving. Yes, it can be subdued, integrated into the system, coopted, and so on. Eventually, the system will have to resort to extermination and annihilation of the anomaly of the self-giving impotentiality of Christ, for this Christ is a being that is not supposed to be and that cannot be. But just as its appearance is in weakness, it survives precisely because the power of the system cannot undo the announcement of its being. Impotentiality is more than potentiality actualized in power.

Whether we are believers or not, Christ opens up to a new form of existence that simply lies outside the Western ideological imagination. It can only be received and thus recognized. It can only be recognized in its enactment. And once that happens, nothing can stop it. That is the dangerous weakness of the cross. That is the meaning of Christ for our world today.

As the theology of the cross moves from naming the gift of God in Christ to the call to be the gift today, so the subversion and displacement of capitalism as the reigning paradigm can and will only be accomplished through people who do the impossible: invest themselves fully, totally, and radically in the praxis of the new ontology of impotentiality in solidarity with those who are assigned the state of nonbeing.

BIBLIOGRAPHY

Agamben, Giorgio. *Homo Sacer: Sovereign Power and Bare Life*. Stanford, CA: Stanford University Press, 1998.

Aquinas, Thomas. *Summa Theologica, Complete and Unabridged*. Claremont, CA: Coyote Canyon Press, 2010. Kindle.

Cox, Harvey. *The Market as God*. Cambridge, MA: Harvard University Press, 2016.

Luther, Martin. *Luther's Works*. Vol. 31. Edited by Jaroslav Pelikan. St. Louis: Concordia, 1964.
Murray, Alex, and Jessica Whyte, eds. *The Agamben Dictionary*. Edinburgh: Edinburgh University Press, 2011.
Pope Francis. *Evangelii Gaudium*. Accessed September 17, 2019, from http://w2.vatican.va/content/francesco/en/apost_exhortations/documents/papa-francesco_esortazione-ap_20131124_evangelii-gaudium.html.
Raschke, Carl A. *Force of God: Political Theology and the Crisis of Liberal Democracy*. New York: Columbia University Press, 2015. Kindle.
Schmitt, Carl. *Political Theology, Four Chapters on the Concept of Sovereignty*. Translated by George Schwab. Chicago: The University of Chicago Press, 1985.
Smith, James K. A. *Desiring the Kingdom: Worship, Worldview, and Cultural Formation*. Grand Rapids, MI: Baker Academic, 2009.
Weber, Max. *The Protestant Ethic and the Spirit of Capitalism: and Other Writings*. New York: Penguin Books, 2002.
Žižek, Slavoj. *The Sublime Object of Ideology*. London: Verso, 2008.

NOTES

1. The deep connection between the political and the metaphysical was already noted by Carl Schmitt who noted that "The metaphysical image that a definite epoch forges of the world has the same structure as what the world immediately understands to be appropriate as a form of its political organization." Carl Schmitt, *Political Theology, Four Chapters on the Concept of Sovereignty*, trans. George Schwab (Chicago: The University of Chicago Press, 1985), 46. Where Schmitt sees metaphysical conception follow from the political imagination, Carl Raschke suggests we need to understand what's happening in the political realm through genealogical work into the religious imagination. Says Raschke: "Political theology is *not* a theology of the political. Instead it aims to inquire into the grounds—or perhaps we should say the *ontological grounding*—of the political as we know it. It inquires into the *apparition* of the political, which has its origins in Greece and has evolved, drawing on the 'metaphysical' superstructure of that inaugural formation or representation, into modern liberal democracy." As genealogy, political theology "leads us to an intuition of the deeper *play of forces* behind the deep politics of not only our era but also previous ones. The play is at the same time a *Wechselspiel*, and "interplay," which both in its origins and in its outtake can be deciphered as "divine" in an authentic political theological entailment of all its inferential possibilities. It is what we will designate as the *force of God*." Carl A. Raschke, *Force of God: Political Theology and the Crisis of Liberal Democracy* (New York: Columbia University Press, 2015), Kindle.

2. James K. A. Smith, *Desiring the Kingdom: Worship, Worldview, and Cultural Formation* (Grand Rapids, MI: Baker Academic, 2009), 19–23.

3. Harvey Cox, *The Market as God* (Cambridge, MA: Harvard University Press, 2016).

4. Pope Francis, *Evangelii Gaudium*. Accessed September 17, 2019, from http://w2.vatican.va/content/francesco/en/apost_exhortations/documents/papa-francesco_esortazione-ap_20131124_evangelii-gaudium.html.

5. Giorgio Agamben, *Homo Sacer: Sovereign Power and Bare Life* (Stanford, CA: Stanford University Press, 1998), 44.

6. Alex Murray and Jessica Whyte, eds., *The Agamben Dictionary* (Edinburgh: Edinburgh University Press, 2011), 160.

7. I'm neither trying to explain Matthew by way of John nor attempting to claim historicity for these words of Jesus. What I'm trying to point to is that in addition to the cross as the ultimate sign of weakness, Jesus's self-understanding as understood by two interpretative frameworks in New Testament literature was rooted in withheld power. For a theology of the cross we do not resort only to the grand Pauline discourse on the weakness and offense of the cross in 1 Corinthians 1.

8. The proof from contingency in Aquinas's words: "The third way is taken from possibility and necessity, and runs thus. We find in nature things that are possible to be and not to be,

since they are found to be generated, and to corrupt, and consequently, they are possible to be and not to be. But it is impossible for these always to exist, for that which is possible not to be at some time is not. Therefore, if everything is possible not to be, then at one time there could have been nothing in existence. Now if this were true, even now there would be nothing in existence, because that which does not exist only begins to exist by something already existing. Therefore, if at one time nothing was in existence, it would have been impossible for anything to have begun to exist; and thus even now nothing would be in existence—which is absurd. Therefore, not all beings are merely possible, but there must exist something the existence of which is necessary. But every necessary thing either has its necessity caused by another, or not. Now it is impossible to go on to infinity in necessary things which have their necessity caused by another, as has been already proved in regard to efficient causes. Therefore we cannot but postulate the existence of some being having of itself its own necessity, and not receiving it from another, but rather causing in others their necessity. This all men speak of as God" Thomas Aquinas, *Summa Theologica, Complete and Unabridged* (Claremont, CA: Coyote Canyon Press, 2010), Kindle.

9. Medieval theology was not a monolithic movement. The soteriology presented here is that from the late medieval nominalists, like Gabriel Biel.

10. Slavoj Žižek, *The Sublime Object of Ideology* (London: Verso Books, 2008), 15–30.

11. The relevant passages in the *Heidelberg Disputation* are: "(19) That person does not deserve to be called a theologian who looks upon the 'invisible' things of God as though they were clearly 'perceptible in those things which have actually happened' (Rom. 1:20; cf. 1 Cor 1:21–25) . . . (20) he deserves to be called a theologian, however, who comprehends the visible and manifest things of God seen through suffering and the cross. . . . (21) A theology of glory calls evil good and good evil. A theology of the cross calls the thing what it actually is." Martin Luther, *Luther's Works*, Vol. 31, ed. Jaroslav Pelikan (St. Louis: Concordia, 1964), 40.

12. This otherwise refers to the Lutheran *sub contrario*, "under its opposite." God reveals Godself under the opposite terms of what we expect from God. The *sub contrario* has both a soteriological and an epistemological component. God saves in ways we cannot fathom (Christ's righteousness becomes ours through faith alone). Knowledge of God is resisted as God resists human frames of understanding and as knowledge of God is practical rather than cognitive.

13. When I talk about Luther like this I extend his theology of the cross into the twenty-first century. Of course Luther did have a traditional metaphysical conception of God. Yet his concept of the hidden God has far-reaching consequences. When the theology of the cross was picked up again in the nineteenth century and later as a major concept by philosophers and theologians alike, it was both the emphasis on the suffering and death of God (Hegel, Moltmann) on the one side and the emphasis on the hiddenness of God that became important themes in Western thought. The hiddenness proved useful to conceptualize God for a postreligious imagination (Hegel) and to focus on the givenness of God to the world in the life of the man Jesus of Nazareth (Tillich, Bonhoeffer). When in this essay I speak of the theology of the cross I have a tendency to conflate the classic sixteenth-century theology of the cross of Martin Luther with the later elaborations in the nineteenth through the twenty-first century. This is deliberate. In doing so, I'm being faithful to the basic thrust of Luther's theology while bringing his thought into conversation with our world today.

14. This is, once again, a modern elaboration of the Lutheran *sub contrario* (i.e., "under its opposite").

15. Of course, I'm contrasting concepts here. I'm not suggesting that scholasticism crucified Christ, but, in a way, Christ was indeed crucified by the religious leaders of his own time in collusion with the worldly power of the Roman emperor and in that sense, inasmuch as the gospel was domesticated and systemized, Christ was and is crucified again and again.

16. It is important to make a distinction between the "from outside" and the theology that seeks to articulate it. There is in fact an inherent contradiction in that the moment the human constructive work of theology attempts to express what this "from outside" means and demands, it becomes a human system that masters what it seeks to serve. Yet we cannot live outside this paradox. The dialectic will simply persist and we should embrace it instead of being paralyzed by it. One way to prevent the givenness of God from becoming part of the

ideological construction is to not turn it into a theory but execute it as a praxis. This, for instance, is precisely what Dietrich Bonhoeffer attempts to achieve in his second dissertation *Act and Being*, in which he paints the Church as the present Christ existing in the form of community.

17. Of course I more or less consciously overlook the fact that the call for justice is often done in the name of the God of power. Justice then becomes a mere proxy for power and punishment. When I say that Luther's God of justice led to a subversion of the system in which God functioned as power, I mean to say that with the emphasis on divine justice in Luther there was also a radical reinterpretation of that term; justice was the free gift of God in Christ for those who did not deserve it.

18. There is an apparent tension between the insistence on the appearance of that-which-is-not-us in the person of Christ and my claim that this appearance is not religious but addresses human reality in its totality. If this appearance is only in Christ, doesn't that undermine its nonreligious status? I offer the following points: (1) That which is given in and with Christ appears elsewhere outside of Christianity. Revelation is always the current event of God's love being lived out in the margin of the world in its cry for grace, forgiveness, mercy, justice, and love. As such, we hear this cry elsewhere and see it in operation. (2) The Church can and will be part of the process to the extent it lives out the life of Christ in self-giving, in radical grace, and in radical justice. (3) For Christians the reference point of revelation is always unequivocally the self-giving of God in the person and life of Jesus of Nazareth. The exclusivity and unicity of Christ refers to faithful discipleship: Christ and only Christ is who Christians are called to follow and emulate.

19. Cf. Max Weber, *The Protestant Ethic and the Spirit of Capitalism: and Other Writings* (New York: Penguin Books, 2002).

Index

absolute monarchism, 240
Accelerated Development, 5
Addae-Korankye, Alex, 107
The African Charter for Popular Participation for Development, 5
African economy, 4
African theology, 8, 11, 27, 150
African Union, xiv, 4, 17n15
Agamben, Giorgio, 234
Ahmed, Abiy, 38, 59n5
American Dream, 241
Amhara, 49, 159n16
Anijah-Obi, 107
Antyo, Joseph, 111
Aquinas, Thomas, 235, 236, 237, 239, 245, 253
Arén, Gustav, 141
Aristotelianism, 243
Aristotle, 234, 235, 236, 239
Atuluku, John, 110
Authoritarian leadership, 56

Bakke, Johnny, 27
Bauman, Zygmunt, 118, 119
Bonhoeffer, Dietrich, 30, 37, 56, 148, 150, 153, 221, 229, 261
Buddhists, xvii, 176, 178, 179, 181, 182, 183, 184, 187, 190
Buhari, Muhammad, 111
Burmese, xvii, 175, 181, 186
Bush, Robin, 81

Capabilities Approach, xvi, 4, 7, 9, 10, 12, 13, 39, 43
Capitalism, xviii, 117, 131, 233, 252
Central America, xiv
China, xiv, 84, 85, 172, 175, 184, 185, 223
Christian mission, xv, 21, 202
Clarke, Matthew, 75
Climate change, xii, 252
Colonial, xvi, xvii, 3, 5, 7, 170, 172, 174, 223, 224, 226, 227, 228, 240
Comprehensive Asian Development Plan, xiv
Cone, James, 44, 47
Corruption, xii, 49, 56, 107, 183
Cox, Harvey, 233
Cultural imperialism, xiii, xv

Dabbs, W. Corbett, 108
DeCampos, Elisabeth, 109
Debela, Daniel, 23
Decolonizing Theology, xvii
Democracy, x, xii, xiii, xv, xvi, 6, 9, 37, 51, 53, 68, 71, 74, 75, 92, 100, 120, 124, 125, 145, 147, 150, 151, 154, 157, 178, 183, 186
Desalegn, Hailemariam, 49
Descartes, Rene, 239
Developing Countries, xiii, xiv, xv, 85, 86, 88, 89, 91
Development models, xiii, xiv, 86

Development plan, 3, 4, 5, 6, 7, 11, 12, 14, 105

Eastern Orthodox tradition, 22
Ecological apocalypse, 252
Economic development, xii, xiii, xiv, 4, 5, 6, 7, 30, 50, 83, 146, 155, 182, 183
Economic Growth, xiii, 3, 13, 39, 67, 68, 82, 107, 183
Ethiopian Evangelical Church Mekane Yesus, 23, 24, 25, 26, 27, 28, 30, 51, 52, 142, 148, 154, 157
Ethiopian Kale Hiwot Church, 52
Enlightenment, 221, 224, 225, 239, 252
Environmental Degradation, 42, 107
Environmental Sustainability, 112, 207
Ethiopia, xvii, xviii, 37, 38, 39, 50, 51, 52, 53, 57, 114, 141, 142, 143, 144, 145, 146, 147, 148, 149, 151, 152, 154, 155, 156, 192
Ethiopian Christians, 48, 152
European Missionaries, 103
Evangelism and Development, xviii, 21, 23, 27
Exploitation, xiii, xv, 5, 28, 57, 100, 103, 107, 128, 169, 170, 187, 188, 209, 213, 240, 250, 252

Feener, R. Michael, 81
Fehintolu, Osamolu Titilayo, 110
Feudal Structure, 237
Fritz, Jan Marie, 100
Foujtaij, Philip, 81
Free Market, xvii, 82, 120, 121, 128, 239, 240, 242, 243, 245, 247, 248, 249, 250, 251, 252
French Revolution, 242
Friedman, Milton, 118, 120, 128

Ganno, Aster, 23
Gebre-Ewostateos, 23, 142
Gobat, Samuel, 141
Goodin, Robert, 68, 74
Global North, xii
Global South, ix, xii, xiii, xiv
Globalization, xvi, xvii, 6, 9, 68, 70, 71, 73, 117, 120, 124, 126, 127, 131
Groome, Thomas, 73
Gutiérrez, Gustavo, xiv, 186

Hailemariam, Mengistu, 143, 148
Halafoff, Anna, 75
Hayek, Friedrich A., 118, 128
Heidelberg Disputation, 243
Heyling, Petter, 141
Holistic Healthcare, 110
Holistic Ministry, 26, 28, 29, 30, 50
Holistic Theology, xviii, 21, 25, 29, 30, 31, 154
Holistic Understanding of Mission, xviii
Human Development, xii, xv, 4, 7, 9, 10, 12, 13, 14, 26, 27, 67, 68, 69, 72, 75, 76, 83, 101, 103, 104, 109, 112, 113, 122, 146, 150, 152, 157, 169, 170, 183, 191, 247
Human Development Report, 68, 83
Human Flourishing, xvi, 37, 38, 39, 40, 41, 42, 43, 44, 45, 47, 48, 49, 53, 55, 56, 67, 72, 74, 83, 145, 154, 176, 177, 182, 183, 191
Human Rights, xiii, xvii, 9, 44, 51, 55, 101, 108, 137, 139, 145, 146, 147, 151, 152, 156, 169, 170, 172, 174, 175, 179, 180, 181, 182, 183, 184, 186, 191, 192, 202

India, xiv, 84, 85, 141, 184
Indigenous Development Plans, xiv
Industrial Revolution, 240
International Monetary Fund, xiii, 5
Islam, 85, 141

Japan, xiv, 84, 85

Kairos Document, 8, 151
King Jr., Martin Luther, ix, 48, 54, 56, 145, 147, 212
Krapf, Johann Ludwig, 141, 142

Legos Plan, 5
Levinas, Emmanuel, 118, 131
Liberation Theology, xvi, 8, 88, 89, 91, 172, 178, 186, 209
Logos Plan of Action for Economic Development, 5
Luther, Martin, xvii, xviii, 23, 28, 103, 138, 139, 141, 171, 209, 234–235, 238, 239, 240, 243, 244, 246, 247, 248, 251, 252

Index

Luther's theology, xviii, 234, 235, 243, 244, 247
Luther's two-kingdom, xvii
The Lutheran Church of Christ in Nigeria, 110, 111
Lutheran Missionaries, 22
Lutheran World Federation, 27, 28, 143, 155

Madagascar, xviii
Marx, Karl, 240
Marxism, 89
Mattes, Mark, 102
Measuring Development, xiii
Medieval Christianity, xviii, 139
Migration, xii, 42, 53
Mugambi, Jesse, 3, 9
Myers, Bryant, 13

Neoliberalism, 82, 91, 92, 117, 120, 121, 122, 128, 243
Neoplatonic Christianity, 235
Neoplatonism, 243
Nesib, Onesimos, 23
New International Economic Order, 4, 5
New Partnership for Africa's Development, xiv, 3, 4, 6, 7, 11, 12, 14
Niemoeller, Martin, 147
Niger Delta Ecosystem, 108
Nigeria, 99, 106, 107, 108, 109, 110, 111, 112, 113
Nussbaum, Martha, xvi, 4, 10, 11, 12, 37, 38, 39, 40, 41, 43, 55, 56, 146
Nwaigbo, Ferdinand, 103

Oluwabamide, Abiodun J., 109, 116n23
Opoola, E. O., 113
Oromo, 22, 23, 141, 142, 146, 149
Orthodox Tewehado Church, 54

Peace and Reconciliation, 46, 51, 52, 210
Pentecostal Movement, 25
Pentecostal church, 25, 30, 99
Petros, Abuna, 54
Platonic thought, 239
Political Theology, xviii, 171, 172, 233, 234
Political Violence, 42, 186
Political Vocation, xvii, 113

Pope John XXIII, 67
Postcolonial Church, 222
Postcolonial Africa, xvi, 3
Postcolonialism, 90, 91
Postmodern Theories, xvi
Poverty, xii, xiv, 4, 6, 14, 31, 38, 40, 57, 67, 69, 83, 84, 86, 88, 89, 92, 100, 106, 107, 111, 117, 120, 145, 150, 169, 176, 177, 178, 191, 209
Priority Program for Economic Recovery, 5
Prophetic Call, xvii, 99
Public Engagement, xvii, 38, 41, 173
Public Responsibility, xvi

Reformation, 141, 189, 226, 234, 239
Religious Violence, xvii, 174
Ritzer, George, 118, 121
Roman Catholic Church, 240
Roman Empire, 141, 238, 240
Romero, Oscar, 54, 139, 144, 210

Sassatelli, Roberta, 125
Scholasticism, 239, 240, 242, 250
Secular age, 238, 240, 241, 242, 248, 249, 252
Selassie I, Haile (Emperor), 4, 24, 142
Sen, Amartya, 10, 39, 68, 83
Shalom, xvii, 45, 170, 173, 201, 204, 207, 210, 211, 213
Social Justice, xvi, 4, 10, 11, 54, 81, 89, 91, 127, 132, 145, 147, 151, 154, 157, 177, 183, 207, 208, 209
Structural Transformation, 91
Sustainable Development, xv, xvi, 3, 4, 6, 68, 69, 72, 99, 100, 101, 105, 106, 108
Swedish Evangelical Mission, 22, 23, 24

Tadesse, Abebe, 48
Taylor, Charles, 38, 43, 118, 126
Tewoflos, Abuna, 54
Thacker, Justin, xiii, 5, 9
Theology of Development, 4, 12
Theology of Glory, 252, 253
Theology of Reconstruction, 3, 9, 11, 13, 14
Theology of the Cross, xviii, 221, 223, 229, 234, 235, 243, 244, 247, 250, 251, 253

Tumsa, Gudina, xviii, 21, 26, 54, 140, 146, 148, 151, 152, 153, 154, 155, 156
Tutu, Desmond, 3, 54, 212

Ucha, Chimobi, 107
Ul Haq, Mahbub, 68
Umo, John O., 109
United Nations, xiv, 10, 68, 83, 100, 184
United Nations Development Programme, 68, 100, 101

Villa-Vicencio, Charles, xiv, 3, 9

Weber, Max, 118, 119
Western capitalism, 233
Western civilization, 226, 241, 247
Williams, Rotimi, 109
Wongel, Mulu, 53
World Bank, xiii, 5, 6, 107
World War II, 87, 171, 221

Žižekian, 252

About the Contributors

Ibrahim S. Bitrus is a lecturer at the Bronnum Lutheran Seminary Yola, Nigeria. He received his BD and MTh from the Theological College of Northern Nigeria and PhD in systematic theology from Luther Seminary. His research interests are the doctrine of the Triune God, Neo-Pentecostalism, and Public Theology. He is the author of *Community and Trinity in Africa* (2017) and many essays and articles, including *The Means of Prosperity: The Neo-Pentecostal Interpretation of the Lord's Supper in Nigeria* in *Dialog*, *Disturbing Unjust Peace in Nigeria through the Church and Legal Reforms: The Contribution of Luther's Critical Public Theology*, in *On Secular Government: Lutheran Perspectives on Contemporary Legal Issues* (2016) and the upcoming article, *Give Us Today Our Daily Bread: Luther's Theology of Prosperity* in the *Journal of Theology for Southern Africa*.

Delfo Canceran, OP, is a Dominican priest from the Philippines. He teaches theology, philosophy, and sociology at the University of Santo Tomas in Manila. He has received his PhD in theology from Katholieke Universiteit Leuven, Belgium, and a second PhD in sociology from the University of the Philippines, Diliman. He has published articles in various journals locally and internationally. His most recent publication includes *Images of God: Provocations of the Others* (2012).

Andrew D. DeCort is president of the Institute for Christianity and the Common Good (www.iccgood.org) and lecturer in ethics and public theology at the Ethiopian Graduate School of Theology. He holds a PhD in theological ethics from the University of Chicago and is the author of *Bonhoeffer's New Beginning: Ethics after Devastation* (2018). Andrew is the editor and wrote the foreword to Professor Donald Levine's *Interpreting Ethiopia: Observations of Five Decades* (2014).

Samuel Yonas Deressa is assistant professor of theology and Global South at Concordia University in St. Paul, Minnesota. He holds a PhD in congregational mission and leadership from Luther Seminary. He was a president of a graduate school in Ethiopia, where he gave training on leadership (Foundation for Academic Excellence Ministry) and was a lecturer at Mekane Yesus Seminary. He is the editor of *Journal of Gudina Tumsa Theological Forum*, and has recently coedited a book titled *The Life, Works, and Witness of Tsehay Tolessa and Gudina Tumsa, the Ethiopian Bonhoeffer* (2017).

Josh de Keijzer holds a PhD in systematic theology from Luther Seminary, St. Paul, Minnesota. He has served as adjunct professor at Augsburg University in St. Paul. His research focuses on the intersections of systematic theology, public theology, and social justice, as well as the dialog between the theology of the cross and radical theology. He is the author of *Bonhoeffer's Theology of the Cross: The Influence of Luther in 'Act and Being'* (2019) on the theological method of Dietrich Bonhoeffer against the background of dialectical and Lutheran theology and phenomenology. He has also authored an article in *The Journal of Religion* titled *Revelation as Being: Bonhoeffer's Appropriation of Heidegger's Ontology*.

Wilfredo A. Laceda obtained his MA in theological studies from Asian Theological Seminary. He is currently a lecturer at Penuel School of Theology in Pasig City, Philippines. He is married to Shelleni Laceda and blessed with two children, Juliana Ysabel and Elijah Amos.

Teck Peng Lim obtained his PhD in religious education from King's College, London, and is currently the associate dean at the Trinity Theological College in Singapore. He writes in both English and Chinese. His research interests include the relationship between Christian religious education and the development of Christian agency in the Asian context, particularly Singapore.

David Thang Moe is a PhD candidate in intercultural theology at Asbury Theological Seminary in Wilmore, Kentucky. He has published numerous articles in peer-reviewed scholarly journals and is an author of *Pyithu-Dukkha Theology: A Paradigm for Doing Dialectical Theology of Divine Suffering and Human Suffering in the Asian-Burmese Context* (2017), with a foreword by Walter Brueggemann. His research areas focus on a Trinitarian theology of religions, public ecclesiology, and Asian theology in the context of Christian-Buddhist dialogue on sin and suffering. He is an editor of the

Journal of Asian American Theological Forum and is associate editor of *Missiology: An International Review*.

Nestor M. Ravilas is the president of Penuel School of Theology in the Philippines. He received a BTh in pastoral studies from Penuel School of Theology, an MDiv in biblical studies from Asian Theological Seminary, and a ThM from the Asian Graduate School of Theology. He has published numerous articles including *Life, Justified Aggression, and Ritualized Violence* and *Embedded Violence: The Evangelical Violent Formation and the Rise of President Rodrigo Roa Duterte to Power* (2018).

Wondimu Legesse Sonessa earned his BTh from Mekane Yesus Seminary and MA from Ethiopian Graduate School of Theology, both in Addis Ababa, Ethiopia. He also received his MTh from Luther Seminary, where he is currently pursuing his PhD in systematic theology. Prior to this, he was lecturer and dean at the Mekane Yesus Seminary. He has authored articles including "Simul Lutheran Et Charismatic in Ethiopia in Lutheran Forum" and two upcoming articles, "The Notion of 'Gumaa' and 'Waadaa' as Traditional Peace-Making Principles among the Oromo of Ethiopia: Contextual Resources for Understanding the Biblical Teachings on Forgiveness and Reconciliation" in the *Asian Journal of Theology*, and "Imago Dei and the Tensions of Ethnic Identity" in the *Journal of Religion in Africa*.

www.ingramcontent.com/pod-product-compliance
Lightning Source LLC
Chambersburg PA
CBHW050900300426
44111CB00010B/1313